VIRTUAL WORLD DESIGN

VIRTUAL WORLD DESIGN

Ann Latham Cudworth

CRC Press
Taylor & Francis Group
Boca Raton London New York

CRC Press is an imprint of the
Taylor & Francis Group, an **informa** business

AN A K PETERS BOOK

CRC Press
Taylor & Francis Group
6000 Broken Sound Parkway NW, Suite 300
Boca Raton, FL 33487-2742

© 2014 by Taylor & Francis Group, LLC
CRC Press is an imprint of Taylor & Francis Group, an Informa business

No claim to original U.S. Government works

Printed on acid-free paper
Version Date: 20140206

International Standard Book Number-13: 978-1-4665-7961-3 (Paperback)

Library of Congress Cataloging-in-Publication Data

Cudworth, Ann Latham, 1955-
    Virtual world design : creating immersive virtual environments / Ann Latham Cudworth.
      pages cm
    Includes bibliographical references and index.
    ISBN 978-1-4665-7961-3 (paperback)
      1. Computer simulation. 2. Shared virtual environments--Design. 3. Virtual reality. I. Title.

    QA76.9.C65C83 2014
    006.8--dc 3   2013044499

Visit the Taylor & Francis Web site at
http://www.taylorandfrancis.com

and the CRC Press Web site at
http://www.crcpress.com

Contents

Preface

A BRIEF OVERVIEW OF THE CHAPTERS IN THIS BOOK

In this section, there is a brief overview of each chapter in this book, and the projects in it. A suggested skill level is included, to guide you in the choice and order of projects.

Chapter 1: Introduction to Virtual Worlds and Designing for Them
    Beginner to advanced levels
        Chapter 1 discusses the history of virtual worlds, how they actually work, and who uses them. How to prepare as a designer when tackling your first virtual environment project is discussed, as well as how to set up a virtual world for your own design usage.
Chapter 2: How to Use This Book and Start Doing Virtual World Design
    Beginner level
        This chapter shows you how to use this book, decide on the appropriate computer configuration, pick your world viewer, and access the additional content for the projects.
Chapter 3: "Build It Once": Optimizing Your Design Workflow
    Beginner to advanced levels
        In Chapter 3, workflow, design practices, and protocols are discussed. The reader will follow through the process of setting up design studios of various sizes and configurations, all the while learning about the concept of "Build It Once" and how the design workflow can be optimized for maximum effectiveness across three platforms: Second Life, OpenSim, and Unity.
        Project: Organizing your design studio with a "critical path" technique. In this project, you will look at your own design methodology and find new ways to streamline the process of project development.
Chapter 4: Concepts in 3D Design for Virtual Environments
    Beginner to intermediate levels
        Chapter 4 delves deeply into the aspects of 3D design and reflects on the qualities that make composition work in 3D, especially from a virtual world point of view. Aspects of compositional methodology, similarity and contrast, are displayed and discussed. Questions and developmental steps for initiating and refining a design are in the latter part of this chapter. Finally, the importance of education, serious games, virtual environments, and the design aspects of each are discussed.
        Project: Designing a virtual classroom with a modular system. This project contains content for the creation of a virtual classroom, which you can do with your class, if you are a teacher. The parts are designed to be modular and provide you with an expandable system so that you can create many sorts of classroom configurations.
Chapter 5: Virtual Terrain and Designing Landscapes
    Intermediate to advanced levels
        Chapter 5 is about understanding the importance of terrain and its design in a virtual world. Aspects of real-world terrain design and landscaping are considered in the Wheely Island

project, which is the majority of Chapter 5. In the process of making Wheely Island, the reader is introduced to the concept of Design for All, all-access design for both the real world and the virtual world.

Project: Making Wheely Island, an all-access terrain. In this project, you will create a new terrain and landscape it for a wheelchair trail on a Second Life or OpenSim platform. This project is a comprehensive lesson in how to create terrain using a height map and relates that construction to the real-world design challenge of creating wheelchair-accessible landscapes.

Chapter 6: 3D Modeling, 2D Graphics, and Data Visualization

Beginner to intermediate levels

This chapter is about modeling with the inworld tools and prims (primitive objects), as well an introduction to designing with mesh models. Also discussed are methodologies for creating and utilizing textures, transparencies, and animated textures for efficient building and clarity of effect.

Project: Designing a data visualization environment: your 3D timeline or personal infographic. In this project, you will make a 3D timeline. 3D mesh model content for the basic milestones, like Work (briefcase) and Love (a heart), is provided, in addition to an info button, and a pushpin icon for adding points of interest. This project is designed to be open ended so that anyone can add their personal images, memory items, or web links.

Chapter 7: Color, Particles, and Sensory Spaces

Beginner to intermediate levels

In this chapter, many aspects of color are discussed, including color basic terminology, color mixing, period and culture-based color, and how color choices will impact the experience of virtual spaces. Particles and particle systems for Second Life and OpenSim-based virtual worlds as well are examined, along with how to design for their inclusion in the environment.

Project: Designing a colored light and particle effect. In this project, you will learn about color and how to use a basic particle script to create a color and light show within a virtual cocoon-like sensory space designed by Tim Widger. The goals of this project are to demonstrate the use of color with the creation of a prim-based structure containing a simple particle system and light sources. When you have finished this project, you will have an experimental space to test and observe color, lighting and particle effects.

Chapter 8: Lighting in Virtual Environments: Second Life and OpenSim

Beginner to advanced levels

Chapter 8 challenges the reader to think about and perceive 3D lighting in a new way. Starting with the fundamental structure of what lighting does in a virtual world, the chapter progresses through lighting methodologies, environmental lighting effects, shadows, and ambient occlusion. Types of lighting rendering are discussed as well as basic lighting setups like portraits, night scenes, and product shots.

Project: Lighting three basic scenes in Second Life and OpenSim. In this project, you will re-create and examine the structure of three basic lighting setups: a portrait, night scene, and a product shot.

Chapter 9: Cameras and Collaborative Spaces (the Ideagora)

Beginner to intermediate levels

In Chapter 9, the reader's attention is directed toward the importance of cameras in a virtual world and how they relate to storytelling, narrative, and social interaction. Aspects of first- and third-person cameras are discussed, along with new interfaces driven by touch and voice. The concept of an Ideagora is introduced as a place where the old idea of a marketplace meets the modern idea of crowdsourcing and virtual spaces.

Project: Installing and personalizing an Ideagora for your team. In this project, you install the Ideagora content and set it up for media viewing. The content is customizable to suit your meeting or demonstration area needs.

Chapter 10: Virtual Goods and Design for Virtual Shopping Environments

Beginner to intermediate levels

Chapter 10 is about making a retail environment in a virtual world. Marketing in a virtual environment is demonstrated, as well as how to design your own virtual brand. Finally, the aspects of building your own virtual store and how that relates to all of the other aspects of the virtual environment are demonstrated.

Project: Designing and building a Pop-up shop. In this project, you will assemble a series of modular components to make a Pop-up shop in your region. The project will explore all the basic aspects of virtual retail, including how to set up the land for search engine optimization, building a Pop-up shop from modular components, and adding interactive elements to respond to your customers.

Chapter 11: Sound Design for Virtual Spaces

Beginner to intermediate levels

In Chapter 11, the aspects of sound, sound design, and accessibility (Design for All) are discussed in terms of how they relate to a virtual environment. Sound creation and sound editing are discussed, as well as how to plan for a soundscape in the virtual environment.

Project: Designing an audio-based role-play/gaming environment. In this project, you will create a sound-based game. This game is loosely based on the Norwegian fable of "Three Billy Goats Gruff" and challenges you to make a sound-based game enclosed in an environment that can only be navigated by following sound cues. This project will teach you about sound design, and a nonvisual approach to game design.

Chapter 12: Avatars and Nonplayer Characters

Beginner to intermediate levels

The avatar and its importance in virtual worlds are examined in Chapter 12. Design considerations for an avatar presence and how nonplayer characters can be used in design are discussed.

Project: Setting up a basic avatar in a virtual environment. Even with the increasing use of premade avatars in virtual worlds, the knowledge of how to set up a basic avatar is a valuable skill to have. In this project you will work with shape, body, and clothing layers on the standard avatar mesh body.

Chapter 13: Prototyping for the Real World in a Virtual Environment

Beginner to advanced levels

Chapter 13 dives into the prototyping methodologies available in virtual environments. Prototyping for math, science, military projects, architecture, entertainment, and gaming is discussed and illustrated.

Project: Prototyping a simple maze space, trying it in a virtual environment, and making a 3D print from it.

Chapter 14: Scripting Basics for the Designer

Beginner to advanced levels

Code writing or the creation of programming scripts in a virtual world is introduced in Chapter 14. This is script writing from a design perspective and endeavors to show the virtual environment designer how to work with simple scripts and with a script writing specialist.

Chapter 15: HUDs in Virtual Environments

Beginning to intermediate levels

Chapter 15 concerns itself with heads-up displays or HUDs. Various types of HUDs and their design approach are illustrated and discussed.

Project: Creating a URL-giving HUD. In this project, you will create a simple three-button HUD that opens access to an external website while you are in a virtual world.

Chapter 16: Machinima in Virtual Worlds

Beginner to advanced levels

The basics of machinima, visual narrative, storyboards, camera use, editing, and an overview of the Phototools module in the Firestorm Viewer are included in this chapter.

HOW THE SKILL LEVELS ARE DEFINED IN THIS BOOK

For the purposes of categorizing the projects in this book by skill level, each skill category is generally described by the following broad qualifications:

Beginner skill level

6 months to 1 year of experience with a 3D modeling system (3DS Max, Maya, Blender, SketchUp, etc.) and 2D graphics program (Adobe Photoshop, GIMP [GNU Image Manipulation Program], etc.) and game-making programs like Unity.

1–3 months of active experience in an online virtual environment such as Second Life, OpenSim, World of Warcraft, EverQuest, and the like.

Intermediate skill level

1–2 years of casual experience (hobbyist or part-time user) with 3D modeling programs (3DS Max, Maya, Blender, SketchUp, etc.) and 2D graphics program (Adobe Photoshop, GIMP, etc.) and game-making programs like Unity.

3 months to 2 years of active experience in an online virtual environment such as Second Life, OpenSim, World of Warcraft, EverQuest, and the like.

Advanced skill level

1–2 years of experience on a daily basis with 3D modeling system programs (3DS Max, Maya, Blender, SketchUp, etc.) and 2D graphics programs (Adobe Photoshop, GIMP, etc.) and game-making programs like Unity.

2 or more years of active experience in an online virtual environment such as Second Life, OpenSim, World of Warcraft, EverQuest, and the like.

Please note that these are broad categories only; you may a have different skill level in 3D than you have in 2D. That should not dissuade you from trying a harder project. Always reach up and try the next-hardest level. Soon you will be looking back at a solid path of progressive skill enhancement.

Acknowledgments

First and foremost, thanks to my family, Dr. Allen and Cynthia Cudworth, for their support and encouragement in this endeavor.

My many thanks to Michael Fulwiler and Tim Widger for their contributions to the richness of visual information presented in this book. They are two of the most talented individuals I know, and I am lucky to work with them.

Thanks to all the people who I know from Second Life and OpenSim, especially those who contributed images of their work and information for use in this book. Their contributions are credited throughout the pages of this book.

Also special thanks go out to people who offered me advice and counsel about my ideas and images throughout this process, presented here in chronological order of their help: Rafael Jaen, Dr. Carl Hunt, Dr. Richard Hackathorn, David Fliesen, Craig Harm, Ghilayne Andrew, Roc Myers, Terry Beaubois, Nic Mitham (KZero), Madeline Gray (Design for All Foundation), Rita J. King, Robert Daniels, James Stallings II (SimHost), David Meschter, Shannon Bohle, Ben Lindquist, Matthew Warneford (Dubit Economy Designer), Emily Short, Maria Korolov (Hypergrid Business), Jeffrey Lipsky, P. J. Trenton, Kathy Ferris, Patti Abshier, Hilary Mason (Script Me!), Cliff Leigh, Maya Paris, Nebadon Izumi, Drew Harry, Sherry Bolton (Avayalive), Don Whitaker, Jon Brouchoud, Ilan Tochner (Kitely), Chris Jaehnig, Kenneth Y. T. Lim, Pat McGillicuddy, Anton Bogdanovych, Bruce Damer, Richard N. Hart, JayJay Jegathesan, and Justin Clark-Casey.

My deepest gratitude to the following people for their consultation and advice:

Doug Maxwell from MOSES (http://brokentablet.arl.army.mil/) for his contributions to Chapter 1 regarding simulator structure;

Jopsy Pendragon, creator of the Particle Lab and Vehicle Lab in Second Life, for his contributions to Chapter 7 regarding particles;

Eva Comaroski, from Wizardry and Steamworks (http://was.fm/start) for her contributions to Chapter 14 regarding scripts and script writing;

Oberon Onmura, noted scripter and artist in Second Life (http://www.flickr.com/photos/oberon_onmura/) for his contributions to Chapter 14 regarding script writing.

Finally, special thanks to Rick Adams, (Executive Editor), Marsha Pronin (Project Coordinator), and Marsha Hecht (Project Editor) for their valuable help and support during the entire process of creating this book.

About the Author

Ann Latham Cudworth is a two-time Emmy award winner who designs virtual and physical scenery for network television. Her passion is to design environments that speak to their audiences visually, aurally, and physically. A transplanted Bostonian thriving in New York City, she has shared her knowledge as a teacher of design and visualization at New York University and at workshops and conferences worldwide for 16 years. Her weapons of choice are SketchUp, 3DSMax, and Photoshop Creative Suite. When not in a virtual world, she can be found listening to a ball game or cycling through the city. More information about her numerous projects are available on her web site, http://www.anncudworthprojects.com.

About the Contributors

After a chance meeting in Second Life, 3D content creator **Tim Widger** has been collaborating with Ann Cudworth and building 3D models for the virtual environments they have created in Second Life and OpenSim since 2008. He originates from Plymouth, England, and currently lives in Cornwall. He has a background in engineering and now works in social care. He is a keen guitarist, motorcyclist, and science fiction fan. He developed the 3D model content, based on concept images from Ann Cudworth, for the projects in Chapters 4–7 and 9 and 10 using the 3D software Blender.

Illustrator **Michael P. Fulwiler** is a native Californian. He transplanted to New York City to choreograph experimental dance theater. While exploring 3D movement on early computers, he began to work as a freelance designer, which continues to this day. His current focus is working conceptually from design programs and attempting to bring that work to life using a variety of natural media. "Stimulate the imagination with concept, form, and color" (http://www.kromaworks.com).

Michael is responsible for the following illustrations, based on concepts developed by Ann Cudworth: Figures 1.1, 1.2, 1.4, 3.6 through 3.11, 4.1, 5.2, 5.16, 6.18, 6.22, 7.1 through 7.5, 8.1, 10.1 through 10.5, 11.1, 11.2, 12.1, 13.1, 15.6, 16.5, and 17.1.

1 Introduction to Virtual Worlds and Designing for Them

Education is not the filling of a pail, but the lighting of a fire.

—William Butler Yeats

1.1 WELCOME TO THE INFINITE VISUALIZATION TOOL, A VIRTUAL WORLD

Like the universe with its glittering galaxies floating over our heads on a summer night, cyberspace continues to expand, full of people like you creating worlds for exploration, entertainment, and learning. Within this three-dimensional manifestation of our collective imagination, you will find new ways of understanding time and space. Terrestrial and temporal identifiers become insignificant as you work with people from around the world. Unlike any visualization tool that precedes it, a virtual world in cyberspace provides you with a place where your creative concepts can be shared as a 3D form with the world, in any scale, at any time. Let your mind unfold to the possibilities of how a virtual platform works, and you will be rewarded with a new understanding of design and the human perception of it. Almost 2.5 billion people are in cyberspace worldwide [1], and according to KZero, the number of registered virtual world accounts has broken 1 billion [2]. Obviously, virtual worlds are here to stay, and they need people who will design and create content for them. If you are interested in becoming a virtual world designer, the virtual worlds that run on user-generated content (UGC), like the open grids created with OpenSim (OpenSimulator; http://opensimulator.org/wiki/Grid_List) or private membership grids like Second Life (http://secondlife.com/), are good places to start. Mesh model based content created for those worlds can also be used on game development platforms like Unity.

1.2 A SHORT HISTORY OF VIRTUAL WORLDS

Figure 1.1 is an illustrated timeline showing an overview of virtual world concepts and how the evolution of presentational devices has created the possibility of immersive virtual environments. This process started long ago, in our ancient world.

1.2.1 Visual Theory and Creation of the First Illusions

Let's jump into an imaginary time machine and look at how historical concepts in philosophy and observations on perception can inform us about virtual reality and the virtual worlds it contains. What is it about perception and illusion that fascinates us? Perhaps when early humans noticed the effects of a flickering campfire on the painted animals that decorated their cave walls, they began to see a story in their minds. This imaginary story was brought into being by their primitive projection technology: firelight. As civilization developed, perceptions of reality and the attempt to describe it gave rise to philosophy, which gave rise

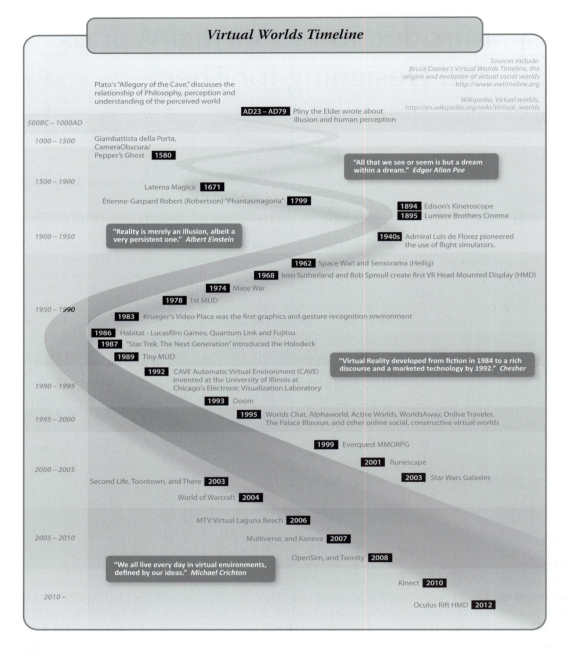

FIGURE 1.1 This timeline shows some of the key ideas, devices, companies, games and projects that have contributed to the development of virtual environments as we know them today.

to theories, experiments, and debate. Early concepts about the nature of reality and virtual reality may have started with Plato (approximately 424–348 BC) and Aristotle (384–322 BC). In his "Allegory of the Cave," Plato constructs a model for reality and how it is perceived [3]. Within the allegorical environment of a dark, deep cave, he describes four kinds of individuals: prisoners, puppeteers, the released prisoners, and observers, all experiencing a different reality. The prisoners are chained to a bench and forced to watch a shadow play performed by the puppeteers, carrying shapes and objects back and forth in front of torchlights. The prisoners think that the moving shadows they see and hear are reality. The third group, the released prisoners, has been unchained from the bench and, as they make their way out of the cave and into the sunlight, they are beginning the process of acknowledging that the shadows on the cave wall are not reality. The observers are standing outside the cave and learning about the sun and how it lights the world.

Plato disagreed with Aristotle regarding how humans perceived reality; he believed that the true "Forms" of natural things or concepts were imperfectly understood by humans, whereas, Aristotle believed that systematic observation and analysis could lead to the human understanding of the "Forms" of natural things or concepts. [4]. Plato's belief that our experience was only a shadow of the real and unknowable "Forms," represents an interesting philosophical juxtaposition to the virtual reality we create today. In today's world, we have another kind of CAVE (cave automatic virtual environment) for virtual reality. Invented in 1992, this CAVE is a virtual reality environment made from projected images on walls surrounding a person wearing a head-mounted display (HMD); it is not a holodeck yet, but it is approaching it.

Almost 400 years after Aristotle, Pliny the Elder wrote about the origin of painting, sculpture, illusion, and human perception in his book, *Natural History,* circa AD 77–79. You can almost imagine Pliny, relaxing on the patio of his villa in Pompeii, telling the story of how Butades of Corinth, seeing a line drawing his daughter had traced on the wall from her lover's shadow, filled it in with clay and fired the relief to make the world's first portrait [5]. Maybe later in the evening, Pliny would tell of the painting contest between Zeuxis and Parrhasius, two great painters of the fifth century BC. Smiling at the memory, Pliny tells you of how Zeuxis created a still life containing a bunch of grapes painted so realistically that the birds flew down from a nearby tree to eat them. Seeing that, Parrhasius invited Zeuxis to remove the curtain from his painting to reveal the image. When Zeuxis tried to do that, he discovered that the painting of the curtain was so realistic, that he was fooled into thinking it could be drawn aside. Pliny concludes with the account of Zeuxis ceding victory to Parrhasius, saying: "I have deceived the birds, but Parrhasius has deceived Zeuxis" [6]. As Pliny undoubtedly noted, the creation of realistic images fascinates us, and each successive development in the visual arts has been influenced by that fascination.

1.2.2 Trompe l'oeil, Photorealism, and the Projected Image

In the centuries from AD 1000 to 1700, great painters and sculptors discovered more ways to make illusions. Trompe l'oeil was invented, and images that could create 3D spaces in our mind's eye filled churches and mansions. The tools to create those illusions involved the scientific analysis of perception and optics by Alhazen Ibn al-Haytham (965–1039), the observations of Leonardo Da Vinci (1452–1519) and others. In 1580, Giambattista della Porta perfected the camera obscura and another device that eventually became known as Pepper's ghost [7]. Pepper's ghost is named after John Henry Pepper, who popularized it in 1862 from a device developed by Henry Dircks. This ancient device finds everyday use in the television studio as a teleprompter and occasionally makes an appearance in a stage show or fashion video when they want to include the animated image of someone in the performance space.

Projected reality began with the magic lantern (mid-seventeenth century); its invention is credited to both Athanasius Kircher and Christiaan Huygens. Étienne-Gaspard Robert (Robertson) and his "phantasmagoria" (circa 1799) used the magic lantern to great theatrical effect with complex shows involving moving projectors, live voices, and elaborate arrangements of curtain masking and projection screens. In one long-running show, staged in the crypt of an abandoned Parisian monastery, he succeeded in creating the virtual reality of a supernatural world in the minds of the audience. As an eyewitness describes: "In fact, many people were so convinced of the reality of his shows that police temporarily halted the proceedings, believing that Robertson had the power to bring Louis XVI back to life" [8]. Once the lens and a reliable source of illumination were worked out, moving images and the cinema were soon to follow.

1.2.3   The Birth of Cinema, Electronic Screens, and the Start of Immersive 3D Design

On December 28, 1895, the Lumière brothers did something that changed our perception of reality again. In the first public screening of commercially produced cinema, they showed 10 short films at Salon Indien du Grand Café in Paris [9]. Later that year, one film in particular captured the public's imagination: *L'Arrivée d'un Train en Gare de la Ciotat* ("The Arrival of a Train at Ciotat Station"). By setting the camera intentionally close to the tracks, they captured a dramatic image of the train as it progressed diagonally across the screen, from long shot into close-up shot. There were many other creators of motion picture devices at the time, including Thomas Edison with his kinetoscope (circa 1891), but the Lumière brothers are credited with being the first to see the potential for cinema and modern filmmaking. They went on to develop and establish many of the filmmaking techniques and cinematographic methodologies that are still used today.

Many of the modern imaging devices have long histories. The ancient Romans, in their time, created wonderful mosaics. They also created a conceptual model for the functioning of a computer screen—the concept of producing an image from many small colored dots, tiles to them, pixels to us.

At some time at the end of the nineteenth century, photographic manipulation began to appear; the Maison Bonfils Company connected four aerial photographs to create a panorama of the city of Beirut, Lebanon. Another step toward illusionary immersion was made and is now shown in the 360-degree panoramic stereographic projections stitched together from dozens of images and seen all over the World Wide Web today [10].

1.2.4   Computer-Created 3D Space and Early Virtual Worlds

The war years gave virtual reality and the means to create it a big boost. Admiral Luis de Florez (1889–1962), who fought in both World War I and II, pioneered the use of flight simulators to save pilots' lives. Military usage of virtual reality and training simulations continues to this day and now includes the use of virtual worlds built on OpenSim platforms and others [11]. In 1962, Morton Heilig built the Sensorama device. It was described by a witness this way: "The Sensorama was able to display stereoscopic 3D images in a wide-angle view, provide body tilting, supply stereo sound, and also had tracks for wind and aromas to be triggered during the film" [12]. Shortly afterward, Ivan Sutherland, working with Bob Sproull, developed the first HMD (head mounted display) and called it the "Sword of Damocles" because of the great elongated cable and arm hanging above the head of the wearer. With this device, they opened the door to full-immersion virtual reality [13].

Meanwhile, haptic devices were being developed at the University of North Carolina's Haptics Research Department; in the late 1960s through the early 1980s, devices like Grope I, II, and III and the Sarcos Arms were created there. At the AT&T labs, Knowlton's virtual push-button device was built. It projected a virtual graphic of symbols on a half-silvered screen above the hands of an operator using a keyboard, effectively combining the virtual with the real [14]. More developments in virtual reality physical feedback (haptic) interfaces started to happen in the 1980s. The Sayre Data Glove (developed at the University of Illinois with a

National Endowment for the Arts grant) lead to the Mattel Power Glove. Thomas Zimmerman, Jaron Lanier, and Scott Fisher met at Atari and later worked on the VPL glove [15].

At the same time, virtual worlds were being created in computers and in the early versions of the Internet. In 1974, Maze War was created, an early ancestor of the first-person shooter game; this included the first appearance of avatars, game space maps, and a first-person 3D perspective within the game space [16]. By 1978, the first MUD (Multi-user Dungeon) arrived. Known as the "Essex MUD" and played on the Essex University (UK) network, it ran until late 1987 [17]. The Essex MUD was a text-based game, creating a "constructivist" approach to virtual reality by allowing the players' imagination to construct the virtual world as they role-play with others online. Also notable was Krueger's Videoplace, created in 1983. It was the first graphics and gesture recognition environment [18].

1.2.5 GAMING AND VIRTUAL WORLDS

By 1986, Lucasfilm Games, Quantum Link, and Fujitsu had opened "Habitat" [19]. This was a significant step toward creating online gaming communities in virtual worlds. The imagination of the public and the appetite for immersive virtual worlds was stimulated by the appearance of the holodeck in *Star Trek, the Next Generation* (1987) [20]. MUDs were reinvented with the appearance of TinyMUD in 1989. This codebase, which created a socially oriented MUD, was based on player cooperation rather than competition and opened the door for socially based virtual worlds [21].

The early 1990s saw the invention and construction of the first CAVE at the University of Illinois in Chicago (1992). In the CAVE, all the technologies that had come before it were combined into one powerful device, creating intense immersive experiences. Still active today, the CAVE has video images projected in stereoscopic 3D. When they are inside it, visitors wear an HMD containing stereoscopic LCD (liquid crystal digital) shutter glasses to view the environment. Sensors collect information about the location and body position of the visitor and adjust the projection fields accordingly [22]. In 1993, Doom started the craze for gamers' first-person shooter games, creating the foundation of a gamer subculture, and was played by over 10 million within the first 2 years of its appearance. Full of graphic violent imagery, Doom has been named one of the 10 most controversial games of all time by Yahoo Games [23].

The mid-1990s ushered in a wave of online, socially based, constructive virtual worlds; among the most popular were, Worlds Chat, Active Worlds, and WorldsAway [24]. Although it seems impossible these days, these worlds functioned on a dial-up connection. In 1995, the ban on commercial usage of the Internet was lifted, and a home-based connection to more sophisticated games became possible. Eventually, broadband cable and Internet connections became available, paving the way for increased popularity of online gaming and virtual worlds [25]. EverQuest and Runescape were early members of the online virtual world MMORPG (massively multiplayer online role-playing game) category [26]. Soon, large, established games and entertainment franchises like World of Warcraft and Star Wars created their own virtual worlds [27]. Also in the early 2000s, the virtual worlds of Second Life and There combined social connection with user-generated content that could be bought and sold in the virtual world market [28,29]. As the midpoint of the second decade of this century approaches, increasing interactivity and immersion is being interwoven into the online home-based experience of virtual worlds. Many game makers and virtual world developers are striving toward creating an open game, one without levels or barriers that creates a compelling story through the emergent play of its visitors [30]. In 2007, OpenSimulator (or OpenSim, the abbreviation used in this book) arrived and started the creation of a system of virtual world grids, the foundation of a 3D Internet. This software, based on the Second Life protocols, does not seek to be a copy of Second Life; it seeks to expand the virtual worlds' Metaverse and provide connectivity among them all [31]. Kinect for Xbox 360 has been hacked to capture real-time motion tracking, and the Oculus Rift HMD holds promise for eager customers looking for immersive visual feedback in their virtual worlds [32]. There is undoubtedly much more to come, and for you, a designer of virtual environments, great challenges await.

1.3   HOW DO THEY WORK?

The best way to understand a virtual world is to visit one. There are hundreds of public virtual worlds online that allow access free of charge or through a subscription. A list of the most popular virtual 3D worlds includes Active Worlds, Minecraft, OpenSim-based worlds, Second Life, and The Sims Online.

Essentially, virtual worlds are persistent 3D spaces defined inside of a computer program running on a server. When you log out of one, the place still remains, it is "persistent," cycling through its daily settings and hosting other visitors to its location. Figure 1.2 shows the generic structure shared by most user content-generated virtual worlds such as OpenSim and Second Life. As you can see, even this bare-bones description is fairly complex. When you want to enter this world, you start with the viewer (or client) interface. This is a program that you download and run on your computer. For the purposes of this book, the Firestorm Viewer was selected since it is the most popular one and provides a customized setup for use in OpenSim as well as Second Life.

Assuming that you have set up an avatar account previously with whatever virtual world you would like to visit, let's look at the process of entering a virtual world.

After you have launched the viewer and logged in to your avatar account, your user name and password are verified by the login service, and if the account is valid, the avatar's last location or home location coordinates (x, y, z) are found on the land map of the world. The login service coordinates with the viewer so that the avatar can view the region it is entering and tells the simulator (sim) to expect an incoming avatar. Once the avatar starts to appear, you can see the landscape on your screen and your avatar standing on it. You are now in the simulator, and it is busy telling the grid service that you are there and that all the simulators around your location should share their data with your avatar and viewer so you can look over at them. There is lots going on in the simulator; it is the central backbone and a switchboard for information being sent to and received from your avatar. The simulator is also running lots of calculations in its physics engine to help objects and your avatar have realistic physics, like keeping your feet on the ground, providing solid walls and open doorways, letting coconuts from the nearby palm tree fall with a soft thump and roll around. The simulator is also keeping track of the objects in your inventory as well as the other assets in the region. This includes information about who made the content you see, who currently owns it, and what kind of permissions they have to modify it, sell it, or give it away. As you build stuff, especially large items like buildings or mountains, the simulator talks to the map database in the grid service, and that updates the look of your sim on the land map, which is shown in the viewer. The simulator also relays information to other servers and services that keep track of who owns land, especially if it is divided into parcels. It relays information about the lists of your friends and groups, what your social/privacy settings are, and other sorts of details regarding your environment and affiliations.

In 2011, a group of fearless explorers called the Alchemy Sims Builders set off across the Metaverse in search of more space and land they could call their own. They settled in on a server maintained by SimHost (http://www.simhost.com) and established the Alchemy Sims Grid (ASG), a 16-region grid accessible via the hypergrid (grid.alchemysims.com:8002:triton). Most of the content and pictures taken for this book were made on this grid, which runs OpenSim 0.7.5. In Figure 1.3, you can see what the "back end" of the system looks like on a computer screen. As you can see there are 17 windows open all the time; 16 of them are for the various regions on ASG, and 1 is for ROBUST, which coordinates the whole grid. Having a system like this gives you the god-like power to make quick and dramatic changes to your terrains, create avatar accounts and such. It also requires that you exercise responsible behavior and dedication to maintaining the persistence of the grid. At least once a month, there are server updates that shut the server down, so you will

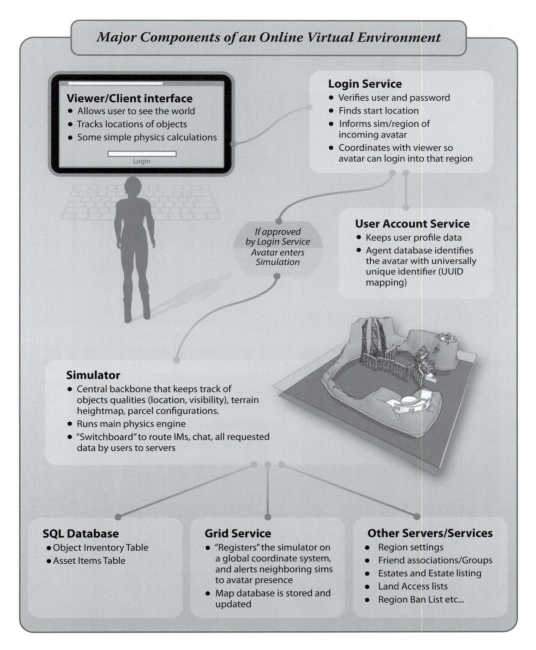

FIGURE 1.2 This is a diagram showing the major components of an online virtual environment, and how these components interact to bring the virtual environment experience to the user.

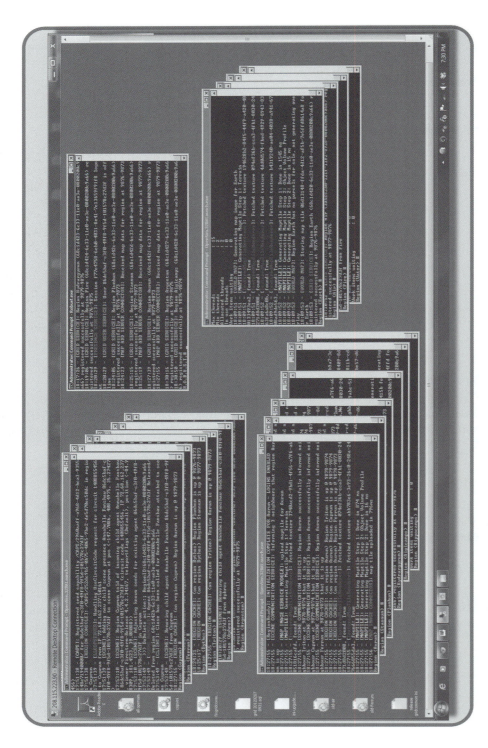

FIGURE 1.3 This is a screen grab of Alchemy Sims Grid server shown via a Remote Desktop Connection login. On the screen are 17 command line windows, one each for the 16 regions of the grid, and 1 for the ROBUST. (Redesigned OpenSimulator Basic Universal Server Technology) program that manages them. Alchemy Sims Grid can be reached via the Hypergrid address of grid.alchemysims.com:8002:triton.

need to know how to restart everything. This is especially true if you share the simulator with other people or have it attached to the hypergrid. They may have plans to build something that day, and if the simulator is down because of the updates or upgrades, that becomes frustrating. Furthermore, never forget that this is alpha software right now, so many weird and unpredictable things will happen. You will need to be diligent in backing up content and reminding the other users on your grid to do so as well.

1.3.1 So Many Worlds, So Little Time

There are many kinds of virtual worlds and the grids they contain; as a designer, you should visit as many as possible to see what the grid "culture" is and how things are organized. Another excellent way to keep up with virtual worlds is to follow blogs like New World Notes (http://www.nwn.blogs.com) and Hypergrid Business (http://www.hypergridbusiness.com) and set up some Google alerts about virtual worlds and virtual design so you receive links to all the latest news in your e-mail.

1.4 WHO USES VIRTUAL WORLDS AND HOW THEY USE THEM

The topic of virtual worlds and who uses them is always under exploration by researchers. Rutgers University conducted an online survey about worlds with UGC (user generated content) and posted some of the initial results (http://player-authors.rutgers.edu/). If you are new to virtual worlds, you would probably like to know how other people use them. An alphabetical set of thumbnail reports about how they are used in various sectors and some specific instances of each is listed below.

1.4.1 Architects/Landscaping Designers

Architects and environmental designers like Jon Brouchoud (http://jonbrouchoud.com/) and David Denton (http://www.daviddenton.com/) utilize virtual worlds like Second Life and OpenSim and the gaming platform Unity. In these worlds, they work with prototyping building designs, building site planning, and developing 3D models of both real and virtual worlds.

1.4.2 Artists/Painters, Sculptors, Dancers, Actors

The number of artists/painters, sculptors, dancers, and actors working in virtual worlds is huge. There are many performing arts groups in Second Life and OpenSim, and the creation of spectacular scenery and performance spaces is standard fare. Linden Endowment for the Arts (http://lindenarts.blogspot.com/) provides grants for full-region builds to artists and creators on a regular basis. In general, the folks in this category use virtual worlds for design planning, performance, environmental art, sculpture, game design, and gallery displays.

1.4.3 Engineers/Medical Professionals

Ever since their beginnings, Second Life, OpenSim, and Unity have displayed virtual versions of engineering problems, chemical modeling, medical models of the human body, and medical care facilities. Pam Broviak is a licensed civil engineer (state of Illinois) who utilizes virtual worlds for engineering training. Currently, she is working on developing virtual builds to simulate the layout and performance of civil engineering designs and plans, educational environments to teach civil engineering concepts, and a virtual learning and reference environment for local government. Other members of this category use virtual worlds for physical engine studies and structural 3D design.

1.4.4   DESIGNERS, SET DESIGNERS, INTERIOR DESIGNERS

Richard Finkelstein, (http://www.rfdesigns.org/), a professional set designer and set design teacher, uses virtual worlds for prototyping real scenery, teaching set design principles, and designing scenery for virtual performances. Other set and interior designers use virtual worlds for space planning and color studies.

1.4.5   SCIENTISTS AND MATHEMATICIANS

Scientists like Andrew Lang (http://journal.chemistrycentral.com/content/3/1/14) have used virtual worlds like Second Life to demonstrate the structure of molecules for chemical models. J. Gregory Moxness (http://theoryofeverything.org/MyToE/) uses virtual worlds to demonstrate models of E8 math, making the conceptual visible and beautiful.

1.4.6   TEACHERS IN PRIMARY, SECONDARY, AND GRADUATE SCHOOLS

Teachers in primary, secondary, and graduate schools quickly recognized the value of virtual worlds. Jokay Wollongong (http://www.jokaydiagrid.com/about/) started with Second Life and now has branches of her educational virtual worlds in OpenSim and Minecraft. Jokaydia, her grid in OpenSim, is made for teachers and their classes in grades K–20 and shares resources across the grid. Since 2009, Kenneth Y. T. Lim (http://voyager.blogs.com/about.html) has developed the Six Learnings curricular design framework, which has been used to inform the conceptualization, design, and development of a series of lessons that leverage the affordances for learning with the use of immersive environments in the Singapore school system. Teachers use this "Six Learnings" program in Singapore with virtual worlds to help students deepen their knowledge of and to examine their intuitions about local environments, as well as to prototype their creative works and to plan the productions and staging of dramatic performances.

1.4.7   TRAINERS AND THERAPISTS

Virtual worlds are invaluable for training, simulations, and therapy. Silicon Valley Media Group's First Responders Simulator utilizes them to create training and practice scenarios for disaster workers and emergency response teams. SVMG, headed by Cynthia Stagner, also develops simulation environments for hazardous occupations, in fields such as utilities, law enforcement, and industrial manufacturing. Other trainers use them to teach languages, practice acculturation for military deployment, and teach military strategy. The therapists working in virtual worlds find that the results are comparable to or better than a real-life meeting with their clients, as they counsel them on motherhood, post-traumatic stress disorders (PTSDs), and even weight loss. Patti Abshier works in Second Life to assist counseling professionals who provide counseling using virtual worlds. Other uses are role-playing for cognitive therapy, technical systems training, and medical training.

1.5   VIRTUAL ENVIRONMENTS FROM A DESIGNER'S POINT OF VIEW

What are the challenges to a designer on a virtual environment project? In some ways, they are exactly the same challenges of a designer in the physical world.

The primary challenge is to keep the client happy by helping define and present his or her message and supporting those efforts within a positive working environment including you and your team. A happy client is a flexible client, and a flexible client will give you the design latitude you need to be creative.

The secondary challenge is to be professional in your demeanor and work ethic. This means that you have taken the time to learn your craft and the working rules involved with your community, and that you strive to maintain the highest professional standards possible.

The tertiary challenge is to understand the needs of people, how that affects the accessibility of a virtual world, and the principles of Design for All.

1.5.1 Defining the Job of a Virtual Environment Designer

At present, there is no union or guild of virtual environment designers to codify the job description or set the working practices, but you will probably want to have those defined in any letter of agreement you have with a new client. A good definition to include in your paperwork would be the following:

> The virtual environment designer shall be responsible for the creation of the following: (1) creative concept representations, including sketches, models, and descriptions that pertain to the client's stated list of requirements for the environment; (2) subsequent rough preliminary 3D models and iterative progress representations as the design process progresses; and (3) the final environment in a virtual space, including all of the following items: terrain, landscaping, buildings, scripted objects, lighting, and sound elements.

You may also want to add in avatars and other kinds of special objects like vehicles if that is what you want to design and the client has requested it.

1.5.2 Being a Designer "In the Know"

As a designer of virtual environments, you should be well versed on the differences and similarities of various virtual platforms. One of the first questions to your client should be: "How many virtual worlds do you want to see this environment on?" If you have been designing for a while, especially if you started before early 2008, you are probably aware of the options provided by OpenSim and Unity. Each platform has created a paradigm shift in design thinking for virtual environments, and as a "metaversal" designer, you need to be aware of that. Figure 1.4 is a schematic drawing displaying some of the differences between Second Life, OpenSim, and Unity in terms of terrains, inventory backup, and content creation. A designer who is "in the know" plans for these differences so that if the client decides to change platforms, the designer is ready to go with it.

1.6 DESIGNING IN A PREEXISTING VIRTUAL WORLD OR MAKING ONE YOURSELF

The decision about where to build your first design for yourself or a client should not be taken lightly. There are many options, so you will need to do your homework regarding what these can provide and match them to your project's needs. Essentially, there are two basic categories: (1) prebuilt grids (or hosted grids) that allow you to have land regions, modify terrain, and create content that is hosted on someone else's server and (2) "do-it-yourself" virtual worlds that you install, run, and build on your own server or computer. Let's look at these and some examples of each.

1.6.1 Prebuilt Grids/Hosted Grids

The category of prebuilt and hosted grids includes the "full-service" grids like Second Life (http://www.secondlife.com) and over 200 OpenSim-based grids, such as 3rd Rock Grid (http://3rdrockgrid.com/),

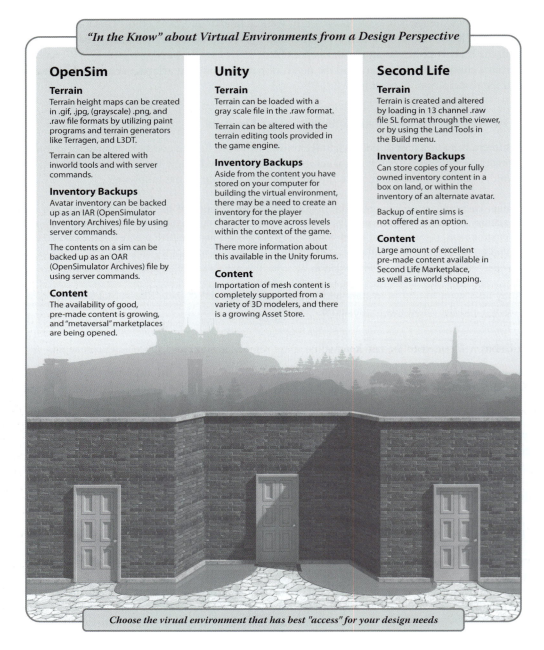

"In the Know" about Virtual Environments from a Design Perspective

OpenSim

Terrain
Terrain height maps can be created in .gif, .jpg, (grayscale) .png, and .raw file formats by utilizing paint programs and terrain generators like Terragen, and L3DT.

Terrain can be altered with inworld tools and with server commands.

Inventory Backups
Avatar inventory can be backed up as an IAR (OpenSimulator Inventory Archives) file by using server commands.

The contents on a sim can be backed up as an OAR (OpenSimulator Archives) file by using server commands.

Content
The availability of good, pre-made content is growing, and "metaversal" marketplaces are being opened.

Unity

Terrain
Terrain can be loaded with a gray scale file in the .raw format.

Terrain can be altered with the terrain editing tools provided in the game engine.

Inventory Backups
Aside from the content you have stored on your computer for building the virtual environment, there may be a need to create an inventory for the player character to move across levels within the context of the game.

There more information about this available in the Unity forums.

Content
Importation of mesh content is completely supported from a variety of 3D modelers, and there is a growing Asset Store.

Second Life

Terrain
Terrain is created and altered by loading in 13 channel .raw file SL format through the viewer, or by using the Land Tools in the Build menu.

Inventory Backups
Can store copies of your fully owned inventory content in a box on land, or within the inventory of an alternate avatar.

Backup of entire sims is not offered as an option.

Content
Large amount of excellent pre-made content available in Second Life Marketplace, as well as inworld shopping.

Choose the virual environment that has best "access" for your design needs

FIGURE 1.4   A diagram comparing some of the key features of 3 popular online virtual environments available for a designer to utilize. Two of them, OpenSim and Unity, are free to download and use. Second Life charges fees for membership and land usage.

Avination Grid (https://www.avination.com), or InWorldz (http://inworldz.com/faq.php). Maria Korolov keeps an updated list on her site, Hypergrid Business (http://www.hypergridbusiness.com/opensim-hosting-providers/). You can also start your own grid and have companies like SimHost (http://www.simhost.com/) and Dreamland Metaverse (http://www.dreamlandmetaverse.com/) host it on their servers. Each hosting company will offer different levels of access to the server on which your grid is hosted, so check their hosting packages carefully so you obtain what you want. If the image in Figure 1.3 makes you nervous, you probably want a hosting service that has created an interface for the server, which simplifies the process of uploading new terrain or saving an OAR (opensimulator archive) file for your built regions. If you want to dive into the system and access all those command windows, look for a host service that will allow that.

1.6.2 Do It Yourself

If you have the desire to create your own grid and host it on your own equipment, and words like configuration, network, firewall, and database settings do not make your head hurt, there are instructions for downloading your very own version of OpenSim and setting it up (http://opensimulator.org/wiki/User_Documentation).

If you want to do the same but use a self-installing version of OpenSim, you should look at New World Studio (http://newworldstudio.net/). While still in its early stages of development, this version of OpenSim holds promise for providing you with a relatively easy way to install OpenSim and get it up and running quickly.

The final option in this category is the simple and elegant SoaS (Sim on a Stick) (http://simonastick.com/). As a single-user, USB (universal serial bus) stick-based version of OpenSim, this software is available in multiple configurations of regions from 1 to 16. This is a good program to obtain if you want to learn about OpenSim, show it to other folks, and keep some spare regions around just for design prototyping.

1.7 CONCLUSION

Designers can "speak for the people" by representing their needs and interests in the virtual world. The designer's job is about being human, thinking about what humans need, solving their problems, helping them communicate, and doing some good in the world, virtual or otherwise. With those goals in mind, this book will at times take the "30,000-foot" perspective on virtual environments and at other times swoop down to obtain a closer look and deal with the details of a virtual environment and how to utilize it for your design purposes. Enjoy the ride.

REFERENCES

1. Internet World Stats, http://www.internetworldstats.com/stats.htm. Accessed August 1, 2013.
2. KZero Virtual World registered accounts statistics, http://www.kzero.co.uk/blog/virtual-world-registered-accounts-breakthrough-1bn/. Accessed August 1, 2013.
3. Allegory of the Cave, Wikipedia article, http://en.wikipedia.org/wiki/Allegory_of_the_Cave. Accessed August 4, 2013.
4. Aristotle, Wikipedia article, http://en.wikipedia.org/wiki/Aristotle#Metaphysics. Accessed August 4, 2013.
5. Butades, Wikipedia article, http://en.wikipedia.org/wiki/Butades. Accessed August 4, 2013.
6. Zeuxis and Parrhasius, Wikipedia article, http://en.wikipedia.org/wiki/Zeuxis_and_Parrhasius. Accessed August 3, 2013.
7. Pepper's Ghost, Wikipedia article, http://en.wikipedia.org/wiki/Pepper%27s_ghost. Accessed August 4, 2013.
8. Phantasmagorica, Wikipedia article, http://en.wikipedia.org/wiki/Phantasmagoria. Accessed August 4, 2013.
9. Auguste and Louis Lumière, Wikipedia article http://en.wikipedia.org/wiki/Auguste_and_Louis_Lumi%C3%A8re. Accessed August 4, 2013.
10. Panorama, Wikipedia article, http://en.wikipedia.org/wiki/Panorama. Accessed August 4, 2013.
11. Luis de Florez, Wikipedia article, http://en.wikipedia.org/wiki/Luis_de_Florez. Accessed August 4, 2013.

12. Sensorama, Wikipedia article, http://en.wikipedia.org/wiki/Sensorama. Accessed August 2, 2013.

13. The Sword of Damocles (virtual reality), http://en.wikipedia.org/wiki/The_Sword_of_Damocles_(virtual_reality). Accessed August 4, 2013.

14. Knowlton, K., Computer Displays Optically Superimposed on Input Devices. *Bell System Technical Journal*, 56(3), 367–383, 1976. http://www3.alcatel-lucent.com/bstj/vol56-1977/articles/bstj56-3-367.pdf. Accessed August 3, 3013.

15. History of Virtual Reality, a slide show by Greg Welch, http://www.cs.jhu.edu/~cohen/VirtualWorlds/media/pdf/Historical.color.pdf. Accessed August 2, 2013.

16. Maze War, Wikipedia article, http://en.wikipedia.org/wiki/Maze_war. Accessed August 3, 2013.

17. Essex MUD, Wikipedia article, http://en.wikipedia.org/wiki/Essex_MUD. Accessed August 3, 2013.

18. Videoplace, Wikipedia article, http://en.wikipedia.org/wiki/Videoplace. Accessed August 4, 2013.

19. Habitat (video game), Wikipedia article, http://en.wikipedia.org/wiki/Habitat_(video_game). Accessed August 4, 2013.

20. Holodeck, Wikipedia article, http://en.wikipedia.org/wiki/Holodeck. Accessed August 4, 2013.

21. TinyMUD, Wikipedia article, http://en.wikipedia.org/wiki/TinyMUD. Accessed August 4, 2013.

22. CAVE Automatic Virtual Environment, Wikipedia article, http://en.wikipedia.org/wiki/Cave_automatic_virtual_environment. Accessed August 4, 2013.

23. Doom, Wikipedia article, http://en.wikipedia.org/wiki/Doom_(video_game). Accessed August 3, 2013.

24. Active Worlds, Wikipedia article, http://en.wikipedia.org/wiki/Activeworlds. Accessed August 3, 2013.

25. Broadband, Wikipedia article, http://en.wikipedia.org/wiki/Broadband. Accessed August 3, 2013.

26. EverQuest, Wikipedia article, http://en.wikipedia.org/wiki/EverQuest. Accessed August 2, 2013.

27. World of Warcraft, Wikipedia article, http://en.wikipedia.org/wiki/World_of_Warcraft. Accessed August 3, 2013.

28. Second Life, Wikipedia article, http://en.wikipedia.org/wiki/Second_Life. Accessed August 4, 2013.

29. There, Wikipedia article, http://en.wikipedia.org/wiki/There_(virtual_world). Accessed August 4, 2013.

30. Open World, Wikipedia article, http://en.wikipedia.org/wiki/Open_world. Accessed August 4, 2013.

31. OpenSimulator web page, http://opensimulator.org/wiki/Main_Page. Accessed August 4, 2013.

32. Oculus Rift, Wikipedia article, http://en.wikipedia.org/wiki/Oculus_Rift. Accessed August 4, 2013.

2 How to Use This Book and Start Doing Virtual World Design

2.1 INTRODUCTION

Virtual worlds are interesting. If you picked up this book because you agree with that statement, these pages have lots to offer you. Let's take a quick glance at the content. The first and last chapters are full of information about what virtual worlds are, who uses them, and where they may be going in our future. In Chapters 3–16, you will find information about design theory and design practice and how those things relate to you as a teacher, trainer, or content creator. In these middle chapters, you will find several design projects that invite you to deepen your understanding as you learn about the topic and solidify it in your memory. If you are a teacher, try these with your class. If you train people or are interested in simulations for training in virtual worlds, you may find that some of these projects will help you bring more immersive aspects to the virtual environment, such as interactivity, universal access, and a virtual/aural gestalt. If you are a content-creating designer, this book will help you understand design parameters in virtual environments and how to leverage them with a comprehensive design methodology that will benefit you and your clients. These projects are of varying levels of difficulty, ranging from a beginner's skill set to an advanced virtual world user's skill set. Here and there you will find references to Unity (http://unity3d.com/), a free game engine from Unity Technologies. You may find it useful to know a little about some of the differences and similarities between virtual worlds and a game development environment like Unity, especially if you are going to repurpose your content.

2.2 HOW TO USE THIS BOOK

2.2.1 IF YOU ARE TOTALLY NEW TO VIRTUAL WORLDS

If you are new to virtual worlds and virtual environments, it is highly suggested that you read Chapters 1 and 2 first. These chapters will lay the foundation for your understanding of how a virtual world works and how to find a viewer interface. After that, if you are a designer and are interested in setting up a virtual world design practice, then Chapter 3 is a "must read." If you are a teacher and want to use this for classwork, then feel free to jump to Chapter 4 for the first 3D construction project. After that, it is a buffet course. Feel free to pick and choose among the rest of the chapters. For the most part, they are stand-alone modules for learning, although there is some cross-referencing, which is noted in the text.

2.2.2 BEEN THERE, DONE THAT: OLD HAND AT VIRTUAL WORLDS

If you have been designing in Second Life for a year or two and are thinking about setting up your own virtual world, then you should read Chapter 1 first and then skip to Chapters 4–16. Chapter 3 is a good one to read if you are thinking of creating a design company. Otherwise, feel free to skip around the book and try things as you want to or need focused information on a certain topic.

2.3 HOW TO GET AND UPLOAD THE CONTENT FOR THIS BOOK INTO YOUR VIRTUAL WORLD

Every effort is been made to provide good-quality content for use in this book. However, since they have no control over how this content is used, modified, or redistributed once released into the world, neither the book's author, Ann Cudworth, nor the content creator, Tim Widger are responsible for anything that happens to your computer or virtual world in which you are working while you are using this content, or anyone to whom you have given it. The content will be periodically reviewed and updated if necessary, and update notes placed on the Ann Cudworth Projects site, http://www.anncudworthprojects.com/.

2.3.1 WHERE TO GET THE CONTENT AND INFORMATION ABOUT IT ONLINE

1. The primary source will be http://www.anncudworthprojects.com/, in the Virtual World Design Book Download section, organized by book chapter. Information will be posted on the blog, and other pages on the site as tutorials are developed and reader feedback posted.
2. Content will be also be available in Second Life and possibly some other grids, as the need develops, and notice of such availability will be made on the website and through social media channels. Feel free to like Ann Cudworth Projects on Facebook, follow Ann Cudworth Projects on Google+, and @afanshaw on Twitter.

2.3.2 BEST PRACTICES FOR NAMING CONVENTIONS WHEN UPLOADING CONTENT INTO YOUR VIRTUAL WORLD

It is highly suggested that you name each mesh model file you upload from the Ann Cudworth Project site, with exactly the same name as the original file, to avoid confusion while you are working on the projects in these chapters.

If you are importing the 3D content from this book into OpenSim or Second Life as a COLLADA .dae (Digital Asset Exchange) file, please be aware that download times may vary significantly depending on your bandwidth, processor speed, and such. Some of these models are large and will take a while to load into your virtual environment. After extensive test analysis, the following guidelines have been written to help you with the content uploads from this book. The Avatar/Upload/Mesh Model menu which you will use to do this is illustrated in Chapter 13, Figures 13.15–13.17.

2.3.2.1 Tab 1–Level of Detail (LOD) Guidelines to Follow on Upload from Source

1. In Second Life for High source setting use "Load from file," for the Medium source setting it should be "use LOD above," and for Low and Lowest source settings use the "Generate" setting. This will give you a good resolution on the model at most distances, without boosting the Land Impact or costing too much in Upload fees.
2. In OpenSim, where the Uploads are free of charge, you can use "Load from file" settings for High and Medium LOD uploads, use "the LOD above" in the Low source, and keep the Lowest at "Generate."

2.3.2.2 Tab 2–Physics Guidelines to Follow

Use this for both Second Life and OpenSim. Please see the known problems section regarding uploading models from SketchUp.

1. Step 1: Level of Detail (for the physics collision shape) Select "From File" and load in the accompanying physics .dae file. This physics file will have a name that matches the mesh model. This is a simplified version of the mesh model structure, with no textures on it, that will be used by the mesh model as a physics collision shape. *Note:* In future usage, on your own models. To use the Upload menu for the generation of a physics shape is a trial and error process. You will save more time, if you make your own simplified versions of your mesh model and use that for a physics shape file.
2. Leave Step 2 and Step 3 alone on this menu tab for these uploads.
3. *Note:* In Second Life, the physics shape type on a mesh is set to "convex hull" under the Features tab of the Build/Edit menu, by default. You will need to change this to "prim" for every mesh you upload. The prim setting for physics shape type is the default in OpenSim.

2.3.2.3 Tab 3–Upload Options to Use

1. Use the scale spinner to enlarge/reduce the mesh model on Upload if the project calls for it.
2. Texture guidelines to follow on Upload: The textures for the model must be in the same folder as the model in order for them to be applied to the surfaces of the model during an upload. They will be included with the model, as long as the Include Textures box is ticked when you upload.

2.3.3 Known Problems with Uploads in Second Life and OpenSim

1. Make sure that mesh models uploaded in Second Life, are set to "prim" under Physics Shape type in the Features section of the Build/Edit menu.
2. In both Second Life and OpenSim, mesh models that have multiple parts may not be uploaded with the same key or main prim with which the mesh model was created. If you are uploading a mesh model, and need a specific part to be key, you may need to unlink it and re-link it when the mesh is rezzed inworld.
3. Loading models from SketchUp into Second Life can be problematic. Even though, SketchUp will save a COLLADA .dae file that will upload to Second Life, you may find that the physics shape will not function properly. If you are going to make many mesh models for Second Life, it is recommended that you use a modeler like Blender or 3DS Max. There seems to be no such problems in OpenSim with uploading a mesh model from SketchUp; it will take a COLLADA .dae from SketchUp as well as the physics "From File" setting.
4. Sections of a model that were built with a transparent material on them may become opaque because of a state change in the upload. To make them transparent again, go into Edit Linked and select that part or face, not the whole linked object. Then, in the Edit Menu, under the Texture Edit tab, change the transparency to what you need.

2.3.3.1 Licensing Information

All the 3D model content, Ann Cudworth's sound content, and other content that she and Tim Widger have created for this book are provided under the Creative Commons Attribution 3.0 license (http://creativecommons.org/licenses/by/3.0/deed.en_US), which means you are licensed to (1) share it (to copy, distribute, and transmit the work); (2) remix it (adapt the work), and make commercial use of the work, under the following conditions:

Attribution: You must attribute the work in the manner specified by the author or licensor (but not in any way that suggests that the author or licensor endorse you or use of the work).

A suggested form of Attribution would be to add "Virtual World Design Book written by Ann Cudworth, model created by Tim Widger, 2013" in the description box of the mesh model you are going to use from this book in your virtual world.

2.3.3.2   How to Use the LSL Scripts Provided

Regarding the utilization of the LSL (Linden Scripting Language) scripts provided with this book, please follow these guidelines. Each script, shown in the tables of this book are available in in the Virtual World Design Book Downloads section, listed by chapter on the website, http://www.anncudworthprojects.com/. If you are going to use the LSL script take it from there, as a WordPad or text file, not from the tables in the book. The tables have extra enumeration, that will not be needed inworld when the script is going to run. Some of these scripts have been created by other people, such as the LSL scripts in Chapter 7 and Chapter 15, are under their own licenses and provided for use under those terms. For the most part, this means keeping the header of the script intact, so the original source of the script is known. Read each script to be sure you know its specific license terms, before you use it.

2.4   OPERATING SYSTEM AND SYSTEM CONFIGURATION FOR YOUR COMPUTER

Throughout this book, there has been an effort to be platform agnostic. You may be a PC user or a Mac or Linux-based system user, and there are advantages and disadvantages to each platform in terms of virtual world design. Whatever computer system you decide to use, it should be of good quality and backed up by warranties. Virtual world graphics are demanding on a computer system, and you may find that your settings in terms of shadows and draw distance cannot be the same as other users if your system is old or on the slower side of processing speeds.

For the creation of this book, two computers were used. The first one was a medium-grade desktop workstation that was 5 years old and died a slow death as its graphics card started to overheat during an early summer heat wave. The second one is a custom build by JNCS (http://www.JNCS.com). It runs on Windows 7 Professional, with an Intel Core i7-4770K CPU at 3.5 GHz. The system RAM is 16 GB, and it is running a 64-bit setup. The graphics card is an NVIDIA GeForce GTX 680. There is much more information about what kind of systems to use with virtual worlds online at http://secondlife.com/support/system-requirements/.

In general, all key commands in this book are given with the PC in mind; the alternative keys for the Mac are given in Table 2.1.

2.5   WHO THIS BOOK WAS WRITTEN FOR

This book is most definitely for you if you have read this far into it. More and more people are using virtual environments and finding uses based on challenges that require new ways to organize and focus the design process. This book is here to help you understand the general principles of 3D design and how to apply them to your specific project. It shows that designing is a way of thinking, a way of seeing patterns and systems, that enables you to support your ideas and get your message across to the visitor in your virtual space. This book will also help you teach others how to do this, to help them build the mental scaffolding neces-

TABLE 2.1
PC Keyboard Commands and the Mac Alternatives

PC Commands (Windows)	Macintosh Commands (Mac System)
Control (Ctrl)	Command (for most shortcuts) or Control
Alt	Option key
Windows/Start	Command/apple
Backspace	Delete
Shift	Shift
Delete	Del
Enter	Return
Right click	Hold Control key and click
Zoom with mouse middle wheel	Control and scroll

sary to understand complex visual systems and 3D environments. Whatever you decide to do in a virtual environment, good design and the understanding of how to create it is fundamental knowledge.

2.6 HOW TO PICK YOUR VIEWER FOR A VIRTUAL WORLD

For the purposes of creating this book, the Phonix Firestorm Viewer version 4.5.1 (Build (38838) Oct 28 2013 01:35:58 (Firestorm-Beta) with OpenSimulator support) and its previous version were used. If you are going to do the projects in this book, it is recommended you download and install this version or higher, since it is referenced heavily. You must use a mesh enabled viewer for the projects in this book as all the 3D content you will download from them is made from mesh. The Second Life wiki has lots of information about requirements for mesh here: http://wiki.secondlife.com/wiki/Mesh. The Phoenix Firestorm Project offers versions tailored specifically for Second Life and OpenSim, so choose the one for whatever type virtual world you find yourself visiting most regularly. There are more details about that on their website, (http://www.firestormviewer.org/). This is not your only option, and having an array of viewers is actually a good idea from a design standpoint. A comprehensive list of all third-party viewers is provided by Second Life (http://wiki.secondlife.com/wiki/Third_Party_Viewer_Directory). Take a look at that list and then consider the following questions:

1. What is your computer system? Mac, PC, or Linux? If your team has a mixed-platform profile, your best bet is to choose client viewers that support all three platforms, which limits the selection immediately.
2. Will you be doing lots of building and creating? If so, then pick from among the viewers designed for that purpose, like Firestorm, Dolphin, Catznip, and Singularity.
3. Do you have special projects in mind? If you want a high-performance viewer for machinima and photography, then Niran's viewer would be your choice, although it does not support Mac.
4. Do you still love the old Second Life viewer and want that look and feel? That would point your choice to Singularity, which incorporates the new code into an older interface.
5. Do you have to create large-scale projects under pressure? Then, you need a viewer with the most stability and lowest crash rate. That would be Firestorm, followed by the Standard SL viewers.

From time to time, you should review the list of third-party viewers to see if there are any new offerings. Radegast, while not a graphic-based viewer, is great for low-bandwidth connections, and there are several mobile tablet-based viewers under development, like Lumiya for Android and Pocket Metaverse for iPhone. New features were being developed by Linden Labs in 2013 for Second Life, such as the server side baking of avatar features, the inclusion of the CHUI (communications hub user interface), and a new materials system (STORM-1905 project). These and other Second Life and OpenSim code changes have had an impact on the third-party viewers and challenge their development groups to keep improving their code.

3 "Build It Once"
Optimizing Your Design Workflow

The supreme accomplishment is to blur the line between work and play.

—**Arnold J. Toynbee**

3.1 OVERVIEW: REDUCING REPETITIVE BUILDING AND INCREASING CREATIVE DESIGN TIME

Design workflow for creative ideas is the circulatory system of your project. It must be kept unobstructed by the blockage of incompatible software formats, inconsistent work standards, and lack of proper planning. In this chapter, you will be introduced to standards and practices that enable your team to function more efficiently, scale up more effectively, and optimize your content creation practices. This is called the "Build It Once" system. As a designer for virtual spaces, you will eventually work in all sorts of environments and will need to repurpose content, as well as refine it in the more advanced systems. No one likes to waste time rebuilding something because it will not load properly into a 3D modeler or a virtual world. The pitfalls are many and can catch the unaware or unprepared designer. By planning your project within the "Build It Once" framework, you create a set of work standards, and you save your team the headaches and lost time of backtracking and redoing work because something got lost or was made incorrectly. Let's get started.

3.2 FIVE BASIC STEPS TO SET YOUR STANDARDS AND PRACTICES

There are five basic steps to help you overcome workflow blockage from inconsistent work standards and lack of planning.

3.2.1 ORGANIZE YOUR FILE STRUCTURE

To drastically cut down on the time spent looking for a previously built item, set up a logical file structure for your project in your computer and duplicate that structure in your virtual world inventory. When you upload a mesh or texture to Second Life or OpenSim, it lands on the top of a pile of items in your avatar's inventory. After a day of iterative design uploads, things can get messy. The first thing to do is to make a "named" project folder for your avatar's inventory, which includes subfolders for all of the components you will be using. The "name" can be an acronym for the whole project. For instance, if you were working on a project called "Our Virtual Schoolhouse," each folder and each item you upload would start with "OVS." Here is how your file structures would look:

OVS Project Folder (contains subfolders)
  OVS Animations (contains subfolders)
    OVS—Animation files and the like

FIGURE 3.1   Screen grab showing Annabelle Fanshaw's inventory file structure for the SL8B project in Second Life. Notice how all the folders start with SL8B, so they congregate in the appropriate place.

    OVS Avatars (contains subfolders)
        OVS—Avatar skins and the like
    OVS Documents, Notecards, Notices
        OVS—Schedules and the like
    OVS Meshes (contains subfolders)
        OVS—Avatars (contains avatar components)
        OVS—Buildings (contains buildings and their components)

This is a sample list only; you may need to add more folders to customize this for a specific project. By following the practice of naming each folder and subfolder with the identifying three-letter acronym, your entire inventory for that project can be isolated with a simple three-letter search keyword. Anything missing or hiding in the lost and found section of your avatar's inventory can be easily located and filed in the appropriate folder. By utilizing this file structure across your virtual world platforms, in the cloud/server storage, and on your computer's file system, you will provide a content structure that you and all of your team will be able to utilize with greater efficiency. A little cleanup and reorganization at the end of each day should be enough to keep it functioning well. See Figure 3.1 for a screen shot of a file structure setup used on a Second Life project called SL8B.

3.2.2 Clarify Your Terminology, Going Even Deeper

Take the time to define what your nomenclature standards will be on the project and make them clear to the entire team. You have started this by naming all of your file folder structures with a three-letter keyword.

Type of Object	Prefix Used	Other Qualifiers (e.g., location/looks at/color/size, etc.)	Resulting Name for Your Inventory Object
Point light	PL	PL is on the ceiling and is pink.	PL-ceil-pink
Spot light	SP	SP points at talent on stage from right side.	SP-talent-SL (SL is stage left)
Direct light	Dir	Direct light acting like sunset on whole scene.	Dir-sunset
Projector light	Proj	Projected movie on northeastern wall of house.	Proj-movie-NE-wall
Camera	Cam	Camera from front of stage in television studio set that looks like an office.	Cam-2-Office
Wall	Wall	Northeastern wall: 1 of 10.	Wall-NE-1
Door	Door	Northeastern door for bedroom.	Door-NE-bedroom
Window	Win	Northeastern window: 6 of 20.	Win-NE-6
Trees/plants/other vegetation	Tree	3-meter tall oak tree in winter look.	Tree-Oak-3m-winter
Architecture/buildings	Bldg	Small guest cottage for estate.	Bldg-cottage
Special effects/particle effect	SPFX	Roaring bonfire for beach scene.	SPFX-bonfire-large
Animations	AN	The lambada dance, male partner's choreography for your party scene.	AN-Lambada-male
Clothing and skins: upper/lower/head/ tattoo/alpha	Up/Low/Head/Tat/Alpha	Dragon tattoos for upper parts of male body.	Tat-Up-Male-Dragon
Sounds	Snd	Large waterfall.	Snd-waterfall-large

FIGURE 3.2   Table showing suggested abbreviations and nomenclature for lights and camera types, 3D model types, scripted particle producing objects, animations, skin textures, and sounds used in virtual environments.

Let's develop this idea. When you also include the "OVS" in front of each texture you make, every mesh, and so on, this organizes your content even more. There are even more ways to use proper naming to clarify each item's identity and function. For instance, suppose you have made a new wall texture, a desk, and you have built an inworld spotlight prim for your OVS project. A clear set of names would be as follows: ovs-insidewall_schoolhouse.jpg, ovs_small_single_desk_schoolhouse.dae, and ovs-SP-wallwash-blue.

In each case, the name starts with the project keyword code "ovs" and then the name continues to define the item by what it is, such as "insidewall," "small_single_desk," and "SP-wallwash" (which means a spotlight that lights the wall at a steep angle, creating a wash of light). The last bit of each name tells us more specific qualities of each texture, object, light, etc. The wall texture goes inside the schoolhouse, as does the desk, and the spotlight is set to a blue color. The use of dashes or underscores is up to your discretion, you may simply leave a space there if you desire.

Try to be as descriptive as you can without getting too wordy. Make up a list of abbreviations that the whole group can utilize so everyone is on the same page. With a logical naming system, any member of your team should be able to quickly find a specific object among the hundreds generated during the creation process. And, they will know exactly what the object is without having to open the file. Even a model or texture that has not been used for years is still useful because it can be easily found with this system and repurposed for a new build, saving you and the team time and money. Figure 3.2 is a table of suggested name abbreviations and a naming methodology that you can use with 3D models and virtual environments to indicate the kind of object, light, texture, and so on in your scenes.

3.2.3 STANDARDIZE YOUR RESOLUTIONS

Set up the resolution standards the team will use for textures in every project. For 90% of your texture work within Second Life, OpenSim, and Unity, an image the resolution of 512×512 pixels will be more than sufficient. Only when you need high fidelity of detail should you go to the maximum setting of 1024×1024 pixels on a texture in Second Life or OpenSim. The resolution can be taken even higher in Unity, but you need to remember most high-end graphics cards and platforms top out at a resolution of 2048×1536 pixels, so your rendering cost may not be worth the extra fidelity [1]. Of course, when you are making a new texture, working from a higher-resolution base image is preferred, so you can max out the detail of the image and then reduce it to the 512 pixel size.

3.2.4 STREAMLINE YOUR UPLOAD METHODOLOGY AND TEST EVERYTHING

Decide ahead of time how you want to upload your mesh models. If you are not sure how much various settings on the upload menu will cost in terms of land impact and upload charges in Second Life, take advantage of the Second Life Beta Test grid, which will not charge you upload fees. You can log in to this right from the viewer's main page, under the Log into Grid menu. After some testing, you can define your preferred land impact for meshes in Second Life, level of detail (LOD), and physics settings and synch this with your 3D model building methods. Like the texture resolutions, you should seek to find the optimum numbers of vertices and faces for your models that give the highest LOD with the lowest land impact.

Cross-check these virtual world settings with the model's appearance in Unity or any other platform you are using so you know your mesh models look good everywhere and run efficiently. If you are adding on to a previous build in your virtual environment, it would be good practice to go through that build and check the relative land impact costs you already have in your objects. You may find some surprising results, especially if you have some old hollowed or twisted prims (primitives) lying about. Just select the objects and compare their relative land impact costs as displayed in the Build/Edit menu under the Create/Land Impact/More info link. See Figure 3.3 for a screenshot of this feature.

It is possible that the land impact of many objects, especially their physics weights, can be greatly reduced without having an impact on their functionality by changing the type of physics settings and making your own physics shape files. There is excellent information available about how Second Life measures land impact here (http://community.secondlife.com/t5/Mesh/Prims-Prim-Equivalent-Land-Impact-a-too-long-guide/td-p/1293579).

Note: It would be good practice to make a habit of reading articles in the creation forums of Second Life (http://community.secondlife.com/t5/Creation-Forum/ct-p/CreationForum) and Unity3D (http://forum.unity3d.com/forum.php) every week so you can stay on top of what is being developed and tested.

3.2.5 CREATE A DETAILED PLAN

Make graphics documents, rough models, storyboards, and even animatic movies (movies made from clipped-together artwork and stills) to organize the project, define your team tasks, and assign them. This is like a "to-do" list on steroids and creates a detailed plan that everyone understands. Figure 3.4 shows an example of how an alien avatar was conceived for a 2010 project in Second Life.

In another example of planning, Figure 3.5 shows how SketchUp (http://www.sketchup.com/) was used for a proposal presentation in 2010 for a game sim built in Second Life. At first, a rough schematic model was made, and from that model a series of sketches was generated so that the client (IBM Art Grant committee) understood the complexities of the build.

FIGURE 3.3 Screen grabs from Second Life showing the process of assessing the land impact of previously built objects on your land by using the advanced information link (center box) under the General Tab of the Build Menu (right side box) in the Firestorm viewer. On the left is the "What is all this?" help browser web link provided by Firestorm to explain the meaning of "weights" and "land impacts" generated by your content.

Taking the time to make a detailed plan serves you in many ways. It can be used to sell the client on the idea and your professionalism, to organize the team and rev them up about the project, and to help you see the overall scheme for workflow for the project.

3.3 LINES AND ARROWS AND CHARTS, OH MY!

The following section presents some large charts that represent possible workflow scenarios for your design studio. As you know already, each project in the virtual environment design is a bespoke creation, but like that great tailor on Savile Row making custom suits, you will need to have your creation methods organized and refined. The best way to utilize the information in this section is to consider these concepts first and then to observe your team's workflow. It may be that you utilize different software or have the need to interact with many other teams. Take the best parts of these ideas for your use and customize the details to fit your particular team and project.

3.3.1 "BUILD IT ONCE" CONTENT FLOW SYSTEM

Figure 3.6 has a chart that illustrates the "Build It Once" content flow for design development in Second Life, OpenSim, and Unity. The software was chosen to fit a work group that utilizes both Mac and PC platforms.

Sy Avatar - Concept Sheet   "Inland - Search for the Sy"

Sources: Silicon based creature based on fractal structures

Sample Looks

FIGURE 3.4 Concept sketch showing ideas for the Sy avatar created for "Inland: Search for the Sy," built in 2010 on IBM exhibition sims, in Second Life.

This design method structure is focused around a "shared content library" full of items with file formats that can be utilized by all the destination platforms. You should look for the common file formats that can be imported and exported from the software your team likes to use. Sure, there are plenty of translators; MeshLab (http://meshlab.sourceforge.net/) is a fine example, but your goal here is to streamline the work-flow as much as possible. Just because the final platform of your project will accept 18 file formats does not

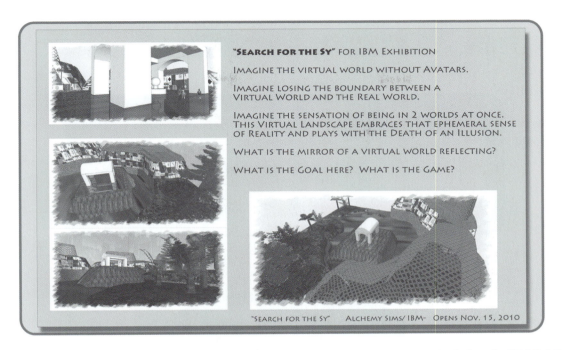

FIGURE 3.5 Initial pitch/proposal sketches created in SketchUp for "Inland: Search for the Sy" on the IBM Exhibit sims, from 11/2010-2/2011.

mean your team should be working with all of them. Try to utilize the most common file formats, like the COLLADA (.dae), the Autodesk .fbx format, and you will have fewer translation issues. Bear in mind that it is the COLLADA (.dae), not the Autodesk (.dae), file format that is universally accepted in Second Life and OpenSim. The strength of using SketchUp Pro in this scenario is that your prototype models can be viewed in the OpenSim and on Unity. Blender is a free 3D modeling program, so you can set up lots of workstations for an expanding team without much overhead. 3DSMax is a widely used professional program for 3D modeling in the entertainment industry. There are probably some more software programs you like and want to include here, but these three will cover most of your needs and offer a wide price range.

3.3.2 "Build It Once" Chart of Studio Skills and Responsibilities

You may be a sole proprietor, but understanding the typical structure of a larger design studio is necessary. There may be sudden growth in your business, or you may take on a new job with a larger studio. Again, you are urged to embrace the "spirit" of this chart and revise the details as they pertain to your experience and needs.

As you look at the chart of skills and responsibilities in Figure 3.7, it is necessary for you to understand that there are important lines of direct communication to be established. While it's crucial that all members of the team communicate well with all the other groups, the big decisions and clearest workflow streams go through these direct lines of communication. As you may note, the art director/creative director position is the very hub of this structure. Everyone needs to talk to the art director for one thing or another, and usually this person's phone is ringing off the hook. However, as important as that position is, these individuals are only as good as the teams that support them. Without great images from the concept artist or clear background stories from

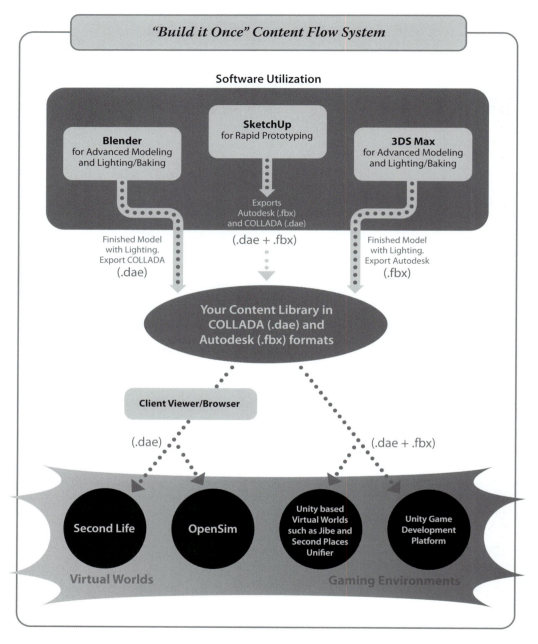

FIGURE 3.6 Chart showing how the "Build It Once" methodology can be utilized with several modeling programs and virtual worlds at the same time. *Note:* See Chapter 2, Section 2.3 for more information on upload procedures.

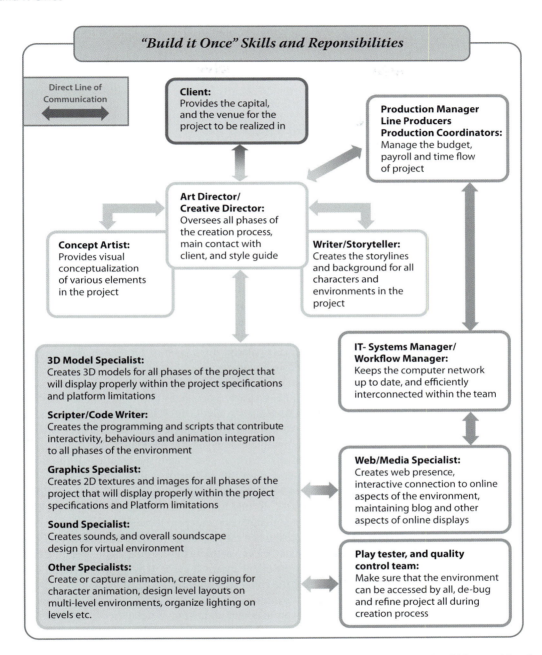

"Build it Once" Skills and Reponsibilities

Direct Line of Communication

Client:
Provides the capital, and the venue for the project to be realized in

Production Manager Line Producers Production Coordinators:
Manage the budget, payroll and time flow of project

Art Director/ Creative Director:
Oversees all phases of the creation process, main contact with client, and style guide

Concept Artist:
Provides visual conceptualization of various elements in the project

Writer/Storyteller:
Creates the storylines and background for all characters and environments in the project

3D Model Specialist:
Creates 3D models for all phases of the project that will display properly within the project specifications and platform limitations

Scripter/Code Writer:
Creates the programming and scripts that contribute interactivity, behaviours and animation integration to all phases of the environment

Graphics Specialist:
Creates 2D textures and images for all phases of the project that will display properly within the project specifications and Platform limitations

Sound Specialist:
Creates sounds, and overall soundscape design for virtual environment

Other Specialists:
Create or capture animation, create rigging for character animation, design level layouts on multi-level environments, organize lighting on levels etc.

IT- Systems Manager/ Workflow Manager:
Keeps the computer network up to date, and efficiently interconnected within the team

Web/Media Specialist:
Creates web presence, interactive connection to online aspects of the environment, maintaining blog and other aspects of online displays

Play tester, and quality control team:
Make sure that the environment can be accessed by all, de-bug and refine project all during creation process

FIGURE 3.7 Chart showing the skills and responsibilities in a larger design office that should be considered when setting up the "Build It Once" methodology.

the writer, the art director has no images or words to impress the client or to guide the model creation team. The producers and production managers have their eyes on the overall picture; every day, they look at what was accomplished and revise their perception of how effectively the whole system is performing. Although estimating the cost of producing creative designs is difficult, a great producer knows how to weigh those intangible factors into their budgeting processes and can diplomatically keep the whole studio on time and on budget.

3.3.3   "Build It Once" Project Development Workflow

Anyone familiar with the tidal changes on a seaside harbor has observed that as the tide comes in, there will be lots of swirls and eddies in the water, all surrounding the main direction of the tidal flow. Project development takes the same sort of shape, conceptually speaking; there are many side circles of development going on, which all contribute to the overall push in the direction of the goal. In the world of software development, there is a term called *Agile development* [2], which has been adopted by the "Lean Startup" business movement to define the process of iteration and incremental development as a productive and successful approach to creating a new business model [3]. This approach has merit in the process of designing a new virtual environment as well.

In Figure 3.8, the project development workflow chart, you will see that the central flow of the project is surrounded by "Agile Cycles." On the right side are the verbal elements of the environment; on the left are the visual elements of the environment. As the project progresses up from concept through development to creation, each level will contain a cycle of iteration and incremental change that is fed into the mainstream for overall construction. This is necessary because each new element added into a virtual environment will affect the overall balance, the load on the server, and the accessibility to its visitors. Of course, there are limits; no one can build a house if the brick maker keeps redesigning the bricks. Most of the cycling will be done in the concept and preliminary phases. These will spin very fast, changing daily, if not hourly. Further up the ladder, the cycles of level design, model making will spin more slowly as changes to those elements take more time and effort. In the center of it all are four important correlated systems: the 3D/2D designing, the coding/script writing, the optimization, and the sound design. All of these systems have an impact on each other, and the members of these groups need to be in constant communication regarding their needs and the impact of other work on their constructions. Finally, at the top of the chart, in synch with the creation of the final virtual environment, will be the creation of the video trailer and website to advertise and promote the new build.

Let's zoom in on one of the Agile Cycles. Figure 3.9 shows how it works in detail. In the center is the iterative/innovative cycle. It follows the "creation/rest/test" format that a global-based design group can provide. While members of one team are creating and testing, members on the team located many time zones away are resting and will pick up the creation and testing cycle when they return to work the next day. Of course, it is optimal to have the global teams close enough so that they can actually have a meeting in real time once a day.

The other important part of this Agile Cycle is the client approval cycle. If your design studio is working with a client from a large company, it is likely that the client will have several levels of approval within their company for each major step in the project. If your immediate client approves something without traveling through his or her own company approval cycle, you may end up having to delay or cancel your project, so watch out for that. With a diplomatic approach, try to learn about the hierarchy of approval in your client's company, so you know what their process is.

3.3.4   Organizational Structure for a Large Design Office

Eventually, your build group, design company, or school may find the need to organize a large group of people for a project. This can be a real challenge to workflow if productivity and creativity are hampered

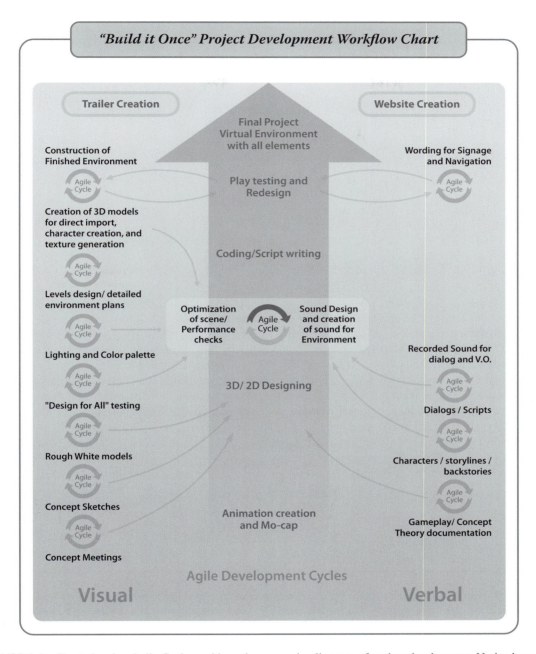

FIGURE 3.8 Chart showing Agile Cycles and how they occur in all stages of project development. Notice how they all feed into the center, while continuing to progress upward towards completion of the project. These cycles should be considered when creating a "Build It Once" workflow methodology.

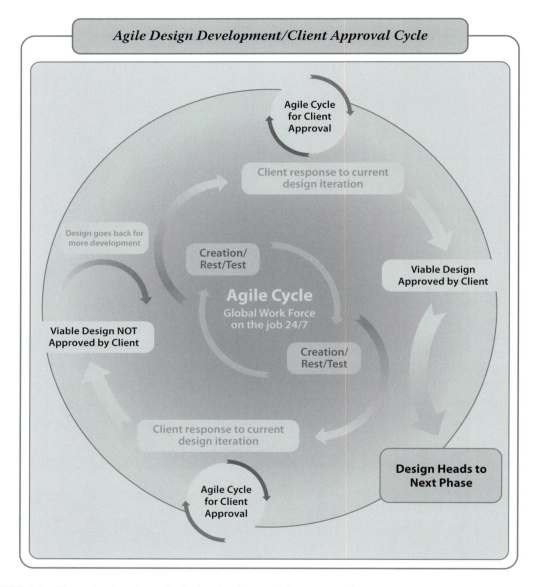

FIGURE 3.9 Chart showing the agile design development/client approval cycle. Note how this cycle is dependant on the client's own approval process. This process should be taken into account when developing a "Build It Once" methodology for your design group.

by excessive layers of management, unproductive meetings, and bureaucratic office procedures. Figure 3.10 shows a basic office structure for a large virtual environment design office. Again, this is a conceptual representation of the structure; your office may need to include additional group modules like an educational planning department, a human interface testing department, or a mobile media integration department. The structure of the team should be flexible enough so it can add group modules as may be required by new

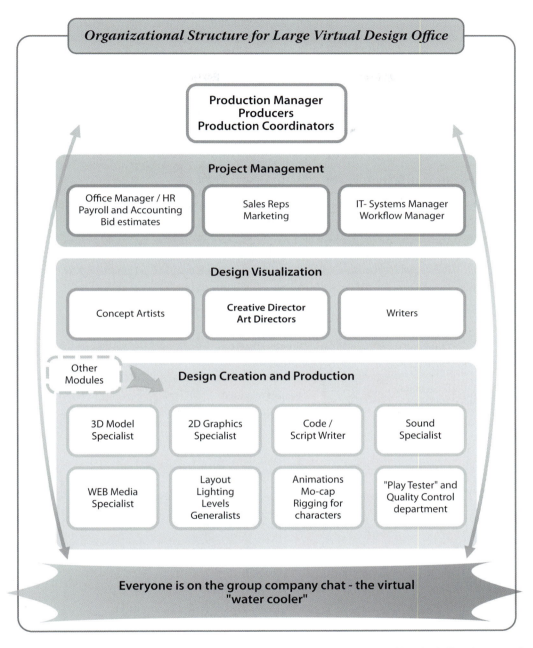

FIGURE 3.10 Chart showing the organizational structure for a large virtual design office, including the general range of groups that will function together on a project. This structure should be considered when applying a "Build It Once" methodology to the workflow.

projects. You may decide to make your company all virtual and have the company headquarters in a virtual world. There are some advantages to this, such as easy scalability of workspace, access control via private or self-hosted islands, and a built-in testing ground for your new designs. The importance of a production manager, who daily takes on the roles of social buffer, traffic cop, and diplomat, cannot be overstated. Daily communication among your groups can be supplemented by having a companywide chat channel, the virtual equivalent of the water cooler meeting, so people can take advantage of crowdsourcing when they have a problem or question. Other key people are the office financial manager and the systems/workflow manager. In a virtual design office, these folks provide a stable base of operations, and an organized, functional environment where the creative and production teams can do their work.

3.3.5 Organizational Structure for a Small Design Office

You may be just starting out or, for project budgetary reasons, need to keep your team smaller. A small dedicated, highly skilled team can accomplish much with careful planning; see Figure 3.11 for an overall picture.

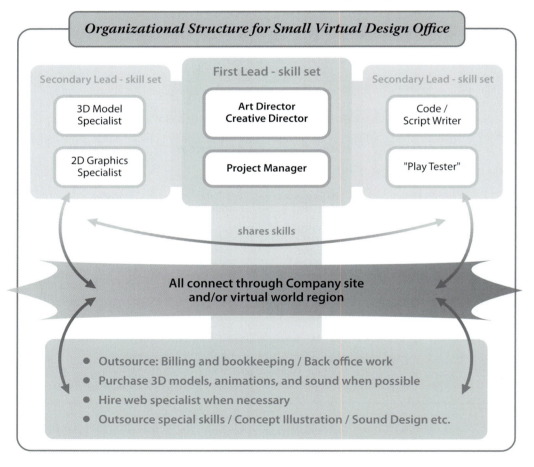

FIGURE 3.11   Chart showing the organizational structure of a small virtual design office and how content purchasing, outsourced office management and web specialists would be utilized.

The first things you should assess are how your skills break out and how they may complement each other. To some extent, you should each know how to do the other person's job so you can step in if a person becomes overloaded. In the 1970s, the Dutch soccer (football) program had a style of play called "total football" (*totaalvoetbal* in Dutch), and for almost 5 years, the Dutch dominated the sport. They trained every member of the team besides the goalie to have an understanding and competency for every position on the field. They saw the flow of the game as a jointly held understanding of the dynamic use of space on the field and strived toward maintaining an organized spatial arrangement that would optimize their tactical advantage on the pitch. This is how a small design team functions best; the individuals exchange tasks and work together to keep as much fluidity and flexibility in the creation process as possible. Of course, good clear, constant communication is of paramount importance here. You should all know both your strengths and your weaknesses and work together to buttress each other's efforts. A team of two or three people should take advantage of outsourcing services available to small businesses. Accounting, billing, and website maintenance can all be outsourced, and there are many small companies dedicated to providing that kind of office support [4]. There are many people in the virtual world community who are reachable by social media and through various groups in Second Life, OpenSim, and Unity. Your small design team should join these communities to benefit from the shared knowledge and skills advice.

No matter the size of your design group, these factors help them become a great team:

1. They have clear, simple goals that are meaningful to them, even if they are working on a very large and complex project.
2. They provide each other with mutual support in skills and morale.
3. All members of the team are constantly striving to improve their skills and understanding of design, and that effort is supported and encouraged by the entire company.

3.4 CONCLUSIONS ABOUT "BUILD IT ONCE"

Workflow optimization and creative development techniques have only been lightly explored in this chapter. You, as a designer, can find deep mines of information about this topic all over the web and learn even more about it from your peers. Always take the time for a "long view" of a project so you can get the structure of the working environment sorted out before the creative tornado sweeps through the system. You will reap the benefits of a quality design delivered on time and on budget.

3.5 PROJECT: GETTING YOUR DESIGN STUDIO ORGANIZED WITH A "CRITICAL PATH" TECHNIQUE

In this project, you will set up your desktop workspace and design studio workflow to create a "critical path" [5]. By doing this, you will see how all the programs you are using interact to export and upload content. You will time the process, to gauge the speed of your workflow, and discover any snags along the way.

You will need some sort of timing device for each step, such as this online stopwatch, http://www.online-stopwatch.com/full-screen-stopwatch/. Also, before you begin, pick out two areas in the Metaverse where you can rez objects. If you do not have your own land in Second Life or an OpenSim region set up, then look for a quiet public sandbox in each world. Now, use the following steps to test your system:

1. The first thing you need to do is to make sure your 3D modeling package can export the COLLADA (.dae) file format. Note, there are other .dae formats available, but to upload mesh models into Second Life and OpenSim, it has to be COLLADA (.dae). There is a list of 3D modelers that export

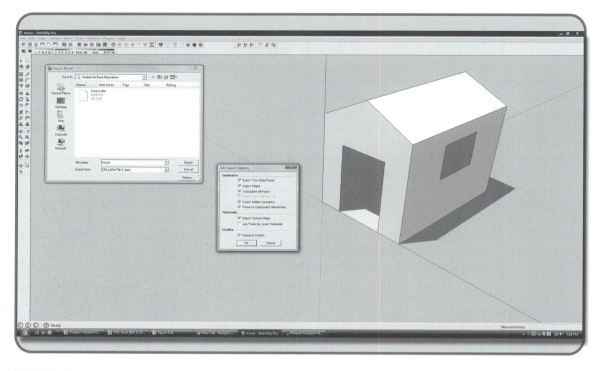

FIGURE 3.12 Screen grab of SketchUp interface showing export menu for the COLLADA .dae format. This file format can be imported into virtual environments such as OpenSim and Unity.

COLLADA (.dae) files here: http://wiki.secondlife.com/wiki/Mesh/Tools. Also, MeshLab (http://meshlab.sourceforge.net/) is a great program for converting files if you need to do that for uploading.

2. Make a quick model of a small, simple house in your modeling program; Figure 3.12 has an image of the sort of house you should build. When you have built the house and saved it as a COLLADA (.dae) file, get your stopwatch set up and proceed to the next step.

3. Start the clock; launch the Firestorm viewer, and log in to your previously chosen location in OpenSim. Now upload the COLLADA (.dae) file with the Avatar/Upload/Mesh menu. For more information on upload procedures look in Chapter 2, Section 2.3. There are images of this Mesh Upload menu in Chapter 13, Figures 13.15–13.17, to provide a quick guide. Once the upload fee of the mesh has been calculated, upload the house into your inventory. When the import is complete, rez the house on the ground in front of you as shown in Figure 3.13.

  Stop the clock when you can fully see the house model in front of you on the ground.

4. Log out of OpenSim and log in to Second Life at your previously chosen location there. Start the clock again and select the same upload settings. Time the procedure and make a note of the differences in the uploads. Does this version of the model behave in the same way as OpenSim and does its physics shape allow you entry into the house?

5. Compare notes on how long each upload took and ask why there might be differences. How about the effect of different servers, different loads on the regions where you were? Did the model look different in any of the locations?

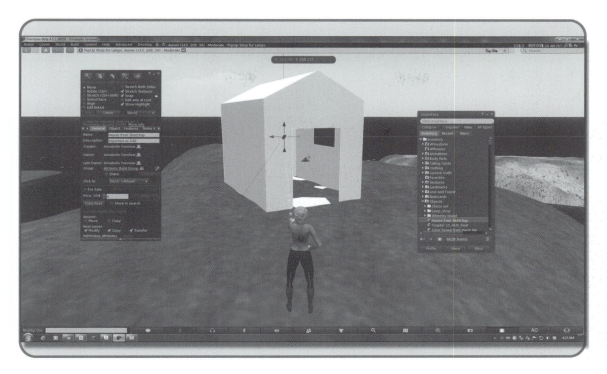

FIGURE 3.13 Screen grab showing the SketchUp house model (saved as a COLLADA (.dae) file) after it has been uploaded into OpenSim.

6. Try another round of uploading with other settings on the menu, changing the physics, LOD, and so on. How were the times for upload then?

Take the time to thoroughly review the upload menu settings in Firestorm so you can obtain a nice-looking (relatively high, but not crazy high LOD) model with the appropriate physics collision shape to the structure.

7. Congratulations, with this simple exercise, you have started the process of analyzing your workflow. Information like this will help you plan for the project and estimate the costs more accurately, which will make you more competent and competitive.

REFERENCES

1. Top Ten Reviews—Graphics Cards 2013, comparative chart published on Top Ten Reviews.com, http://graphics-cards-review.toptenreviews.com/. Accessed April 25, 2013.
2. Agile Software Development, Wikipedia article, http://en.wikipedia.org/wiki/Agile_software_development. Accessed April 30, 2013.
3. Green, Amanda, 5 Lean Business Tips for OpenSim Startups, Hypergrid Business, March 16, 2013, http://www.hypergridbusiness.com/2013/03/5-lean-business-tips-for-opensim-startups/. Accessed April 30, 2013.
4. Jackson, Nancy Mann, How to Build a Better Business with Outsourcing, *Entrepreneur*, http://www.entrepreneur.com/article/204652. Accessed May 1, 2013.
5. Critical Path Method, Wikipedia article, http://en.wikipedia.org/wiki/Critical_path_method. Accessed May 1, 2013.

4 Concepts in 3D Design for Virtual Environments

Design is in everything we make, but it's also between those things. It's a mix of craft, science, story-telling, propaganda, and philosophy.

—Erik Adigard des Gautries

4.1 INTRODUCTION TO 3D DESIGN

4.1.1 A UNIVERSAL LANGUAGE THAT YOU EXPERIENCE CONSTANTLY

For a few minutes, imagine your favorite childhood space. Perhaps it was the dinosaur exhibit of your local museum, the art room of your elementary school, or your own backyard. In your mind's eye, take a walk through that place, remembering the size and shape of each area and the objects, furniture, and architectural elements it contained. Everything in that environment has been stored in your memory in a "canonical" form [1]. Whether you call it a tree, *arbre*, or *árbol*, in your native speaking language, it represents a 3D form in your mind, and that form is part of the universal language of forms we create in a virtual 3D environment. This collection of forms, stored in our memory, also lets us "time travel" to places that may no longer exist. As a designer, you need to allow yourself to be inspired by your encoded memory containing this database of forms. By utilizing your "Visuospatial Sketchpad" (or inner eye), which stores and recalls these forms for you when inspiration strikes, you are accessing a powerful tool for design, as shown in Figure 4.1 [2]. Rediscover this great repository you have been adding to since you were a child and utilize it as often as possible when you are designing, teaching, or just showing your children how to imagine new places.

4.2 DESIGN ELEMENTS IN VIRTUAL ENVIRONMENTS

Every language in the world shares common concepts about identity and classification, and that is true for the language of 3D design. There are six fundamental elements found in 3D no matter where it is created: line, space, shape, form, color, and texture. Many 3D designs utilize all six elements in their composition (or arrangement of objects); some simply use two or three of these. Let's focus in on these elements and examine how various artists in Second Life have used them to create 3D designs. Figure 4.2 has examples of the six fundamental elements of 3D design.

4.2.1 LINE

A line creates a linear, spatial connection between two points. A line can also create a temporal connection between two events, such as a timeline does, and a line can define the direction of a moving object, as trajectory does. Every drawing starts with a line, but lines do not need to be trapped on the 2D plane. Think of how a smoke

FIGURE 4.1 (See color insert)   Schematic chart of the Visuospatial Sketchpad as it processes your observations on shape, size, color, texture and relative location of a 3D form into your memory. These observations are stored in the Visuospatial Sketchpad (inner eye) as a recoverable database of forms for your use in designing.

trail follows a jet plane or how a long ribbon creates lines in space when the rhythmic gymnast moves through a routine. These are common examples of lines in 3D space. Picture 1 in Figure 4.2 is Werner Kurosawa's design for the Linden Endowment for the Arts (LEA) Media Arts Center SE. Werner used lines to create an interesting gallery space. As your eye moves down the shiny chrome beams toward the light wood colored floor, notice the shadows. With the movement of the virtual sun, another dynamic linear composition is created as the 3D linear elements are converted into a 2D composition of shadow lines that move along the floor and walls. Werner created yet another line pattern on the wall elements, with the black lined glass, which is reminiscent of the horizontal black-and-white marble detail on the walls of the Siena Cathedral (*Duomo di Siena*) in central Italy. Line is always with you in 3D design, even if you are working with massive forms. There will always be the edge of the object and the line created when it occludes another object. There will be lines created by the shadow edges on an object or from the change in your point of view on an object. The camera through which you look at the 3D world you are creating has a linear axis pointing directly at the object, and the build editor in your viewer displays infinite lines in the x and y directions when an object is selected. The more you look, the more lines you will see in 3D.

4.2.2 SPACE

Every 3D design defines itself in space. Space can surround the design, the design can surround a space, or the space can flow through and around the design simultaneously. A 3D design can make the space feel claustrophobic or expansive; it can hide and reveal space in multiple ways. In *listen ...* (Figure 4.2, picture 2), a sound-based exhibit by Alpha Auer for the HUMlab exhibit "Tropophonia," Auer works with lots of open space. As you enter this exhibit, you find that you are standing on a translucent plane of glass under a black, starry sky filled with fast-moving clouds. The plane is decorated with black squares, from which light beams emanate, and the surface is covered with concentric rings of glowing dots. These graphic features serve to define the center and an internal grid simultaneously. Whirling around you like planets circumscribing their orbits are animated avatars wearing armatures reminiscent of planetary orreries. As you walk across the plane, you discover a trio of avatars performing synchronized movements, and further exploration will trigger delivery of wearable art, so your avatar may become part of the environment. As you can see, with every element she has created, Auer has sought to define the spatial quality of the environment. With its ephemeral lighting and orbiting avatars, it has become a dynamic, ever-changing space that at once has infinite scale and human scale. The use of a dark surreal sky for this exhibit contributes to the sensation of infinite space.

4.2.3 SHAPE

Shape is the most primal of elements in 3D design. To our eyes, the shape of something serves to identify it immediately, and the potential for danger or friendship, to our brains. Shapes can be protective when used with camouflage, shown on butterflies that sport large "eyespots" on their wings. These eyespot shapes serve to mislead a predator into thinking the butterfly is a much larger, dangerous animal. Shape in a 3D world appears everywhere, shadows cast on the face of a 3D object, or a very thin 3D object that resembles a shape from a certain view are two such examples. Shapes also can be created in a virtual world through the use of particles. These are elements created by code such as Linden Scripting Language (in Second Life or OpenSim) or JavaScript (Unity) that is running inside an object in the virtual environment. When the script is running, it will cause the object to emit planar shapes with a texture image on their surface, which will always turn to face (or billboard) the camera. The particle script can be written to generate a profusion of these images, spray them in a certain angle, maintain a certain frequency, and to let them follow the winds or gravitational forces of the environment where they exist. Collectively, as these images are generated by the particle-producing

FIGURE 4.2 (See color insert)   Images of artwork that embody the six primary principles of 3D design. From the top, these principles are (1) "Line," from a build by Werner Kurosawa (a Belgian architect and artist in real life) for the Linden Endowment for the Arts (LEA) Media Arts Center SE; (2) "Space," from *listen ...* , a sound-based exhibit by Alpha Auer (Elif Ayiter, an artist in real life) for the HUMlab exhibit "Tropophonia"; (3) "Shape," from *Le Cactus*, by Maya Paris (an artist working in the United Kingdom); (4) "Form" from *The Arrival of the Fish*, by Rose Borchovski (a Dutch artist in real life); (5) "Color" from *plante**, by Betty Tureaud (a Danish artist in real life); and (6) "Texture," from an educational project at the Possibilities Unlimited Museum, by Quinlan Quimby (artist and content creator for virtual worlds).

script, they can create effects like rain, smoke, and fire, as well as graphic shapes in a 3D design. In *Le Cactus* (Figure 4.2, picture 3), Maya Paris (an artist working in the United Kingdom) displays the usage of all three sorts of shapes in her 3D design. There are the textual shapes of words like "what" and "not" hanging in the air, and consistently throughout the environment she has used circular and semicircular shapes to create old phonograph records and art deco motifs. The environment becomes filled with additional shapes when avatars are seated on an interactive carnival ride located within the space. As they rotate, the seats they ride in (shaped like bananas) give off particles with shapes that look like cherries, bananas, and other fruit. The visual fruit salad piles up and fills the environment with shapes generated by the ride, complimenting the general ambiance in this lounge, a playful homage to Josephine Baker's (1906–1975) cabaret acts.

4.2.4 FORM

Form is often the most recognizable element in 3D design and probably the one you would think of first. The form of an object is at once its identity to us and its impact on our senses. The volume of space that a form occupies defines its relative importance and implies mass and weight to our perception. The form of a cavity surrounded by 3D design defines our relationship to the environment, our relative scale, and our sense of importance in it. In *The Arrival of the Fish*, Rose Borchovski has many forms, animal and human, arranged in a surreal assemblage. In one part, she has a series of penguin forms (Figure 4.2, picture 4) that displays multiple versions of the penguin, in a sort of stop-motion effect. This series of forms creates a sequence that explains to the observer what the form of a penguin is and allows the observer to create a mental "animation" of the penguin diving off its perch. By inverting the form as the penguin takes a dive, the observer is allowed to see many sides of the penguin in a single glance, enriching the experience of encountering a penguin form.

4.2.5 COLOR

The element of color is subjective and emotional. Like shape, it connects with your brain on a primal level. Colors in the natural environment warn us of poisonous vegetation or animals. Our society attaches meaning to the color of roses and other flowers, and we use color words to describe a state of mind, such as "feeling blue" or "green with envy." Many of these color meanings are also tied into cultural structures, such as the white wedding dress or the orange robes of Buddhist monks. Color can also define and influence our perception of space because warm colors such as red and orange seem to move toward us, and cool colors like blue and purple seem to recede. In her fractal-like sculpture called *plante**, Betty Tureaud (a Danish artist in real life) creates a sense of iridescence with the application of rainbow colors and implied reflection on the surfaces (Figure 4.2, picture 5). Because the texture is set to self-illumination, no shadows are rendered, and the eye is free to bounce among the cluster of structures that make up the sculpture. By utilizing color in this way, she creates a sense of flowing motion across the 3D surface.

4.2.6 TEXTURE

Texture, the sixth element of 3D design, belongs to two senses, touch and sight. You can speak of "visual texture," but the understanding of that concept resides in our tactile experiences. When you reach to touch the surface of unpolished granite, you know it will feel rough, and you also know that visually it will look pocked and catch tiny shadows across its face. The visual texture of light and dark across the face of an object can also be created with color contrasts. In her prototype for an educational project at the Possibilities Unlimited Museum, Quinlan Quimby used texture to redefine the concept of the Blue Willow china pattern (Figure 4.2, picture 6). In shades of blue and white, she has borrowed from the famous blue willow china pattern to create an environment filled with blue willow buildings, trees, and landforms. Every surface is defined by its texture as part of the whole, which is visually united by the color scheme.

4.3 COMPOSITIONAL METHODOLOGY FOR THE SIX BASIC ELEMENTS IN VIRTUAL ENVIRONMENTS

Once you have grasped an understanding of the basic six elements of 3D design, the challenge of using them in an effective way will become easier. Standing on the vast plane of a virtual space, trying to organize your elements to make a cohesive visual statement can be daunting at first. Have no fear; you can break this down into manageable pieces and grapple with them one by one. With reference to Wikipedia's comprehensive list of the design elements and principles [3], this section shows you a series of relationships between 3D elements that create comprehensible arrangements or composition in a virtual world.

4.3.1 DEFINING THE LEVEL OF DIMENSIONALITY

Think about the theater for a minute. You have probably been to see performances done on standard proscenium stages and have watched the actors break the vertical plane of that proscenium by coming out to the edge of stage. When a theatrical production demands more interaction with the audience space, there is a move to a three-quarters thrust stage, and the audience is put on three sides. In the arena stage, built like the Roman Coliseum, the ultimate immersion is achieved with the audience completely surrounding the performance, or chariot race as it were. The same sort of "drama" exists in 3D design, as illustrated in Figure 4.3. Bas-relief or "low relief" (from the French interpretation of the Italian term *basso-relievo*) is created by allowing the 3D designs to just break the background surface. Of course, in 3D design bas-relief can be done on all surfaces surrounding you, not just the walls.

Sculptural is the next stage of this process, shown in Figure 4.3 as the shapes start to break free of their background surface. In the last stage, the 3D design becomes immersive and surrounds you with its elements.

4.3.2 ESTABLISHING UNITY

One of the fundamental methods for creating a composition with visual impact is to establish visual unity. As noted in the images in Figure 4.4, there are three ways to do this: using proximity, similarity, and rhythm.

You can use proximity, or the "closeness" of the elements, to unify the composition. Your eye will group objects that are close together and perceive them as major elements. In Figure 4.4, look at the cluster of objects on both sides of the space. Notice how they seem to create groups in your mind's eye, and even though the arrangement on the right side may seem very dissimilar, you will still probably group it, thinking (box + sphere) as opposed to (box) and (sphere). Similarity of elements also unifies composition. As you can see in the second image from the top, the arrangement of cubes and boxes is unified by their rectilinearity. In the third image, several patterns of rhythm have been established to unify the whole. With the rising sections on the surrounding walls and another repetition of the boxes and cubes on the ground, the arrangement has two sorts of rhythm, one that travels vertically and one that travels horizontally.

4.3.3 POINT, LINE, AND PLANE

In good composition, you should include at least one point, line, and plane. In Figure 4.5, there is a virtual world composition to represent the concept. Here, it is visualized as a sphere, a long thin box, and a flat cut

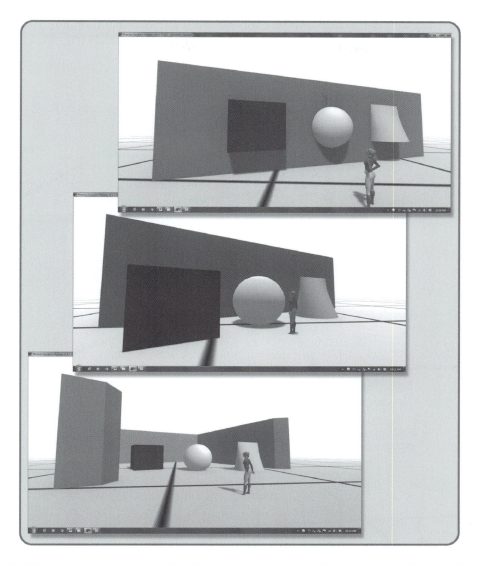

FIGURE 4.3 Three screen grabs from an OpenSim virtual environment showing the three levels of dimensionality that can be perceived in a virtual environment: (1) bas-relief (top); (2) sculptural (middle); and (3) immersive (bottom).

box on the ground, but this compositional harmony could be created in numerous ways, including by the use of textures on the forms. For instance, the point could be made with a white texture that has a small black dot, and the line could be a texture that has a single line on a transparent background, applied to two sides of a very thin box. These are obvious examples to make the concept clear; you should try to have some representation of a "point-line-plane" composition in your creations. By changing the spatial relationships, the overlap, and the repetition of the points, lines, and planes in your design, you can create extremely interesting compositions. It has been proven that humans prefer a certain mathematical density in our visual field [4], so let your visual field guide you to the best composition.

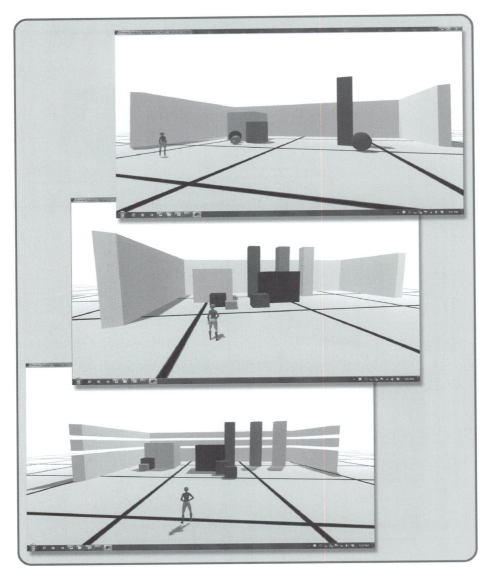

FIGURE 4.4 Screen grabs from OpenSim showing 3 examples of visual unity: (1) using proximity of forms, which collect as groups in our mind's eye (top image), (2) unity with similarity demonstrated with a range of box-like forms (middle image), and (3) visual unity created with rhythm, a repetition of similar but derivative forms (bottom image).

4.3.4 BALANCE

Balance comes in many forms. In Figure 4.6, you will see the three most common forms of spatial balance: symmetry, asymmetry, and radial symmetry. The location of the fulcrum or "tipping point" is the most important factor for creating balance in a composition. Like a seesaw, the visual weight of elements in a symmetrical composition will find a point where they are at equilibrium. In a symmetrical balance, that

FIGURE 4.5 Screen grab from OpenSim showing a virtual interpretation of the 3 fundamental elements of composition: a point (shown as a sphere), a line (shown as a long thin box), and a plane (shown as a flat box on the grid surface).

point will be the center on a line between the two sides, and in radial symmetry, that point will be at the intersection of all visual lines that connect the elements in the composition. Asymmetrical balance is more abstruse; the center between unequal sides can become a visual tug-of-war, as you look back and forth between the elements on each side, weighing them in your mind's eye. Symbol and meaning can enter into this balance as well. Suppose a tiny mouse was on one side and a huge elephant on the other. They are facing each other in a standoff. The elephant's legendary fear of mice makes its huge scale less important, and the mouse standing his ground bravely makes the mouse seem more important in the composition. This is an example of psychologically based asymmetrical balance.

4.3.5 Hierarchy

The hierarchical aspect of design composition is seen all around you. Think of the position of carved animals on a totem pole or the height of a king's throne in relationship to the rest of the room. Higher, taller, and nearer imply importance in a composition, as you can see in Figure 4.7. If there is something in your 3D design that you want the observer to consider important, try to put it in a place where it will be seen immediately and seems to be a focal point from all directions. You should lead the eye of the observer to the most important element in a balanced composition with clear hierarchy.

4.3.6 Scale

Figure 4.8 shows some extreme examples of the use of scale in a composition. The relationship between the avatar and the surrounding objects is always a source of dynamic tension in a visual composition. It is always interesting to play with unexpected scale. For instance, you could enlarge the scale of something typically small into a gigantic form, just as Claes Oldenburg has done with his giant clothespin in downtown Philadelphia. Of course, this is a much easier endeavor and requires much less public funding when you do it in a virtual Philadelphia.

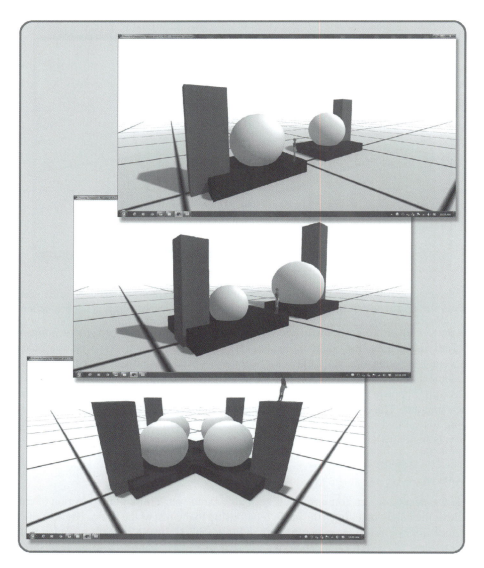

FIGURE 4.6 Screen grabs from OpenSim demonstrating a virtual interpretation of the 3 kinds of symmetrical balance: (1) equal visual balance or symmetry (top image), (2) unequal visual balance or asymmetry (middle image), and (3) center based or radial symmetry (bottom image).

4.3.7 DOMINANCE

Some examples of dominance in 3D design are shown in Figure 4.9. For any object to dominate all the other objects requires that it have an appropriate amount of overscale qualities, be in a dominant position compositionally, and otherwise exhibit qualities that draw attention to itself. This is different from hierarchy and asymmetrical balance because the dominant object will not let the eye move away from it much. However, you cannot freeze the eye to it, or the composition becomes too static. It is entirely conceivable

FIGURE 4.7 Screen grab from OpenSim showing a virtual interpretation of hierarchy in 3D composition. Note the relative importance of objects in the visual field, and how the less-important elements in the foreground lead the eye to the most important element in the center of the image. This effect is achieved by shrinking and lowering the foreground objects, while enlarging and raising the background object. The linear pattern on the ground also moves the eye toward the focal point on the largest object.

FIGURE 4.8 Screen grab from OpenSim showing a virtual representation of the impact created by changing scale in a 3D composition. Notice how the avatar establishes a visual measurement from which you judge the relative scale of these chairs.

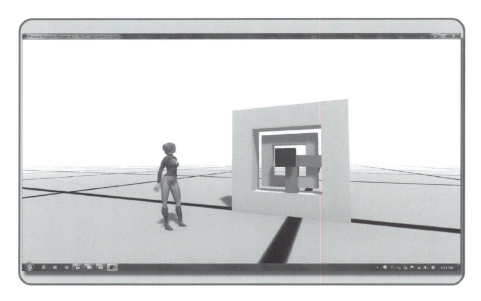

FIGURE 4.9   Screen grab from OpenSim showing a virtual representation of dominance in 3D composition. Notice how the small dark cube moves the eye toward the middle of the composition and holds it there like the center of a target. The avatar's eyeline also creates a subtle directional indicator, moving your eye in the direction of the center of the composition.

that a dominant object could be a very small object and yet have the gravitational force of a collapsing star on your attention. The object can achieve this focus by being the brightest object in an arrangement or the shiniest or perhaps by being positioned at the center of your eye line.

4.3.8   MOVEMENT

The involuntary movement of your eyes as they gaze at a new 3D form will inform you of its internal compositional movement. How the design directs your eye to look around and through its arrangement of forms, shapes, symbols, colors, and lines in the composition is also compositional movement. If your 3D design is kinetic and has moving parts, orbiting or changing their positions in space, you have the challenge of blending spatial movement with an ever-changing compositional movement, as shown in Figure 4.10. The observer may pause in one position to view this composition, so he or she has a static frame of reference from which to judge the sequence of movement. If you desire that the observer walk all around your sculptural composition or through it if it were designed to be immersive, you should design your moving parts to encourage that. When you add moving parts to a static composition, it is best to design your animations to complement the innate visual movement you initially created.

4.4   USING SIMILARITY AND CONTRAST IN 3D DESIGN

Similarity, also defined as likeness, is an element that can help underscore the message you wish to convey with your design. Similar colors, shapes, forms, and textures help to unify the visual impact of your design. However, too much similarity can lead to visual fatigue, boredom, and loss of focus on the composition, so it should be used judiciously.

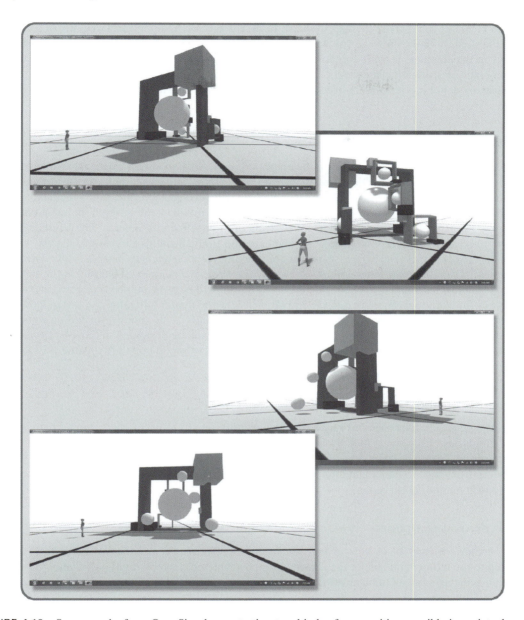

FIGURE 4.10 Screen grabs from OpenSim demonstrating two kinds of composition possible in a virtual environment: (1) static 3D composition is created with a non-moving sculptural structure that is viewed from 2 sides (top two images) and (2) kinetic 3D composition created by scripting several of the spheres to orbit around the structure, viewed from 2 sides at various times during the movement (bottom two images).

Contrast elements can include changes in shape, form, color, scale, and lighting. Good use of contrast will reinforce the strength of the message you wish to convey. If you go too far with inclusion of contrasting sizes and shapes in the elements in your composition, your meaning may be obscured. Likewise with too much contrast in color or shadow on the forms, an observer will not experience a meaningful viewing progression because his or her eye is being pulled all over the composition as a meaningful pattern is sought by the mind's eye.

4.4.1 Managing Similarity and Contrast

Let's look at how similarity and contrast can be employed in 3D virtual design. There are many elements to organize in a 3D environment, the forms and shapes, textures, colors, and sometimes textual information. The last is a component in just about every 3D environment; you will need signage, titles, and other text to help the visitor navigate the space. These "informational" parts of the environment are different in intent but visually related to the "structural" assemblies of bas-relief, sculptural, or immersive objects. The similarity/contrast quotient of both parts should be complementary and balanced from all angles and views. One way of managing and balancing this visual structure when you are working with a team is to make a "style document" or "style manual." Deciding what fonts will be used in the signage, what colors will be used in the surrounding walls, and how other such repeated elements in your 3D design will be used and then collected into one document allows your team to work more quickly and efficiently while maintaining the visual standards.

The short sections that follow provide examples of various kinds of 3D contrast, including some that are intrinsic to designing for multiuser online environments. When you are designing in those environments, be aware that there are also the intrinsic contrasts within the ranges of social popularity, game skill levels, and interactivity of virtual worlds.

4.4.2 Spatial Contrasts

"You are in my space!" Everyone has heard that statement in one form or another. Human beings identify with the boundaries of the space they occupy and how near or far they are to others. They also notice it in a 3D composition. Figure 4.11 provides a basic example of how spatial contrast can be achieved. Notice the arrangement, the change in depth and dimensionality for the elements as well as their relative "nearness" or "farness" to the point of observation.

4.4.3 Positional Contrasts

Figure 4.12 shows images of objects in positional contrast. Notice the grouping of the objects and their relationship to the left or right side of the screen. Are they centered, thereby implying balance? Or, are they off-center, leaving a feeling of unbalance? Position is important; it implies hierarchy and relationships as well as the overall structure of the composition.

4.4.4 Form Contrasts

What are the qualities of form? Subjectively, you may divide forms into those you find attractive and those you do not. Objectively, you may find a collection of forms can be created from many parts or one whole, or they can be made from a simple, smooth form or a series of rough, complex forms. The vast language of form is at your command, and finding similarities and contrasts within them creates visually rewarding compositions. Look at Figure 4.13 for an example.

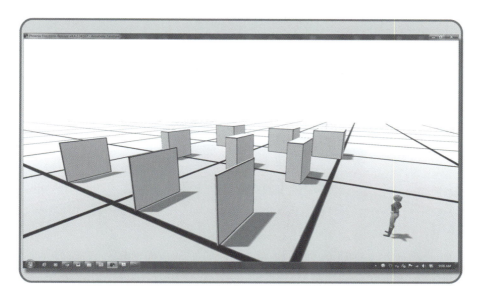

FIGURE 4.11 Screen grab from OpenSim showing a virtual representation of spatial contrast in 3D composition. Notice how as the cubes get larger and farther away, the "visual pressure" or sense of space between them creates a contrast to the slimmer versions in the foreground.

FIGURE 4.12 Screen grab from OpenSim showing a virtual representation of positional contrast and grouping in 3D design. Notice how your mind's eye groups the spheres near each other, and contrasts them to the singletons in the surrounding area.

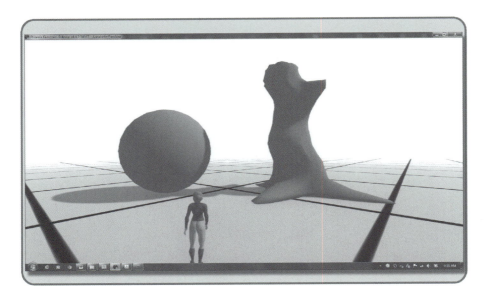

FIGURE 4.13 Screen grab from OpenSim showing a virtual representation of contrast of form in 3D, with two objects that exemplify this: (1) a geometrically based object (sphere) and (2) an organically based object (tree trunk).

4.4.5 DIRECTIONAL CONTRASTS

When you see a weather vane spinning on the top of a house or a flag flying straight out from a pole in a strong wind, you are seeing two simple examples of directional contrast. In each case, there is a stable element (the house and the flagpole, respectively) as well as the moving or "unstable" element (the weather vane and the flag, respectively). The visual direction of the stable elements in these compositions is generally vertical; both the house and the flagpole rise from the ground. The visual direction of the weather vane and the flag while generally horizontal will also change orientation with the wind and create a directional contrast. Figure 4.14 provides a simple example of sculptural directional contrast.

4.4.6 STRUCTURAL CONTRASTS

Structure in nature tends to follow some standard rules. Small on top of large, such as in the branching of a typical tree, or graduated volumes, such as you might find in a chambered nautilus shell. In buildings, you tend to find some sort of internal structure that connects the floors and rooms in a cohesive pattern, until there is an earthquake. By utilizing the physics engine in a virtual world, you can create lovely random structural contrast as stacked objects fall to the ground. Figure 4.15 presents an image of a structural collapse and the structural contrast it creates. On one side, the elements stand straight and tall, and on the other side, they are in a complex pile at the base.

4.4.7 SIZE CONTRASTS

The creation of size contrast can have profound effects on how a 3D design is understood and accepted. The contrast in size between the elements contributes to the observer's understanding of the relative importance

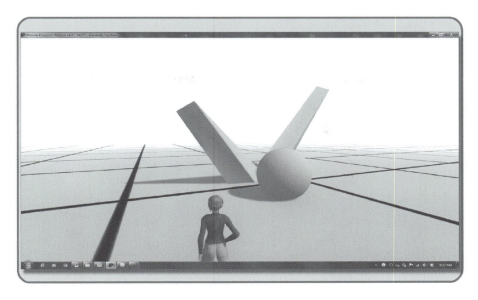

FIGURE 4.14 Screen grab from OpenSim demonstrating directional contrast in a virtual environment by using angled lines and tapering shapes to move the eye in different directions.

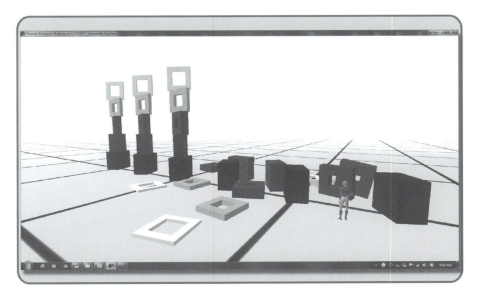

FIGURE 4.15 Screen grab from OpenSim illustrating a virtual version of structural contrast in 3D composition that was created by the actions of inworld physics on columns of physically enabled objects.

FIGURE 4.16 Screen grab from OpenSim, virtually demonstrating size contrast in 3D. Here this is shown by using in a box-like family of forms.

of the elements, and the contrast between the observer's scale, as either an avatar or a real person, contributes to the psychological impact on the observer. Imagine how it feels to walk from a wall diagram displaying the various sizes of whales and into the great hall of a museum where a full-scale model of a whale is hanging over your head. This experience is memorable in both virtual and physical worlds. Size contrast can also occur within a family of forms, such as the relative scale of the planets in our solar system or all the various frames in the window of a framing shop. Look at Figure 4.16 for an example.

4.4.8 COLOR CONTRASTS

Your 3D design will benefit from the application of color contrast. This contrast does not need to be profound if the style of your design does not ask for it. In fact, a subtle range of color, punctuated with some spots of intense color, is visually interesting. Likewise, the use of light and dark, warm and cool colors playing across your composition can inject energy and excitement into the message embodied in your design. There is much more discussion about color and its uses in 3D design in Chapter 7. Look at Figure 4.17 for shades of gray color contrasts in a 3D design.

4.4.9 TEXTURE CONTRASTS

Until haptic devices allow us to "feel" virtual surfaces, texture is only visual in a virtual environment. This is not a setback to 3D design if the visual textures are chosen and applied properly to your objects. Figure 4.18 comprises an assemblage of objects with various textures to show the dynamic range (smooth, rough, shiny, dull, complex, simple) that can be achieved in visual textures. Also for your consideration is the script-driven interactive possibility that these textures can be animated or the objects could change textures in response to an avatar's presence or touch (mouse click).

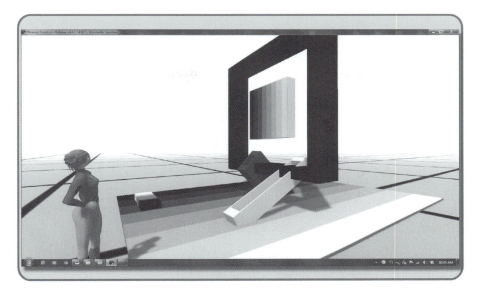

FIGURE 4.17 Screen grab from OpenSim showing a virtual version of color contrast in 3D design using shades of gray.

FIGURE 4.18 Screen grab from OpenSim virtually demonstrating texture contrasts shown on the forms of a 3D design.

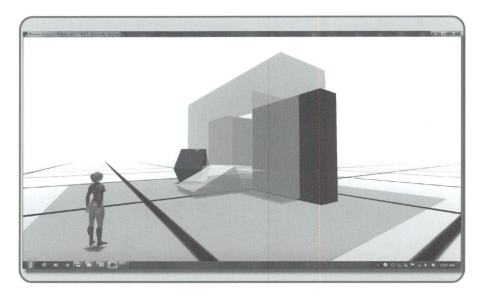

FIGURE 4.19   Screen grab from OpenSim virtually showing an example of 3D design with a variety of density and opacity in its composition.

4.4.10   Density/Opacity Contrasts

Density is defined in the *Encarta Dictionary* as the "concentration of things within an area in relationship to the size of that area," but the word also means the relative transparency of a surface or an atmosphere. Great quantities of particles in a virtual environment can create dense visual effects like smoke and fog, and at the virtual shoreline, there is a horizontal line of contrast between a transparent virtual liquid and an opaque virtual solid. Figure 4.19 shows a 3D design that utilizes elements with varying kinds and degrees of density.

4.4.11   Gravitational Contrasts

The laws of gravity have a part to play in 3D design. When a 3D design seems to defy these laws, the visitor will experience things like excitement, anxiety, and possibly fear. In Figure 4.20, you will see some simple examples of how a stacked form can create gravitational contrast by simply turning it upside down. There is a sense of stability on one side and instability on the other. In more complex designs, you can incorporate multiple instances of this kind of contrast to create sophisticated contrast patterns.

4.4.12   Social Contrast

In some ways, social contrast is related to density, especially when defined in terms of visitor numbers in your 3D environment during an event and afterward. There is also the social contrast between the more popular versus less-popular destinations in virtual worlds, one region teeming with many avatars next to a region that is completely empty. As a 3D designer and builder of virtual environments, you should be aware that there

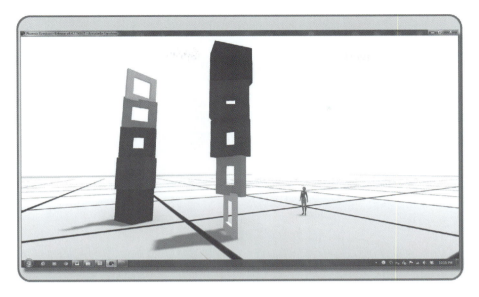

FIGURE 4.20 Screen grab from OpenSim demonstrating in the virtual space an example of gravitational contrast and its psychological impact in 3D design.

are ways that social contrast can be manipulated within an environment. With the addition of pathways and obstacles, meeting circles, and hidden cul-de-sacs, you create an environment that energizes social contrast for your visitors. The creation of designed social contrast within the space gives your visitors an interestingly complex environment that stimulates social contact and that invites them to return frequently. The most popular spots found in a virtual world are plaza meeting areas and sandboxes. Figure 4.21 has an image of the world map from Second Life showing regional areas. The current avatar population of the region is indicated with dots (shown green on the world map of the client viewer) and a number next to the name of the region (e.g., Mauve (23)). The avatars in this area maintain a steady visitor density, even though they come and go, implying that this is a "home base" or log-in area for most of them. Notice how it compares with the vast emptiness of the surrounding regions. Successful use of social contrast in 3D design would include a popular meeting area in any region as well as an area encouraging solitude.

4.4.13 Gaming Contrasts

In addition to social contrast, the quality of gaming contrast (game-like vs. work-like) can deeply affect how the visitor views and behaves in your virtual environment. For instance, Figure 4.22 provides an image of Jopsy Pendragon's Particle Lab in Second Life, where visitors can learn how to create and script objects that emit particles. This region is filled with games and toys, such as a Ferris wheel, hot air balloons, gondolas, trains, and a giant whale mouth that you enter for a tour. The whole place resonates with the message of "learning is fun." On the work-like end of the gaming contrast scale, you will find the kind of informational displays with a structured virtual interface. Often, they are attractive buildings with many signs and displays in them, but the message is more like "Welcome to our virtual corporate environment; let us give you the information you seek." Each type of environment has its place, and once you have established

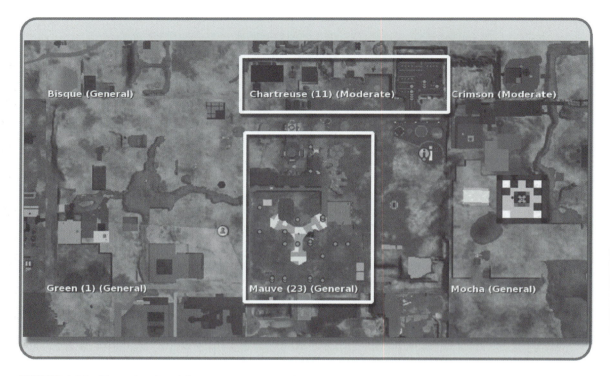

FIGURE 4.21 Example of social contrast on regions in Second Life. Note how Mauve contains 23 visitors, while Mocha is empty. Mauve has a large public sandbox that encourages social gathering.

the message you would like to deliver, the amount of game-like versus work-like contrast in your design will sort itself out.

4.4.14 Interactivity Contrast

In a 3D virtual environment, lots of magic things can happen. The environment can be scripted to sense the presence of a visitor and respond by activating interactive visual or audible content, to be seen by all in the area or specifically by the person who just arrived. You might think of this as "automatic interactivity." In contrast, there is "manual interactivity," which requires that the avatar take action to initiate the interactive behavior. A manually interactive typewriter design by AngryBeth Shortbread (a designer, scripter, builder in the United Kingdom) is pictured in Figure 4.23. When you click your mouse on the keys of this giant typewriter, written text appears on the page of paper above you, and the message also connects to a Twitter feed. This kind of interactivity is obviously designed into an object, but there are other kinds of interactivity that can emerge within the virtual environment. Consider a scenic landscape, a park, or forest. While such a vista seems to provide no such built-in interactive connection with the visitor, do not think that kind of an environment will never be used interactively. You will find that, even with a modicum of accessibility to a method that will change their environments, your visitors will respond interactively and "play" with the elements they can change. Interactivity, with its range of levels and effects and its close or distant relationship to the actions of the visitor, is another powerful tool in your 3D design kit.

FIGURE 4.22 Screen grab from showing gaming contrast in 3D design with the game-like atmosphere of Jopsy Pendragon's Particle Laboratory Learning Center in Second Life, Teal Region.

4.5 DESIGNING "FLOW" INTO VIRTUAL ENVIRONMENTS

Let's think about the concept of "Flow" and how that relates to being a virtual environment designer, a teacher, and a game maker. Each of these professions has at its core a fundamental goal to create environments that allow Flow to happen. Flow is defined as a state of mental being where the visitor, student, or gamer has become so absorbed and involved in his or her interaction and progress within the environment, project, or game that the individual loses him- or herself for a while. You have probably experienced it yourself, becoming immersed in content creation, losing track of time, maybe forgetting to have lunch, just gliding along on the wings of inspiration as you create, teach, or play a game. As you have experienced Flow, understand that you should strive to pass it on in your designs. It is one of your primary goals to create an environment with mechanisms and objects that help the users of your game or visitors in your environment attain Flow on their own.

4.5.1 FIRST QUESTIONS A DESIGNER SHOULD ASK BEFORE DESIGNING ANYTHING

One of the best things a designer can do is ask lots of questions. This section suggests some questions you can ask yourself about the project at hand, to the client if the design work is for hire, or to your class if this is a group assignment. These questions are just to get the ball rolling, and you will probably discover more as you go. Take the time to jot down what the answers are and add them to your journal, along with any images you

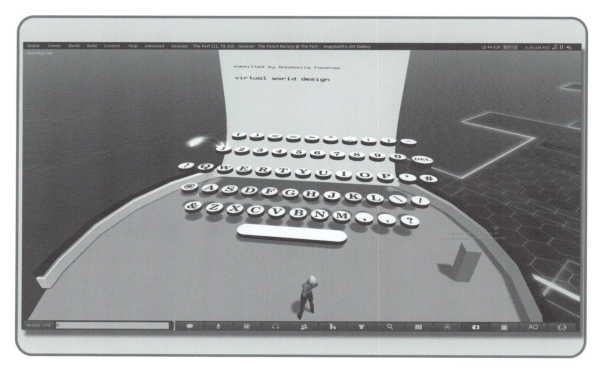

FIGURE 4.23 Screen grab showing an interactive typewriter, designed and built by AngryBeth Shortbread (a designer, scripter, and builder in the United Kingdom). This can be found in Second Life, The Port region.

have shared with your group. This will form the start of your style document or style manual. The questions are arranged by topic:

Concept
  What is the message that you are trying to convey, for the client, group or yourself?
  Do you have any favorite websites/image sites that inspire you about this design?
  Does this environment relate to surrounding spaces, both virtual and real?
  Is it to be mixed reality, real and virtual together?
Budget
  What is your overall budget?
  How many people will be in the environment at any given time?
Purpose/meaning
  How do you or your organization want to be represented by this design?
  Who is your audience or intended target?
Parameters
  What is your time frame for production?
  What activities does this space have to support? Shopping, dancing, education, games?
  If this design is for an event, what is the duration of the event?
  What is the future of this build? Will it continually be developed as a "permanent" project?

When you have answered all these questions and collected information in your journal, it is time to start designing, sketching out your plans visually, and coordinating the team with an overall view of the project.

4.6   EDUCATION, SERIOUS GAMES, VIRTUAL ENVIRONMENTS

With the growing acceptance of virtual worlds as viable environments for teaching, there is an increasing need to design virtual spaces that facilitate learning. New uses for virtual worlds are continually developed by teachers and learning technologists. These technology-savvy individuals are always seeking better ways to communicate with their students and utilize all sorts of digital systems to design new learning tools. Often, they create what are known as "serious games" or games that are primarily created to support the enhancement of learning or training. Even though the technology of virtual worlds is fairly new to the academic world, the use of games to teach serious lessons, strategies, and concepts is not. Historic evidence points to games being played as far back as 3000 BC. Games like chess, dominos, and Go have been played for more than a thousand years [5]. It is clear that games like these, while providing entertainment, also teach strategy, 3D conceptualization, and probability theory.

Ever since people have been building games for virtual worlds and online sites, these classics have been replicated and incorporated into expansive game-like environments. The next section provides a project that lets you (and your class) design an environment for learning. If you can, work with your students, helping them to create their own virtual learning space, and let them take "ownership" of their virtual learning environment.

4.7   PROJECT: ASSEMBLING A MODULAR VIRTUAL CLASSROOM

Some of the latest research shows that classroom learning can be enhanced by good lighting, flexible furniture arrangements, serious consideration of the visual background, and a color scheme that is age appropriate [6]. If you are a teacher, you know how much the students want to personalize their environment. Generations of names scratched into desktops attest to that. Now you can provide them with the ultimate in customization, a modular virtual classroom that they can configure as desired. You can easily provide a virtual location for this project with a SoaS (http://simonastick.com), a virtual environment that runs on a USB stick, or set up a private grid with one of the many sim hosting services listed on Hypergrid Business (http://www.hypergridbusiness.com) in the OpenSim Vendors section.

4.7.1   CREATING A PLAN

To get organized, try using Dio (https://www.dio.com/), some other kind of visual journal, or use a bulletin board to display pictures that inspire you and your class about their virtual classroom design. Where will class be today? Perhaps the spring season is just around the corner, and you would like to have some nature studies. Letting the outdoors into your classroom, real or virtual, is good for learning, provided it does not become too distracting. Since this is a virtual classroom, you can have class on the moon or inside a human brain. Developing classrooms that access those kinds of imaginary spaces may be a good homework assignment to give your students. Since the components for this project are modular, the design possibilities are almost infinite. Recent research has shown that students can focus more when they are within a rectangular room, as opposed to a square one, so perhaps this is a good plan with which to start [6].

For the purposes of this sample project, the modular classroom is placed on the surface of Mars. Mars photos from NASA were examined, and a terrain was developed to support the look and feel of this planet.

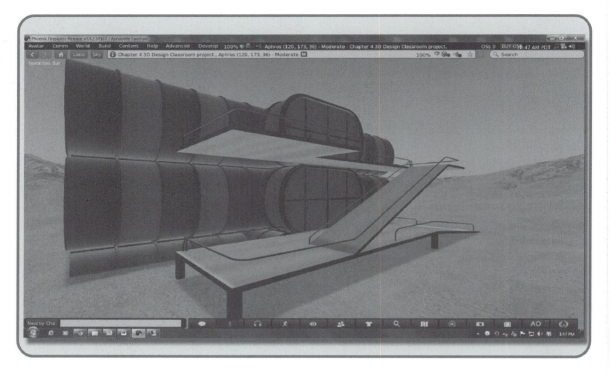

FIGURE 4.24   Screen shot from OpenSim showing final assembly of modular classroom for Martian terrain.

4.7.2   SETTING THE FOUNDATION AND LEARNING ABOUT THE PARTS

This modular classroom was designed to be part of any kind of environment. It is almost infinitely expandable due to the nature of its interchangeable parts. Figure 4.24 shows the configuration that was used for the Martian surface setup.

First things first. Once you have downloaded the Chapter 4 content from the Ann Cudworth Projects website (http://www.anncudworthprojects.com), in the Virtual World Design Book section, you should upload all the .dae files into your inventory for use in the virtual environment. As you do that, make sure to name the classroom parts in the same way. For instance, Airlock.dae would become a linked object named Airlock in your inventory.

Now would be a good time to review the notes on uploading procedures in Section 2.3, and to look at Figures 13.15 through 13.17. Make sure to include the textures on your Upload, by checking that box in the Upload menu, see Figure 13.17 for an image of this menu. Also included in the online content, are Physics .dae files. It is very important that you utilize the physics files on your upload, by selecting "From file" in the Step 1: Level of Detail section under the Physics tab located within the Upload Menu of the Firestorm viewer. This will ensure that the each part has exactly the physics level of detail it needs for your usage. As you upload them, make sure you tuck all the parts away in a special folder, and make a copy of it as backup.

There are several basic parts to this system: Airlock, Base, Crossroads, Door, Door_Trim, Railings (1,2,3), Ramps (1,2,3), Tunnel, and Windows. Later on, you will add in some Ramps for access to the airlocks. Figure 4.25 shows them laid out across the landscape of the sim.

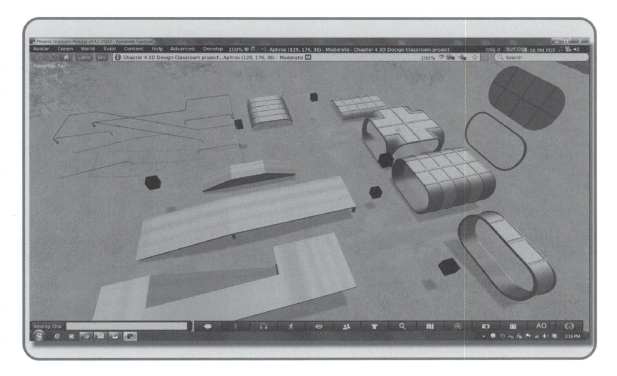

FIGURE 4.25 Screen shot from OpenSim showing the modular parts of the classroom laid out on the Martian terrain. Note the black alignment cubes.

Please note the black alignment cubes that are attached to each element, except for the outermost glass doors (these you can easily align by eye). These are important parts to help you align the various model sections for this particular configuration of the classroom.

After you upload these models into your world and have them rezzed on the ground near each other, check to make sure that the alignment cubes are the key prim (the prim all other prims are linked to) on these elements. As you probably know, the key prim is indicated with a yellow outline when you have a linked object selected in the Build/Edit menu, and the rest of the linked objects will be highlighted in blue. Sometimes, when a model is uploaded into OpenSim or Second Life, the key prim is changed. If the .dae model files have not uploaded into your virtual environment with the alignment cube as the key prim, go into the Edit Linked mode (check the box on the Build/Edit menu), and unlink the alignment prim. Without moving it, deselect everything by clicking on the ground or sky. Now, re-select the model, and then the alignment cube, and link them back together. The cube should now be the key prim, and show a yellow highlight, while the rest of the model is highlighted in blue.

Now, you are good to go. Let's start the construction by opening the Build/Edit menu. If you have the space on your region, you could just lay out all the parts and shift/copy or drag a new one from your inventory as needed.

4.7.3 Assembling the First Floor

Set up your build editor to with the Edit Axis at Root box checked; that will allow you to align the parts of the classroom because it will let you select the center of the Root (or key prim) of the linked parts. You will be centering the classroom at the coordinates of $x = 128$, $y = 128$, $z = $ whatever your terrain height is. All of your parts will be aligned to those coordinates, with a variation in z to accommodate the various levels in the classroom structure.

For the initial step, set up the support structure of the building, called Base, by aligning three of these pieces, with the center one at $x = 128$, $y = 128$, $z = $ height of your terrain, as shown in Figure 4.26, top image. Note that the middle base piece is rotated 90 degrees to the end pieces; this is purely for aesthetic reasons, and they can all be set in a straight line if you wish. For the purposes of this project, the foundation is laid running East to West on the terrain, so that the airlocks can be added on the North and South sides. Then, add in the Crossroads section of the structure and align it to $x = 128$, $y = 128$ as well. After that, add in the Tunnel sections, which will be linked up to the crossroads section, along the $y = 128$ axis, so they are in line. See Figure 4.26 for these three steps.

4.7.4   ADDING THE DOOR AND WINDOW DETAILS TO THE FIRST FLOOR

Once you (and the class) have set up the Tunnel sections, you can now add the Door_Trim, Windows, Airlock, and Doors mesh model components. The Door_Trim will go onto every opening, the Windows will go onto the ends of the Tunnel sections, and the Airlocks will go onto the Crossroads openings without the Tunnels in this build. You then will add in the Doors for the Airlocks, leave them up or open so that the avatars can walk in and out. Later, you may want to add a door moving script that allows it to function like an airlock door. The windows may be opaque in your components because of a state change in the upload. To make them transparent again, go into Edit Linked and select a window section or glass wall only, not the whole linked object with its alignment cube. Then, in the Edit Menu, under the Texture Edit tab, select the face of each window and change the transparency to 20%. See Figure 4.27 for progressive images of this assembly. The outermost doors will not will not have their alignment cubes at $x = 128$, $y = 128$. To align with the front door frames, they will be moved 3.34 m out from the center, or you can do that by eye.

4.7.5   CREATING THE SECOND FLOOR

Once you have gotten the first-floor building assembled the way you want it, hold the Shift key to group select the entire first floor. Shift+drag it to make a copy, moving straight up on the z axis to make the second floor. You are doing great! See Figure 4.28 for images from this step.

4.7.6   REMOVING THE ALIGNMENT CUBES AND CREATING A "HANDLE"

If you are comfortable with the process of linking and unlinking elements in a virtual structure and have everything in its final position, then go ahead and unlink the alignment cubes and delete them. Create a new prim, located at $x = 128$, $y = 128$, $z = $ above the structure of the whole classroom to serve as a "handle" for moving it all around easily. Then select all the parts and relink the entire structure to the "handle" prim, selecting it last, so it becomes the new key prim. If you plan on putting some LSL scripts into the doors, to them to make them move, unlink them from the handle first. There are images of this process in Figures 4.29 and 4.30.

4.7.7   ADDING IN THE RAMPS

In the spirit of "Design for All," the ramps and rails are added to the exterior for ease of access. Now let's add in the Ramps and Railings mesh models. Put Ramp_1, on the ground to have access to the South side

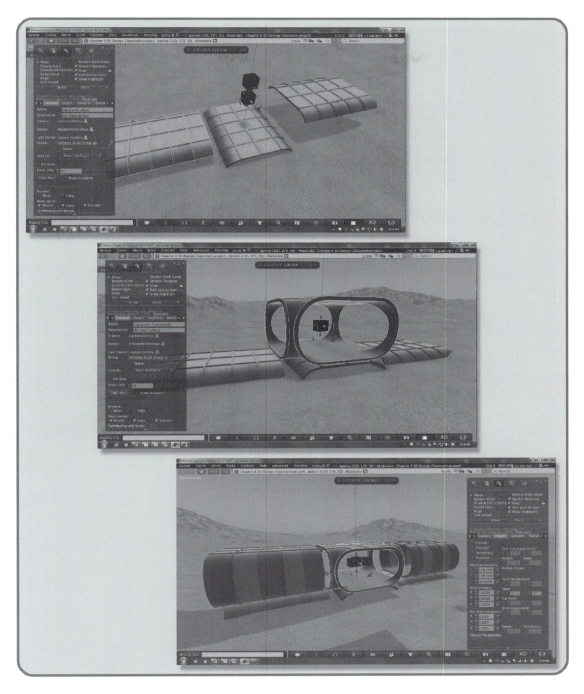

FIGURE 4.26 Screen shots from OpenSim showing (1) the assembly of the three base pieces (top image), (2) placement of the crossroads piece (middle image), and (3) placement of the 2 side tunnel pieces (bottom image).

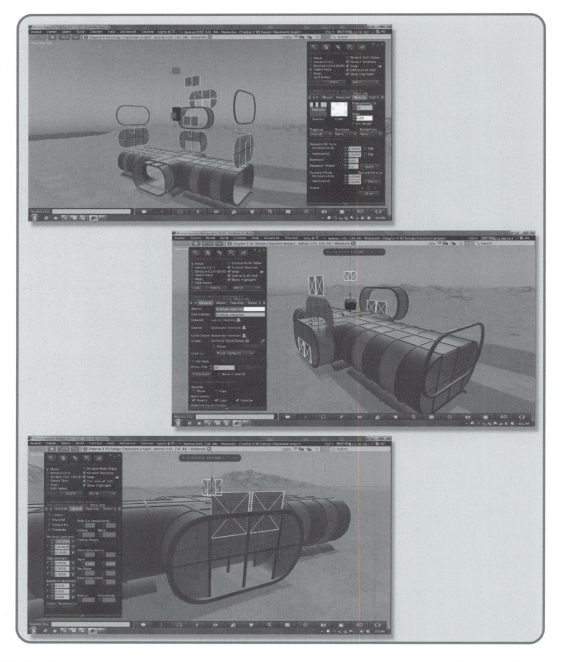

FIGURE 4.27   Screen shots showing assembly of doors and windows on modular classroom. Shown are (1) windows and door trim being dropped into place on the ends of the tunnel sections (top image), (2) door trim and airlocks being dropped into place on the crossroads section (middle image), and (3) doors being set into position in the window frames on the airlock.

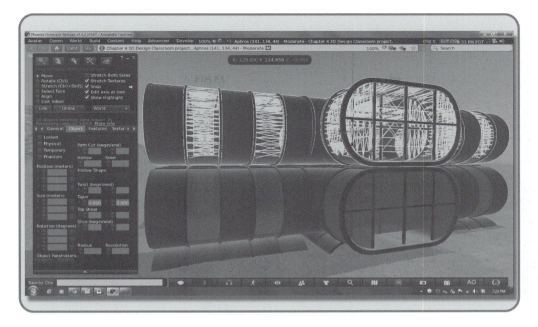

FIGURE 4.28 Screen grab showing the cloning of 1st floor elements to make the second floor of the modular classroom.

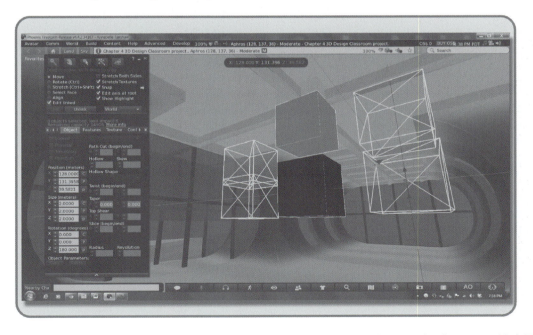

FIGURE 4.29 Screen grab showing alignment cubes insited the structure when classroom has been assembled. These cubes can be unlinked, and the entire structure relinked to one key cube. The door elements, should be left unlinked if they are to be scripted.

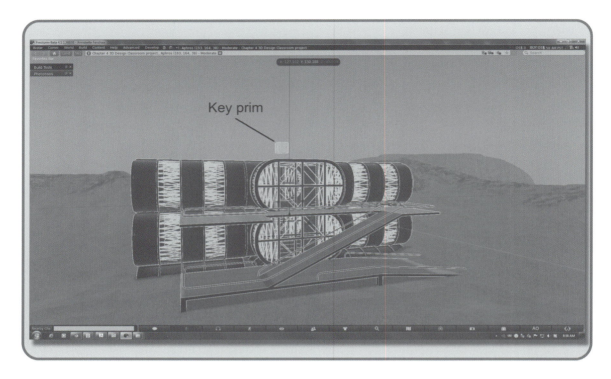

FIGURE 4.30 Screen shot showing completed modular classroom, all of it linked to a key "handle" prim (shown as light colored cube floating above the structure).

Airlock. Stack Ramp_2 and Ramp_3 on the North side Airlocks so there is access to both levels on that side. Install the railings as shown: Railings_1 running up the first ramp and airlock side, Railings_2 on the outside edge of the top platform, and Railings_3 running up the second ramp and inside edges of the top platform. Refer to Figure 4.24 for details.

Now that you have finished your first build, take some pictures and post them for your friends.

4.8 CONCLUSIONS AND TAKE-AWAY IDEAS

You have come a long way in this chapter, moving from the basics of 3D design to creating your own design from modular components. What you will bring along into the next chapters is a sense of good composition in 3D design and how to achieve it. That information is universal and applicable to all virtual environments.

REFERENCES

1. Neuroscience of Visual Object Recognition, Wikipedia article, http://en.wikipedia.org/wiki/Cognitive_neuroscience_of_visual_object_recognition. Accessed February 16, 2013.
2. Visuospatial sketchpad, Wikipedia article, http://en.wikipedia.org/wiki/Visuospatial_Sketchpad. Accessed February 16, 2013.
3. Design Elements and Principles, Wikipedia article, http://en.wikipedia.org/wiki/Design_elements_and_principles. Accessed February 18, 2013.

4. Hosey, Lance, Why We Love Beautiful Things, *New York Times*, February 15, 2013, http://www.nytimes.com/2013/02/17/opinion/sunday/why-we-love-beautiful-things.html?smid=tw-share. Accessed February 18, 2013.
5. History of Games, Wikipedia article, http://en.wikipedia.org/wiki/History_of_games. Accessed February 20, 2013.
6. Barrett, Peter, Yufan Zhang, Joanne Moffat, and Khairy Kobbacy, A Holistic, Multi-level Analysis Identifying the Impact of Classroom Design on Pupils' Learning, *Building and Environment*, 59, 678–689 2013, http://www.sciencedirect.com/science/article/pii/S0360132312002582. Accessed February 22, 2013.

5 Virtual Terrain and Designing Landscapes

I don't divide architecture, landscape and gardening; to me they are one.

—**Luis Barragan**

5.1 TERRAIN IS MORE THAN JUST DIRT

Our terrain defines us; we are mountain people, coastal dwellers, or plains residents. Terrain can provide our physical defense or force us to recognize our physical weakness, and throughout the world, sacred places on our terrain are a source of mythology or spiritual beliefs [1, 2].

From an aerial perspective, a cityscape might appear to be primarily flat, but even New York City has hills, and that terrain overlooks valleys filled by the mighty rivers that surround it. As a designer, you can create a terrain that has a powerful effect on the experience of your visitor once you have mastered the fundamentals of loading and editing it in a virtual environment.

5.1.1 FUNDAMENTAL ASPECTS OF A VIRTUAL TERRAIN

In a virtual world, terrain is a surface patch or netlike structure of interconnected vertices. On a terraformed sim (virtual environment simulation), this looks like a fisherman's net thrown over a bumpy, irregular surface, but on a new sim, it is displayed as a flat plane. Typically, upon creation, the flat plane of land is elevated to just above the standard sea level of 20 meters so the avatar is not walking underwater. By accessing the wireframe render style, you can see how the mesh of the landscape is altered once it has been terraformed, as shown in Figure 5.1. The wireframe mode can be accessed in the Develop menu, which along with the Advanced menu, is activated on the top bar of the Firestorm viewer after the basic installation is done. Use the key commands of (Ctrl+Alt+D) and then (Ctrl+Alt+Q) respectively to turn on these hidden menus. Using (Ctrl+Shift+R) will let you see the wireframe once the Develop menu is showing. Note more information about key commands and the Firestorm viewer is available here, (http://wiki.phoenixviewer.com/keyboard_shortcuts).

As you can see in Figure 5.1, after the land has been terraformed, the surface patch or terrain takes on the distortions that provide for the creation of hills and valleys, mountains, and coastlines in your virtual environment.

Just changing the landscape from flat into low hills adds more visual interest to your developing virtual scene because it allows for the visitor to "discover" your space. Think about how you enter a great valley from a mountain overpass or how hills flatten to the coastline as a river nears a sea. Each landscape we create in a virtual world can tell the story of a voyage. If you utilize that "storytelling" concept in your design, it will have great influence on your visitor's perception of the environment and the contents you have built in it.

FIGURE 5.1 Screen grabs from OpenSim showing virtual terrain using two kinds of rendering. In the top two images, the flat initial terrain and its wireframe structure are shown, and in the bottom two images, a "terraformed" landscape and its wireframe structure is shown.

5.1.2 RESEARCH AND FINDING INSPIRATION FOR MAKING COMPELLING TERRAIN DESIGNS

There are many places you can find inspiration for your landscape designs. Watching documentary films like *The National Parks: America's Best Idea* by Ken Burns [3] or looking at the 3D worldwide terrain geography available on Google Earth should provide you with a broad range of excellent examples displaying the magnificent compelling terrains we have around us.

For more aesthetic inspiration, to find the "mood" and "personality" in a landscape, look to the great landscape paintings throughout history. As early as the Minoan and Roman eras, we painted images of our landscapes, inspired by what we saw around us. Worldwide, our common desire to make images of our landscapes is shown in the work of Chinese painters like Fan Kuan, Tabriz from Persia, and Toyo and Hiroshige from Japan. In Europe, there were painters such as Friedrich from Germany, Turner from England, and Corot from France. In more modern eras, Van Gogh, Cezanne, O'Keefe, Thiebaud, and Sanchez have created landscapes that speak to our souls. Online searches for "great landscape paintings" and "best landscape painters" will bring up hundreds of examples for you to examine.

For inspiration of a more virtual nature, visit places in Second Life and OpenSim. Examples of several interesting landscapes are shown in Figure 5.2. In the top picture, you see the sculpted mesh mountains surrounding the Oni Kenkon Creations Tower built by Nebadon Izumi on the OS Grid. In the middle picture is an image of Shambala, a massive multiregion build surrounded by an estuary, built by Hiro Protagonist. The bottom frame shows a two-picture sequence of Mac Kanashimi's "Scripted Fractal Landscape," built in Second Life, in the LEA27 region. This incredible build constantly shifted its underlying shapes to create an ever-changing landscape for the visitor.

5.2 METHODOLOGIES FOR TERRAFORMING USING INWORLD TOOLS

There are two inworld methodologies for creating changes in your terrain, and they are not mutually exclusive. The first and most universally accessible is using the Land Tools in the Build menu of your Firestorm Viewer. Anyone can utilize these tools, provided the Edit terrain permission is granted to them by the owner or they own the land themselves. The second method is uploading a grayscale height map (or height field) image file specifically created to generate terrain on your region. Please note the second method for terraforming is only available to owners of the land; estate managers and land renters will be locked out of that menu on the viewer.

5.2.1 IMPORTANT SETTINGS AND LAND TOOLS IN THE FIRESTORM VIEWER

Before you start terraforming on your land, and if that land is accessible to the public, there is one important detail to check in the About Land menu. In the Firestorm Viewer, in the World tab/About Land/Options section, there is a set of check boxes under "Allow other residents to:," and you want to make sure the box next to "Edit Terrain" is left unchecked (see Figure 5.3). If you leave it checked, other residents of your world will be able to alter your terrain and possibly ruin your carefully built landscape.

There are three basic menus you will need to know about when you are doing terraforming: the Land Tools in the Build menu, the About Land tools, and the Estate/Region tools.

Let's start by looking at the Land Tools in the Build menu. This method is useful for terraforming a land area or parcel that is under one Region in size (less than 256 meters square). You can see the Land Tools by opening your Build menu and selecting the tiny bulldozer icon on the top right. Let's go through them one by one (see Figure 5.4 for images of this).

Fantastic Landscapes

Nebadon Izumi - Oni Kenkon Creations Tower on the OS Grid

Hiro Protagonist - Shambala on the OS Grid

Mac Kanashimi - Scripted Fractal Landscape in Second Life, LEA 27

FIGURE 5.2 (See color insert) Screen shots of amazing landscapes created for OpenSim and Second Life. Notice how they can vary in composition, with the usage of outlying mountain meshes (top image), composite terraforming that combines many regions into a whole large structure (middle image) and the creation of a landscape made from scripted objects (bottom image).

FIGURE 5.3 Screen grab from OpenSim showing the About Land/Options menu for securing terraforming rights. It's very important to turn off the terraforming option for other users (see circled box on menu image), in order to preserve your terrain.

1. On the top line of the open Build menu, you will see five icons; the last one is a tiny bulldozer. That should be highlighted, indicating that you have activated the Land Tools.

2. Below that, it says "Click and Drag to Select Land." What this means is that when you pick the radio button next to Select Land on the list, you can select portions of the terrain to terraform.

   Using this option is like selecting a mask for creating a stencil effect. Just as your brush will only paint the areas open in a stencil mask, the selected area on the terrain will be the only part affected by the Land Tools (e.g., flatten, raise, lower, etc.). When your terraform work is done on the selected terrain, you can use the smooth button to blend into the adjacent land.

3. Below the Select Land button are the six land editors: Flatten, Raise, Lower, Smooth, Roughen, and Revert. With the exception of Revert, the names clearly describe the effect each editor will have on your terrain.

   Note: Revert is a special editing tool, and it is tied in to one of the features available to you if you are the owner of the region or estate. In the top bar, under the World tab, there is Region Details, which will bring up the Region/Estate menu. On that menu, under the Terrain tab near the bottom, is the Bake Terrain button. By "baking" the terrain, you set the terraforming heights on the region as a baseline configuration. If you want to experiment with new changes in your terrain and then return to the baked configuration, you can do that by using the Revert tool.

4. Back in the Land Editing menu, next to the Edit tools are slider bars for your bulldozer. The Size button on the slider affects the size of the patch moved by the bulldozer to let you work in large

FIGURE 5.4 Screen grab from OpenSim showing aspects of the Build/Land Tool menu: (1) bulldozer icon that opens the terrain tools from the build menu, (2) the select land button for selective terraforming, (3) the terrain modifying tools, (4) the bulldozer settings, (5) the parcel information that shows terrain subdivision, (6) the parcel join or subdivide tools, and (7) the land transactions buttons allowing purchase or abandonment of land.

strokes to create a prairie or little touches to create a small plateau. The Strength button on the slider below Size will change the power of the bulldozer and how much the land will move with each mouse click or the duration of your click-and-drag action.

5. Below this is the Parcel Information, letting you know the land area and who the owners are. Also included is an About Land button, which is a good reminder to go back to About Land and make sure the terraforming option is not checked, and no one else can edit the terrain on your parcel.

6. Under that is Modify Parcel, which allows you to Subdivide and to Join selected land parcels. This tool is very powerful and will allow you to divide land for the purposes of setting music and media streams, rental properties, group access, and other property-related attributes. When dividing or joining land, you should always check the About Land settings and the Region/Estate settings to make sure that they are where you want them to be on that parcel after you have completed the changes. The resulting combined parcel inherits the properties that were assigned to the last parcel selected to be joined. Also, these Modify tools may make landmarks and landing points invalid, so you should also recheck those.

7. And finally, the Land Transactions buttons. Obviously, if you are in a world that uses currency, and you desire to own the services provided by buying the land, this is where you do it. You can also give up all ownership to the land, and in Second Life the ownership will go back to Governor Linden.

5.2.2 Testing the Functionality of the Built-in Land Tools

Let's take the Land Tools out for a test drive so you can get the feel of them. In Second Life, Torley Linden has provided a terrain testing ground (http://slurl.com/secondlife/Here/173/165/23), or you can try this on your own land in an OpenSim region.

First, let's try selecting an area about 20 meters square. You can check your dimensions by laying out a 20 m × 20 m × 1 m box, making it hollow and using it to frame your terraform area.

Practice selecting the terrain inside the box, and practice selecting the terrain outside it. *Note*: You cannot select anything but a square shape, so you will have to work section by section around a center area. You will also see by just clicking on the land that the minimum size of a section is 4 meters square.

When that feels comfortable, select an area. Make the bulldozer about 25% of its full size and set the strength at 50%. With Raise selected on the Edit tool, hold the left mouse button down and circle the bulldozing patch over the selected area. You should see the ground start to move and raise itself. Do not hold the mouse on it too long if the reaction is slow. Give the server time to make many calculations for you; this is a complex command for it. When the ground stops moving, use your camera to look at it from all angles (holding the Alt key down and using the arrow on Page Up and Page Down keys). Note how it changed and what it felt like to do that change. Good terrain sculpting is a tactile as well as a visual task, so you need to learn how it feels and how long you should run the bulldozer tool over the land to obtain the effect you want.

Try the rest of the tools and see how they work on that patch of the terrain. You will notice that by changing the sliders for size and strength of the bulldozer you can greatly affect the look and the speed of the terraforming. See Figure 5.5 for comparative images of how these tools work.

Another factor to be aware of are regional limits on terrain settings. For instance, on the Second Life mainland, the land cannot be elevated or lowered more than 4 meters. Elsewhere in the Metaverse, land can be elevated or lowered plus or minus 100 meters unless the owner has set limits on the terraforming in the Region/Estate/Terrain menu.

How you design with these parameters in mind is a decision related to the needs of the environment you are creating. Making really tall mountains over 100 meters high on a relatively small patch of ground (one region or less) will probably not look good. Overly high terrain looks unnatural and disproportionate,

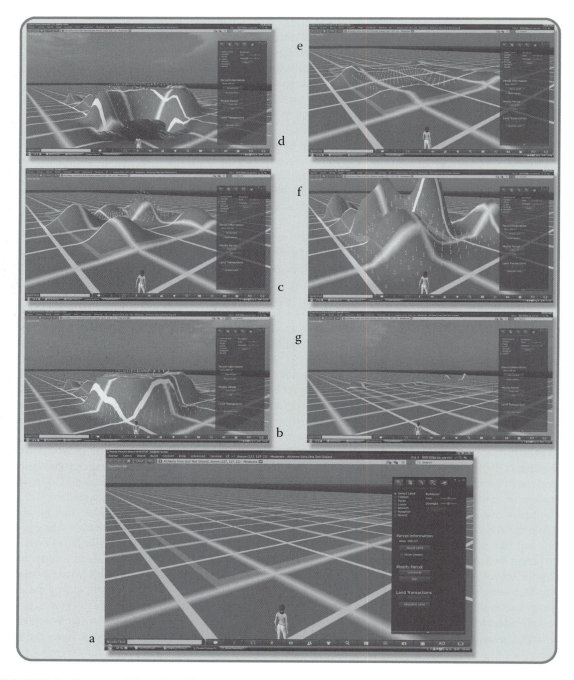

FIGURE 5.5 Screen grab from OpenSim showing use results of the terraforming tools available for manipulating the land surface in the Land Tool Menu. They are: (a) Select, (b) Flatten, (c) Raise, (d) Lower, (e) Smooth, (f) Roughen, and (g) Revert. Note the different kind of icons that appear on the ground surface with each tool used.

and the rock, grass, or dirt textures become stretched and distorted. A good rule of thumb is to keep the highest peak one-fifth of the distance of your longest view, measured from the seabed or lowest terrain point. That is, if you have a parcel 100 meters square, keep your highest peak at 40 meters (20 meters over the standard sea level of 20 meters). Also, remember that high mountains usually need big bases to look natural; the land grade should start to rise from some distance away from the peak of the mountain.

5.3 METHODOLOGIES FOR TERRAFORMING USING HEIGHT MAPS

In larger-scale projects such as entire regions or grids, it is more efficient to utilize a height map to create your landscape design. Height maps, or height field maps as they are sometimes known, are powerful tools for quickly creating lots of varied terrain. These are RGB (red, green, blue) images (256 by 256 pixels per region) that define the height of the terrain by the color values in the red channel. They are saved in the RAW file format, and although only 3 of the channels (red, green, and blue) actually affect the landscape now, they still need to be saved with the legacy 13 channels to be loaded in properly in Second Life and OpenSim through the viewer interface. *Note:* if you have your own region or grid in OpenSim with total server access, then terrain manipulation can be accomplished with a simple 256 × 256 pixel grayscale image installed with the "terrain load" server command. When you manipulate terrain with your bulldozer tool, you are actually using "brushes" to change the values on an underlying height map, and those changes are interpreted by the simulation program into changes in the elevations on your land surface patch.

5.3.1 Region Controls for Terrain Loading and Textures

Before we load in a dramatic example of how a height map works, let's look over the Region/Estate/Terrain menu. You will find it under World/Region Details in Firestorm.

Here are all the options on that menu; their location on the menu is indicated by number in Figure 5.6. These are available to estate owners and managers:

1. Water Height is the setting that is your "sea level." This is typically 20 meters from the bottom of the sea, the lowest point on your land.
2. Terrain Raise Limit is the setting for your highest peak, above the baked default level set on the land.
3. Terrain Lower Limit is the setting for your lowest valley, or ocean bottom, below the baked default level.
4. Terrain Textures for the land surfaces are the dirt, grass, and rock textures applied to the terrain.
5. Texture Elevation Ranges is the location and range covered by these textures on the terrain.
6. Download RAW terrain … will allow you to download a RAW file snapshot of your grayscale height map onto your computer to be opened in a paint program such as Photoshop or GIMP (GNU Image Manipulation Program).
7. Upload RAW terrain … will allow you to upload your preformatted RAW file to the server and install your new terrain. This is one of the most fun things to watch in a virtual world as the terrain starts to fill in row by row. *Note*: Again, remember only owners have the rights to upload and download terrain files.
8. Bake Terrain freezes the present terrain as the middle level for the Terrain Raise and Lower limits.

5.3.2 Examining a Benchmark Terrain for Your Region

Now, you have a general overview, let's proceed with the loading of your first terrain. To prepare for the terrain tests and projects in this chapter, you should now go to http://www.anncudworthprojects.com, and download

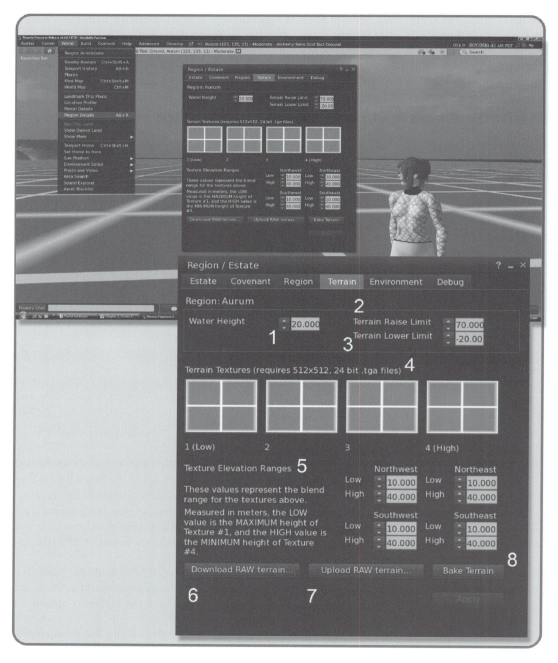

FIGURE 5.6 Screen grab from OpenSim showing terrain setting options on the World/Region Details/Region-Estate/Terrain menu screen, such as (1) the Water Height setting, (2) and (3) the Terrain Raise and Lower limits, (4) the palette of Terrain Textures, (5) the Texture Elevation Ranges, (6) the Download RAW file start button, (7) Upload RAW file start button, and (8) the Bake terrain start button.

the content for Chapter 5. Find the two RAW files called Benchmark_heights.raw and Benchmark_255.raw and save them to a special folder called Terrain Benchmarks. Use the terrain upload options in the Region/Estate menu under the Terrain tab to load in Benchmark_heights.raw for the first test, and then replace that with the Benchmark_255.raw file. In the upper image of Figure 5.7, you can see how Benchmark_heights.raw will step the terrain in response to the values in the RAW image and in lower image of Figure 5.7 you can see what a smooth steep terrain Benchmark_255.raw will produce. Try landing your avatar on various parts of these two terrains, to see what the elevation is at various locations. This will give you a good idea of how your sim will react to various values in a height map field. Notice that the terrain textures in Figure 5.7 have been made in 4 simple shades, white, light gray, dark gray and black. Notice how the simulator program makes splotchy blurs on the edges of the terrain textures where they meet on the terrain.

Let's utilize the information you have discovered from these benchmark examples of land heights and proceed to making an accessible terrain called Wheely Island.

5.4   MAKING WHEELY ISLAND, A WHEELCHAIR-ACCESSIBLE VIRTUAL PARK

Before you start terraforming, consider this question. Virtual environments have been used extensively to train motorized wheelchair users since the late 1990s [4], and the numbers of wheelchair-accessible nature walks in our national parks have been increasing every year. Let's take on the dual challenge of making a beautiful virtual landscape that is also accessible to all, designed for ease of use in movement and visibility. In real life, you may not need a wheelchair to get around, but understanding how to build for accessibility in a virtual space is the sign of a well-rounded virtual environment designer. For the purposes of building this park, you are going to follow the guidelines set out by the American Trails Organization, specifically the guidelines utilized by Malibu Parks, California (see pp. 7 and 13) [5].

In general, we want to consider the width of the boardwalks (5 meters wide is acceptable), the cross slope (no more than 1:50), and a running slope of 1:20 for our Wheely Island visitors. The maximum running slope of 1:12 for 60 meters (200 feet) will have to be interspersed with level resting spots. Turnaround spots will have to be provided, as well as railings to prevent a wheelchair from running off the boardwalks. This environment should also be fun to visit, so you should consider the idea of running the boardwalk near the water as well as making platforms overlooking some interesting features like cliffs and perhaps a sea volcano. In this project, the initial design concept was roughed out in SketchUp, as shown in Figure 5.8.

5.4.1   ROUGHING IN THE TERRAIN SHAPES OF WHEELY ISLAND USING THE SECOND LIFE TERRAIN FORMAT

Now that you can see the overall plan for this island, let's move onto making the actual terrain height map for it. Assuming that you have downloaded the content for this chapter, open up the pre-made files for each step in a paint program such as Photoshop or GIMP so you can reference them as the project proceeds. Note that the RAW file must be opened as a 256 × 256 pixel image in RGB with 13 channels, and you should open both the Layers menu and the Channel menu, if you are working in Photoshop, or their equivalents in your favorite graphics program. The 13 channels are a legacy structure for terrain height maps. These were originally used to control land properties such as parcel division, flying, and such. Now, the simulator just uses three of these channels: the red one (channel 1) defines the height field as 0–255 meters; the green one (channel 2) defines the height multiply factor, allowing for the elevation value of a terrain to be raised by multiplying it with a chosen number; and the blue one (channel 3) defines the water height in meters on the sim, which is typically 20 meters. More detailed information is found in the Second Life wiki [6]. Although there are many channels in the file, you will only need to concern yourself with the all-black image on the red channel. At first, the

FIGURE 5.7 Screen grabs from OpenSim showing, in the top view, a region loaded with the Benchmark_stepped.raw terrain file. The water level is set to 0m. Note, a thumbnail of the actual terrain height map is shown in the upper left section of each image. In the bottom view, a region is loaded the Benchmark_255.raw file and the water on the adjacent region is lowered to 0m. These are benchmark terrain files that will show you how your simulator responds to a height map, so you can accurately gauge what grayscale value will produce a given terrain elevation.

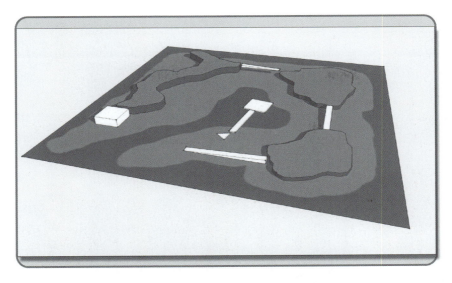

FIGURE 5.8 Screen grab from SketchUp showing initial rough mockup of terrain design for Wheely Island.

red channel will look completely black because all the terrain is at zero elevation, but as you paint in your landforms, gray shapes will emerge to indicate the new land heights.

Note: As mentioned before, if you are working with an OpenSim-based region and have access to the server command window, you can load the terrain there as a flattened grayscale file (.png, .jpg, etc.), rather than as a RAW file through the viewer interface. This is convenient if you are interested in modifying your terrain quickly and on a more granular level. There are several terrain server commands available, allowing you to "tweak" the results. More information on that is available (http://opensimulator.org/wiki/Server_Commands). Now on to making the actual terrain files.

5.4.1.1 Making the Coastline
In your paint program, open the the Step1_Wheely Island.raw file as shown in Figure 5.9. Open up the Window/Channels tab, select and make sure you are only drawing on the Red Channel, which will look like a grayscale. Using the color picker on your paint program, set the paint brush color to (R = 30, G = 30, B = 30) on your color picker and trace over in the coastline shown in Figure 5.9 with a hard-edged brush of about 9 pixels, being careful to stay at least 20 pixels from the outside edge of the image.

5.4.1.2 Filling in the Landforms
Continuing with the terrain making, use the image from the previous step (Step1_Wheely Island.raw) and fill in the whole island shape with the same coastline gray color. Move inland and pick a gray that is (R = 58, G = 58, B = 58) and draw in the first hilltop, bottom right. Moving counterclockwise, draw in the next hilltop with the gray set at R=63, G=63, B=63) high, and finally draw the volcano crater edge on the top left-hand corner with the lightest gray at (R=67, B=67, B=67). Look at the Step2_Wheely Island.raw file to see a completed version of this, also shown in Figure 5.10.

5.4.1.3 Smoothing the Terrain
Continuing with the same image you started with (Step1_Wheely Island.raw), you will now modify it some more with the smudge and blur tools. To create more natural land forms, use a 9-pixel smudge tool (normal

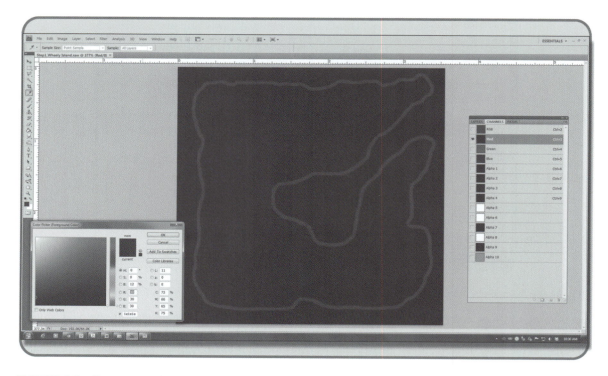

FIGURE 5.9 Screen grab from Photoshop. Note that the coastline is drawn on the red channel for the Wheely Island terrain file. This file, "Step1_Wheely Island.raw," can be downloaded from the Chapter 5 content at http://www.anncudworthprojects.com.

mode, strength at 50%) to soften the outside edges of the hills onto the surrounding coastal plains. Use the smudge tool and the blur tools to blur the edges of the coastline into the ocean bottom so the coast drops off gradually. When you like how it looks, put an overall Gaussian blur of 3 pixels on the image, to further smooth the terrain as shown in Figure 5.11. You can see the final result of this step in the file Step3_Wheely Island.raw, from the Chapter 5 content. Save your final as "Wheely_Island.raw" for use in the first upload of your terrain.

5.4.1.4   First Upload of Your Terrain

Upload the last Wheely_Island.raw file through the Region/Estate menu, under the Terrain tab, and look at Figure 15.12 for an example of what this looks like. This process may take anywhere from 1 minute to 15 minutes depending on your Internet connection and traffic on the server. Make sure your avatar is hovering above the ground, not standing on it, when the terraforming is going on; otherwise, you might be thrown up into the air.

5.4.2   REFINING THE TERRAIN

Now that you have loaded the terrain onto your region and watched it magically appear, disable the camera constraints under the Advanced Menu tab (Ctrl+Alt+D to make this show) so you can pull back to see the whole sim and examine for the need for refinements. You may also have to increase the draw distance in the Avatar/Preferences menu.

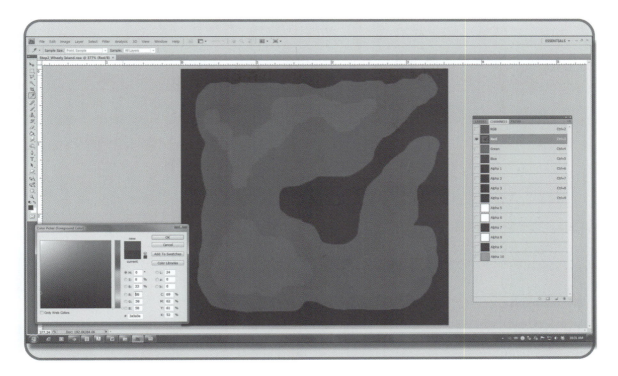

FIGURE 5.10 Screen grab from Photoshop showing process of filling in the land masses on the red channel in the Wheely Island terrain file. "Step2_Wheely Island.raw"can be downloaded from the Chapter 5 content at http://www. anncudworthprojects.com.

Walk your avatar around the landscape so you can compare the difference in actual terrain height you get in the sim (use your avatar's Z coordinate) with the grayscale scale values you painted in the height map. If you like the configuration of the landmass, but find that it is just a little too high or too low, you have a few options.

1. You can go back into the paint program and lighten or darken the overall file to raise or lower the entire landscape.
2. You can turn to third-party software such as Bailiwick (PC) or Backhoe (Mac) to adjust the region multiplier and raise or lower the entire region.
3. You can select the whole region or the parts you want to change with the terrain editing tool and set the bulldozer strength to the weakest settings and raise the landscape "by hand."

If the land is just too bumpy, you can smooth it again with the Gaussian blur in your paint program. Be aware that this will start to lower the hills as it blends them into the surrounding areas. You can also smooth the landscape with the inworld bulldozer, just make sure you bake the terrain first and set the Terrain Raise and Lower limits to small numbers.

Have patience as handmade terrain making is not an exact science and requires a bit of practice to get the land just the way you want it. Once you think it looks good, take your avatar for another "walk about," paying attention to the views you obtain, as well as the accessibility of the landscape.

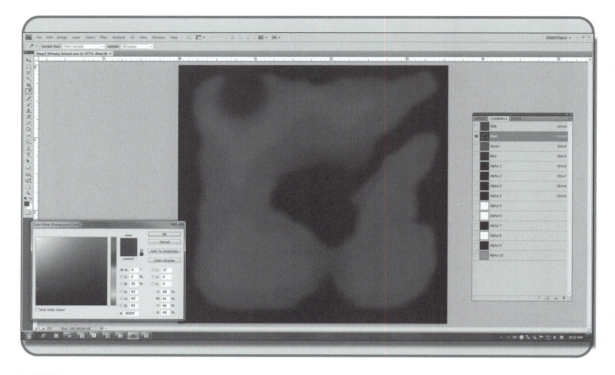

FIGURE 5.11 Screen grab from Photoshop showing the use of a Guassian blur in the Wheely Island terrain file to smooth the terrain. The completed file "Step3_Wheely Island.raw," can be downloaded from the Chapter 5 content at http://www.anncudworthprojects.com.

You should ask yourself these questions:

1. Do I like the views from the middle looking in all directions?
2. Do I like the views looking from the corners in all directions?
3. Do I get a sense of "discovery" as I walk around?
4. Are my hills or coastlines too steep to walk up?
5. Does this terrain seem easy to access from all directions?

You can also do a little fine-tuning of the terrain surfaces now, using the built-in Land Tools that you explored previously and are shown in Figure 5.5. It is advised that before you start to do the final terraforming that you bake the terrain and set the tools to a limited range, say 2 meters for the Terrain Raise Limit and –2 meters for the Terrain Lower limit.

5.5   ADDING TERRAIN TEXTURES TO YOUR LANDSCAPE

Assuming that you are satisfied with the shape of the terrain, let's turn our focus to the terrain textures and how to get the most out of them. These are required to be of a specific format in Second Life and OpenSim. The texture terrain menu will only accept images that are 512 × 512 or 1024 × 1024 pixels, 24 bit, TGA-type files.

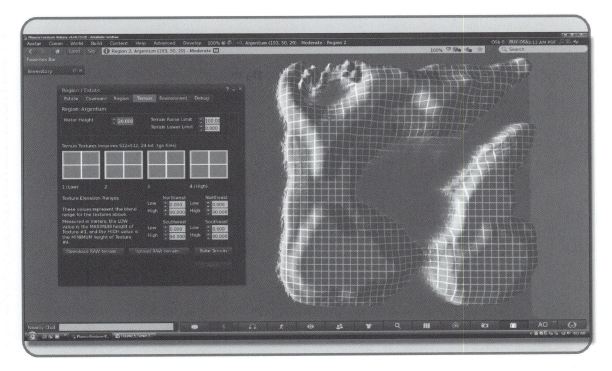

FIGURE 5.12 Screen shot in OpenSim showing terrain initially generated from Wheely_Island.raw terrain file, and then embellished with the built in terrain tools in the Edit menu. On the left is the Region/Estate upload menu and terrain texture tools. Note, a simple grid texture has been applied to all 4 quadrants to bring out the surface contours on the new land, it is not the final texture.

Since you now have some nice coastline, let's go with sandy and volcanic tropical beach textures. Included in the assets for Chapter 5 are some terrain textures that you are free to use for the purposes of this project. Once you have them, these should be loaded into your avatar's inventory and then into the Terrain Texture slots on the Region/Estate/Terrain editor.

Starting with the far left window, number 1 or the lowest elevation, drag in the ocean bottom texture (WI_ocean_bottom.tga) from your inventory; drag in the white sand (WI_white_sand.tga) in window number 2; grassy sand (WI_grassy_sand.tga) in number 3; and the volcano stone (WI_volcano_stone.tga) in number 4, the highest elevation of the island. Once you have loaded them in, click the Apply button and they will appear on the landscape.

1. WI_ocean_bottom.tga
2. WI_white_sand.tga
3. WI_grassy_sand.tga
4. WI_volcano_stone.tga

Take a walk around and look at where the textures are blending on the landscape. To see the ocean bottom clearly, change the Water Height to 0 in the Region/Estate/Terrain menu and apply your texture, noting where the blend lines occur.

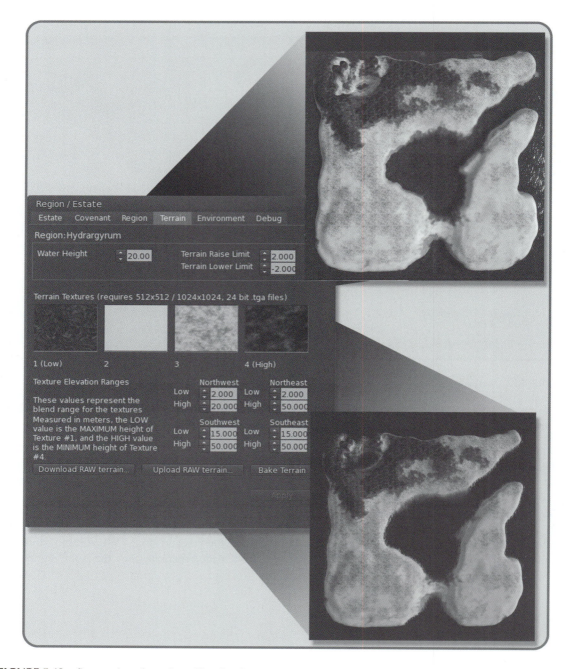

FIGURE 5.13 Screen shots from OpenSim showing terrain textures applied to Wheely Island terrain. In the top right image, the ocean bottom is shown with the water height at 0, and in the lower right image the water height is at 20 m. Notice how the texture elevation ranges affect the appearance in different quadrants of the terrain by revealing varying amounts of the four terrain textures used.

Following the logic of the landscape is important in deciding where the textures will show on a terrain, as shown in Figure 5.13. Let's start with the volcano in the northwestern quadrant of the sim. Obviously, here we would like to show the burned stone and darkened ground seen around a volcanic crater. By setting the Texture Elevation Ranges in the northwestern quadrant first, we can effectively set the scheme for the whole sim. Set the Low setting in the northwestern quadrant to 2.0 meters and set the High setting to 20.00 meters. By doing this, you are pulling the volcanic stone texture down low, all the way to the 20-meter waterline, and pushing the ocean bottom texture to the lowest depths of the undersea area.

Now, fly over to the southeastern quadrant of the sim. On this side of the sim, we want a tropical paradise, and we are assuming that there is no volcanic heat to kill the vegetation. By putting the Low setting to 15.0 meters and the High setting to 50.0 meters, we will see a nice grassy, sandy beach surface. Now that you have established the looks of the two definitive environments on the island, you can fill in the transitional quadrants. The northeast will have Low = 2.0 meters and High = 50.0 meters, and the southwest will have Low = 15.0 meters and High = 50.0 meters. These settings should provide you with a nice transition from tropical paradise to volcanic crater on the terrain settings. Again, if you have not baked your terrain, please do so now. Put the water level back to 20 meters and admire your work so far.

5.5.1 CONSIDERATIONS FOR MAKING GOOD TERRAIN TEXTURES

Eventually, you will want to make your own textures for terrain. Three important things to remember as you generate them in Photoshop or GIMP are tiling, scale, and saturation of color.

Since a texture is tiled many times across the sim, if it is not blending smoothly on all four sides, it will start to make its own pattern across the simulator terrain, which looks distracting. You can avoid this effect by testing; save your new terrain image as a fill pattern, create a new test file at 4× the size of your terrain image in your paint program and fill it with the terrain pattern you are developing. Immediately, you will see if the texture creates an unwelcome pattern across the landscape. Pushing the texture off center a little bit with an offset filter and adding some border blurring will help that. Filter Forge (http://www.filterforge.com/) is also an excellent tool for seeing how a pattern will tile; it plugs in to Photoshop and comes with access to a large online library of procedural texture generators. In terms of scale, keep an eye on recognizable terrain elements such as flowers or seashells on the landscape. You do not want them too big or too small, as they cover the terrain, unless you are going for a fantasy or "Alice in Wonderland" effect. Finally, you should pay close attention to saturation of color. As you work, think of how mountainous landscapes look and how they tend to soften in color and go a bit gray with the atmospheric perspective created by the distance. If there is a way you can work this effect into your landscape textures, such as toning down the colors on mountain peaks or deepening the saturation of color on the ocean textures, a greater and subtler sense of depth will be created in your terrain.

5.6 OTHER APPLICATIONS FOR CREATING LANDSCAPES

When you start to design terrain it is handy to have a few other software tools around to alter, view, and transfer terrain files. Two simple terrain editors are the freeware programs Bailiwick (for Windows; http://www. spinmass.com/Software/Bailiwick.aspx) and Backhoe (for the Mac; http://www.notabene-sl.com/Backhoe/). On the more professional or "pro-sumer" level are terrain programs like Terragen (http://planetside.co.uk/) and L3DT Pro (http://www.bundysoft.com/L3DT/). If you really want to go crazy making huge and varied terrain, there is the World Machine program (http://world-machine.com/index.php).

5.7 DESIGNING ACCESS FOR ALL

Now, we are ready to set up our visitors' trail on Wheely Island. Again, it may help you to plan this out with an overhead shot of the sim at hand. Any good nature walk is a loop that brings you back to where the car is parked or, in this case, where you teleported in. When you design for "all access," you need to think of access in several ways. Imagine if you could not actually move the mouse with your hands, if you only saw things that had a high contrast on them, or if you were there to experience only the sounds of this place. Being aware of the differing levels of a visitor's virtual experience will enhance your ability to create access for all. It is far better to begin these considerations in the planning phase of a build than to have to retrofit a sim after it is finished.

5.7.1 LAYING OUT THE WALKWAYS FOR WHEELY ISLAND

Once you have downloaded the Chapter 5 content from the Ann Cudworth Projects website (http://www.anncudworthprojects.com), in the Virtual World Design Book section, you should upload all the .dae files into your inventory for use in the virtual environment. As you do that, make sure to name the classroom parts in the same way. For instance, 45_Degree_Walkway_Left.dae would become a linked object named 45_Degree_Walkway_Left in your inventory. Now would be a good time to review the notes on uploading procedures in section 2.3, and to look at figures 13.15 through 13.17. Make sure to include the textures on your Upload, by checking that box in the Upload menu, see Figure 13.17 for an image of this menu. Also included in the online content, are Physics .dae files. It is very important that you utilize the physics files on your upload, by selecting "From file" in the Step 1:Level of Detail section under the Physics tab located within the Upload Menu of the Firestorm viewer. This will ensure that the each part has exactly the physics level of detail it needs for your usage. As you upload them, make sure you tuck all the parts away in a special folder, and make a copy of it just in case.

Let's continue building. From the Wheely Island content you have uploaded inworld, take out the elements called "Turning_Point_Walkways I, II, and III." These are the turnaround areas and focal points on your walkways path. It is best to lay these out first and "connect the dots," so to speak. The approximate coordinates, <x,y,z> for the Turning Point elements (in clockwise order are: (1) Turning_Point_Walkways_I at <189.086, 213.149, 36.7237> (2) Turning_Point_Walkways_II at <217.029, 161.037, 29.8943> (3) Turning_Point_Walkways_I at <139.536, 111.79, 24.9081> (4) Turning_Point_Walkways_III at <217.181, 45.6227, 28.5412> and (5) Turning_Point_Walkways_III at <42.6837, 46.624, 31.0233>. Note, these elements are enumerated in the top left image on Figure 5.14, and their coordinates are mentioned in the caption. Once you get the turning points in place, use some large box prims that are 5 meters wide and about 100 meters long to line them up as shown in the top left image of Figure 5.14. By using these box prims as simple yardsticks, you can quickly get a good idea of how the walkways can be laid out. Remember from Section 5.4, there is a limit to acceptable gradients on the ramping, and you should endeavor to stay within those guidelines if you can. You can quickly measure the height of something by rezzing a box on that location and reading the z coordinate.

Once you have roughed it out, then start laying down sections of walkway using the following mesh model components provided: Long_Straight_Walkway, Medium_Straight_Walkway, Short_Straight_Walkways, Medium_Straight_Walkway_Planks, as well as the 90_Degree_Walkway_Left, 90_Degree_Walkway_Right, 45_Degree_Walkway_Left, 45_Degree_Walkway_Right, 90_Degree_Walkway_Left and 90_Degree_Walkway_Left_II mesh parts to connect the turning points. Use the Bridge_Support_Walkways when the walkway travels over a valley on the sim. Note, these components may be used at your discretion, and in any arrangement you choose. Continue up the path, laying in sections of boardwalk, until you have laid out the whole walkway. Don't be afraid to move the turning points to "snug up" the fit between the walkways you are laying down. Once you have the whole path done, upload the mesh model Wheelchair.dae into your

FIGURE 5.14 Screen shots from OpenSim showing the "Flow of Process" used during the placement of the major elements on Wheely Island. The approximate coordinates, <x,y,z> for these (in clockwise order are: (1) <189.086, 213.149, 36.7237> (2) <217.029, 161.037, 29.8943> (3) <139.536, 111.79, 24.9081> (4) <217.181, 45.6227, 28.5412> and (5) <42.6837, 46.624, 31.0233>. Top left image shows the turning point elements placed on the landscape and aligned with large box prims. Middle two images show how these box prims guide alignment of walkways and how various turns and connectors are used. Bottom image shows completed boardwalk view.

avatar's inventory and then assemble and "wear" the wheelchair. It should attach itself to your avatar's body and put you into a sitting position. Because this object is attached to your avatar, it will move up steep hills and ramps more easily than a real wheelchair would, so you want to double-check your ramp rise again, by the numbers, to make sure it is not too steep. The wheelchair attachment should help you make sure there is enough room for turning around and width for two people in wheelchairs to pass each other. Roll down onto the lower platform and check the view from there. All around the entire path, there should be a barrier just high enough to stop a wheelchair from rolling off, but not so high it blocks the view from the avatar's camera.

5.7.2 Safety Barriers on Wheely Island

Another thing to consider is the inclusion of "invisible" barriers or transparent prims that keep people from entering an area. In fact, you may want to consider some of these around the volcano to prevent a visitor from wandering a bit too close to the edge and falling in or on turnaround areas where you have not added in the wooden barrier from the walkway. It is not that the virtual lava will hurt them, but falling down into a pit can make it difficult for a novice visitor to escape, especially when there is lots of smoke particle activity blocking the view.

5.8 MAKING AN "ALL-ACCESS" ELEMENT: THE BASIC SIGN

For the last bit of this chapter, let's consider signage and its relationship to the concept of all-access building. You will probably want to make some signs for Wheely Island that say things such as, "Welcome to Wheely Island" or "This way to the volcano." Assemble a three-prim sign from 2 cylinders and one box, so that it resembles the one in Figure 5.15. From the content you downloaded for Chapter 5, find the 5 Wheely Island

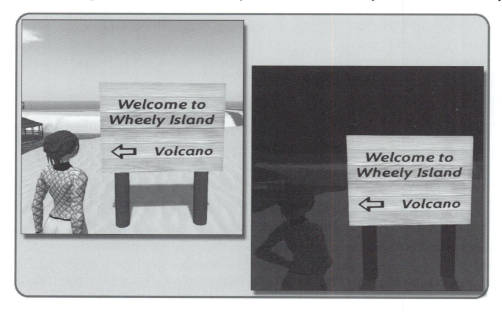

FIGURE 5.15   Screen shot in OpenSim showing a sign with "Design for All" considered in its construction. This is readable by most vision types. The front face is set to full bright so that the sign is visible even in a night setting.

sign files that start with "Wheely_island_sign...", and apply one of the lettered textures to the face of the box element, and the wood plank texture to the back face of the box. Keep the default plywood texture on the cylinders and darken the underlying material color to weather the look a bit.

5.8.1 CONSIDER THE VIEWER

With a few changes to the textures on a simple three-prim build, as shown in Figure 5.15, you can make an accessible sign fit into the overall look of the hiking trail. Your new sign should read "Welcome to Wheely Island" or "Caution! Volcano. May erupt without notice." Using the content for this chapter, you can take the .jpg files provided for the signage, and save them as templates for other signs on the island. Included are: Wheely_island_sign_back.jpg, Wheely_island_sign_front_arrow_l.jpg, Wheely_island_sign_front_arrow_r.jpg, and Wheely_island_sign_front_caution.jpg.

As you make signage, think about the "readability" of the sign and make sure you have created lettering that is large and clear enough to be read easily. Look at the visual contrast and ask yourself if you can see the edges of the letters clearly in all kinds of light. Go into the Sun Position menu and try looking at the sign during all times of day. If it is hard to read at night, try making the sign face prim into a light source or changing the glow brightness on that face of the prim in the Texture menu.

5.9 PLANTING TREES AND OTHER LANDSCAPING ON WHEELY ISLAND

By now, you are becoming pretty confident with terrain and how to manipulate it; so it is probably time to start landscaping your terrain. Again, there are several choices depending on what world you are working in. In Second Life, the default library folder in your inventory under Objects/Trees, plants and grasses, contains some plants and trees with which you can landscape Wheely Island. This gives the new builder a quick-and-easy way to add low-impact landscaping to the terrain, and it is always there if you need it. You can then "plant" them from your inventory into your landscape by dragging them onto the land. If you are working in OpenSim, there are other options.

5.10 MAKING YOUR OWN TREES FOR LANDSCAPING

If you are working in OpenSim, there are many options in the Metaverse for getting and making trees. The main things to consider are your time and money budget for landscaping the build, and your climate/aesthetic look for the landscape elements. Try to estimate how may trees, shrubs etc, you will need to have for a virtual environment in the planning stages, so you have an appropriate amount of time and money dedicated to obtaining pre-built or making your own landscape content. In consideration of the climate/aesthetic, if you have spent time making a South Pacific-based Wheely Island landscape terrain, placing a maple tree into the scene is just going to undercut your visual coherence and your visitors' "sense of place." Try to plan for landscaping elements that will support the story of the landscape from the "ground up" as it were. Before your head starts to hurt with the thought of making all that content, let's look at these options:

Option 1. Snappy tree (http://www.snappytree.com) is a wonderful free online tree generator that exports its custom tree meshes as a COLLADA file (.dae) that can be uploaded into your modeling program or the virtual world for texturing. You can also use this in conjunction with CanTree (http://arnaud.ile.nc/cantree/) another online tree generator, which makes excellent 2D images suitable for branch textures. In fact, you can combine the tree base and branch planes of Snappy Tree with the CanTree images and make an excellent composite tree.

Terrain and Landscape Shots of Wheely Island

Wheely Island looking Southwest

Wheely Island looking East

Looking West at Sunset

FIGURE 5.16 (See color insert) Screen grabs in OpenSim from Alchemy Sims Grid, showing the finished Wheely Island terrain at sunset.

Option 2. Make some trees and grasses from the landscaping content in the OpenSim texture library, utilizing the time-honored structure of three thin box prims intersecting at a common point with the textures on their flat sides to create an illusion of a 3D tree.

Option 3. Free landscaping content. Many of the grids now have freebie stores, and there are several sites offering free content (http://www.hypergridbusiness.com/opensim-content-providers/).

When you are landscaping a terrain, it is helpful to remember scale, pattern, and color. Keeping the scale relative to the avatar's size creates believable perspectives. If you want to make the avatar seem small, then scale up your trees, but by doing that, you risk creating a diminished sense of distance. Even in the most profuse vegetation on our planet, there is a structure and pattern to how it grows. Smaller plants tend to cluster under larger trees and carpet the ground. If you work with images from the kind of forest glade or tropical jungle you want to imitate, you will see the small details in placement and scale that can be put into your virtual environment to make it look better. Color in landscape is always necessary, and it should be used judiciously. Unless you are making a coral reef or the flower fields of Holland, color in the landscape is muted, and only pops when you are near the plant. Of course, if you are doing a fantasy alien landscape, you may want to break all these rules to increase the strangeness of it all. Whatever you do, have fun with it. Figure 5.16 has some shots of how Wheely Island was landscaped utilizing a combination of Second Life library trees and some handmade grasses from the textures in the OpenSim library.

5.11 CONCLUSIONS AND RECAP

Well, you have come a long, long way in this project. What started out as a flat piece of virtual terrain is now an all-access wheelchair trail walk with exciting features. Congratulate yourself and take the time to show this off to your friends. Maybe you should throw a beach party? If you are interested in learning more about how to design with access for all in mind, check out the Able Gamers Foundation (http://www.ablegamers.com/).

REFERENCES

1. Hodges, Jim, Cover Story: Human Terrain Experts May Help Defuse Future Conflicts, *Defense News*, March 22, 2012, http://www.defensenews.com/article/20120322/C4ISR02/303220015/Cover-Story-U-S-Army-8217-s-Human-Terrain-Experts-May-Help-Defuse-Future-Conflicts. Accessed August 26, 2012.
2. Sacred Mountains, Wikipedia article, http://en.wikipedia.org/wiki/Sacred_mountains. Accessed August 26, 2012.
3. Burns, Ken, *The National Parks—America's Best Idea*, http://www.pbs.org/nationalparks/. Accessed August 26, 2012.
4. Harrison, A., G. Derwent, A. Enticknap, F.D. Rose, and E.A. Attree, Application of Virtual Reality Technology to the Assessment and Training of Powered Wheelchair Users, http://www.icdvrat.reading.ac.uk/2000/papers/2000_03.pdf. Accessed September 2, 2012.
5. National Trails Training Partnership, Resources and library, http://www.americantrails.org/resources/accessible/index.html; Specific to Malibu Parks, California, http://atfiles.org/files/pdf/Trail-Accessibility-Design-Malibu.pdf. Accessed September 2, 2012.
6. Tips for Creating Heightfields and Details on Terrain RAW files, http://wiki.secondlife.com/wiki/Tips_for_Creating_Heightfields_and_Details_on_Terrain_RAW_Files. Accessed August 30, 2012.

6 3D Modeling, 2D Graphics, and Data Visualization

Living at risk is jumping off the cliff and building your wings on the way down.

—**Ray Bradbury**

6.1 SPATIAL PERCEPTION AND HOW THAT APPLIES TO THREE-DIMENSIONAL MODELING AND VIRTUAL ENVIRONMENTS

You can model, build, or create whatever you can visualize if that visualization is based on careful, complete observations of what you see in the real world. Look around your desktop. What are the qualities of the three closest objects? What basic form do they remind you of most—a sphere, a box, or a cylinder? Where do the highlights and shadows fall? What does the space around the object look like? Take a look at the basic prim (primitive forms) in Figure 6.1. Note how they bend space around themselves by showing changes in the lighting on their surfaces. Each one has its own signature pattern. The sphere has a small round highlight, while the shadows hug the opposite side like a dark band. The ring has a streak of highlight, and the shadow on the back side starts with a straight-edged gradient. The box has no such gradients; each face is shaded in a solid color, a highlight on the top face, deep shadow color on the back-facing side, and a somewhat middle tone on the other visible side. You can never see more than three sides of a solid box from a single point of view. Rez a few of these basic prims inworld and take a few minutes to observe the light and shadow qualities of the cylinder, the torus, and the tube as well.

The knowledge that these basic forms can be combined to create any complex 3D content is the fundamental key to modeling with the build tools provided within a virtual environment such as Second Life or OpenSim. As you build, these forms should be constantly compared to the imagery recorded on your visuospatial sketchpad, your observations of the general scale of the avatar within the virtual environment, and how that relates to what you are making. With this process you can maintain a context-related cohesive look to all that you build.

Remember, you are designing not only the 3D object but also the 3D space around it in a virtual environment. You control how 3D is seen and felt in your space, so why not make the most of it? One way this can be done is by using the land controls in your viewer. With them, you control access to various areas or parcels and thereby define a path for the visitor. You can also control access by putting the avatar inside solid structures such as tubes or hallways, or you can give them a tour vehicle with which to experience your virtual environment. With scripting, you can change the size, position, color, texture, and visibility of your 3D models and have them transform as they are approached and viewed, a great way to keep the experience fresh and interesting.

In the real physical world, we perceive 3D objects and their relationship to each other in space through a variety of "depth cues." Our brains observe the relative size of two objects, and we often assume the larger one is closer to our position in space. By using the time-honored technique of forced perspective by building objects some distance away in a smaller scale, or diminishing these objects in actual scale as they progressively become distant, we can fool the brain into thinking these objects are even farther away. This is done

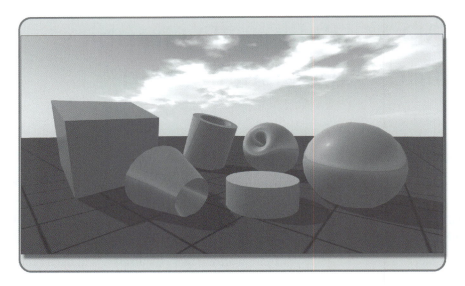

FIGURE 6.1 Screen grab from OpenSim showing the basic 3D solids called prims that are available in the Build Menu. They are shown with lighting to display their unique forms. Pictured here from the left side are: a cube, ring, tube, cylinder, torus, and sphere.

to great effect on Cinderella's castle in Disney World. The upper battlements are reduced in scale proportionally, making the structure look twice as tall as it actually is [1].

Changes in contrast, detail, and focus will also cause our brains to assume changes in 3D spatial relationships. An object that has more contrast with a greater range of light and shadow on its surface will look closer to the observer, whereas an object that is grayed out and muted in shadow and highlights will look more distant. You can see examples of this on a foggy night in a city environment as the haze in the air makes buildings down the block look more distant. This atmospheric perspective can be utilized in virtual worlds by changing the WindLight Settings (Second Life) or Light Share (OpenSim) for your environment (see Chapter 8 for more details on lighting). Diminishing the amount of surface detail in distant objects and softening their edges with semitransparent textures will also increase the feeling of distance. Conversely, if you add more detail to your 3D model and enhance the edges of your object's textures, it will seem nearer to the observer. In Figure 6.2, examples of these kinds of perspective are displayed: contrast, detail, and atmospheric. As you can see, they are very effective ways to alter how 3D form is perceived. They are used all around you in the real world—in theme parks, on the stage, or in store displays—so why not put them to use in a virtual one?

6.2 PICKING A 3D MODELING PROGRAM AND A METHODOLOGY FOR BUILDING

You have numerous choices as there are many 3D modeling packages. 3DS Max, Maya, Blender, Modo, Cinema 4D, Cheetah3D, SketchUp—the list goes on and on, lengthening with each year as new 3D modeling programs and interfaces are developed. As a designer, you are used to making choices, so look for the 3D modeler that will work best for you in these three ways: (1) operating system, (2) price, and (3) capacity (or software features). Grade them on a scale of 1 to 10 and try the demo versions of the top three on the list.

Granted, learning your first 3D program and developing your 3D mind-set may seem a bit overwhelming at first, but as you progress, you will find that many of these programs utilize similar tool sets. You may have a limited budget for software, but that should not stop you. In almost all categories, there is a free or low-cost

FIGURE 6.2 Screen grabs from OpenSim displaying a virtual representation of the alternate types of perspective that can be used to enhance the feeling of depth in a virtual scene. Shown are (1) contrast perspective (top), (2) detail perspective (middle), and (3) atmospheric perspective (bottom).

option for the software you need. On Wikipedia there is a comprehensive comparison chart of this software (http://en.wikipedia.org/wiki/Comparison_of_3D_computer_graphics_software).

It is imperative that you decide early how your 3D modeler will be used to support your design message at every step of your project. It may be that you utilize one kind of modeler to create preliminary presentation models (a light, fast modeler such as SketchUp) and another type (a solid modeler with more robust capacity, such as 3DS Max) to create the fully textured, finished models for your virtual environments.

Deciding what you want to do and where you want to take 3D modeling is often the most difficult aspect of a project. As you remember from the workflow charts in Chapter 3, there is a huge benefit to be gained by deciding this process ahead of time.

Here are some questions you should ask:

1. Regarding the final output: What is your desired finished quality for your project presentations? Would a rough, nontextured white or gray "massing" model that shows the general overview of the design suffice for a planning meeting, or do you need to present a full-blown colored model with multiple views to obtain the funding for the project?
2. Regarding the team and workflow structure: Are you working on the project alone, or do you have a team that can divide the work into specialized areas of expertise? The simplest structure for a virtual world build team would be three or four people, one designer/overall coordinator/pitchperson, one master builder, one coder/scripter, and possibly one web specialist. The web specialist may not be needed until you are further in the project; however, if you are planning to interact with 2D web pages and databases, it is advisable to bring the web specialist into the group as soon as possible.

6.2.1 Three Possible Scenarios for 3D Modeling Methods

6.2.1.1 Scenario 1: The "Basic Geometry/Basic Textures" Approach

The "basic geometry/basic textures" approach to the design and building of your virtual environment takes advantage of the native tools and assets that are provided in Second Life and OpenSim, and to some extent Unity. The Build editor in the Firestorm Viewer has various "built-in" prims or basic geometry available for your use. Because these are already defined in the database of the virtual world, they are readily accessible, quick to rez, and have no upload charges. When you think about it, most of the things built in our real environments can be made from simple geometric forms. Our buildings have walls made from boxes or cylinders; our vehicles are various sorts of spheres and cones. Almost anything man-made in real life lends itself to fabrication with prims in a virtual environment. Figure 6.3 shows a "Guitarlale" built by Vicki Brandenburg entirely from the standard prims.

In Scenario 1, the textures are derived from the basic "in-house" textures that come with the standard inventory of the avatar's account. At the bottom of the inventory list in the Library/Textures file folder of Second Life and the OpenSim Library/Texture Library are loads of prepared textures for use in your builds. The best feature about them is that they load instantly, so no visitor will ever see blank gray objects when initially visiting your virtual world. Bear in mind that, since these textures are within the common database of each virtual world, they cannot be exported along with the object since you were not their creator.

If you are thinking of utilizing prims in a Unity build, the Unity Asset store has some plug-in tools for that. In 2012, Pro-Builder (http://www.sixbysevenstudio.com/wp-flexible/project/probuilder-for-unity-3d/) was introduced, which allows building/editing of mesh right in the Unity environment [2].

6.2.1.2 Scenario 2: The "50/50" Approach

By utilizing the inworld prims for 50% of your build and imported meshes for the other 50%, you are setting up for a build that has a more realistic and organic look. This approach will provide more flexibility

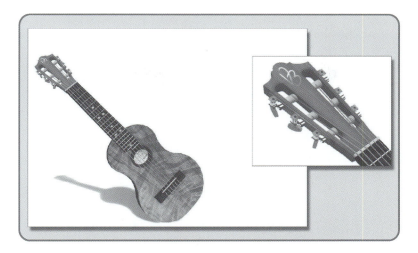

FIGURE 6.3 A virtual "guitarlale" built entirely from inworld prims. Created by Vicki Brandenburg in Second Life circa 2009. Inset shows the level of detail in the head and tuning pegs that she achieved.

with import/export and supports the "Build It Once" approach for your project. It is also conceivable that the imported mesh objects will have less "land impact" on the virtual region and will render more quickly if they were built for a real-time rendering environment and have made efficient use of their faces and vertices. The downside of Scenario 2 is that it may take longer to create as you will be making 50% of the textures and geometry from scratch, and it will require the real-world expense in Linden dollar "upload fees" if you are bringing the meshes into Second Life.

6.2.1.3 Scenario 3: The "90/10" Approach

The "90/10" approach is the most complex and most expensive scenario of the three. In this scenario, 90% of the 3D geometry is created from external meshes, and all related textures include lighting and baking of shadows for each specific object. This is a professional level and requires a serious commitment to learning the 3D modeling software you have chosen. Again, this could allow for efficient object construction if built properly, which would lessen land impact and increase real-time rendering speeds. This approach also fully supports the "Build It Once" method because the models are usable in many programs, platforms, worlds, or games. If you want to proceed this way, you would be well advised to take a class in 3D modeling or at least do many tutorials for the software of your choice if you have not been trained on 3D modeling software previously. It will lower your frustration level considerably.

Whatever scenario you choose, make sure that the rest of the team is on board with the decision, and that you clearly delineate where each major element in your design will originate. You may find it helpful to do a rough model of the build in SketchUp first just to get a sense of the scale of the effort that will be required.

6.3 BUILDING WITH THE INWORLD PRIMS (PRIMITIVE OBJECTS)

If you choose Scenario 1 for a project, the seven-member family of prims—the box, cylinder, sphere, prism, torus, ring and tube—is all you will use to build your virtual world. Lots of possibilities open up once you understand how they can be carved, cut, and twisted into various forms. In the Firestorm Viewer, there is a whole suite of Edit modifiers available for each prim. Let's go through each one and see what kinds of diverse forms can be made. Feel free to open up your viewer, find a virtual sandbox somewhere, and build these as they are shown below.

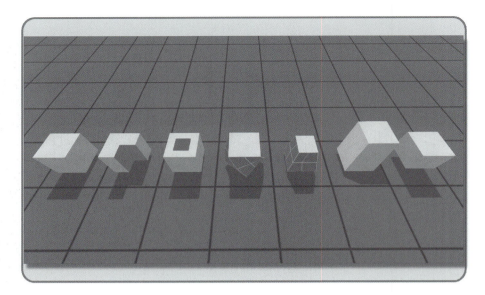

FIGURE 6.4 OpenSim screen shot of the range of virtual forms that can be made with a box and its modifiers: shown from the left going right they are: none, path cut, hollow, twist, taper, shear and slice. On the fifth sample from the left, the grid texture demonstrates how a Taper modifier will affect the look of a texture. Distortion of a mapped texture on the tapered box is removed with a Planar mapping setting in the Build/Texture menu.

6.3.1 THE BOX

Box, our basic building block, has six faces when it originates. However, this box has numerous polygons per faces to accommodate form-changing edits like hollow, taper, twist, and path cut. From this simple form, an abundance of architecture can be generated—walls, steps, doors, windows, the list is long. Take a look at Figure 6.4 and try to make each of these forms using the path cut, hollow, twist, taper, shear, and slice modifiers in the Build/Create menu. They have all been applied to the same basic box, and as you can see, there are many variations. *Note:* if you are curious about how many triangular polygons are being rendered on a selected object, go to the Develop/Show Info/ menu, and select Show Render info. At the bottom of the onscreen list that appears, the number of Ktris (triangles) will be displayed for the prim you have selected. You will notice how the number decreases as your avatar walks away, and another Level of Detail takes over.

6.3.2 THE CYLINDER

Cylinders are another useful form for architecture (Figure 6.5). With three faces (top and bottom caps and one side surface) in its beginning form, this prim can take the form of columns, machine parts, and other elements of the mechanical world. Try creating these forms with the cylinder modifiers that are similar to the box modifiers and available in the Build/Create menu when you create a cylinder form.

6.3.3 THE PRISM

Prisms are three-faced wedges that can come in handy for many things, like ramps, weapons, and even cheese. Try to make these forms with the available modifiers shown in Figure 6.6 with the prism modifiers in the Build/Create menu.

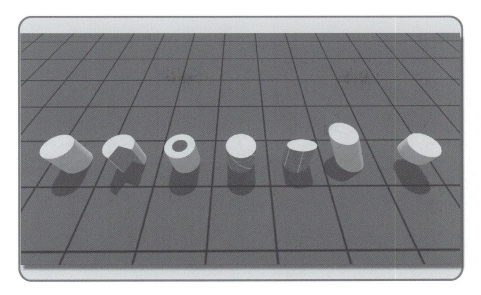

FIGURE 6.5 OpenSim screen shot of the range of virtual forms that can be made with a cylinder and its modifiers: shown from the left going right they are: none, path cut, hollow, twist, taper, shear and slice. Note how in the twist modifier, fourth from the left, the texture shows more of the effect of the modifier than the form.

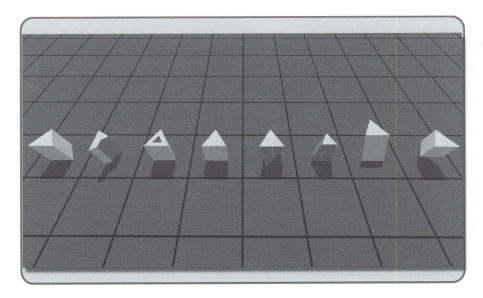

FIGURE 6.6 OpenSim screen shot of the range of virtual forms that can be made with a prism and its modifiers: shown from the left going right they are: none, path cut, hollow, skew, twist, taper, shear and slice.

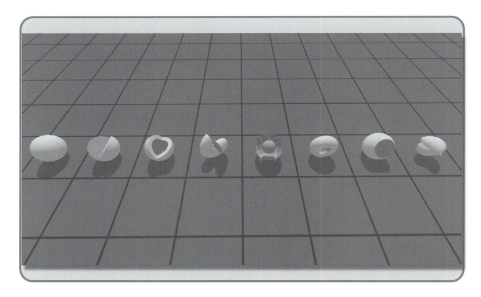

FIGURE 6.7 OpenSim screen shot of the range of virtual forms that can be made with a sphere and its modifiers: shown from the left going right they are: none, path cut, path cut and hollow, skew, hollow and twist, taper and hollow, dimple begin and end, taper profile.

6.3.4 THE SPHERE

Spheres are geometrical perfection, one face; all vertices are equidistant from the center. You will note that once you make a sphere that slice is no longer an option, and a new modifier has appeared called dimple. Try twisting the sphere with the slice modifier in the Build/Create menu for some interesting forms (Figure 6.7).

6.3.5 THE TORUS

The torus is an interesting form. Created from an oval or circle that has been stood on edge and extruded on a circular path, it looks like a doughnut and can be modified into making car axles, bar stools, and elf house roofs. This prim introduces another modifier, hole size, and now the modifiers profile cut, taper profile, and revolutions will have some interesting effects. Look at the samples in Figure 6.8, and try out these modifiers in the Build/Create menu.

6.3.6 THE TUBE

Tubes may fool you into thinking that they are cylinders with a hollow center, but in virtual worlds, they are a different type of form. You will find that the top and bottom faces of the tube will display a texture map differently from a hollowed cylinder, and that is useful when you want a radiating texture on a curved walkway. When a tube is created, the hole size setting is at 0.5; you will need to change that to actually see that it is a tube. Try making the tube-based forms in Figure 6.9 with the modifiers in the Build/Create menu.

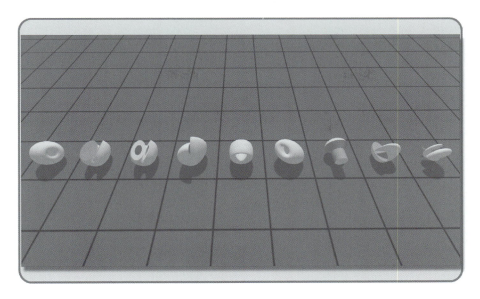

FIGURE 6.8   OpenSim screen shot of the range of virtual forms that can be made with a torus and its modifiers: shown from the left going right they are: none, path cut, path cut and hollow, twist, hole size, top shear, profile cut, taper profile, and skew with revolutions.

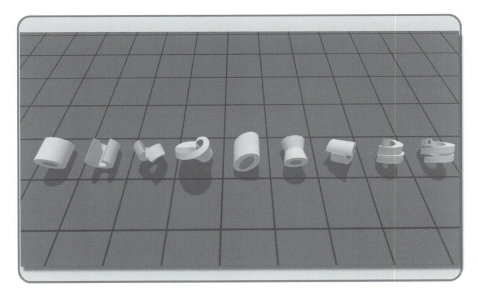

FIGURE 6.9   OpenSim screen shot of the range of virtual forms that can be made with a tube and its modifiers: shown from the left going right they are: hole size, path cut, skew, twist, top shear, profile cut, taper profile, skew and revolutions, and revolutions with a hollow modifier.

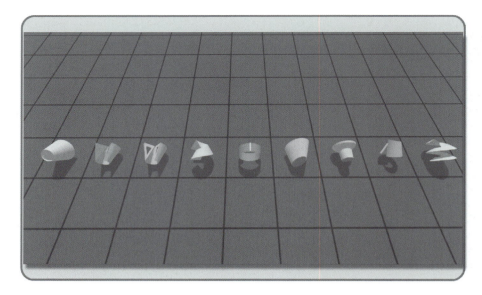

FIGURE 6.10 OpenSim screen shot of the range of virtual forms that can be made with a ring and its modifiers: shown from the left going right they are: none, path cut, path cut and hollow, skew, hole size, top shear, profile cut, taper profile, and revolutions.

6.3.7 THE RING

Rings are what you get when you stand up a triangle and extrude it around a perpendicular circular path. They are useful for mechanical parts, clothing like collars and cuffs, and all sorts of surface details. Try making the modified ring forms in Figure 6.10.

All of the other forms that are offered in the creation menu (the pyramid, hemisphere, hemicylinder, and tetrahedron) can be made from the basic seven forms. To derive the greatest benefit from this exercise, it is recommended that you spend some time creating these families of forms, and saving samples into a "building component" folder for future reference and usage.

6.4 MESHES AND HOW THESE CAN BE IMPORTED

Since 2011, the 3D objects made with externally generated meshes have been available for a builder's use in Second Life and OpenSim. In fact, meshes have always been used in builds; the standard prim objects native to the virtual worlds are simply custom meshes designed for use with the modification tools included in the viewer. For the purposes of this book, the instruction in various methodologies for building meshes in Blender, 3DS Max, or any other 3D modeling package are left to the wide range of tutorials available online or through your local educational institutions. It is highly recommended that you take an online or in-school course in your chosen program so that you learn to model quickly and efficiently. One of your most valuable assets is interaction and social networking with your peers. Join the inworld groups, visit the software bug tracking and program development pages (JIRA) to comment on the new programs you use, and share what you have learned freely with your peers. When you start to make your own meshes in a modeling program like 3DS Max or Blender and want to import them into Second Life, you should be aware of what the options and costs are. Fortunately, the Firestorm Viewer has an easy-to-use importation menu that allows you to see what the import will cost in Linden dollars for Second Life. This is a no-cost procedure in OpenSim.

6.4.1 The Basics of Importing a Mesh Model

Let's go through the basics of importation in the Firestorm menu. You can activate it by selecting Avatar/Upload/Mesh Model from the top bar of the viewer menu. This will bring up the first page of a three-page menu but do not be put off by the complexity. You really need to know only a few settings to do a basic import. There are images of this menu in Figures 13.15, 13.16 and 13.17.

Once the menu is up, use the Browse button, open the COLLADA (.dae) file you want to import from your computer in the top box, next to High and below Source.

Name your model in the top left box and choose a Type that represents its use, such as architecture, vehicle, and so on. Make sure that the Textures box below the Preview window is checked if you have applied textures on the model. Now, let's go on to the Tabs and their various settings. There is a complete list for the settings on these tabs in Chapter 2, Section 2.3, as well as known problems with uploading to OpenSim and Second Life.

On the first tab of the menu, you are given options for importing your model at various levels of detail (LOD). As you develop building/import skills, this menu will give you the opportunity to "tweak" the LOD yourself and upload lower-detail models when you need to without sacrificing visual quality. Building with that factor in mind will save you time during the importation process.

Under the Physics tab, you are setting the physics collision "shape" for your object, and since this also has an impact on server performance, the lowest setting possible is desirable. However, if you need to walk on or inside the object, you may need a higher physics setting, or make a custom one for the model.

In the third tab, you will set up the Upload options for your model. This is where you can add the textures to the model for simultaneous importation. Check the box (under the Scaling section) that says "Include Textures."

Once you have gone through the three tabs, checking the guidelines from Section 2.3, and set up your model for importation, click calculate weights and fee and review the fees for importation, the resource weights, and land impact. If this is all acceptable, click Upload.

Shortly afterward, you will see the object appear in your inventory. Drag it out of your inventory to rez it on the ground and check your results. For more detail and information on uploading meshes, please refer to the wiki for Firestorm (http://wiki.phoenixviewer.com/fs_mesh_upload).

Sometimes, with a very complex object, such as the motorcycle from Layton Destiny (Figure 6.11), it will have to be designed and imported in sections. In Figure 6.11, there is a snapshot of this beautiful work. Layton has also provided special physics files for the content of this book. By utilizing these files define the LOD under the Physics/LOD section of the importer, the uploads can be faster and with a lighter land (server) impact.

6.5 SCULPT MAPS (SCULPTIES) AND HOW THEY LED TO MESH

For those of you who are not familiar with them, a sculpted prim (sculpty) is created when a sculpt map is applied to the surface of a special prim. Essentially, the rainbow-hued sculpt maps work like a 3D displacement map on the vertices of the prim. Each pixel on the sculpt map image has a specific 3 number color value relating to the amount of red, green and blue it contains. That numerical value is translated into x,y, and z coordinates which are assigned to displace the vertices on the prim, for example, changing a sphere into an apple-shaped form. For a time, in the years between 2007 and 2011, these sculpt maps were the best way

FIGURE 6.11 Motorcycle model built by Tim Widger (Layton Destiny in OpenSim and Second Life). This complex model was created in Blender as a series of mesh parts, imported into OpenSim and reassembled.

to make organic forms such as plants and animals in Second Life, then mesh imports were allowed, and it all changed. Sculpted prims are not dead, however, there are several programs still available for use that can make sculpt maps directly, like Sculpty Paint [3] and the Kanae Project suite of tools [4].

In the Build menu, a rezzed prim can be converted into a sculpted one by using the drop-down menu on the Object tab and selecting Sculpted.

Once the basic sculpty has formed (it looks like a wooden apple), you can drag your new sculpt map into the loading box, and your prim will take on the sculpty form from the sculpt map you made. Do some experimenting with the sculpt map stitching to see how various ways of applying the sculpt map to the prim affect the way its form looks and where the seams appear. Figure 6.12 shows the sculpty editor and the resulting form used in a dragonfly vehicle, made by Annabelle Fanshaw.

As a designer, you have to make constant adjustments in your methodologies to suit the needs of your various projects. Sculpties are still used to great extent in virtual worlds, and for making large one-prim structures like a cloud or sequoia tree trunk, they still probably have an edge in terms of cost and ease of use. Utilizing the inworld premade sculpts available through the Second Life Marketplace or applications like Sculpty Paint are good ways to start building new things, especially if you are still learning how to use a 3D modeling program.

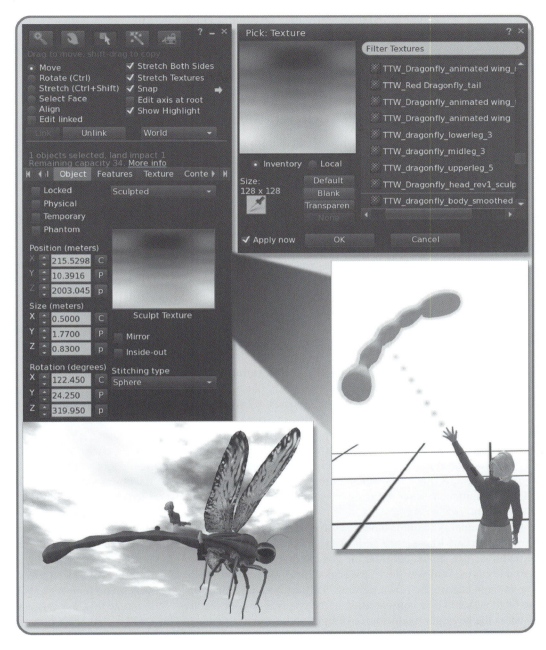

FIGURE 6.12 Screen grabs from Second Life showing process of making parts for a dragonfly vehicle. Top left and right shows the application of a multicolored sculpty map to the object in the Sculpt Texture box. Lower right shows the resulting organically shaped tail form of the dragonfly, and lower left shows the whole vehicle when assembled. Wing outline shapes were traced from a photograph on Wikimedia Commons, http://commons.wikimedia.org/wiki/File:Cloudwing_bangalore.jpg, Photography by L. Shyamal, Creative Commons license.

The downsides of this type of building—including lack of fine control over the vertex positions displaced by the sculpt map, high rendering cost due to collisions on its default spherical physics hull, and difficulty with editing the forms inworld—have eventually paved the way for the widespread adoption of mesh use in virtual worlds. Eventually, sculpted prims will probably become a footnote in the history of virtual world building as mesh content replaces it.

6.6 CONCEPTS IN TEXTURE CREATION, 2D GRAPHICS

Texture creation is the other primary aspect to the design of beautiful forms. Nothing enhances a form or embellishes it like a well colored, nicely rendered texture on the faces.

6.6.1 QUALITIES OF GREAT TEXTURES

What makes a great texture? Strive for five qualities: (1) efficient use of resolution or size of the graphic file; (2) color harmony; (3) a sense of lighting and shadow; (4) "tile-ability"; and (5) specificity.

Efficiency: The size of your texture makes a difference in the efficiency with which your virtual world can be produced on a visitor's screen. Unless you need to make a sign with lots of text and graphics on it, the overall sizes of your textures should not exceed 512 by 512 pixels, and if you can make it with 256 by 256 pixels, then go for it. You should note that textures always have to be made in the "power of 2" formats (1024, 512, 256, 128, 64, and so on), thereby providing nice, easily stackable texture blocks for the computer's memory. Getting into the habit of using the smallest possible textures can save you loads of grief by avoiding slow rezzing times and complaints from your visitors, who have to look at a gray model while the textures load for them.

Color Harmony: To create color harmony in your textures, think about the environment in which they will be. Sunset in Paris covers the buildings with a rosy blush, tropical reefs have a lovely aquamarine glow, and wintertime in Helsinki is full of firelight and snow. If you are making a full-blown model with baked textures in Blender or 3DS Max, then the lighting in your scene could provide the color harmony as well as shadows for your textures that will be imported with the mesh. If you are just making a single texture to apply to an object inworld, then it would be wise to select a dominant color in the environment and put a little of that into your graphic. Of course, all is not lost if you find that your graphic looks out of place in the virtual environment. A quick adjustment of the underlying material color on the object and you can blend it all in. This phenomenon, observed in an environment that is unified in overall color, is called the Harmony of Dominant Tint.

Lighting: All quality textures have a sense of lighting and shadow. To get the "visual texture" of a rough or convoluted surface like a stone wall or even a brick face, built-in shadows and highlights are necessary in your textures. You should consider the general direction of the overall lighting in the environment as you create your textures. Will you "lock" the region into a WindLight setting and offer that file to your visitors, or will you let them choose their own lighting? Perhaps you have a custom day cycle set up for your region. All of these factors should be a consideration in the creation of your textures. To organize this, ask this question first: What is the key light (main source of light) in my environment, and how will it change? You may want to make only subtle shadows on your built elements and let the visitors activate their own real-time shadows for the full effect. Whatever you do, make sure that you test it under all sorts of lighting conditions and take pictures so you have a record of how it looks as you change things.

The 3D modelers like Blender and 3DS Max allow you to apply textures to your models, light the scene, and then "bake" the shadows onto the surface as you render the sides of the model into a flat texture. These textures can actually be unwrapped from the model and manipulated as 2D files in a graphics program like Photoshop or GIMP (GNU Image Manipulation Program). For instance, you could add sparkling icicles around the windows of your bakery model texture for the winter season look and not have to rebuild any models.

If you are feeling adventurous and want to try some additional material features, look under the Texture tab in the Build Editor for the options in Shininess (specular) and Bumpiness (normal). Here is a place to add in additional textures in the form of specular maps and normal maps which you build with your 3D modeler to enhance the surface appearance of textures inworld. There is more information about these here: http://community.secondlife.com/t5/English-Knowledge-Base/Materials-Normal-and-Specular-Mapping/ta-p/2034625/.

"Tile-ability:" The capacity for a texture to be repeated seamlessly across a surface, is an essential quality in good textures. To develop a texture that looks great across a terrain and does not have a "quilted" feeling is a fine art. About 80% of the textures you will use have to be tiled, so it pays to learn a few ways to make them look good. Depending on the graphics program you use, there are probably some tutorials available to show you how to match the edges with the native tools like Blur or Copy Stamp in Photoshop. There are also various texture plug-ins for Photoshop, like Filter Forge, which are useful when you need to make tile-able textures and are well worth the investment. When you are making textures to be tiled, make sure to allow extra time in your building phase for the testing of the tile-able texture on a variety of forms inworld. Sometimes, a texture that looked good on your desktop will look badly matched on the terrain or large wall structures you are building, and you will need blur/blend the image and modify it further. You may find that by working along the diagonal axes of the image you can create better tiling adjustments as it will draw the eye away from the edges.

Specificity: This defines a great texture; few of the surfaces in our real world look identical. This starts with research. As a designer, you should get a good small pocket camera and have it with you during projects. All around us every day are surfaces with incredible details and visual texture. Get into the habit of looking at the environment around you and snapping a picture of any wall, floor, or surface that interests you. A good collection of images like that, which are copyright free for you, is invaluable. As you develop as a designer, you begin to get picky, and that is a good thing. For instance, you may learn through your research and observation that brick in Amsterdam looks different from brick in New York. The clays that were fired to make these bricks were different, and they are exposed to different climates. Eventually, you will immediately see these differences in various textures and know that even the most subtle changes will evoke a different mood in the visitor.

There are many good 2D programs that can help you make stunning textures. Adobe Photoshop and Illustrator are the workhorses of the graphics industry, but if your purse is smaller, GIMP (GNU Image Manipulation Program) [5] is an excellent freeware program for graphic production.

6.7   UTILIZING THE TEXTURE MENU IN THE BUILD EDITOR

Let us assume you have now created a fantastic texture and would like to show it off on the surface of your prim built object. There are lots of ways you can make your textures stand out by utilizing the built-in texture tools. Before you move to the Texture tab in the Build menu, take a few minutes to look at some of the general options in the top section. Two of them, Select Face and Stretch Textures, are crucial to mastering texture application on virtual objects. Farther down in Section 6.7, under mapping, you will see the impact of Stretch Textures, but for now let us focus on Select Face. A prim can have seven faces counting those that appear when you use the Hollow and Path Cut options on a cube. Sometimes, you may want to apply a special texture to just one of those faces. If you are zoomed in on the object and have a clear shot at it, you can simply drag the texture out of your inventory and onto that face. Otherwise, you can turn on the Select Face button in the top section of the Build Editor and select the face with your mouse cursor. This will highlight the edges of the face and give you a crosshair target in the middle of it that is useful for centering the texture you are applying.

Now, select your whole object and bring up the Texture tab in the Build editor, but rather than using the menu to fiddle with Transparency, Glow, or any of those goodies just yet, let's create a lighting effect that does not stress the server too much or require that we make any special textures.

Take a few minutes to decide how the lighting will be set up in your scene. In Figure 6.13, there is a stone arch in need of some texturing. Let's suppose that for the most part the sun or the moon will light this scene. On the underside of the arch, rather than take the default white base color in the Texture (diffuse section of the Texture tab), why not take that down to a 60% or 50% gray color? In the example shown in Figure 6.13, bringing down the base material color to a gray on the undersides and off sides of the arch creates the sense of overall lighting without adding immovable baked shadow textures to the structure. If you do this consistently all over your build, you can create a sense of light and shadow without making any special shadow-based textures.

Now that you have tried a little base material shifting to add some lighting, let us proceed with a quick tour around the rest of the Texture tab menu (Figure 6.14).

The Transparency spinner obviously allows you to make the prim or object translucent or even invisible by changing the alpha value on your texture. Be aware that by using this, the server will change a 24-bit texture into a 32-bit one to accommodate an alpha effect, and that change could cause alpha sorting glitches or flickering in your scene where two layers of transparent objects overlap. There is little you can do about this except to plan carefully when you build to avoid overlaps of alpha-based textures and to use them as judiciously as possible. Also, be aware that when you turn on Transparency, bump mapping and shininess are deactivated on the object.

Glow and Brightness were added to the texture options in Second Life in 2009. This vertex shader will cause a minor performance hit, but most graphics cards these days would barely notice. When activated, the surface is rendered to show a radiating light from the edges and faces. It is effective for fire and radioactive fuel effects, although the glow itself will not cast light on the scene or create any shadows. The Shininess and Bumpiness modifiers contain the legacy settings, and are still one of the simplest ways to put some life into your textures. For even finer, more realistic effects, it is worth your time to experiment with specular and normal maps to take advantage of the newer options in these modifiers.

Mapping comes in two basic categories: default and planar. Each type of prim has its own default mapping format, called UV mapping, which determines how a texture is wrapped around or mapped onto the form. The U represents the horizontal direction of the texture image, and the V represents the vertical direction of a texture image. Look at Figure 6.15 to see how each of the primitives will take on a texture map and how they orient the UV coordinates.

The planar mapping does what its name says; it will make your texture align itself to the plane of a box or prism. This can be used to help correct the distortion you will see on the sides of a tapered box or prism as shown in Figure 6.4, and the arch base prims of Figure 6.13. Please note that the planar mapping of a texture will affect the tiling as it changes from repeats per face to repeats per meter. This can easily be set back to the appropriate size with the spinners on the lower part of the menu if you so desire.

Tiling the texture you have made on the surface of a prim or object is a bit of a fine art in itself (Figure 6.16). When you build something, the first place to check is at the top of the Build menu and make sure that the stretch texture box is checked on. When you rez a prim, its default texture mapping setting is one repeat both horizontally (U) and vertically (V), and the default size of the object (usually a box) should be 0.5 meters to the side. At this point, you can decide to utilize a little math and take advantage of the built-in stretch textures option. Suppose you wanted to make a tile floor that was 10 meters square. You could make a huge

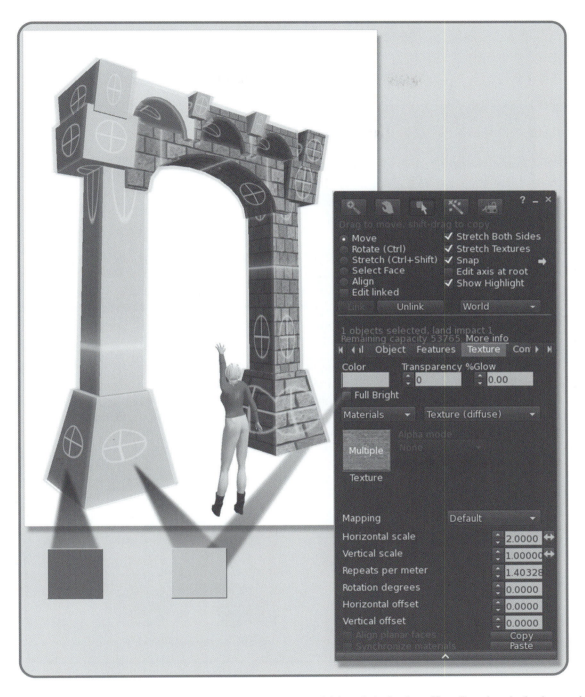

FIGURE 6.13 Screen shot from Second Life, showing a material-based shadowing effect. By using the background color of the texture material judiciously, you can obtain a "shadow" effect as demonstrated on this stone arch.

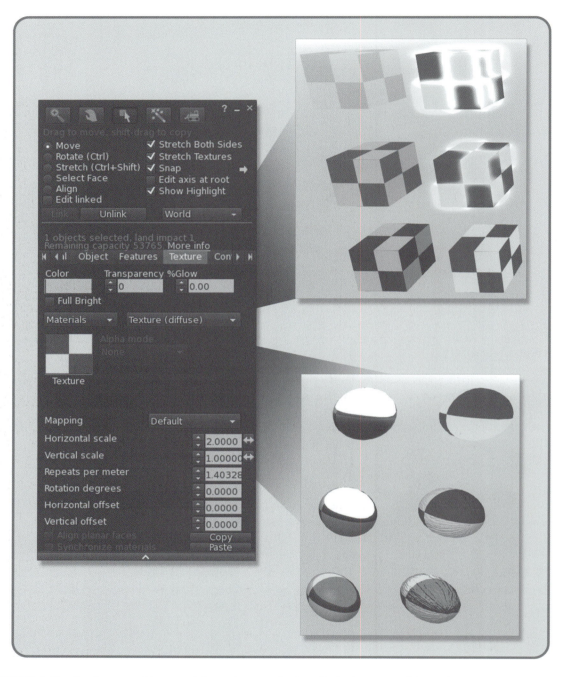

FIGURE 6.14 On the top and bottom right are images of prims displaying some of the various settings available in the texture tab of the Build menu (left side). Options for brightness and glow are shown on the cubes, and options for shininess and bump textures are shown on the spheres.

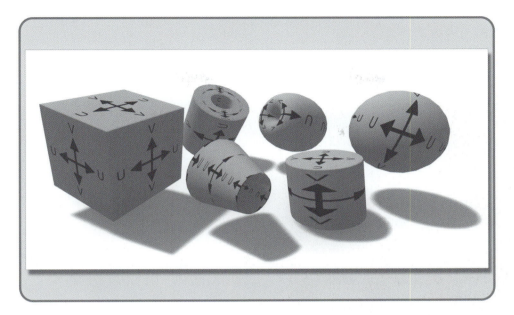

FIGURE 6.15 Screen shot in OpenSim showing the default UV mapping for each of the basic prims. The UV coordinates are used to place the location of textures on a 3D object. V represents the vertical direction, and U represents the horizontal direction.

texture—1024 × 1024 pixels—and repeat it once on the top surface of that floor, but this approach will greatly increase the load on the server and may cause your neighbors to experience lag as well.

To solve this problem in the most efficient way possible, you should ask yourself: What is the smallest texture size that can be tiled or repeated across the surface to create the look I want? You may find that you could use a texture that is 256 pixels or possibly even 128 pixels square and obtain the same effect with a much shorter loading time for your viewer. Remember that these textures are packed into the graphics memory like tiles themselves, squashed into a square format with their resolution defined by the power of 2. In fact, if you upload a texture that is 300 × 400 pixels, the virtual world uploader will make a 512-pixel square image out of it. This will look fine proportionally once you stretch it across a 3 by 4 meter prim, but you will lose some resolution on the upload.

Rotation of a texture is pretty straightforward. The texture on each face can be selected and rotated around the center axis. This can become interesting when combined with the Align Planar Faces, which allows you to align a texture across the faces of several prims. There is a fine example of this in Figure 6.3. There is even more information about how to utilize this feature in Torley Linden's video tutorial collection (http://community. secondlife.com/t5/Tips-and-Tricks/VIDEO-Align-planar-faces-for-easier-texture-mapping-in-Viewer-2/ ba-p/669471).

Repeats per Face and Repeats/Meter can be utilized in your building when you need to work with realistic sizes on the surfaces of your architecture. Obviously, real ceramic floor tiles around the world vary in size. If you know the real size of the floor you intend to make and the real size of the tiles, you can create a tile-able texture in your graphics program (256 pixels square should be sufficient) that will tile properly. If the virtual floor surface is the same size as the real one, then you can use the Repeats/Meter to create a realistically scaled version of your real-life floor.

FIGURE 6.16   Screen grab from OpenSim, showing various ways to tile a single texture on a 10 m square prim. From the top down on the right, these modifiers are shown: default, planar, offset on the U and V, 10 repeats/meter, and rotation of texture 45 degrees. On the left is the texture tab of the Build menu, tiling options for textures are in the lower section.

Offset is a valuable tool as well, especially with textures that have an alpha channel and may have had the image placed just a little too close to the edges. Primarily, the Texture Offset will slide your texture along the horizontal (*U*) or vertical (*V*) axis. If you turn on Select Face while doing the offset, you will see the center of the texture moving back and forth when you run the spinners. It is always wise to make sure that any texture with a transparent background, like a tree or bush, does not go all the way to the edge of the image. It is best to leave a 4- to 6-pixel gap at the edge so you are not fiddling too much with Offset modification of the texture on your form.

6.8   SPECIALIZED TEXTURES: ANIMATED, TRANSPARENCY, AND BAKED LIGHTING WITH AMBIENT OCCLUSION

In the next 3 sections you will explore some of the more exotic forms of texture creation: animated textures, textures with transparency, and textures that have the lighting in the scene added on their surfaces (baking) with ambient occlusion.

6.8.1   TEXTURES WITH ANIMATION

At times, you may want to create objects that have moving surfaces, things like water, spinning targets, flapping wings, or whatever captures your imagination. There are several ways to produce these effects by the use of simple scripts and special textures. The most basic way to animate a texture is to use a script to move it around on the face of a prim. If you animate the offset, then the texture appears to slide across the surface, just as water flows down a channel. Animate the rotation and you can have a spinning wheel image. If the scale is animated, you can make a surface appear to "breathe" or inflate.

If you want a cycling animated effect, perhaps a crackling fire, then a series of flame images when played in sequence can create a realistic effect. The initial texture is laid out in a specific grid so that the animate texture script can find that section of the texture and project each image in sequence. Figure 6.17 illustrates a texture that creates flapping dragonfly wings. Each "frame" has the wings in a slightly different position, and that creates the illusion of rapidly beating wings as the images are flashed on the surface of the prim as rapidly as possible.

As you start to dive into animated texture creation and want to get scripts that create animated textures, pay a visit to Robin Sojourner's Texture Learning Exhibits on Living Tree Island in Second Life.

6.8.2   TEXTURES WITH TRANSPARENCY: TWO METHODS FOR CREATING THEM

At some point in your virtual building career, you will need to make a texture that has transparency on it. You may need to make a frosty window for your gingerbread house or a leafy branch for the new tree you are building. There are several methods for creating these types of textures, and two of the most useful ways are by using a 24-bit PNG file (easy; good for beginners) or making a TGA 32-bit file (less easy; good for advanced graphics users). Torley Linden has a useful tutorial about the PNG method (http://youtu.be/ekLIgpRHSq4) [6].

In textures that have varying levels of transparency, like a frosted window or a dragonfly wing, you may need to utilize the alpha channel of a 32-bit Targa file. For more information on creating these kinds of transparencies, check out Robin Woods's excellent tutorial (http://www.robinwood.com/Catalog/Technical/SL-Tuts/SLPages/WhiteHalo.html).

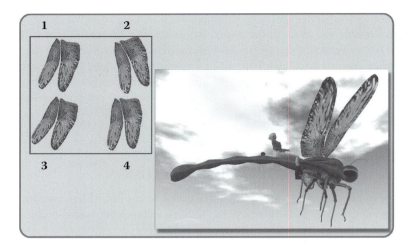

FIGURE 6.17 Screen grab from Second Life showing the texture needed for animated wings (top left) and its application to a dragonfly vehicle. When the animation script is added, each wing picture (1–4) is displayed the face of the prim sequentially for a fraction of a second, giving the overall effect of a fluttering movement.

6.8.3 TEXTURES WITH BAKED LIGHTING AND AMBIENT OCCLUSION

When you get your final mesh object build textured and lit in your 3D modeler, you will probably have the option to add in Ambient Occlusion to the render process. Essentially, Ambient Occlusion is a rendering process that calculates how the surrounding hemisphere of ambient light in the scene will be obstructed or occluded by the existing objects or buildings. Once this is initiated, it creates a "dirt map" or soft-shadow map on the entire scene. When this graduated tone is layered into the overall colored rendering of your model, it can enhance the lighting effects, especially when you have soft daylight or indirect glow in the scene. At this point, the shaded and lit texture can be unwrapped from the surface of the model and saved as a flat texture file or "Baked texture." When the model is imported into Second Life or OpenSim, the mesh model and its lit, shadowed, and colored baked texture comes with it and is reapplied to the surface. 3D Modelers like 3DSMax and Blender offer Render to Texture (creating a baked texture), and UV unwrapping features in their programs to help you create this effect.

All of this effort in prerendering or "baking" the shadows and lighting of Ambient Occlusion onto the surfaces in your model is to encourage a speedy graphics performance for the visitor in your game or virtual world. The less work the graphics card has to do with each texture, the smoother and faster the frame rate will be for the visitor. If you have a model that you would like to view with Ambient Occlusion before you go through the baking process, you can see how this effect looks inworld by turning on Advanced Lighting and Ambient Occlusion in the Avatar/Preferences/Graphics menu (Figure 6.18).

6.9 PROJECT: DESIGNING A DATA VISUALIZATION ENVIRONMENT: YOUR 3D TIMELINE OR RÉSUMÉ

Virtual environments connect with external databases via specialized LSL (Linden Scripting Language) functions. The introduction of real-time data visualization or data display within the 3D environment has created some sensational results in the art and communication design sectors. This connectivity gives you many interesting ways to explore a database and your relationship to data being collected in real time worldwide.

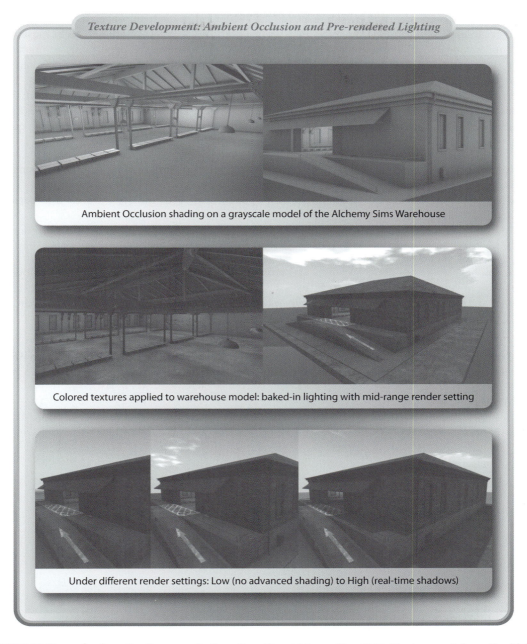

FIGURE 6.18 (See color insert) Screen grabs from OpenSim, Alchemy Sims Grid. The top panel shows the Alchemy Sims Warehouse model with just the ambient occlusion lighting on while it was being built in Blender. In the middle panel, the effect of ambient occlusion and the colored texture maps is displayed. In the bottom panel are three views of the warehouse showing various render settings available inworld and how they can enrich the image.

The relationship between a virtual environment and the visible data it can represent creates opportunities for the designer to express information in many new ways. Like great architecture, these spaces must be inviting and understandable all at once. This "hands-on" project will give you the opportunity to practice your building skills and to create a 3D "infographic" in a virtual space, which is based on your personal profile, timeline, or CV (curriculum vitae; résumé).

To start this project, you will need your résumé or chronology. If you have one listed on LinkedIn, then you can access the Visualize Me site (http://vizualize.me/) to create an instant graphic display of your work history.

The first decisions you need to make are about the environment for your display. Here are some questions to ask:

1. How will this be viewed by the visitor? For instance, will they walk among the display elements, like an exhibit, or look down on it like a map?
2. What aspects of the exhibit structure and color palette will focus the eye towards your personal timeline data.
3. How can you make your personal data come "alive" and display new, meaningful connections to the visitor?

Once you have answered these questions and broken down your personal history to some infographics, download the content for this chapter from http://www.anncudworthprojects.com/Virtual World Design Book Downloads and upload it into your avatar's inventory. Let's start building a timeline display of your chronology.

6.9.1 Make the Timeline Base

As shown in Figure 6.19, the decades of your lifespan are represented with a series of 10 m long boxes. Now build a 100 m long box as the back wall, and stand it up behind the base sections. This represents a 100 year

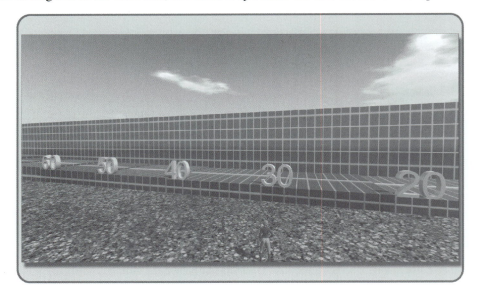

FIGURE 6.19 Screen grab from OpenSim showing the setup for the basic structure of the timeline. The base elements are covered with a tiled texture to divide them into 10 increments—each block representing a decade. The back wall is 100 m long, divided into 100 increments representing 100 years.

lifespan—may you live that long! Once those elements are built, add a grayscale grid texture to all surfaces. Set the horizontal repetition of the grid texture on the bases, so that it divides each decade box into 10 sections. If you wish, each decade section may be color coded by changing the underlying color in the texture tab. On the back wall, repeat the texture to match the base decade sections, making sure the textures align between the wall and base sections. Once you have the base and back wall done, download the number models (Numbers_0-9.dae) and add them along the timeline to enumerate the decades. Note, these meshes (made in SketchUp) will come in as a linked set, so you will need to unlink them, and save them as separate numerals for usage. With the standing numerals at the end of each decade box, there is a clear display of chronological order.

6.9.2 Adding Details

To add details along decade boxes, build some simple 3D content from prims like a graduate cap and wedding bands to represent your education, and family. You can also upload the Icon_Briefcase.dae and the Icon_Heart.dae meshes that you downloaded from the chapter's content and add them to the timeline you are building. You can see that in Figure 6.20. These can even be identified by the use of "hover text" (a simple script that is widely available) if you desire. In addition to the heart and briefcase, there are two other icons: the Icon_Information.dae, and the Icon_Pushpin for use in your timeline.

6.9.3 Landmarks and Focal Points

Looking at the structure you have so far, what do you see? 3D arrows (mesh model called Arrow.dae in the content) were added to this timeline as shown in Figure 6.21, to draw the visitor's eye toward information on which they should focus. What can you add to the collection that personifies you? In Figures 6.20 and 6.21, some geographical shapes have been added to the back wall indicating international trips and countries

FIGURE 6.20 Screen grab showing the icons added along the timeline to represent your work, school, and personal relationship chronology.

FIGURE 6.21   Screen grab showing the timeline with arrow and pushpin focal points added as well as "Post-it" notes on the back wall.

visited. These were created in SketchUp from simple geographical outlines. Along the timeline, find some times or locations that you would like to "landmark." Graphic directionals like the arrows and push pins (also available in the mesh model content) will encourage the visitor to stop at various locations and learn more about your personal history. You may also want to add some "Post-it" notes or written signage, which are made with simple prims and texture files, on your timeline.

The forms and objects you choose could be based on your infographic in Visualize.me or on some theme completely designed by you. Something to experiment with is making a basic element or two in an external modeler like SketchUp, Blender, or 3DSMax and seeing how this imports into your build. This array of forms and graphics is all about *you*, so express yourself. If you are a pilot, bring in a plane model; if you are a swimmer, make a moving water texture. Whatever you do, "own this build."

To inspire you further, the next section of this chapter has images and discusses some art/database projects that were created in Second Life and OpenSim. You will see that there are few limits on this kind of design.

6.10   ART AND DATA VISUALIZATION IN A VIRTUAL WORLD

There are two systems that have to work in concert for data-influenced art and data visualizations in a virtual world. One is the external server where the data are stored in a database, and the other is the internal server that holds the virtual world system. As Ben Lindquist said: "To put it in the simplest terms possible, virtual world data visualization is a mapping of data dimensions—a column in a spreadsheet, for example—to virtual world dimensions such as color, height, or distance along an axis" (from email conversation, 2012).

In Figure 6.22 (top section) are images from three works created in 2010 on the Beach Ride region of Second Life for a Sculpture Park sponsored by Alchemy Sims. Layton Destiny created "Ancient Sun and a Fresh Kansas Breeze," a windmill that responded to the winds of Second Life. Arrehn Oberlander built

FIGURE 6.22 (See color insert) Screen grabs from Second Life and OpenSim, showing several examples of how external data can be introduced and utilized to create artworks in the virtual environment.

"Barometric Bubbles," which filled the air with bubbles in response to the rise and fall of barometric pressure in his real world environs.

Ben Lindquist and Ann Cudworth created a data visualization art piece called "Tidal Mills." Their initial concept was to display a dataset in an "artful" way. Readily available complex datasets are hard to come by, but they did find a good one in the tidal predictions for the New York City and Long Island area. Together, they created kinetic sculptures on a virtual beach that moved in response to the shifting tides. More information about how "Tidal Mills" was designed and made are available on the Alchemy Sims You Tube channel (http://www.youtube.com/watch?v=Lw1IQ7nTTJs).

Glyph Graves, a prize-winning virtual world artist, has played with physical world/virtual world inter-relationships in many of his works. For instance, in "Reflections within Diversity," he created a virtual sensing environment that mapped the avatar's spoken language to a colored light in a real-world glass sculpture. Using real-time data from all manner of natural (river heights/temperatures, the earth's magnetic field, solar wind from space, data from Antarctic weather stations) and man-made phenomena (stock market indices), he creates conceptual art in sound, color, and space that are captivating to the visitor. In Figure 6.22 (middle section), you can see images from "Forest of Rivers," "I Thought I Hated Him," and "Enfolded," which interact with the visitor or move and create sound in response to real-time events. Movies of these artworks can be seen on his You Tube channel (http://www.youtube.com/user/GlyphGraves).

In Figure 6.22 (lower section) is a data visualization sim called "Memonic" built by Ann Cudworth and Ben Lindquist. This environment showed the visitor a countrywide slice of Twitter activity in real time and allowed the visitor to "call" the tweets (linked to color coded spheres) to his or her location by saying keywords in chat.

Although not shown in pictures, other notable data visualizations have been done by David Burden with Daden Limited (http://www.daden.co.uk/solutions/datascape/about-datascape/) and by Eric Hackathorn at Fragile Earth Studios (http://fragileearthstudios.com/).

6.11 CONCLUSION

This chapter has covered a lot of ground and presented a survey on 3D modeling, and 2D graphics that are the essential elements of a virtual world. The textures, prims and meshes can be used by you in a million ways, so dive right in! When you get more experience, you can start to relate the things you make in a virtual world, through the application of scripting and databases, to the outside world, and create a "mixed reality" experience for the observer.

No matter what modeling program or what paint program you choose, what is most important is that you come into the project with a clear idea of what your message is and how your team will tackle it, step by step. By doing that planning, not only will you make it easier to complete the task, but also you will find it easier to budget.

REFERENCES

1. Cinderella Castle, Wikipedia article, http://en.wikipedia.org/wiki/Cinderella_Castle. Accessed December 17, 2012.
2. ProBuilder, company website, http://www.sixbysevenstudio.com/wp-flexible/project/probuilder-for-unity-3d/. Accessed December 17, 2012.
3. Pixel Lab, Sculpty Paint, company website, http://elout.home.xs4all.nl/sculptpaint/. Accessed December 21, 2012.
4. Kanae Project, company website, http://kanae.net/secondlife/index.html. Accessed December 21, 2012.
5. GIMP—The GNU Image Manipulation Program, organization site, http://www.gimp.org/. Accessed December 22, 2012.
6. Making Transparent Textures—Second Life Video TuTORial, You Tube, http://youtu.be/ekLIgpRHSq4. Accessed December 23, 2012.

7 Color, Particles, and Sensory Spaces

Mere color, unspoiled by meaning, and unallied with definite form, can speak to the soul in a thousand different ways.

—Oscar Wilde

7.1 THE IMPACT OF COLOR AND THE POWER OF PARTICLES

Color is like dynamite: It must be handled carefully. If used thoughtfully, color will clarify and reveal your designs' forms and internal meanings. If used carelessly, it will undermine and collapse the design composition by diverting the visitor's eye and fracture the underlying harmony of form and pattern. That said, sometimes as a designer, you do want visual pandemonium. If you really want to blow things up, particle systems will create the resultant dust clouds, as well as rain, snow, fire, hair, fur, and many other "fuzzy" chaos-based events in a virtual environment [1].

7.2 UNDERSTANDING THE BASICS OF LIGHT AND COLOR

From the vast expanding sphere of electromagnetic waves emitted by our Sun, there is a narrow band between the infrared and ultraviolet called the visible spectrum. These wavelengths slip through the "optical window" in our atmosphere to light Earth. When one of these wavelengths is scattered by the atmosphere, the air takes on that color. For example, when clean air scatters the blue wavelengths at midday, the sky becomes blue, and at sunset, the red wavelengths tint the skies pink. Your eyes are sensitive to three ranges of light wavelengths, each range centering on the red, blue, and green areas of the visible spectrum [2]. Proof that a trichromatic sensitivity in your eyes (Young-Helmholtz theory) exists is only a recent finding (in 1983 by Dartnall, Bowmaker, and Mollon), and there are still many questions about how your eyes actually see color, what part of color vision resides in the brain, and what is in the retina.

7.2.1 DEFINING THE RAINBOW AND CREATING THE COLOR SCALE OVER HISTORY

As human cultures evolve and develop their languages, more color terms are added to their vocabulary. A primitive culture may only have two color terms, and say that the color is bright/warm or dark/cool. Eventually, the need arises to be more descriptive, and the culture adds more color terms. The stages of color term development are thought to be a product of both biological and linguistic influences [3].

Isaac Newton's scientific experiments on the refraction of light along with other seventeenth century natural scientific theories led to the establishment of red, yellow, and blue as the primary colors in the eighteenth century. This standard is still around even though it is not applicable to the commercial and digital uses of color we have today [4]. When additive and subtractive color mixing was refined and standardized, the color wheel was reinterpreted. Now, you use the red, green, and blue (RGB) light as the primary colors in the additive RGB color-mixing system. This system most closely approximates how your eyes see colors, and it is utilized in television, computer monitor displays, as well as web graphics and virtual worlds. The subtractive CMYK color-mixing system for painting, printing, and dyeing uses cyan, magenta, yellow, and black (known as *K* for key) as the primary colors [5,6]. Figure 7.1 shows how these color-mixing systems relate to the visible spectrum and what their internal components are.

As you see, there are secondary colors that can be made from mixing two primaries in each system. Tertiary colors are made from mixing one primary and one secondary *or* two secondary colors in a color system like RGB or CMYK.

7.2.2 Basic Color Terms You Should Know

For clear communication about color with your team and clients, you should know the meaning of these six terms:

1. **Hue** is the actual color. For instance, blue is a hue, as is yellow.
2. **Grayscale** is the range from pure white to pure black, with a 50/50 mix in the middle.
3. **Value** is the "brightness" of the color. Colors look bright or dark because of the amount of light they let the surface of an object reflect back to your eyes. A color with a high value would let more of the visible spectrum back to your eyes, and a color with a low value would let less light come back to your eyes. For instance, if you had two pieces of cardboard, one painted light yellow and one painted dark blue, laid out on a table under natural light, the yellow card would have a higher value than the dark blue card. If you imagine the underlying grayscale in the color, the yellow card would be near the white end of the grayscale, and the blue would be near the black end of the scale.
4. **Saturation or luminosity** (the latter term is used by painters) is the intensity of the color. A highly saturated color would be close to the spectral color and have almost no gray in it. Saturated colors can be seen in corporate logos like those of Coca-Cola (the red) and Gulf Oil (the blue and orange). Perception of a color's saturation is relative to the observer's position and the environment where the color is viewed.
5. **Complimentary colors** are colors that live across the color wheel from each other. Red is complimentary to green, blue to orange, and yellow to violet. One way to find the complimentary color of any color you see is to take advantage of the afterimage effect in your eyes. If you gaze at an isolated square patch of color for 30–60 seconds and then look at a blank white area, you will see the complimentary color of the previous color. Gazing at a red square will produce a green square in the afterimage. This effect becomes useful when you need to mix a complimentary color on the fly. Once you have found the complimentary color, you can test its accuracy. Complimentary colors, when mixed together, will produce a shade of gray. A truly great online resource is available at http://colorschemedesigner.com/. This online application will help you pick all sorts of complimentary color schemes and to view them with a variety of color-blindness filters to help you achieve visible accessibility for all. This is exceptionally important when you are designing signage and graphics for your environments. There is a built-in color preview with color-blindness filters built right in Photoshop, as well as a plug-in for GIMP (GNU Image Manipulation Program) that will also allow you to check your color choices to make sure you are designing for all visitors.
6. **Tint, tone, and shade** are terms that relate to the amount of white, gray, or black in a color. A lighter tint of red is pink, while a deeper shade of red is reminiscent of the color of dried blood. A tone falls in between and indicates that a certain amount of gray or another color has been added to the original color. Figure 7.1 shows a color sample and how it can become a tint, tone, or shade by using a grayscale and how that affects its value.

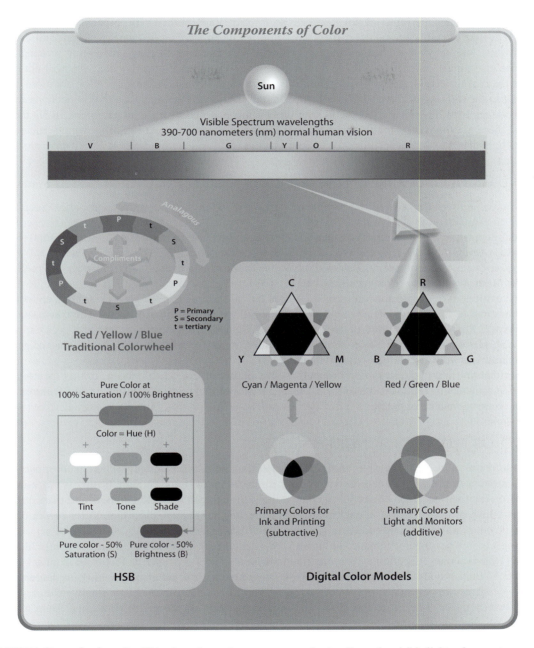

FIGURE 7.1 (See color insert) This chart shows the components of color. From the visible light color spectrum on the top, color models are pulled out to display the RYB (red, yellow, blue) wheel, CMYK (cyan, magenta, yellow, key-black) model and the RGB (red, green, blue) model. Subtractive color mixing is shown under the CMYK model and additive color mixing is shown under the RGB model. Also included is the HSB (hue, saturation, and brightness) structure, bottom left.

Now, let's consider the effect of color reflection and saturated colors. Color, especially saturated color, can be reflected off adjacent surfaces onto what you are viewing. For instance, a green wall next to a red-and-white logo may act to dim the apparent colors of the logo by reflecting green on it, making the red look more grayish and the white look like pale green. This is a real-life phenomenon; you will not see this effect in the real-time rendering of virtual worlds until graphics cards and bandwidth allow for more detailed rendering in the lighting of the virtual world scene. However, since you are aware of this phenomenon, you can provide textures for your virtual builds with these kinds of color effects added to them. In 3D modeling systems, there are many lighting features, such as those for ray tracing and radiosity, which calculate this reflected light effect in the scene and add it to your model's textures for export into a virtual environment [7].

7.2.3   Using the Color Menu in the Texture Editor for Color Settings on Particle Systems

When you begin to set the color of the particles in an LSL (Linden Scripting Language) script (Section 7.6.2 provides an example table of a basic LSL particle script), you will note that the 0–255 range (integer format) of the red, green, and blue system in your graphics software has to be converted into a range from 0 to 1.0 (or a percentage format) for the LSL code to use it. In this system, 1.0 is 100% of the color, and 0 is 0% of the color. For instance, to obtain purple, you would have 0.5 in red, 0.0 in green, and 1.0 in blue, and pushing the red up to 1.0 makes the color change to magenta.

In the texture editor of Firestorm (Figure 7.2), three tabs are given in the Color Picker submenu so you can switch back and forth between the integer, LSL percentage, and hexadecimal formats. There is also a button that gives you the additional option of copying the RGB values into the format <r,g,b>, so you can paste it into an LSL script. For example, the color magenta will be converted to <1.000, 0.000, 1.000> and stored on your clipboard for your use in the LSL particle script.

Notice that you have spinners on the menu for Hue, Saturation, and Luminance. In this menu, you can think of Luminance as lightness or value. All in all, this little menu has some very useful features for the designer working on a color palette.

7.3   COLOR FROM A DESIGNER'S PERSPECTIVE

In all cultures of the world, color has emotional overtones, spiritual meaning, psychological impact, physiological influence, and a socioeconomic relationship. The most obvious example of this is represented by the flags of each nation. Each country has created a design using colors and symbols and placed them on a banner, which provides a cultural anchor and iconic identity for them. Colors chosen for corporate logos, seasonal fashion, uniforms, and industrial signage are all fascinating examples of how color serves global marketing, creates a company's image, and is utilized to communicate with all cultures. Because blue is the universal favorite color, it is often used in multinational corporate logos, such as that of IBM, also known as "Big Blue." When you are designing a virtual world environment, you are also designing for the real world.

Every designer working must have an awareness of what colors mean in the client's native culture because it helps communicate ideas with the client and ultimately supports the client's message. Here are some questions you should ask yourself as you prepare to design the color scheme of a new virtual environment.

1. Who is your client, and what kind of culture does the client want you to represent?
2. What is the climate like in the virtual environment?
3. What country/region will this virtual environment represent?
4. What demographic is this virtual environment designed for?
5. What goals/effects/moods does your client hope to achieve?

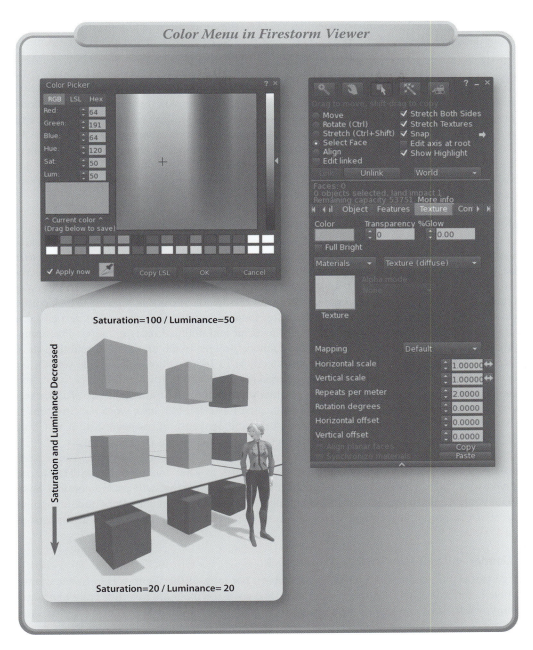

FIGURE 7.2 (See color insert) Screen grabs from OpenSim showing the texture tab in the Build menu (top right) and Color Picker sub-menu (top left) that provides color tools for the designer. In the lower left is a sampling of the saturation/luminance range on a series of prims.

Let's look at some color-based phenomena that relate to these questions, and reflect on how that might influence your design choices.

7.3.1   WHO ARE YOU DESIGNING FOR? FIVE FACTORS THAT AFFECT COLOR PREFERENCES

Every second of the day, people make decisions based on color. Decisions on the ripeness of fruit, the vitality of a patient's liver, or the appeal of a new hat, dress, or shoes are made on the basis of what color is perceived, what that color means in the observer's experience, and what attributes the observer gives that color. From a virtual environment designer's point of view, there are five broad categories of human life that have an impact on color choice preference and how you might use color in your designs. A virtual world environment designer should be aware of these and how they will have an impact on the design and another person's perception. Let's examine them one by one.

7.3.1.1   Cultural and Geographic Influences

The actual climate, the geopolitical structure of the country, its history, and the relative level of globalization are all major factors in color preference. For instance, in the cool climate of Sweden, light, pale colors such as sky blue, light yellow, and white are preferred, while in the warmer climates of Brazil, highly saturated versions of green, yellow, and red are preferred. The color preferences of cool versus warm climates are related to the look of color in the sunlight of those climates. Under the blazing sunlight of Brazil, colors have to be saturated to have any impact, and under the softer light of Sweden, the paler colors rest easier on the eye. Worldwide, the nations have wrapped color up in social and political representation. The orange and green of Ireland's flag represents the Protestant and Catholic groups. In the modern German flag, the black, red, and gold tricolor represents the Republican democracy. In India, yellow symbolizes wealth, and the world over for centuries, the color purple has represented royalty.

Over the last few decades, globalization has gradually influenced the traditional use of color in many countries. Western brides have traditionally worn white, and Eastern brides have worn red (in China, India, Pakistan, Vietnam) for hundreds of years. This historical/traditional custom has been shifting in China, and now you will see Chinese brides wearing white dresses with red decorations or accessories.

As a successful designer of a globally accessible virtual world, you always do your research to understand the cultural meanings of color and how that information relates to what you are building. That knowledge will serve you well when the time comes to design evocative palettes that will pack emotional as well as informational content into the visual environment. Table 7.1 presents the major colors (red, orange, yellow, green, blue, violet or purple, black, and white) and some of their meanings and cultural affiliations around the world.

7.3.1.2   Gender and Self-Identity-Based Influences

Color and gender identification starts when we are babies. For most of the Western Hemisphere, pink is for girls, and blue is for boys. However, in Belgium, pink is considered the more assertive color and is used for boy's clothing, while blue, which has long been associated with the Virgin Mary, is used for girls. A perfect example of gender identification combined with political symbolism is the Transgender Pride flag, which displays two light blue stripes, two pink stripes, and one white stripe in a horizontal composition.

For the most part, children's cartoons, clothing, and toys, and sometimes their living spaces, are decorated with bright primary colors such as spectrum red, blue, yellow, and green. As they age and start forming their personal identities and tastes, children will experiment with color. In 2013, color palettes for teen products were influenced by fantasy, gothic themes, urban gaming, and television environments. Small wonder that teens want to try out a Gothic Vampire bedroom or have multicolored graffiti on the walls. Designing the

TABLE 7.1

Psychological Effects of Hue, Color Response, and Meanings by Global Location/Culture

Psychological Effects	Africa	Asia	Australia	Europe	N. America	S. America
Red Hue effect: rousing and motivating Advances in visual field; implies confidence, protection	South Africa: mourning Pan-African flag color: courage	China: good luck India: purity Bridal color Shinto/ Buddhism Singapore: joy	Aboriginals: the land, earth National flag: bravery, valor, strength	Russia: Communist Beauty Sweden: high class England: phone booth Celtic: death	Cherokee: success Love, passion Danger, stop Jamaica: drunk	Aztec: blood Combined with white means religion
Orange Hue effect: exciting and welcoming Implies appetite, social activities	Ancient Egyptian paint color	Happiness and love India: saffron is sacred Middle East: mourning	Ayers rock/Uluru at sunset, dreamtime, creation mythology	Ireland: Protestant Netherlands: House of Orange Autumn, extroverts, danger Lascaux cave	Native Americans: kinship Amusement, food Autumn, Halloween Safety	Sweet potatoes
Yellow Hue effect: encouragement and radiant effect Implies thinking and memory	Egypt: mourning Pan-African flag color: sun, wealth, justice High rank in society	China: royal color Japan: courage India: wealth India: saffron is sacred Middle East: mourning	National color: wealth, seashore, deserts Aboriginals: represents the sun	Nazi yellow star for Jews in World War II Crime stories: real and fictional in Italy had yellow covers	Hope Caution, hazard Cowardice School bus	Aztec: food, corn Mexico: mourning Mayan color for direction of south Columbian flag: wealth of gold
Green Hue effect: relaxes the eye Implies peace and tranquility Color of almost every active military worldwide	Pan-African color found in many flags; earth, fertility, Muslim religion	India: Islam China: cuckold Iran: paradise China: jade-virtue Indonesia: forbidden color	National color: forests, eucalyptus, meadows	Ireland: national Portugal: hope Scotland: honor	Spring season Traffic: go	Aztec: royalty Death in countries with jungle climates

(Continued)

TABLE 7.1 (Continued)
Psychological Effects of Hue, Color Response, and Meanings by Global Location/Culture

Psychological Effects	Africa	Asia	Australia	Europe	N. America	S. America
Blue						
Hue effect: recedes in the visual field. Worldwide favorite color; calming; spiritual	The sky On South African flag: Dutch and U.K. colonists	Iran: heaven China: spring India: Krishna Middle East: heaven	National flag: vigilance, truth, loyalty	Greek: protection from evil Holy Spirit Virgin Mary	Cherokee: defeat Conservatism Corporate Uniform Postal HTML links	Mexico: mourning Columbia: soap Mexico: trust and serenity
Purple						
Hue effect: calming Implies spirituality and creativity	Egypt: virtue and faith Middle East: wealth	Thailand: mourning (widow) Iran: future omen	Weather map color indicating extremely hot weather	Royalty UK: royal mourning Italy, Rome: Caesar First color in prehistoric art	Purple Heart medal	Mayan color for religious ceremonies Aztec color for royalty
Black						
Hue effect: context driven Implies power, mystery, magic, and death	Primary art color	China: boy's color Japan: wealth	Aboriginals: the color of the people	Mourning Spain, Portugal, Italy: widows Scandinavia: bride's color	Funerals Death Power Rebellion Anarchy	Aztec: war Mexico: widow's color Masculine color for clothing
White						
Hue effect: context driven Implies purification, clarity	Primary art color On South African flag: Dutch and U.K. colonists	Japan: funeral wear and bride's first dress symbolizing her "death" as she leaves her parents	National flag: peace and honesty	Purity, peace Mourning color for French queens	Bridal color Goodness Clean Cherokee: peace	Aztec god Quetzalcoatl

Source: Based on information provided by these sites: http://colormatters.com/, http://webdesign.about.com/od/color/a/bl_colorculture. htm, and http://en.wikipedia.org/wiki/Wedding_dress.

color palette of a virtual environment for an adult client should take into account the color appeal that is influenced by the client's gender. In general, studies have shown men prefer brighter and cooler colors, while women prefer warmer and less-saturated colors, favoring tints rather than tones. Research has shown that women will tend to have more diverse color tastes, while men will be more tolerant to more achromatic or black-and-white palettes [8].

Over the last few decades, the rigid color preferences defined by gender differences have been fading; you now see men wearing sport uniforms from the secondary or tertiary palettes, such as purple, orange, and teal. Do not be afraid to push the color envelope. Sometimes, clients just need to be shown that the right shades of lime green and magenta will actually enhance their blue and red color scheme, giving the overall design more impact.

7.3.1.3 Educational and Socioeconomic Influences

Consider the difference in the colors of the website for McDonald's restaurants and the Per Se restaurant in New York. The McDonald's website impacts the eye with bright primary colors like red, green, and blue. The Per Se website has sliding image panels in muted browns with gold highlights. Dinner at McDonald's will cost about $20; the tasting dinner with wine at Per Se will cost much more. All around, in everything you buy, every advertisement you see, a carefully chosen color scheme is used to market those goods and services. You should begin to make it a habit to notice how color is used for that purpose and be aware of the ways you can utilize it in your virtual world design. Generally, the higher the economic class and educational level of the customer, the more sophisticated and nuanced the palette used for representing those goods and services will be. Complex colors like mauve, teal, and celadon green are used to create the idea of rarity, preciousness, and good taste. Simple colors like red, blue, and black are used to create the feeling of strength, solidity, and power. For instance, if you are building a virtual world dedicated to opera, consider a sophisticated palette with tints and tones of colors such as you might see in a French rococo painting by Jean-Honoré Fragonard, and if you are building a virtual world dedicated to Formula 1 racing, you could use a palette from the high-energy images of Pop Art artist Roy Lichtenstein. The tints and more complex colors of the Fragonard will denote sophistication, and the bold primary colors of the Lichtenstein will create power and movement in the visual field.

7.3.1.4 Chronological and Generational Influences

The age of your client will influence color preferences in a couple of ways. Color preferences are influenced by past experiences in the childhood and teenaged years [9]. If someone had happy experiences as a teenager sipping cherry coke in a hometown pastel-colored sweet shop, the person will most likely enjoy pastel colors his or her entire life because of the fond memories. These specific color preferences will be subjective, client by client, but there are also age-related cross-cultural preferences that develop based in the client's generational color history. You should think of your client's cultural age as well as the chronological age. Is he or she a Millennial (born 1980–1996), a Generation Xer (born 1964–1980), or a Baby Boomer (born 1945–1964)? The color palettes of these three generations are very different. A boomer may fondly remember the pop colors of a Peter Max painting, while a Gen Xer favors the colors of his or her first video game. By understanding the history of color and how it applies to your client's cultural group, you will easily find common ground with the client for discussion about the color palette of the design. Figure 7.3 shows a chart of some colors from each decade, derived from images of the popular culture in that decade.

Today's children and young adults have more color choices than ever, and many of them enjoy experimenting with color in their graphics programs and games. Undoubtedly, they will grow up expecting this customization in their virtual environments and be very sophisticated consumers, able to enjoy many complex color schemes.

7.3.1.5 Psychological and Experiential Influences

Finally, you should remember that color, above all, is a subjective preference. Your client's childhood memories and collective experiences, good and bad, will affect the client's likes and dislikes for color. Knowing

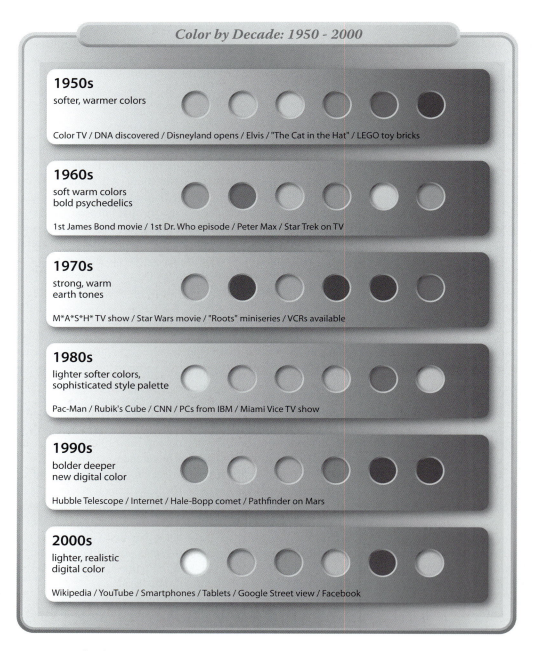

FIGURE 7.3 (See color insert) Chart of color palettes by decade (1950–2010) based on color samplings from pop cultural images from these times.

your client's preferences will help you avoid the pitfall of picking a color the client hates for your virtual world design, and it will also help build a basic color framework to expand your palette. Not all clients can tell you what color cerulean blue is, but if you show them a cerulean-based palette, they may like it. Perhaps the first thing you should do is to ask your client to name a few of his or her favorite colors. You can also look for the client's color preferences in what he or she is wearing. If the client only wears black, be bold. That powerful color goes well with red and blue, as well as silver and gold, so try that combination if you are designing a personal space for that client.

7.4 COLOR, COLORED LIGHT, AND PERCEPTION

In general, someone with good color vision can see 10 million different colors. In fact, color perception is so constant that the human brain will even compensate for the effect of colored light. When tested, most people were able to find the white color sample even when it was shown to them under different colored lighting. This phenomenon is called *color constancy* [10]. Color vision starts with the rods and cone cells in your retina, but color perception starts in the brain. Understanding how color and its use in architectural spaces can affect the psychological perceptions and physiological state of the observer gives you an incredible tool kit for creating unforgettable virtual spaces. Color is fleeting, color is ephemeral, and yet it can be remembered forever. As you settle down to design, ask yourself: How can my sculptural and architectural forms be enhanced and empowered by colors in ways to make a virtual environment more visually interesting and emotionally moving?

7.4.1 COLOR, PERCEIVED SCALE, PERSPECTIVE, AND PROGRESSION IN AN ENVIRONMENT

Color in the environment can change the way you perceive scale, perspective, and the progression of surrounding space in an environment. To perceive these effects within an architectural space, you will need a series of testing rooms. Figure 7.4 shows a simple connected box room design; it has a doorway in each wall, so multiple rooms can be seen at once. Try building this simple model for yourself in your favorite modeling program and import it into your virtual sandbox. *Note:* this model, called House.dae and its physics file House_Physics.dae, is also available for download in the Chapter 7 content for this book at http://www.anncudworthprojects.com/. In the Firestorm Viewer, under Avatar/Preferences, turn on the Advanced lighting settings and Ambient Occlusion for your scene, lowering your draw distance so your computer can handle the extra computation easily. Try changing the ceilings, walls, and floors by selecting the appropriate faces of the model and modifying the settings in the Color Picker submenu.

1. Make the first ceiling red (RGB=255,0,0); the second ceiling light gray (RGB=198,198,198); the third ceiling medium blue (RGB=125,175,255); the fourth ceiling orange (RGB=255,111,0); the fifth ceiling light yellow (RGB=255,255,195), and the sixth ceiling dark green (RGB=50,110,0). Stand your avatar in the corner of one room; go into Mouselook and check out the walls and ceiling in your camera view. Take a walk around, looking at all the rooms. Did you notice how aggressively the red ceiling advances toward you and how the cooler blue ceiling pulled back? Look at the top panel in Figure 7.4 to get a sense of this effect.
2. Turn the ceilings back to white (RGB = 255,255,255) and now try that same color progression on the walls: red, gray, blue, orange, yellow, and green. How does this wall placement of color feel different from ceiling placement? What color on the walls makes you feel more secure, more energetic, or more relaxed? In Figure 7.4, the second panel down, this effect is illustrated.

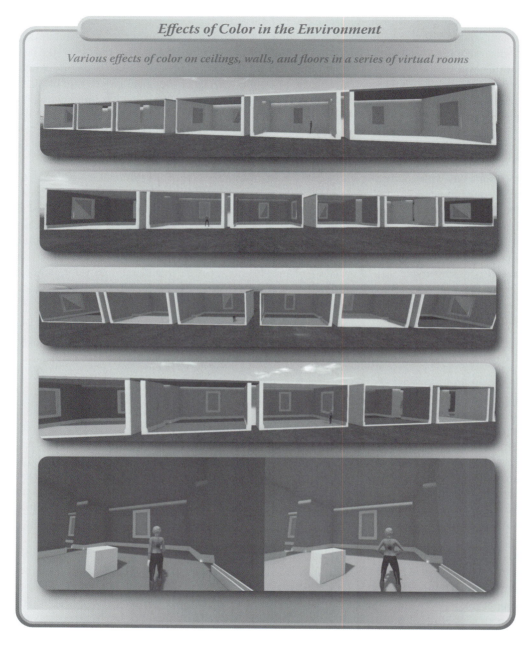

FIGURE 7.4 (See color insert) Screen grabs from OpenSim showing the effect of color changes on the ceilings, walls, and floors of interconnected rooms (top four images). In the bottom two images, the effect of a warm color on the perception of the virtual space is contrasted with that of a cool color.

3. Turn the walls back to white and try the color progression on the floor. How does that affect your sense of gravity? What color on the floor makes you feel more "grounded"? What color makes you feel a bit weightless? The third panel down of Figure 7.4 shows this effect.

4. Now, try various combinations of your color palette on the ceiling, walls, and floor. You may notice that when you use the strong red on all the surfaces, the energy of the room maxes out and cancels out the overall advancement effect, but when you combine it with some yellow surfaces, it becomes more exciting due to the contrast of the two warm colors. Highly saturated colors will advance and make the space stimulating, which is good for a nightclub but not as good for a workspace where people need to focus.

Cross-cultural studies, even interspecies studies (monkeys to humans) have indicated that there were physiological and psychological responses or color-mood reactions common to all participants [11]. The color red excites the observer emotionally and physically more than any other color in the spectrum, while viewing shades of blue and green tend to relax the observer. In Table 7.1, the major physical and psychological effects for each color are listed in the far left column under the hue.

7.4.2 Color and How It Affects Your Perception, Judgment, and Senses

Color can powerfully affect your ability to judge space, time, and mass. To see how it affects our sense of volume and distance, try these changes in your virtual test room. Recolor the walls to a very pale blue, put a bright green cube in the middle of the floor, and set the sun position to default afternoon. Take a snapshot to record how this looks and save it to a file. Now, change the walls to bright saturated red and take another snapshot. When you compare them, you will probably feel that the red walls are closer in space, and the volume of the room has diminished. This effect is shown in the bottom panel of Figure 7.4.

Now, try changing the illumination level by changing the sun position in your world (World/Sun Position in the top tabs) setting to default midnight. Try both the pale blue and red walls again, recording the same point of view under the low-light/blue-light conditions. You will probably notice that the darker color under the dimmer/bluer lighting makes the room seem even smaller.

Your estimation of density, mass, and the apparent weight of an object can be greatly affected by its color [11]. Generally, the darker and more saturated a color is, the heavier the object will appear to be. You can test this by creating a series of large spheres 2 meters in diameter. Make one a deep blue tone and one a light blue tint. Which seems heavier, more massive? Now, copy those two spheres and color them with a deep red tone and a light red (or pink) tint. Compare the deep red to the deep blue sphere. The warmer color will appear heavier than a cooler color with the same tonal (value and saturation) color base. So, if you want your virtual machinery builds to have a more realistic sense of weight, make the colors of these components a dark, deeply warm, saturated color. This sense of apparent weight can be used with ceiling heights and color. A very high ceiling can carry off a saturated warm color, while a low ceiling painted the same way may seem oppressive.

The color of the walls in a lecture hall, meeting room, or classroom seems to affect how we perceive time. Conflicting results have come in regarding whether time seems to pass more slowly or quickly in a warm or cool color room, but in each experiment, a difference has been observed in how time is perceived in rooms with different colors while the same presentation was made [11]. Perhaps you would like to test this phenomenon yourself by creating a color changing lecture room that records the attendance of each visitor during a given lecture and surveying them about their perceptions on the length of the presentation.

The color of an environment can also affect your perception of the ambient temperature. Studies have shown that cool colors will make people less tolerant of a cool room where warm colors will help them tolerate lower temperatures [11]. Sound level is also affected by the color of the environment. We speak of a color, such as a highly saturated orange, as being "loud." Environments that are colored with bright, loud colors will seem to be louder, while cool colors help to tone down the background noise and make a work space seem quieter.

Color is also affiliated with your sense of taste and flavor. A walk through your local supermarket chain store will provide you with abundant examples of how color is affiliated with food and utilized to market to your sense of smell, sight, and taste simultaneously. In work spaces, various smells can be compensated for by using the complimentary color on the walls. For instance, sweet smells that are affiliated with warm colors like red and pink can be reduced in pungency by the addition of greens and blues to the environment [11]. Granted, we do not have smell functions in a virtual world environment yet, but we do make many visual associations with smell, so it is something to consider in your overall palette.

7.4.3 COLOR, ENVIRONMENTAL ENERGY, AND PLANNING FOR AN OVERALL PALETTE

Now that you have tried various color combinations on your test rooms (Figure 7.4) and observed the effects, let's consider how these factors can be used in larger, multipurpose spaces. Color, and the environmental energy it creates, should be considered in the planning for an overall palette in your virtual design. Suppose you are designing a multiroom conference center for Second Life or OpenSim. It will have a large lecture hall, two or three smaller meeting rooms, a main lobby, and some outside breakout areas. The pace of a conference is probably familiar to you. Early in the morning, people arrive for coffee, sign in, and settle into whatever room has the meeting they would like to attend. Every hour or so, they change rooms, and then at midday they all congregate for lunch.

Figure 7.5 displays the floor plan of these rooms, the coffee bar, and the breakout space. Now, imagine that you are using color to enhance the flow and energy of these spaces, silently encouraging people to move into areas where they will get the most from the conference at any given time. Also note in Figure 7.5 the color-coded arrows showing major traffic patterns for a day's activity at the conference. There is lots of circulating at the coffee areas, branching off into the breakout areas and into the meeting rooms. At first, many more people will head to the lecture room to hear the keynote speaker than to the meeting rooms, but later in the morning, they will fill the meeting rooms, leaving the lecture hall half empty. Midday, you see everyone heading out for a lunch break, and at the end of the day, they all head to the terrace for drinks and conversation.

As you design this kind of space, think about these questions:

1. How would you encourage rapid movement through the hallways and allow for settling in the meeting rooms and lecture hall?
2. What colors would you choose for the walls in those areas?
3. How would you make the breakout areas stimulating to conversation and mingling?
4. What kind of gradation in tint, tone, and shade would you use for a visual transition from one area to another?

One way to think of the energy flow is to compare the sense of centrifugal (spins outward) versus centripetal energies (spins inward) within the space [11]. You probably want people to get their coffee and spin off outward toward the meeting rooms and to spin inward once they are inside the meeting rooms and lecture hall. Warm colors tend to encourage centrifugal energy; cool colors will encourage centripetal energy. Of course, painting your coffee area spectrum orange, your hallways red, and your meeting rooms deep green and blue might be overkill, but the warm-to-cool progression is a good place to start. It is the overall palette that is

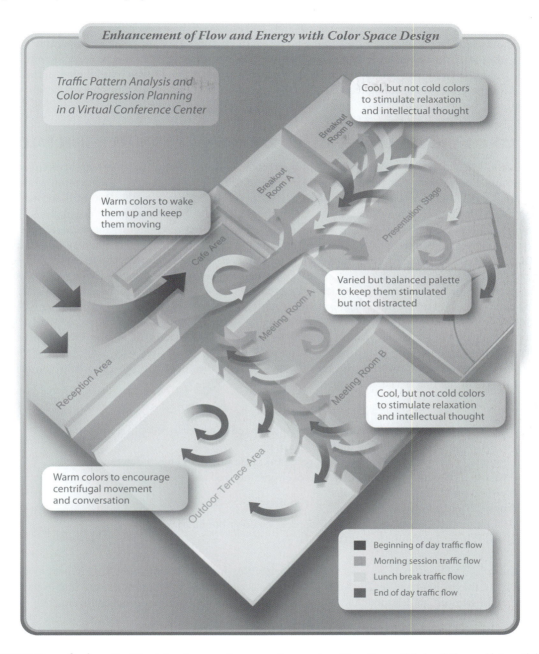

FIGURE 7.5 (See color insert) Chart showing a conference environment, and how the spatial circulation and interactivity during the event could be analyzed and influenced with a color space design.

important, as well as how it is lit and the various tints and tones used to accent it. Remember that it is not only the color of the walls but also the colors of the floors, ceilings, and furnishings that are important.

The most important thing to remember is that one hue, one color is like a single musical note. You will have to compose from many colors to create a rich visual composition in your virtual environment. Like a symphony, there will be repeating themes of secondary and tertiary color as well as major chords composed of dominant, saturated, and primary color combinations in your overall design.

7.5   COLOR AND DESIGN FOR ALL: WORKING TOWARD AN ACCESSIBLE PALETTE

Design for All is a very important factor in your color choices, overall palette, textual options and the color/contrast choices of your project. Consider some of the following aspects of perception while you are designing, so that your project gains greater visual accessibility. Approximately 200 million people in the world are color-blind to some extent, about 8% of the male and 0.5% of the female populations. The most common forms of color blindness are protanopia (less sensitive to red wavelengths) and deuteranopia (blind to green wavelengths). As a responsible designer interested in creating virtual environments that are accessible to all visitors, you will need to check your color palettes for readability by those who are color blind as well as people with low vision. If you are doing disaster simulations, you will need to make sure your colors can be seen by people under the stress of an emergency situation, when the human visual system may only operate with shades of gray. For the most part, utilizing color combinations of yellow/blue or red/blue will provide universal color-coded readability. Sometimes, changing the brightness, the saturation, or the background texture of a color will add to the visibility, useful for those with low vision [12]. Adobe offers an accessibility overview that explains how to utilize their color-blindness filters (http://www.adobe.com/accessibility/products/photoshop/overview.html). In general, they suggest the following things to help you bring your palette into a format that is visible by all:

1. Change color brightness or hue.
2. Pure red tends to appear dark and muddy; orange-red is easier to recognize.
3. Bluish green is less confusing than yellowish green.
4. Gray may be confused with magenta, pale pink, pale green, or emerald green.
5. Avoid the following combinations whenever possible: red and green; yellow and bright green; light blue and pink; dark blue and violet.
6. Apply different patterns or shapes.
7. Add large white, black, or dark-color borders on color boundaries.
8. Use different font families or styles.

If you are a GIMP user, there is a color vision deficiency plug-in available (http://registry.gimp.org/node/24885). By applying these filters and testing your palettes for accessibility, you can make sure that everything you create can be enjoyed, understood, and interacted with by all who visit the virtual environment.

7.6   PARTICLES AND THEIR USES IN DESIGN

7.6.1   WHAT ARE PARTICLE SYSTEMS?

Particles used in real-time games and virtual worlds are "sprites" or one-sided planes with four vertices and two faces, displaying a texture element such as a droplet or snowflake. Every particle generated will "billboard," or always face the camera, to create the maximum visual density possible. Many particle systems or engines are used in the gaming industry to create the various effects of fire, rain, snow, smoke, fog, gun muzzle flares, explosions, dust clouds, and so on [1].

7.6.2 Particle System Basics in Second Life and OpenSim

In Second Life and OpenSim, particles can be generated from any sort of mesh object or prim that contains an LSL-based particle script. Refer to Table 7.2, which shows the text of a basic particle script from the Particle Lab in Second Life, to see how these qualities are delineated in the code. In the LSL code, PSYS means Particle System, and SRC means Source or the particle emitter prim or mesh object.

Read through the LSL code and then double back to look at it while comparing the various modifiers in the script from the modifiers list below Table 7.2.

There are many qualities to a particle that can be affected with a script, and they can be divided into the following groups: physical attributes, temporal attributes, and movement attributes.

Refer to the list that follows and the lines of the LSL particle script from Table 7.2 once you have put it into an empty script inworld to see how this simple script provides lots of ways to affect how the particle looks and behaves. This script should create a basic particle effect that starts as cyan streaks, which gradually turn into circular dots that bounce away as they are affected by the wind. Please note, the LSL scripts in this book should be downloaded from the website, http://www.anncudworthprojects.com/, and copied from its text files to be pasted into a new script. Please see Chapter 2, section 2.3 for more details on downloading scripts.

7.6.3 List of Modifiers in a Particle Script

1. Important physical attributes and the LSL basic particle script:
    a. *Texture*. Line 7: This is a texture image that the system is using from your inventory. The LSL script will use the default particle set in your basic inventory if you have not added the texture to the content inventory of the prim that holds this script.
    b. *Scale or size*. Line 8: This is measured in *x* and *y* directions only, in meters; the maximum is 4.0 meters.
    c. *Color*. Line 9: Colors in percentage of R, G, and B.
    d. *Alpha or level of transparency*. Line 10: 1.0 = totally opaque, 0.0 = totally transparent.
    e. *Emissive quality*. Line 30: The // was removed in this line to make these particles self-illuminating.
    f. *Burst count*. Line 12: Sets how many particles come out on each timed burst.
    g. *Burst radius*. Line 19: Distance from emitter the particles originate, 0.0 = center.
    h. *Bounce*. Line 33: Flagged on/off; works sort of like a force field located at the center of the emitter to reflect and redirect the movement of the particles back in the opposite direction. The particles will bounce up and then fall down to hit it again, each time with a little less rebound.
2. Important temporal attributes and the LSL particle scripting code line:
    a. *Life span of particle*. Line 14: Determines how long a particle will be shown in the client viewer once it comes into the avatar's view or its emitter has been rezzed inworld. The maximum is 60 seconds.
    b. *Burst rate*. Line 13: Sets how often per second the emitter will create a burst of particles.
3. Important movement attributes and the LSL particle scripting code line:
    a. *Pattern*. Line 17: Basic starting configurations for flow.
    b. *Burst speed*. Line 18: Speed of particle through its lifetime.
    c. *Angle*. Line 21: Sets the width of the angle; with pattern 8, will make a 3D cone.

TABLE 7.2

Basic Particle Script from Jopsy Pendragon/The Particle Lab

Line#	LSL Code or Comments

```
0     //Simple Particle Script - by Jopsy Pendragon
1     //The original version of this script came from THE PARTICLE LABORATORY in Second
         Life
2     //Usage: (Touch) the scripted prim to start and stop this particle effect.
3
4     default {
5       state_entry() {
6       llParticleSystem([
7         PSYS_SRC_TEXTURE, llGetInventoryName(INVENTORY_TEXTURE, 0), //or a "TEXTURE-ASSET-
      UUID-KEY"
8         PSYS_PART_START_SCALE, <0.1, 0.3, 0.0>, PSYS_PART_END_SCALE, <0.5, 0.5, 0.0>,
9         PSYS_PART_START_COLOR, <0.0, 1.0, 1.0>, PSYS_PART_END_COLOR, <0.5, 0.5, 1.0>,
10        PSYS_PART_START_ALPHA, 1.0,        PSYS_PART_END_ALPHA, 0.0,
11
12        PSYS_SRC_BURST_PART_COUNT, 1,
13        PSYS_SRC_BURST_RATE,        0.02,
14        PSYS_PART_MAX_AGE, 4.0,
15        PSYS_SRC_MAX_AGE,  0.0,
16
17        PSYS_SRC_PATTERN, PSYS_SRC_PATTERN_ANGLE_CONE, //or _DROP, _EXPLODE, _ANGLE
18        PSYS_SRC_BURST_SPEED_MIN, 0.75, PSYS_SRC_BURST_SPEED_MAX, 1.00,
19        PSYS_SRC_BURST_RADIUS, 0.5,
20
21        PSYS_SRC_ANGLE_BEGIN, 0.2*PI, PSYS_SRC_ANGLE_END, 0.3*PI,
22        PSYS_SRC_OMEGA, < 0.0, 0.0, 0.0 >,
23
24        PSYS_SRC_ACCEL, < 0.0, 0.0, -0.5 >,
25      //PSYS_SRC_TARGET_KEY, llGetLinkKey(LINK_ROOT),
26
27        PSYS_PART_FLAGS, (0
28            |PSYS_PART_INTERP_COLOR_MASK
29            |PSYS_PART_INTERP_SCALE_MASK
30            |PSYS_PART_EMISSIVE_MASK
31            |PSYS_PART_FOLLOW_VELOCITY_MASK
32            |PSYS_PART_WIND_MASK
33            |PSYS_PART_BOUNCE_MASK
34        //|PSYS_PART_FOLLOW_SRC_MASK
35        //|PSYS_PART_TARGET_POS_MASK
36        //|PSYS_PART_TARGET_LINEAR_MASK
37          )
38        ]
39      );
40    }
41
```

TABLE 7.2 (Continued)
Basic Particle Script from Jopsy Pendragon/The Particle Lab

Line#	LSL Code or Comments
42	`    touch_start(integer n) {state particles_off;}`
43	`    }`
44	
45	`  state particles_off {`
46	`    state_entry() {llParticleSystem([]);}`
47	
48	`    touch_start(integer n) {llResetScript();}`
49	`    }`
50	

   d. *Acceleration on a vector* xyz. Line 24: Accelerate in a direction; adding a minus value for *z* will create gravitational effect on the particle.

   e. *Wind response*. Line 32: Allows the particle direction to be affected by inworld winds. This is flagged on and off by removing the // at the front of the line.

   f. *Follow the emitter*. Line 34: Flag on/off to have particles follow a moving emitter.

   g. *Target a position*. Line 35: Enables the particles to find a target, which is defined in Line 25.

   h. *Target linear*. Line 36: Sends particles in a straight line toward the target, ignoring wind and the like.

Once you have an understanding of these modifiers, you can affect the look of your particle systems easily. If you have an interest in targeting prims in various ways or simply want a fine collection of basic scripts for fire, snow, and so on, then you should head over to the Particle Lab in Second Life. Founded by Jopsy Pendragon, this entertaining and educational region has much more information about particles available at the interactive displays (http://maps.secondlife.com/secondlife/Teal/191/56/21).

7.6.4 Basic Rules for Using Particles and Instantiation

In the virtual worlds of Second Life and OpenSim, particles are rendered by your client viewer. The Firestorm/Preferences/Graphics menu has a slider setting that allows you to see up to 8192 particles in a scene. That may sound like a lot, but get a snowstorm particle system going and add in a few avatars shooting off fireworks and soon you will see a diminished effect. Particles do not cause lag in a virtual world, but their scripting can. Care should be taken to make the scripts as efficient as possible, and if you do not code yourself, you should make sure your code writer has knowledge of how much server lag each script the writer makes adds to your region. There is a limit on visibility for particles, dependent draw distance, and size of the emitter. If you need to see a particle from across the sim, then your draw distance will have to be turned up, and the emitting prim may need to be scaled up. By varying the size of your emitters across the landscape, you can keep the particle load on the observer's viewer at a manageable level. When you are making particle systems for a Unity-based game, beware of too many particle instantiations happening in a short time. This additional amount of work for the game engine may slow the game play, and it is better to recycle a group of objects with particle systems in them than to constantly create new ones during game play.

7.6.5   Textures for Particles

When you make a texture for particles, be careful of the edges on the image; if they are not 100% clear alpha, your particles will look like they have little frames around them. Creating particle textures for particle systems is more art than science, but there are a few good tips to remember.

Tip 1. Unless you require a specific image for your particle, make the texture as a white pattern over a transparent background so you can color shift it to any palette you want using the PSYS_PART_START_COLOR, <1.0, 1.0, 1.0>, PSYS_PART_END_COLOR, <1.0, 1.0, 1.0>, line in the LSL script.

Tip 2. If you need copious amounts of particle flow, such as a waterfall, follow this advice from Jopsy Pendragon and utilize a texture with lots of smaller dots on it rather than one dot in the middle. The collective presentation will look denser with a lower particle emission rate saving processing time.

Tip 3. Pay close attention to the duration of the particle's life span; do not let the particle live one bit longer than necessary for your effect.

Tip 4. When you have the particles flowing the way you want and you do not think you will need to copy the object in your build, you might consider the option of deleting the script from the object; the particles will keep flowing, and you have removed a script from the server load.

Tip 5. Remember that particle scripts may cause server lag; particles are rendered in the viewer. A script that creates too many particles may crash your graphics card.

Tip 6. Jopsy Pendragon, creator of the Particle Lab in Second Life, gave me this tip: "Consider and tune for the intended 'viewing distance.' For large far-off effects use fewer and larger particles rather than trying to compensate with quantity. For small up-close particle effects, use small prims/small object because they won't get rendered for people far away, and won't cause them unnecessary lag."

7.6.6   Designing with Particles

As a designer, you will probably find many needs for particles in your builds. It is relatively common to see them used for fire, fog, fountains, and atmospheric effects, but have you thought of other ways these elements can be used? Now, it is up to you to push the particle creative boundary outward; they can be made into the feathers of a wing, the crystal beads on a chandelier, or a glowing moon. Let your imagination push you to more diversified usage.

7.7   PROJECT: DESIGNING A COLORED LIGHT AND PARTICLE EFFECT

The goal of this project is to design and build a colored light and particle show for installation in a pre-built structure called the Sensory Space. When you start to design this kind of thing, you should ask yourself: What is my central image, my inspiration, for this space? For you, perhaps it the darkness of a womb, the magnified lens of a drop of water, or possibly the fragrant heart of a rose. If you want this space to be a volume full of moving light colors, then you may be inspired by the artwork of the Light and Space movement, which originated in California in the late 1960s [13].

For the purposes of this project, the concept of a nebula was chosen; inspiration was drawn from the magnificent images the Hubble Telescope has sent back to us (http://hubblesite.org/gallery/album/nebula/).

7.7.1 Setting Up the Sensory Space Inworld Using WindLight to "Set the Scene"

Begin by downloading the Chapter 7 content from http://www.anncudworthprojects.com/ in the Virtual World Design Book Downloads section. There are 2 COLLADA (.dae) files needed create the Sensory Space in your virtual environment: Sensory_space_meditation_chamber_inner.dae, and Sensory_space_meditation_chamber_outer.dae. It is very important that you utilize the corresponding physic shape files for these on your upload, by selecting "From file" under the Step 1: Level of Detail section in the Physics tab located within the Upload Menu of the Firestorm viewer. This will ensure that the Sensory Space has exactly the physics level of detail it needs for your usage. For more detailed information on uploading the content for this chapter and how to utilize physic shape files, please go to Chapter 2, Section 2.3.

Like the modular classroom project in Chapter 4, these parts have an alignment cube so you can match them together. After you upload these models into your world, and have them rezzed on the ground near each other, check to make sure that the alignment cubes are the key prim on these elements. As you know, this is indicated with a yellow outline when you have the object selected in the Build/Edit menu. Sometimes, when a model is uploaded into OpenSim or Second Life, the key prim is changed. If the COLLADA (.dae) model files have not uploaded into your virtual environment with the alignment cube as the key prim, go into the Edit Linked mode (check the box on the Build/Edit menu) and unlink the alignment prim. Without moving it, deselect everything by clicking on the ground or sky. Now, re-select the model, and then the alignment cube, and link them back together. The cube should now be the key prim, and show a yellow highlight, while the rest of the model is highlighted in blue.

See Figure 7.6 which illustrates how these parts should be aligned on your terrain. Place the Sensory_space_meditation_chamber_inner.dae section on your terrain first, setting it at the coordinates you want, then move the Sensory_space_meditation_chamber_outer.dae section in the same x and y coordinates, but above it at a higher z value. Now lower the "outer" section down onto the "inner" section, until the x,y,z coordinates match.

Once you get them in place and properly aligned, it is a good idea to link them, so you can move the whole structure around easily. First, select each part, and unlink and delete the alignment cubes. Then select the "inside" first, with a right click and go into the edit menu. Then hold the shift key down and select the "outer" with a left click. When you have both selected, click the Link button on the Edit menu, and they will be linked. Since you selected the outer shell last, it will become the key prim in the structure, and show a yellow outline when selected. If you have gotten them aligned, and linked—Great Work! Now you have a "lab" place to test color and lighting effects in your virtual world.

This seashell-shaped environment is colored in a neutral gray to start. (*Note:* This is a baked texture, and if you decide to use another texture on this form, it will lose its subtle surface shadows created by the Ambient Occlusion rendering in Blender.) Inspired by the general shape of this, you may want to put it on a special landform in this project; the Sensory Space was centered on a "spiral jetty" in the Alchemy Sims Grid, as shown in Figure 7.6. The grayscale height map texture used for this island is provided in the content for this chapter as well.

Now that you have your Sensory Space situated on your terrain, let's look at your new environment in various WindLight settings to see what looks best. For the purposes of this project, the default midnight setting in WindLight was used, because it enhanced the visual effects of the star particles and lighting. Feel free to experiment with other settings in WindLight, found in the World/Photo and Video/Phototools menu under the WL tab.

Also, some manipulation of the materials and features of this object will add some nice effects without much effort. Try making the Sensory Space its own light source so the interior spaces take on some more definition. You can do this in the Build menu by selecting the Sensory Space, and checking the Edit Linked

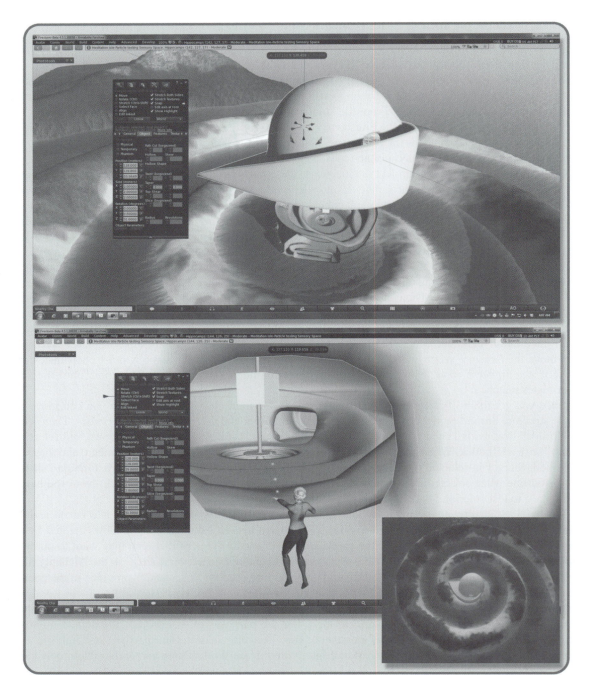

FIGURE 7.6 Screen grabs from Alchemy Sims Grid showing assembly of the Sensory Space (top image), alignment of the inner and outer shells (bottom image), and layout on the sim with a "spiral island" land form (inset image-bottom right).

box. That will allow you to select the inside section only. When you have it selected, go to the Features tab of Build menu, and check the Light box. Make it take on a nice 10-meter light glow that is not overpowering but adds a spirit of light to the interior. Now add in a slight surface glow to the interior section by changing the Texture settings in the Build menu, when you have that part selected. A glow of 0.05 adds just a nice ambient light feel to the surfaces inside and augments the effect of making the inner section into a light source. You should try changing the Texture color to a light purple and Shininess (specular) to low, so the inside, like a real shell, takes on a nice iridescent tone.

7.7.2 Creating Particle Emitters, Lights, and Making Them Move

Now, let's set up a primary particle generator that can be modified and augmented with other features. Utilizing the star research from our Hubble Telescope for inspiration, a star-shaped particle is made as a layered PNG file. Figure 7.7 shows the layered file and how the star is made as a white shape on a clear background. Note that, for visual clarity, the image is shown with a black background in the screen grab of the Photoshop interface. Included in the content you should upload for this project are the particle textures: Galaxy_gobo_black.png, and Star_particle_final.png. Later on, when you are making your own particle images, remember no particle image should be larger than 512 × 512 pixels.

Once you have uploaded your star particle texture, the next step is to drop it into the content of a cylinder prim and add in the LSL script shown in Figure 7.7 and Table 7.3. You will find this script in its LSL format, named "VWD_book_Project Particle Script," in the Chapter 7 download content. Open this in a text based document like WordPad, select and copy it onto your clipboard, and paste it into a New Script inside the contents of the cylinder prim. Save and close the Script Editor menu showing the new script in the cylinder.

Once you drop the script in the cylinder and it starts up, you will see that these particles are moving upward, expanding in a narrow explode pattern, scaling up, starting at full opacity, and ending with less opacity. They are being generated at a set rate per second and living for a certain number of seconds. They are forming a little distance out from the center of the prim and accelerating in the z direction. The wind is masked, but the emission is on, so they are going to be bright inside dark surroundings and will not move according to the winds.

Once you have made a particle prim and it is generating stars nicely, you can duplicate it and modify it to make a whole particle-emitting structure for use inside the Sensory Space. Remember that, for good building practices and to lower the script load on the server, you should delete the particle scripts from prims once you get them running; the particles will keep flowing. However, you will not be able to adjust them since you have deleted the script, so save this step for last and make a copy of the structure for your inventory, just in case. If you need to adjust the particle flow in a prim from which you have cleared the script, just drop the script back into the prim again and save it.

Once you have the cylinder giving particles in the pattern you want, select it, and hold the Shift key down while you drag it over to clone it and then change the shape into a sphere. Do this a few more times and arrange the spheres into a "planetary" system around the center cylinder; change the scale a bit on these spheres to give some visual variety. In Figure 7.8, you will see how this is done, and as you can see, each prim is emitting particles just like its fellow clones.

Now, in the Build/Texture menu, change the surface texture to "blank" (to remove the plywood texture) and color each one of the "planets" a different color. Red, yellow, green, and blue were chosen for this project. Once you know the color of the sphere, add some glow under the Textures tab (0.2 is fine), and, in the Build/Feature section, make it a light source with the same color light. Set each light as Intensity = 1.0, Radius = 10 meters, and Falloff = 0.5. Also, go into the particles script of each prim and change the particle

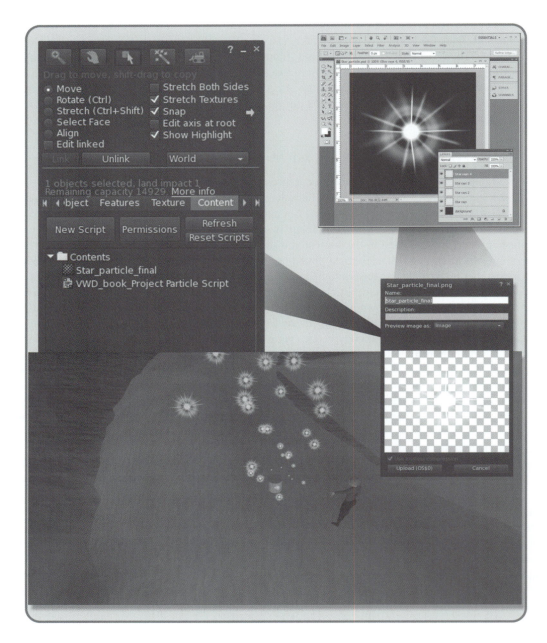

FIGURE 7.7 Screen grabs that show the process for making a star particle texture. In the top right corner, the star texture is made as a layered PNG file, in white with a clear background (the black background was added for clarity of the illustration, but turned off when the file was saved). In the top left image, the texture called "Star_particle_final" is added to the contents of the emitter prim, along with the "VWD_book_Project Particle Script" LSL script. The middle right image shows the particle as it appears inworld on your viewer, and the bottom image shows the star particles being emitted from the prim as the script runs.

TABLE 7.3
WWD_book_Project Particle Script—Chapter 7 Project

Line#	LSL Code or Comments
0	//Copy and paste everything here into an EMPTY Second Life or OpenSim Script!
1	//This script is based on the Basic Particles Script available at the Particle Lab, in Second Life
2	//Usage: Paste into an empty new script and click (save), to create an 'always on' particle effect.
3	
4	default {
5	state_entry() {
6	llParticleSystem([
7	PSYS_SRC_TEXTURE, llGetInventoryName(INVENTORY_TEXTURE, 0), //or "TEXTURE-ASSET-UUID-KEY",
8	PSYS_PART_START_SCALE, <0.01, 0.01, 0.0>, PSYS_PART_END_SCALE, <1.5, 1.5, 0.0>,
9	PSYS_PART_START_COLOR, <1.0, 1.0, 1.0>, PSYS_PART_END_COLOR, <0.0, 1.0, 0.0>,
10	PSYS_PART_START_ALPHA, 1.0, PSYS_PART_END_ALPHA, 0.25,
11	PSYS_SRC_BURST_PART_COUNT, 5,
12	PSYS_SRC_BURST_RATE, 1.0,
13	PSYS_PART_MAX_AGE, 8.0,
14	PSYS_SRC_MAX_AGE, 0.0,
15	PSYS_SRC_PATTERN, PSYS_SRC_PATTERN_EXPLODE,//or _DROP, _ANGLE, _ANGLE_CONE
16	PSYS_SRC_ACCEL, <0.0, 0.0, 0.2>,
17	PSYS_SRC_BURST_RADIUS, 0.5,
18	PSYS_SRC_BURST_SPEED_MIN, 0.1, PSYS_SRC_BURST_SPEED_MAX, 0.3,
19	//PSYS_SRC_ANGLE_BEGIN, 45*DEG_TO_RAD,
20	//PSYS_SRC_ANGLE_END, 45*DEG_TO_RAD
21	//PSYS_SRC_OMEGA, < 0.0, 0.0, 0.0 >,
22	//PSYS_SRC_TARGET_KEY, llGetLinkKey(llGetLinkNum() + 1),
23	PSYS_PART_FLAGS, (0
24	|PSYS_PART_INTERP_COLOR_MASK
25	|PSYS_PART_INTERP_SCALE_MASK
26	|PSYS_PART_EMISSIVE_MASK
27	//|PSYS_PART_FOLLOW_VELOCITY_MASK
28	//|PSYS_PART_WIND_MASK
29	//|PSYS_PART_BOUNCE_MASK
30	//|PSYS_PART_FOLLOW_SRC_MASK
31	//|PSYS_PART_TARGET_POS_MASK
32	//|PSYS_PART_TARGET_LINEAR_MASK
33	)]);
34	}
35	}
36	

FIGURE 7.8   Screen grab showing the creation of sphere prims around the cylinder for the particle "planetary system."

color "PSYS_PART_END_COLOR" to match the color of the sphere. For instance, in the bright red sphere, this change will generate particles that start white and end up bright red.

Remember in the color menu of Firestorm that there is a converter, so you can change the RGB values into the percentages that the LSL particle script code needs, and they give a handy button that will copy these values to your clipboard, so you can paste the numbers into your script in place of the number that is already there. The red sphere code line would read PSYS_PART_START_COLOR, <1,1,1>, PSYS_PART_END_COLOR, <1,0,0>.

The final thing to do in this section is to link these elements together and move them into the Sensory Space. To do this, select all the planets first, holding the Shift key down so they are selected collectively, and then select the cylinder as shown in Figure 7.9. Pick the Link button on the Build/Edit top menu. The planets should have blue halos, and the cylinder will have a yellow halo, indicating that they are linked and the cylinder is the key prim.

If you have more questions or need a more detailed description about linking prims, that is available online (http://community.secondlife.com/t5/English-Knowledge-Base/Build-Tools/ta-p/700039).

You are in the home stretch! Take this linked structure into your inventory as a backup. Rez a copy on the ground near the front door of the Sensory Space and move it into the center of the inner space. Orient the cylinder around the center column of the Sensory Space, and when it's set, change the texture on just that part into a 100% transparency, so it disappears. You will see the light sources from the spheres affect the internal walls of the space immediately, especially if you have your graphics levels set up in High or Ultra.

Figure 7.10 is a view of this setup of the planetary system inside the Sensory Space model. For even greater visual effects, you can do these two additional things: (1) add a spin script into the cylinder to make the whole particle/planetary system rotate around the center column and (2) turn on the advanced lighting (sun, moon, and projectors) and change the lights into projectors that use the Galaxy_gobo_black texture to project a star image on the surrounding surfaces. This additional texture is included in the Chapter 7 content.

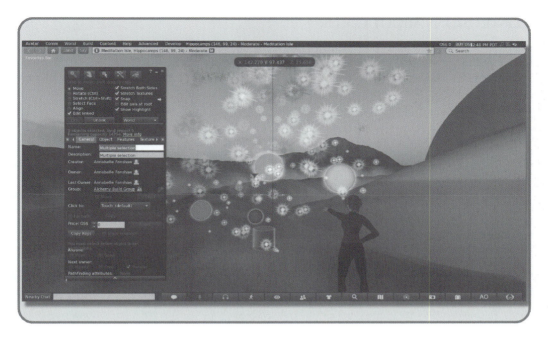

FIGURE 7.9 Screen grab showing result of making the particle emitting prims into light sources, coloring their texture, and linking them to the central cylinder.

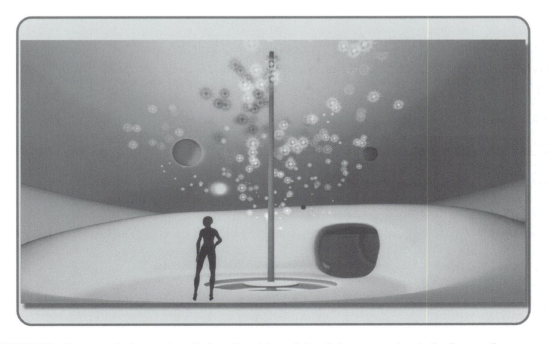

FIGURE 7.10 Screen grab showing installation of particle-emitting, light source prims in the Sensory Space.

7.8 CONCLUSIONS ABOUT COLOR

Colors and particle systems are two of the most magical elements in a virtual environment. Both add dynamism and depth to the visitors' experience in a virtual space. Both can be used to support and enhance the impact of your client's message. Becoming a "power user" with color and particles is one of the perks of being a designer. Enjoy it.

REFERENCES

1. Particle System, Wikipedia article, http://en.wikipedia.org/wiki/Particle_system. Accessed April 7, 2013.
2. Young-Helmholtz Theory, Wikipedia article, http://en.wikipedia.org/wiki/Young%E2%80%93Helmholtz_theory. Accessed April 5, 2013.
3. Linguistic Relativity and the Color Naming Debate, Wikipedia article, http://en.wikipedia.org/wiki/Linguistic_relativity_and_the_color_naming_debate. Accessed April 22, 2013.
4. MacEvoy, Do Primary Colors Exist? *Color Vision* blog, http://www.handprint.com/HP/WCL/color6.html#materialtrichromacy. Accessed April 17, 2013.
5. Subtractive Color, Wikipedia article, http://en.wikipedia.org/wiki/Subtractive_color. Accessed April 7, 2013.
6. Tertiary Color, Wikipedia article, http://en.wikipedia.org/wiki/Tertiary_color. Accessed April 7, 2013.
7. Global Illumination Wikipedia article, http://en.wikipedia.org/wiki/Global_illumination. Accessed April 7, 2013.
8. Khouw, Natilia, Gender Differences—The Meaning of Color for Gender, *Color Matters*, http://www.colormatters.com/color-symbolism/gender-differences. Accessed April 15, 2013.
9. Fields, R. Douglas, Why We Prefer Certain Colors, *Psychology Today*, April 1, 2011, http://www.psychologytoday.com/blog/the-new-brain/201104/why-we-prefer-certain-colors. Accessed April 13, 2013.
10. Color Vision, Wikipedia article, http://en.wikipedia.org/wiki/Color_vision. Accessed April 15, 2013.
11. Mahnke, Frank H., and Rudolf H. Mahnke, Characteristics and Effects of Major Hues, in *Color and Light in Man-made Environments,* Chapter 2, Location 166, 209, 217, 231, 1222, Wiley, New York, 1993.
12. Color Blindness, Wikipedia article, http://en.wikipedia.org/wiki/Color_blindness. Accessed April 20, 2013.
13. Light and Space, Wikipedia article, http://en.wikipedia.org/wiki/Light_and_Space. Accessed June 21, 2013.

8 Lighting in Virtual Environments
Second Life and OpenSim

It is still color, it is not yet light.

—**Pierre Bonnard**

8.1 LIGHTING IS CRUCIAL

Light is the great transmitter that slips through the tiniest aperture, carrying crucial information about form, texture, and color to our brains. Light is also a transcendent medium of emotional cognition, providing us with a daily spectrum of visual moods and meanings. For these reasons and some more you are about to discover, lighting is a crucial element of great design.

8.2 THREE MAIN JOBS THAT LIGHTING HAS TO DO

In a nutshell, there are three basic things that lighting should do within a virtual environment. However you structure the arrangement of these lights or change the materials on your forms and no matter how complex the environmental structures or characters, your lighting must (1) illuminate the meaning (or purpose) of this environment, (2) support the mood(s), and (3) augment the visual style. Let's go into the details of how lighting does that.

8.2.1 ILLUMINATING THE MEANING (OR PURPOSE) OF YOUR VIRTUAL ENVIRONMENT

One of the most interesting things to do is to design lighting that illuminates the meaning or purpose of your virtual environment. To do this, you will need to find the key concept. In fact, that concept may be a "moving target" in the early developmental stages of your project. What you are looking for is one or two key words that will anchor your lighting design to a solid conceptual foundation from which you can create a dynamic lighting structure throughout the environment.

Let's look at three very different environments: your high school cafeteria, the center ring of a circus, and the interior settings of a film by Stanley Kubrick (1928–1999) called *Barry Lyndon* (1975, produced by Warner Brothers). Just now, these examples probably created three wildly different images in your imagination. Let's break them down into descriptive components, emotive aspects, and key concepts so we can understand what lighting might contribute to the environment.

Use your visuospatial sketchpad to call up memories and think about describing your high school cafeteria. Quite possibly, it was a large, open space organized by the various levels of social status within the school. In many ways, it was like the throne room of a castle, full of courtiers and court members surrounding the royalty. The nerds and geeks (courtiers/advisors to the royalty) sat with each other, the cheerleaders and athletes (royalty) sat together, and the unpopular and unattached (court members) mingled randomly. You might choose *hierarchy* as your key word in the concept for this scenario.

What about the center ring of a circus? Standing in the center of that area, one is the focus of the audience's attention and yet is all alone. It is where you face your inner stuff and show the audience that you have the skills to entertain them. You have seen many examples of people being in the "center ring," someone delivering an impassioned speech, someone defending a dissertation, or perhaps someone just standing in the middle of Grand Central Station, isolated by a shaft of light that comes in from the upper windows. It is possible that the key word for your lighting concept is *isolation*.

In the movie *Barry Lyndon*, the main theme is about the attraction of a man to his own destruction, like that of a moth to a flame. Barry Lyndon, the character, is driven to choose that which ultimately destroys all he loves [1]. In the interior scenes, the light is actually candlelight, which is used extensively throughout the movie to support the look of the historical period while casting a warm glow overall. The shadows take on as much meaning as the light in these chiaroscuro scenes, so you might decide that the key words for this lighting concept are *obscured truth*.

What key word and concepts formed in your mind? Each of these environments has many aspects to its meaning; there are no right or wrong choices. The best choice is a meaningful concept that supports your lighting design efforts by helping you organize and focus the look of your overall lighting plan in the virtual environment. Once you find this, you can associate colors, patterns, and styles of lighting fixtures with it to create a cohesive plan for the lighting on the design of your virtual environment.

8.2.2 Support the Mood or Emotion of the Environment

The classic way to learn about how lighting supports the mood of an environment is to study the great painters. Artists such as Artemisia Gentileschi (1593–1656), Johannes Vermeer (1632–1675), and Rembrandt van Rijn (1606–1669) created images that conveyed mood through the arrangement of light and shadow on the subject matter. Each painting has a personal mood to convey. Study the flare of light capturing the anger and violence in *Judith Slaying Holofernes* (ca. 1614–1620) by Gentileschi, the longing and precious tenderness in the luminance of *Girl with a Pearl Earring* (ca. 1665) by Vermeer, or the mystery conveyed by the facial shadows in *Rembrandt: Self Portrait* (ca. 1660). The baroque, neoclassic, romantic, impressionistic, and post-impressionistic art periods are full of examples that have inspired generations of lighting designers.

8.2.3 Augment the Visual Style of the Project

There are several ways that lighting can augment the visual style of the structures in a virtual environment. Once you know what kind of environments you will be lighting, whether a medieval castle or a jazz club, you should plan to coordinate your lighting of the environment with the existing architectural lighting fixtures or add them yourself. At this point, decisions need to be made regarding the actual style of lighting fixture and what kind of light it would most likely generate. For instance, in today's world, it is entirely possible that the interior of a castle could be lit with fluorescent lighting, although it is hoped not. A jazz club could be underwater and lit with the glow of deep-sea creatures. To make these finer artistic choices based in the combined knowledge of historical period, décor, and lighting, you need to do some research. Even if the environment is from a time period far into the future, there is some sort of imagery, either pictorial or literary, that will give you a sense of what the lighting fixtures would be. Our civilization has progressed from campfires and oil lamps, to electric lights, fluorescent bulbs, and LEDs (light-emitting diodes). Each of those types of lighting has its own specific range of color, intensity, and movement, and each can be used in ways that support the meaning, mood, and narrative of your virtual environment.

8.3 SPECTRUMS, COLOR, AND LIGHT

Sunlight travels to us in a spectrum of wavelengths that are revealed in numerous ways. We see color on objects because the surface reflects that wavelength back at us and absorbs all other wavelengths (i.e., a red ball only sends red wavelengths back to our eyes). When we put a piece of blue glass or gel in front of a stage light, the light beam is blue because the colored filter absorbs all the other wavelengths of light, letting only the blue light pass through it. Color sensitivity is wired deep in our brains because our survival depends on it. Think of stoplights and other color-coded symbols so prevalent in our lives and realize that these colors also have deep emotional connections. The color of passion or love is red, hatred is black, and envy is green. When you weave these cultural and emotional connections into your lighting design, it becomes all that more powerful. Ask yourself: Would it be possible to have a depressive orange color or a happy blue color if I needed it? Making these kinds of sophisticated lighting design choices plays against the obvious assumptions and deepens the experience for the visitor to your virtual environment.

In a virtual world, the images of the environments we light are made from a combination of the red, green, and blue diodes on the screen's surface. These computer screen diodes, interestingly enough, mimic the color-sensing cones inside our eye structure that are sensitive to red, green, and blue frequencies, respectively. When various amounts of these three colors are mixed, the entire spectrum of colored light and its colored environment can be displayed for us on the screen's surface. Figure 7.1, the components of color, shows the additive color model (lower right). There you can see how red mixed with green will create amber yellow, how red and blue will make magenta, and how green and blue will make cyan. All three together will make a white color that our eye cannot distinguish from the white color we see under full-spectrum sunlight [2].

The color of light in the real world changes throughout the day and is measured by a standard called "color temperature." This phenomenon is imitated in the Second Life WindLight system. As you can see from Figure 8.1, the color temperature and color of the light change dramatically during the arc of a virtual day. During the midday period, the light has a high color temperature number of 5,500–10,000 K (Kelvin temperature scale) and creates a "cool color" in the bluish range to our eyes (12 p.m., top picture). Conversely, sunrise and sunset lighting produces a "warm-color" or yellow-orange light to our eyes but has a low color temperature number of 2000–3000 K.

The color temperature changes that we see during the course of our day are something worth considering when we design lighting for a virtual world such as Second Life and OpenSim. The WindLight system found in Second Life and Open Sim are useful design tools. They are always running in the default cycle unless you have set your virtual land to a fixed sky or you have designed a specific WindLight setting for your virtual environment and ask that your visitors utilize it in their viewers. Because this system affects the work of designers, artists, and photographers, learning how to manage the color temperature of the WindLight settings is of paramount importance. Note, LightShare is the OpenSim term for WindLight.

8.4 SPACE TO COLOR TO LIGHT: FORMING A LIGHTING METHODOLOGY

Developing a strong, efficient methodology for lighting your virtual environment comes from the practice of observing space and relating it to your decisions about illuminating the meaning, supporting the mood, and augmenting the visual style.

Ask this question: What kind of lighting progression is needed in this space, and how will it support the meaning and mood? Of course, in virtual environments, this can vary wildly. A first-person shooter game needs a progression of illumination that supports the game play by allowing the player to find the

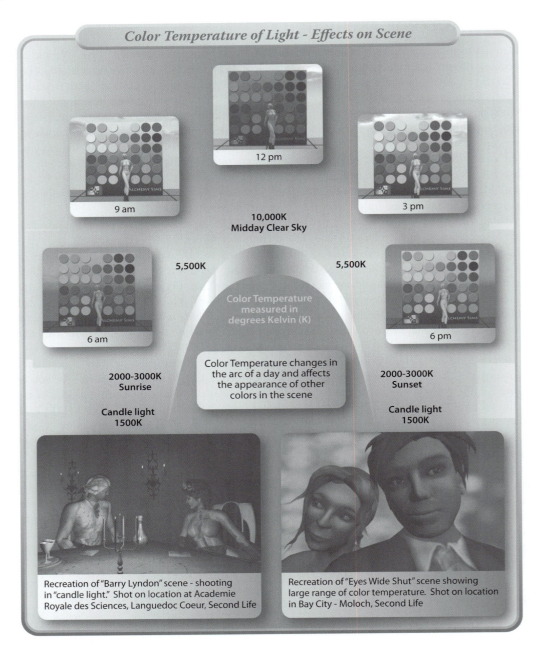

FIGURE 8.1 (See color insert) Chart showing how the color temperature of virtual light effects the look of a virtual environment. These frame grabs from Second Life show how the color temperature of virtual light changes throughout the day cycle. These observations can be compared to the physical world color temperature scale in the middle. In the lower section, two scenes from Stanley Kubrick's films "Barry Lyndon" and "Eyes Wide Shut" have been re-created to display how color temperature in a virtual scene can be manipulated for machinima just as it was for these films.

enemy, feel the ambiance of the space, and witness the effects of weapon fire. A virtual environment that emulates a spiritual retreat, such as a monastery, needs to create a progression of enlightenment—both visually and emotionally. In a virtual environment that is being used to stage a theatrical presentation, you may have a script with lighting cues to work from or the patterns of a dance performance to follow with your lighting progression.

Once you have organized your thoughts regarding the kind of lighting and are comfortable with your lighting plan and its capacity to support meaning, mood, and style, you need to document the actual position and settings of the lights before you decide how they will be sequenced in time. A theatrical lighting designer would call this a "light plot" and would create a drawing by cross-referencing the location of the circuits overhead with the stage setting below. From that information, the designer would make a "magic sheet," which is a simple one-page illustration utilizing various symbols to represent the location of lights and circuits being used. You also can do this for virtual environments. Take an overhead screenshot of the virtual landscape or building you are lighting. Bring that picture into your 2D graphics program and make an overlay that indicates the position of each light with a number. Next to that, in a table format, record the position (x, y, z), the light color and brightness, focus, and other settings for each light so you have a quick organized reference sheet. Figure 8.2 provides one example of how you can set up this magic sheet for yourself.

By utilizing a magic sheet, you are able to quickly set up the illumination ranges on the lights in your environment and design the optimal pattern for them along the visitor's or game player's path. As your visitor travels through the environment, the lights will come on and go out in a progression relative to your avatar's camera and the draw distance the visitor has set up for his or her computer.

8.5 THE THREE BASIC ELEMENTS INVOLVED IN LIGHTING A SCENE: LIGHTS, SHADERS, AND BAKING

The three main elements involved with lighting a virtual environment are light sources (inworld objects or geometry); shaders, textures and materials that affect the surface appearance of objects to make them appear to be shiny, transparent, glowing, and the like; and "baked lighting," which is the creation of a texture with the lighting prerendered on it, sort of like "painting" the light and shadow onto a surface of your objects in a scene. Let's explore.

8.5.1 Light Sources and Their Characteristics

Because Second Life and OpenSim use the OpenGL standard, the overall limit on light sources is 8 and two of them are reserved for the Sun and Moon. The rendering of lighting is handled by your graphics card, so results may vary from computer to computer. In Second Life and OpenSim, there are two basic types of lights: the point light, which emits light in all directions like a light bulb, and the projector, which works like a spotlight and gives off a cone or frustum of light. Both of these are made from setting the parameters of the basic building element, the prim or object. For instance, you could have a prim that is shaped like a hat that emits light in all directions (point light) or a prim shaped like a rock that projects a beam with a pattern onto a surface nearby. If you have lots of prims available on your land, then feel free to create a whole set of lighting prims; if you are getting short on server capacity for them, then look for ways to make your building walls, furniture, and even landscaping objects do double duty and serve as light sources.

Number of Light	Type of Light- Point, SP or Projector Area or Direct	Position of Light on Region in x,y,z coordinates	Color of light in RGB/LSL percentages	Range of Light in Diameter (meters)	Script in light	Type of prim that is light source	Notes
1	Point	73,38,40	1,1,1	20	no	Middle of fountain	Gradual Color Change
2	Point	72,68,40	1,1,1	20	no	Middle of fountain	Gradual Color Change
3	Point	40,71,40	1,1,1	20	no	Middle of fountain	Gradual Color Change
4	Point	39,39,40	1,1,1	20	no	Middle of fountain	Gradual Color Change
5	Spot (SP)	187,109,40	1,0,0	50	Yes, rotation	Cube (100% transparent)	Make slower
6	Spot (SP)	204,186,40	0,1,0	50	Yes, rotation	Cube (100% transparent)	Make static
7	Spot (SP)	205,207,40	0,0,1	50	Yes, rotation	Cube (100% transparent)	Make faster

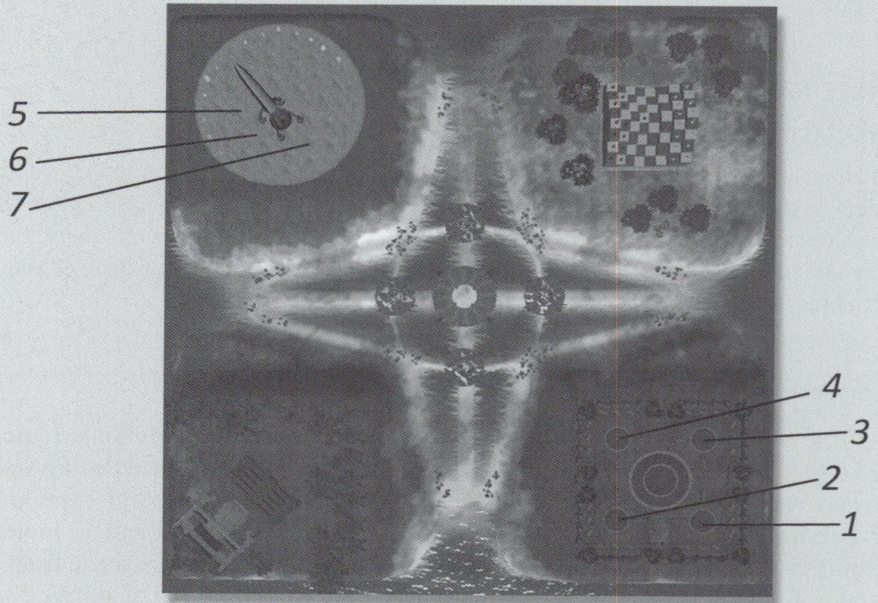

FIGURE 8.2 Chart showing the components of a "Magic Sheet." In the top half, the lights are identified by name, location, color, range, scripting, type of source, and given special notes, if necessary. In the lower half is a schematic map, showing where each of these lights are placed on the sim.

8.5.2 SHADERS AND TEXTURES AND HOW THEY MAKE MATERIALS

Now, if you remember that the color on the surface of an object occurs because it holds on to all the other wavelengths and only lets you see the color wavelength of the material, you are beginning to understand how shaders work. This kind of selective specificity extends to all manner of surface properties in a virtual world, and by controlling them you can affect the quality of "perceived" light in a scene. Imagine the difference in a sphere that looks like blue felt versus a sphere that looks like blue glass. Because of the soft surface on a felt sphere, you may not actually be able to see a highlight on the surface, and the lighting would seem general and diffuse, as if from an overhead fluorescent panel. On the glass sphere, you may see very bright highlights on the surface, showing you the positions of all the lights around it. These extreme examples are to make the point that the choices you make in the properties of the surfaces on your objects in a virtual environment are a vital part of the lighting design. In virtual environments, all of the 3D surfaces are covered with materials or shaders.

Just so you have a clear understanding of the terms and there is no confusion between the term *shader* and the related terms of *texture* and *material*, let's look at the differences in meanings for this terminology.

8.5.2.1 Defining Shaders, Textures, and Materials in Second Life and OpenSim

1. A shader defines the look of a surface of an object. Shaders make up the underlying surface of a material without color or just a basic color tint. They have little "character" other than how shiny, transparent, or smooth they make the surface of a prim or object look.
2. Textures can be added to the shaders to make a surface take on more detailed characteristics such as wood grain, mineral flecks, or animal skin coloring.
3. Materials are the combination of textures and shaders and can be stored on prims in Second Life or OpenSim as shown in Figure 8.3. The menu for creating them is found under the Texture tab of the Build/Edit menu.

Beautiful models covered with "baked" or prelit textures are almost indistinguishable from models lit with real-time light. The limitation to this process is that your shadows are static and especially noticeable if you have any moving lights or a sun/moon cycle. A walk down the street on a sunny day will show you how highlights move across the surfaces as you change your point of view and how shadows move in response to changes in the lighting in the environment.

8.6 ENVIRONMENTAL MENUS AND SHADERS IN SECOND LIFE AND OPENSIM

Shaders in Second Life and OpenSim are influenced by the Graphics settings controlled by Firestorm. The environmental settings you see in the Avatar/Preferences/Graphics menu when you have the quality set as medium or higher include shaders such as Lighting/Shadows and Ambient Occlusion. These Advanced Lighting shaders greatly affect the look of the materials in the world, as you can see in the lower panel of Figure 8.3, and they are in turn affected by the WindLight settings of the entire environment. In Second Life and OpenSim, after you have applied shaders such as transparency, glow, shininess, and bump textures to an object, you can then universally affect the appearance of your water, land, sky, and all the objects on it with the choice of different overall settings in the Avatar/Preferences/Graphics menu and in the World/Environment/Editor/Environment settings menu.

Compare the two menus so that you understand how they differ and overlap in functioning. In Figure 8.4, you can see the Advanced Lighting and Shader controls under the Avatar/Preferences/Graphics tab. Below it is the World/Environmental Editor/Environmental Settings menu, where you can customize your sky and water environments and the overall lighting of the scene.

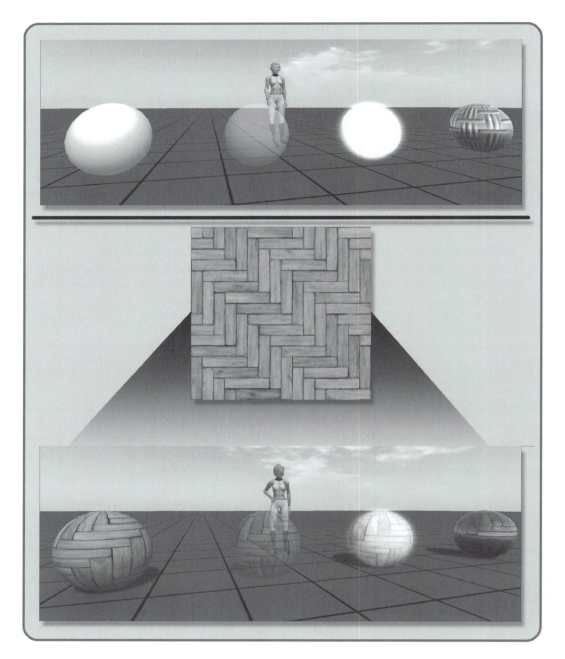

FIGURE 8.3   Screen grabs from OpenSim showing a comparison of four spheres with the following shader/material effects: (1) blank texture/white color, (2) 50% transparency, (3) 0.01 glow, and (4) low shine with bump map (top panel). Also shown are the same four spheres with a herringbone parquet wood texture (bottom panel). This texture is utilized as a bump map in the shiny sphere at the far right of the lower panel. The spheres in the lower panel are shown with the highest level of advanced lighting with real time shadows and ambient occlusion turned on.

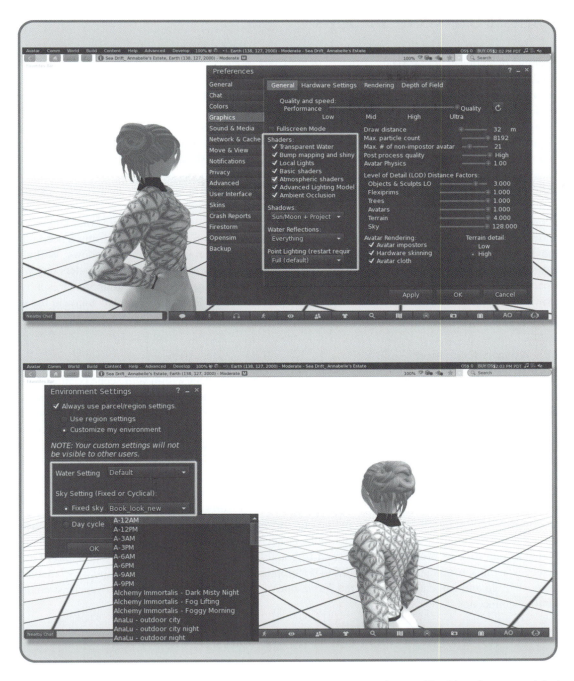

FIGURE 8.4 Screen shots from OpenSim. The top image shows the Avatar/Preferences/Graphics tab menu, and the bottom image shows the World/Environmental Editor/Environmental Settings menu. Both of these menus are crucial to creating lighting, shadow, and color temperature effects in your virtual environments.

8.7 THE IMPORTANCE OF SHADOWS

Understanding shadows and their importance is crucial to lighting design. Shadows tell us what the shape and volume of an object are by the gradation of light to dark along the object's surface; shadows tell us where the location of an object is by their angle and shape on the surrounding surfaces and ground plane, and they reveal the detail of a surface texture when we are close to an object. Shadows also support the emotional dimension of a scene; they help to convey the message and mood just as powerfully as the light does.

How do we see shadows from lights in a virtual environment? Simply put, in a computer rendering a real-time display of geometry with lighting on it, the most common way real-time shadows are created is from a "shadow map" and the application of that map to the scene [3]. Much more is happening of course; your computer is making several calculations, creating a depth buffer, and comparing the locations between lights and objects. Control over the look of shadows, whether real-time or baked into the textures, is available in varying degrees to the lighting designer of a virtual world. Each person visiting your virtual environment may have the menu to activate the real-time shadows for his or her screen viewer, but some may choose not to because his or her computer's graphics system lacks the capacity to display them. This creates a need for you as the designer to make the important decision regarding how your project will show shadows. Will all the shadows be baked in, or will you rely on people to come by with their real-time shadow shaders on? Which approach supports the look of your design in the strongest way? Sometimes, the best approach is a hybrid shadow plan. Use baked shadow textures on architectural details and let visitors know to augment the scene themselves by putting on the advanced lighting system if there is the capacity to view it.

8.7.1 AMBIENT OCCLUSION

As described in Chapter 6, another sort of "shadow" effect that can occur within your scene is called ambient occlusion. This type of shading adds the effect of soft shadows and shades of gray in areas that are occluded or blocked from a source of global illumination. Imagine what your street looks like at noon on an overcast day. None of the shadows are hard edged or dark; they are soft and blurred and directly under most over-hanging objects rather than being cast out onto the street surface. This kind of shadowing is not created by calculating from a single light source; it is created by calculating from an area light that spreads through the scene. Soft shadows appear where spaces are blocked by objects, such as the area behind the pillows on a couch or the floor under a sofa. Ambient occlusion is a favorite rendering effect for 3D model makers because it adds depth to the surface of a model and can be baked into textures [4].

In Figure 6.22 (top panel), you see an image of a virtual warehouse while it was being built in Blender. You can clearly see the textures showing its ambient occlusion shadows and shading. This effect can also be added in real time to your scenes in Second Life and OpenSim through the Firestorm Viewer Graphic Preferences menu. Currently, ambient occlusion is a graphics-processing intensive or "expensive" method for creating shading and can cause "lag" in the frame rate of the image unless you have a superfast computer and online connection.

8.8 HELP YOUR DESIGN LOOK GREAT IN ALL SORTS OF LIGHTING

With every generation of graphic processing cards, the world of 3D graphics shown to you in video games and virtual worlds includes more lighting and shadow effects that are rendered in real time. Viewer settings, computer graphics card capacity, Internet bandwidth, complexity of the geometry in the scene—all affect the actual frame rate that the observer or game player will experience in an online world.

8.8.1 Making Sure Your Lighting Is Seen

Because you are a diligent designer and want your project to look its best, you should plan from the very beginning to test the performance on all sorts of platforms and under various conditions. Remember to consider the slower machines your audience or visitors may use. In Second Life and OpenSim, take a look at your environment using the various types of draw ranges and quality settings in the Preferences/Graphics menu. It also behooves you to look at your scene under a variety of WindLight (or LightShare) settings in Second Life or OpenSim because people visiting your build will do that.

8.8.2 Per Vertex Lighting versus Per Pixel Lighting

As you seek to pack more detail and "realism" into your scene with numerous complex materials/shaders and lots of light sources, the demand on the graphics processor starts to elevate. This is especially the case if your scene is being rendered as "per pixel," meaning that the level of illumination is being calculated for each pixel on the screen. With this approach, creation of the rendered image becomes "expensive" in terms of processing resources. While some of the high-powered game engines like Unreal, CryENGINE, and Frostbite Engine can utilize this form of lighting, most other game and 3D world engines need to have another option. The use of "per vertex" lighting, which calculates the illumination at the vertex and then interpolates the color/shading across the surface until it reaches the next vertex, is much more economical in terms of system resources. This type of lighting is also known as Gouraud shading and is a common feature in most 3D modeling software [5]. In Second Life and OpenSim, you can make your objects take on a richer look by combining the basic default lighting with shader settings and special textures with baked in lighting. Also consider exploration of the newer material settings that utilize bump maps and specular maps, as it will provide even greater latitude in your lighting design.

8.9 PROJECT: LIGHTING THREE BASIC SCENES

The best way to learn about lighting and how to light something, or someone, is to do it. This project will help you create three of the most basic scenarios in lighting: a portrait/daylight scene, a large night scene with an avatar, and a still life or "product shot."

The first thing you should do is make sure that all ambient light in your real environment, the room around your computer, is off or very low so you have the best view of how the lights are being displayed in your scene. Put a small light behind your monitor so that it shines only on your keyboard from below the monitor's frame if you need to see the keys more clearly. Having a keyboard with lit keys is useful in this situation. Also make sure you have turned your render settings up as high as they can go, in Avatar/Preferences/Graphics under the General tab. You should have the Advanced Lighting Model and Ambient Occlusion boxes checked for on. Turn down your draw distance if this drives your computer into a frenzy.

8.9.1 Lighting for a Portrait of an Avatar in a Daytime Outdoor Environment

As a designer, you will need to illustrate how your client's visitors will look in the environment you are building for them. One simple way is to show the avatar within the environment in a flattering light. In Figure 8.5, the avatar is showing how she looks while visiting Wheely Island at sunset. The sky is deeply colored as the custom WindLight setting "Shambala" has the Sun/Moon color set at orange, and this strongly colored light is showing on the screen left side of the avatar's face.

FIGURE 8.5 Screen shots showing "Portrait Lighting" for an avatar. Top left image shows the Atmosphere settings for the Shambala sunset lighting, top right image shows light position for the main (key) light, and bottom image shows the resulting light on the face of the avatar.

To practice this lighting step, find a scenic spot for your avatar and open up the Phototools menu (under the World/Photo and Video tab on the top bar). On the main menu that appears, look under the WL (WindLight) tab for your sky settings. Select a new sky preset and create a new sky setting in the menu panel that appears. Name your new WindLight setting "Portrait Light" and adjust the Sun/Moon color (S/M color) and Ambient colors to cast a warm, orangy sunset color on the scene. In the project example, these settings were (R=1.000, G=0.500, B=0.000) for the Sun color, and (R=0.192, G=0.152, B=0.152) for the Ambient setting, defined in LSL color enumeration in the color picker. With the LSL settings in the color picker, add in a deep red color, (R=0.477, G=0.000, B=0.000) for the BluHrz (Blue Horizon) and a deep blue color, (R=0.073, G=0.200, B=0.400), for the BlueDepth. These will add to the richness of the background of the sky in the scene. Feel free to slide the HazHoz (Haze Horizon), HazDen (Haze Density), DenMult (Density Multiplier), and DistMult (Distance Multiplier) around to shift the look of the sky and ambient environment until you like the look of it.

When you think you have a good background, go to the next step. To round out the sculptural aspects of the avatar's face, a front light source is added in a color matching the overall sky and ambience you just set up. The position for this kind of portrait face lighting is usually from above and pointed down at a 45° angle, from either side or sometimes both. This will bring out the sculptural qualities of most faces but can also bring out the depths of older faces. A flatter angle (one more parallel to the horizon) will soften older faces but tends to wash out the sculptural qualities. In Figure 8.5, this front light source, or "key light," gives you the sense of reflected light (off the water, perhaps) on the avatar's face. The light source and its primary focus are indicated in the right side image at the top of Figure 8.5, and in the lower panel you will see how it targets the upper right side of the face. Try toggling this light on and off to see what it is actually lighting in your scene.

Work back and forth between the WindLight settings and your face lighting. You should be able to obtain some interesting and dramatic lighting with just these simple steps.

8.9.2 Lighting for a Night Scene in a Large-Size Indoor Environment

If you want to show off a large area of the virtual environment, you will need to utilize the Sun or Moon as effectively and dramatically as possible. To achieve the dramatic moonlit night shot you see in Figure 8.6, the standard WindLight setting of Lunar Morning 7 was used for the basic environment lighting. Once you have loaded this WindLight setting in your Phototools menu, click the Edit Sky Preset button, so you can see the Atmosphere settings in it. Because Lunar Morning 7 has a low HazHoz setting, an almost pure black Ambient setting in LSL color notation (R=0.030, G=0.030, B=0.010) and an almost pure white Sun/Moon (S/M color) setting in LSL color notation (R=0.840, G=0.840, B=0.804), the moonlight comes blasting in like there is no atmosphere, creating strong shadows and highlights. To effectively show off the architectural detail of the scene, a large, soft glow called a "fill light" (casting a deep blue color of light) was added behind the avatar and raised to light the background. To accent the "moonlight" on the avatar's face, a projector light was added in the foreground, high and out of the camera framing. This white light projector was angled toward the avatar's left side, and she was turned toward it slightly, so her face would catch more light. Projectors are more difficult to focus and will cast shadows on your avatar, but the dramatic effects created are interesting. Try setting this scene up for your avatar and see if you can create a sense of drama on the background while lighting the avatar's face.

8.9.3 Lighting for a Product Shot

Sometimes, as a designer, you will be building props, furniture, or sculpture for inclusion in a virtual environment, or you may simply want to create a nice image of an object you made to sell on the Metaverse's marketplaces. In Figure 8.7, a couple of abstract chess pieces (knights) are positioned on an endless chessboard.

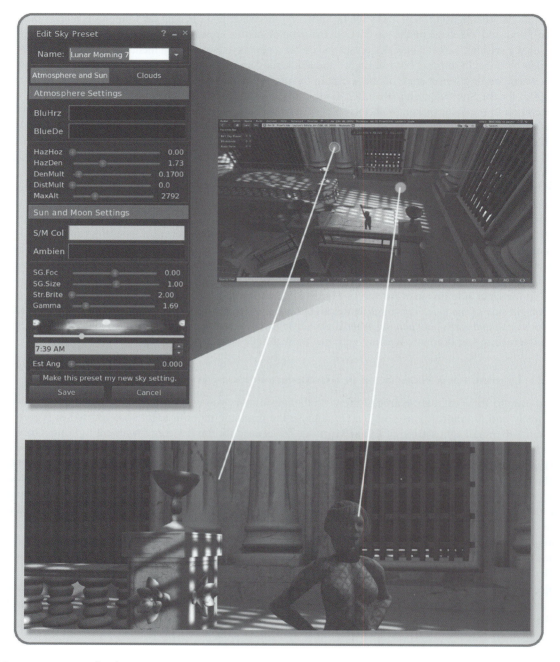

FIGURE 8.6 (See color insert) Screen shots showing lighting for a night scene inside a large indoor environment. Top left image shows the WindLight setting for Lunar Morning 7. Top right image shows positioning the background (fill) light on the left side and the front (key) light on the right side. In the bottom image, the lines point toward the targets of these lights.

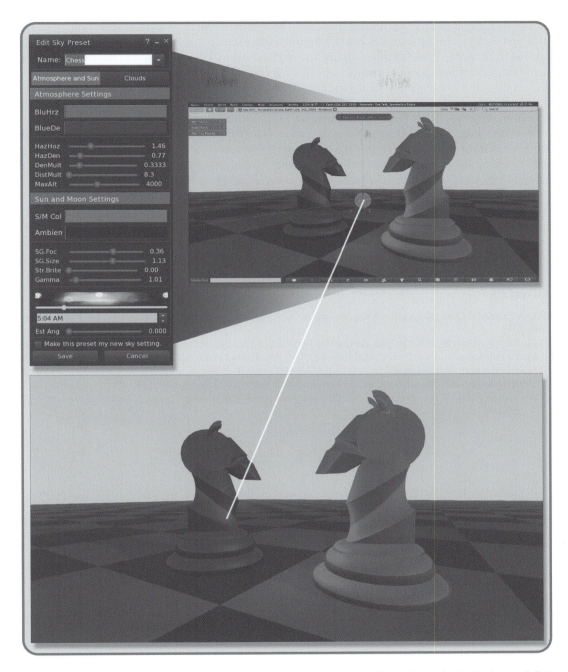

FIGURE 8.7 Screen shots of settings and lighting used in a product shot of two chess pieces. In the top left image is the Atmosphere Settings submenu from the Phototools menu and in the top right image is the composite look of the atmosphere and the product light on the chess pieces. In the bottom panel, the targeting of this product light and the final image are shown. The product light has been made transparent to hide it from the observer.

Again, the WindLight settings are adding a dramatic flair to the ambient (or overall scene) lighting. To support that and underscore the dramatic conflict between these iconic game symbols, a single point light has been added to the scene between them. Unlike the physical world, where you would have to find a place to hide a lighting instrument, you can simply make this light completely transparent, and it will hide itself from view. Even though it is completely transparent, it will still give off the light you need for the scene, and by positioning it between the pieces, it contributes to a deeper sense of reflection and space. The sense of shared light between these two chess pieces pulls them out from the background composition and draws the focus of the observer's eye. Try this setup on some of your inventory objects and strive for a clear, simple lighting design that enhances their inherent qualities and overall eye appeal. If you have made some of your lights invisible by changing their texture to 100% transparent, the easiest way to find them again is by using these three keys: Ctrl+Alt+T (on a PC) simultaneously to reveal all transparent objects.

Knowing how to light effectively is essential to any virtual environment designer. You will find these skills come in handy for presentation "sketches," detail images, sales and promotional displays, and your own portfolio. Do as much experimentation as you can, trying all sorts of WindLight settings, lights, and projectors in combination. Save your settings for the custom WindLight settings in your Phototools listings for future use. Keep looking at great paintings and try to notice the lighting around you as often as possible.

REFERENCES

1. *Barry Lyndon*—Cinematography, Wikipedia article, http://en.wikipedia.org/wiki/Barry_Lyndon. Accessed January 16, 2013.
2. Shimbun, Yomiuri, Blue Streetlights Believed to Prevent Suicides, Street Crime, *Seattle Times*, December 11, 2008, http://seattletimes.com/html/nationworld/2008494010_bluelight11.html. Accessed January 21, 2013.
3. Shadow Mapping, Wikipedia article, http://en.wikipedia.org/wiki/Shadow_mapping. Accessed January 26, 2013.
4. Ambient Occlusion, Wikipedia article, http://en.wikipedia.org/wiki/Ambient_occlusion. Accessed January 26, 2013.
5. Per-Pixel Lighting, Wikipedia article, http://en.wikipedia.org/wiki/Per-pixel_lighting. Accessed January 27, 2013.

9 Cameras and Collaborative Spaces (the Ideagora)

The camera makes everyone a tourist in other people's reality, and eventually in one's own.

—Susan Sontag

9.1 OVERVIEW OF CAMERAS, NARRATIVE, AND SOCIAL SPACES FOR MEETINGS

Forty thousand years ago, in the Paleolithic caves of Spain [1], it is possible that early humans had their first business meetings. They gathered in one special space, signed in by painting outlines of their hands, defined their goals with images of their hunting targets, and listened to what the leaders had to say about the group. Survival in a dangerous, dynamic environment was the main business in those days, as it is today. Our technology has replaced the stone cave with a CAVE (cave automatic virtual environment), our handprints are log-ins, and we watch video images of our leaders speaking. The circle around a campfire was replaced by a conference call and replaced again by a circle of avatars around a virtual campfire. You might say that not much has changed, except that now, with a virtual presence, we can attend meetings in several places simultaneously. Our modern world puts our brains under the constant pressure of assimilating many layers of information simultaneously. Day to day, we are almost always surrounded by multiple screens and immersed in a collective point of view that looks in multiple physical and temporal directions at once. Look around you when you walk down a street or in an airline terminal or even examine what is on your desktop computer. Odds are you are observing through many windows, many screens, and many cameras simultaneously, and your visual memory is filling with images that are a bricolage of daily observation, news media images, websites, and digital content. This is not just an internal phenomenon, collected in your visuospatial sketchpad. The Internet has become a social memory, creating the fabric of our collective experience and the widest-ranging evidence of our existence. Babies are born with their Facebook pages set up by their socially networked parents [2]. These children will grow with their life's memories recorded and shared socially; their personal narratives will be lived collectively with their peers and then perhaps stored and downloaded to the next generation after they are gone.

As a designer of social spaces for meetings, or the "Ideagora," you will find the these three factors are very important aspects of your design methodology.

Factor 1. The relative importance of an idea or the importance of the person presenting that idea is enhanced by the camera's point of view.

Factor 2. The observer's personal, subjective needs for involvement in the presentation will influence their choice of camera view and/or positional location during the presentation.

Factor 3. The ability of the attendees to see and hear the presentation can be influenced by the design of the meeting space.

Furthermore, the design of your meeting space must recognize your audience's desire to remain connected to their entire social network while they attend your presentation, especially if they are blogging or text reporting through Twitter or some other live report. Also, if given the opportunity to run a local chat in text while the audio/voice chat presentation is running, the audience will be commenting simultaneously, filling up a visual chat channel somewhere on the screen.

So, how do you focus the audience's attention, direct their cameras to collect the appropriate visual narrative, and allow them to connect with their networks in a meaningful supportive way? Three words define the solution: presence, affordance, and participation.

9.1.1 PRESENCE

Right now, you are probably logged in to at least one social site such as Facebook or Google+. Usually in the chat box menus, there is an indicator that shows your presence there as well as your current ability or desire to receive contact from others. This is a baseline virtual presence. From there, it ramps up, through tweets, Facebook "likes," blogs, and websites to the most important presence of all. This is known as stage presence to some, charisma or personal magnetism to others. Stage presence is a combination of direct eye contact, physical domination of the surrounding space (and this is not always directly related to your size), and the sonority of the speaking voice. Without a stage presence, the speaker's message will be lost, no matter how compelling the speaker's information is.

How do you support stage presence in a virtual meeting? There are several tools to utilize, but consider the visual first. We are visually oriented creatures, so the image of your speaker will be of paramount importance. Remember, when the speaker looks into a camera, or webcam, he or she makes direct eye contact with whoever is watching. In this way, the speaker can make direct eye contact with the entire audience simultaneously. The background behind the speaker should not be distracting or compete with the skin tones, and if possible, it should be slightly out of focus. The lighting on the face should be comfortably bright and consistent over the whole face. The speaker should not look trapped in the frame, so make sure the camera is far enough away to have a little visual space above the speaker's head. You should also consider the emotional quality of your background design and how that enhances the speaker's presence. Does it make the speaker look beautiful or nondescript, important or insignificant, competent or merely functional? If you are putting the speaker on a big screen inside a virtual world, how is that screen presented to the audience? Giving the audiences an attachable HUD (Heads-up Display) object containing streaming video of the real person speaking on camera while the person's avatar speaks in a virtual world makes for a desktop full of compelling visuals, and the device allows your audience to arrange the screen elements to their own specific preference.

If your speaker is using an avatar, does that avatar represent the speaker in a way that supports his or her message? If your speaker is using a nonhuman avatar, does your audience understand that avatar's symbolic form or why the speaker chose to be a nonhuman manifestation in the virtual space?

Now, consider the audio. Make sure the microphones work well and are adjusted far enough away from the speaker's mouth so he or she does not pop "p's" or you hear breathing. The sound of a human voice, produced clearly in a virtual space, immediately pulls the observer into the environment. When amplified and projected, a voice with a strong resonant sound can powerfully influence the experience of the audience. All of these elements, great and small, add up to creating a strong memorable presence in a virtual environment.

9.1.2 AFFORDANCE

In the physical world, affordance is the perceived and implied use of an object, or 3D space, usually indicated by its design or markings [4,5]. For instance, if you set up a half ring of chairs in a room surrounding a podium, almost everyone who looks at this arrangement would understand that people sit in the chairs to observe the central speaker's presentation. This is pretty basic, and almost universal, in terms of its meaning. What makes designing virtual meeting spaces so interesting is that you can abstract the design of these elements and still imply the same kind of affordances. If the affordances have been transmuted and abstracted and still communicate to the users of your designed environment, you have created a good design. Look around you for more abstracted affordances, and you will see them on signage, on buttons and switches, and even on web interfaces.

Once you understand how people perceive the affordances presented to them in a virtual space (the furnishings, seating arrangements, and visual screen access), you can broaden your scope. Consider the affordances defined by Dr. Janet Murray [6]. She defined the affordances in a computer medium as containing procedural, participatory, encyclopedic, and spatial qualities. If you put yourself back into the Paleolithic cave while you consider them, you can see how these four qualities have long been in existence and just subsumed by the new media.

Procedural. Early cave dwellers did not have the skills to write artificial intelligence programs, but they did have keen eyes for behavior patterns and the understanding of procedural structures. You can see that in their art, in the herds of animals drawn as they moved across the landscape, the positions of the predators and the ecologically aware hierarchies between the predators and prey. This was the procedural system of hunting described in pictures.

Participatory. Like our online social sites, the prehistoric peoples created a participatory environment, demonstrating the importance of the group by putting their handprints on the wall and by visiting and marking the caves repeatedly over long periods of time.

Encyclopedic. On their cave walls, they stored encyclopedic information, just as we do in our computer files. The walls on the caves of Lascaux appear to contain star charts, useful no doubt for determining the best time for hunting and how to navigate in the wilderness [7].

Spatial. The use of the space in prehistoric caves is notable in that it creates a 2D interface in a 3D space. Each location inside the cave gave you a different perspective on the story that was painted on the walls, and as the images danced in the firelight, the observer must have felt a sense of movement and life in those symbols. As they added cave art, the internal surface of the cave became the projection screen of their dreams and experiences.

As you design your Ideagora, think about how these four affordances can support the message of the presentation more efficiently and comprehensively in the meeting space. You are creating the place for your social group to communicate their experiences, to record information, and to develop procedural structures. For instance, how would you present a surface in your meeting space that allows for accessing websites related to the topic? This element alone could be participatory and encyclopedic. Spatially, perhaps that element can be the floor or some lower area that all can see when their cameras are in the default positions. Can you make the room smart? Where can you add some artificial intelligence to help your attendees get more out of the meeting? Finally, are the design and intent of your devices clear to all who enter the space? The most important thing about affordances is that we perceive and understand them quickly and easily in our meeting and community spaces.

9.1.3 PARTICIPATION

How can you encourage participation by the attendees at your meeting? If their smartphones and tablets are all out on the table in your real-space meeting room, and the virtual meeting room is one tab over from their

Facebook page, how do you keep them focused on the virtual meeting? Immersion is the key word here. Break through the "fourth wall," the space between the presenter and the audience, and invite attendees to enter the entire space visually and aurally. Ask them to respond to your speaker's presentation by voting, questions, or moving around the space. By immersing the audience in the presentation as a collaborative event, by putting them in a place where they can move and even make themselves into part of the presentational information, you will encourage a much higher level of engagement and participation from your audience.

For example, imagine your next physical world business meeting being held on a gymnasium floor instead of a conference room. All the team members are standing around the basketball center court circle. Every time your boss wants you to report or comment on something, he or she tosses a basketball at you. When you want to make a comment about a concurrent discussion, you have to roll a ball into the middle of the circle. If you agree with what a team member is saying, you step into the circle and prepare to receive the ball, which your team member will toss to you, allowing you to comment on the team member's discussion. If you disagree with the idea being discussed, you step out of the circle. To reenter the circle and make a comment, you are required to go to the ball rack and get another ball to roll into the center. If the speaker steps in and picks the ball up, you have the floor to air your opinions.

This example has been described to make the following points: (1) Game-like design of a meeting space enhances communication and participation; (2) the physical activity required (with your real body or your avatar's body) to engage with the information being shared sharpens your attention span; and (3) each team member's opinion on the topic is immediately known by all and shared collectively in a visual way.

Breaking your design perception away from the mindset that meeting rooms must look like their real-space counterparts allows you to invent new usage patterns for a virtual space and new ways to communicate and engage. In 2007, Drew Harry from the Massachusetts Institute of Technology Media Lab designed a non-literal conference room in Second Life that looked like a football field gradated in color from orange to green [8]. Those members of the meeting who agreed with the topic discussed were to congregate in the green end of the field, where it said "Agree," and those who disagreed were to be found at the orange end, where it was marked "Disagree." Various other tools, such as a task list and dashboard, allowed for the delegation of tasks to be assigned and accepted by participants and for the moderator to change the overall look and resultant purpose of the environment by selecting new textures for the floor. Images from Drew's designs are shown in Figure 9.1.

Fundamentally, the level of participation, when supported by the environment, increases when the environment interacts with the participants. Interactivity, when it is not complex or distracting, engages the attendees, asks them to communicate, and encourages memorable experiences.

9.2   PRESENTING AND COLLABORATING ON IDEAS IN A VIRTUAL WORLD

Let's time leap from the prehistoric era to ancient Alexandria, in the time of the famous female philosophy and mathematics professor Hypatia (ca. AD 350–370). Before her untimely death [9], this polymath taught the people of Athens about Platonic philosophy in a public space, called the agora, meaning gathering place or assembly space. Agoras were used throughout the ancient world for all kinds of meetings and political discussion. It was in the ancient agora of Athens that the concept and practice of democracy began.

We still need these places; in fact, we probably need them more now than ever before. As our capacity for communication extends itself across the globe and greater amounts of ideation flow through the Metaverse, we must have spaces where these concepts can be presented, discussed, and acted on. This virtual agora, this Ideagora, should be a place that exists without temporal restrictions (open 24/7) and is accessible to all levels of ability. It should embody the four affordances mentioned in Section 9.1.2, and it should encourage the following activities: serious games and storytelling.

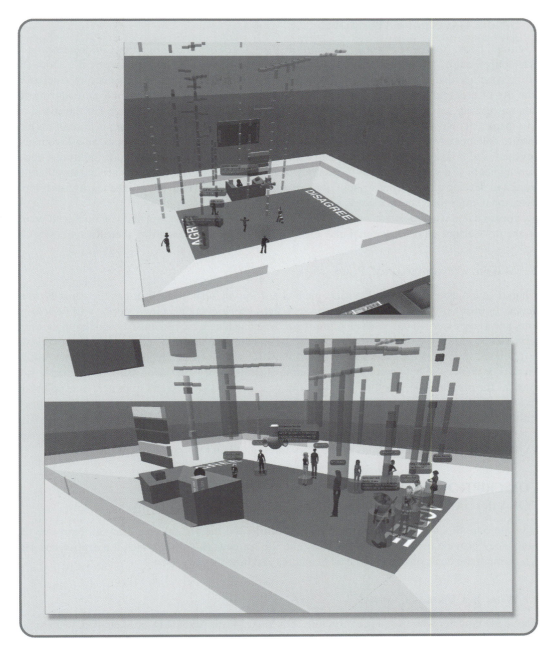

FIGURE 9.1 Drew Harry's virtual environment that explores the design possibilities for meeting spaces. Screen grabs from Second Life, showing images from "Information Spaces—Building Meeting Rooms in Virtual Environments" (https://raw.github.com/dreww/dissertation/master/figures/meeting_space_trial_2.jpg). (Drew Harry and Judith Donath, Massachusetts Institute of Technology, Cambridge, MA, USA. Full article available at http://dl.acm.org/citation.cfm?id=358923.)

9.2.1   SERIOUS GAMES IN THE WORKPLACE

In her seminal book, *Reality Is Broken: Why Games Make Us Better and How They Can Change the World*, Jane McGonigal said: "Collaboration isn't just about achieving a goal or joining forces; it's about creating something together that would be impossible to create alone" [10]. This is the essence of true collaboration, the act of creating something together. It can make an ordinary workday into an inspiring flow of self-value-affirming acts. All the gamification, staff leaderboards, and award badges in the world are not going to inspire people as much as the joy of creating something together. The first purpose of an Ideagora is to inspire collaborative creation. How is that done, you ask? Look toward your team and ask yourself what inspires them and how it can be translated into a virtual space. For instance, if you are creating a new office design, why not have a virtual sandbox where they can push the walls and furniture around together? If your team needs to develop a marketing strategy for street fair advertising, why not ask the team to develop a tour of international cities together on Google Earth.

How you do it and what tools you use to do it are not as important as the fact that you do it with your team. In fact, the first serious game they could play together is a game about designing their Ideagora.

9.2.2   MAKING A "STORYTELLING" PLACE

In the hands of a master salesperson, a sales pitch is a story you want to hear. It has the capacity to inspire its listeners to invest time and money in the project and ideas it contains. Great stories will be told in your Ideagora, just as they were in the caves of Altamira or the ancient agoras. You must design the space to support the storyteller by giving the storyteller a place to stand and face the listeners and a screen to show pictures or video. If you are streaming the event to a website from your virtual space, the production of that broadcast is important. The choices of how you use the camera to show the storyteller addressing the audience is just as important as the presentation, whether you are using your avatar-based camera to switch your points of view or activating a scripted camera as AngryBeth Shortbread (Annabeth Robinson in real life) [11] does in her Machinima Studio in Second Life (http://www.annamorphic.co.uk/studio.html; shown in Figure 9.2). You might compare this kind of exposition to making a live television drama, as you cut from camera position to camera position to "capture the action" of the story in progress and the rapt faces of the audience.

9.3   DESCRIPTION AND FUNCTIONAL ASPECTS OF VIRTUAL CAMERAS IN A PRESENTATION

Cameras come in all sorts of forms in both the real world and the virtual one. They all have one thing in common: They provide us with a point of view and the framework within which a narrative can be built. Let's go through the basic qualities of virtual cameras and how they are used.

9.3.1   WHAT IS A VIRTUAL CAMERA?

If you are a 3D modeler who uses a program like 3DS Max, Maya, AutoCAD, or SketchUp, you are familiar with the way a program opens a new file. Typically, there will be one or more images on the screen, perhaps the top and the side view of a model as the program opens the creation space. These spaces will not have any sense of a lens or depth of field, although they can have perspective. If you wish to display a "parallel projected" view, the default view camera will look at any object as if it were parallel to the drawing plane or computer screen. Adding a new camera in addition to the default viewer makes a big difference in your observation of the model scene. With this new camera, you have control of the width of the frame or view angle,

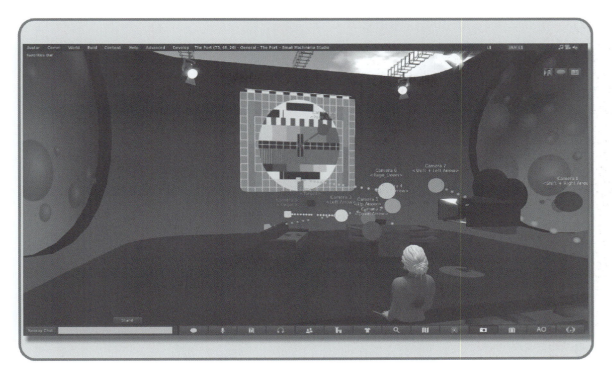

FIGURE 9.2 Virtual television studio in a virtual world. Designed, built, and scripted by Annabeth Robinson (AngryBeth Shortbread in Second Life). This virtual studio can be found in The Port region of Second Life.

as well as control of the depth of field. As you can see from the middle and bottom images in Figure 9.3, once this effect is added into your scene, the difference a lens makes on the view and the resultant change in a sense of perspective when the camera is at eye line level is very clear.

This view of digital information, with the addition of lens distortion and perspective, is what an avatar's camera presents to our eyes. Very subtle changes in this effect can have great nuances of meaning in the way we perceive things in a virtual world. Knowing what cameras do and how to utilize them for storytelling is of paramount importance.

9.3.2 First- and Third-Person Points of View in a Virtual Camera

The two most common points of view that a virtual camera employs in a virtual world are (1) first person or "mouse-look," which shows the virtual world from your point of view with little or none of your body showing in the frame, and (2) third person, which shows a typically wider and higher shot that includes your avatar's body as well as the surrounding environment. Some shooter-based video games employ both first- and third-person points of view simultaneously since it is difficult to aim a weapon from the third-person camera view.

Obviously, in a game or a virtual world, the camera direction and movements are determined by where the player decides the game character or avatar is going to travel in the environment. The carefully planned arrangement of camera shots that build suspense or tell a story in a feature film cannot be achieved with this kind of camera unless the control of the camera is taken over by a scripted device or the camera views are recorded and edited into the desired sequence.

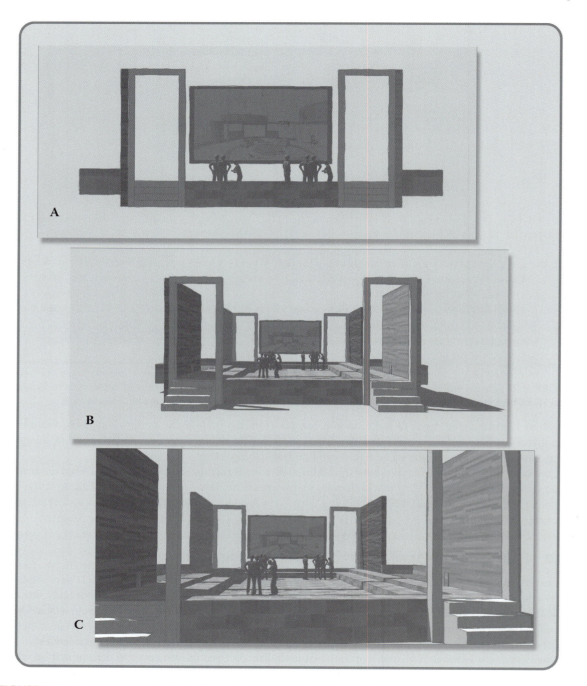

FIGURE 9.3 Screen grabs from SketchUp showing a comparison of the view options. In the top panel is a parallel projection (A), in the middle panel is a perspective view (B), and in the bottom panel is a camera view that imitates a lens effect (C).

9.3.3 TYPES OF CAMERA CONTROL FOR PRESENTATION PURPOSES

One of the most interesting things about camera control in a virtual world is that the cameras can be scripted to do just about anything. For instance, at the T2 Education Island conference center created by the 2b3d Studios team in Second Life, when your avatar sits down, your camera locks into a preset system that allows you to switch views by using the Page Up and Page Down arrow keys. In Figure 9.4, you will see the various angles the camera control has in that conference area. For new virtual world visitors who are not used to moving and focusing the camera for their avatars, this is a welcome device. Conveniently, the information about how to use the system and other guidelines is given out with a note card when you arrive.

9.4 DESIGNING FOR A PRESENTATION

As the designer of an Ideagora, which is a collaborative, storytelling, and information-sharing environment, you will need to establish the basic parameters of your client's needs. You should ask the following questions as you prepare to start designing:

1. What are the maximum and minimum numbers of people expected to use the area?
2. What kind of presentations will be done: 2D, such as website/media based; or 3D, such as architectural models/designs; or both 2D and 3D?
3. Can the presentation area be present all the time, or should it be temporary?
4. What is the aesthetic/architectural style desired?
5. Will the presentations be streamed?
6. How many people will be presenting at a time?
7. Do you need an interview area?
8. Do you need a "demo" area?
9. Will the space be "branded" with the client's logo?
10. Does the client need a teleportation system to connect this venue to others?

More questions may occur to you as you discuss the design with the client, so be prepared for a long, detailed chat before you design a single thing.

9.4.1 GENERAL QUALITIES OF A GOOD PRESENTATION SPACE

Although Intel has been able to run a region with 100 avatars or more [12] in the Science Sim, this is far from the usual use case scenario. In the planning of your Ideagora, a conservative estimate of 25–30 avatars attending at any given time on one region would be more realistic, especially in Second Life. Listed next are some general qualities that all good presentation spaces should have. This is not an exhaustive list but should get you off to a good start.

1. The background should be of a neutral (but not boring) color. Its textures should tile cleanly, with no eye-catching repetition or excessive busyness.
2. If possible, have your conference area face the water. The presenters or leaders should be on a platform with their backs to the open ocean as they face the audience. By doing this, you reduce the number of textures and objects that each avatar has to load into cache memory while watching the presentation.
3. If you are incorporating screens into your design, make sure the size and shape relate to the content shown. For instance, if you are showing high-definition (HDTV) images, then the ratio of length to width should be 16:9 [13].

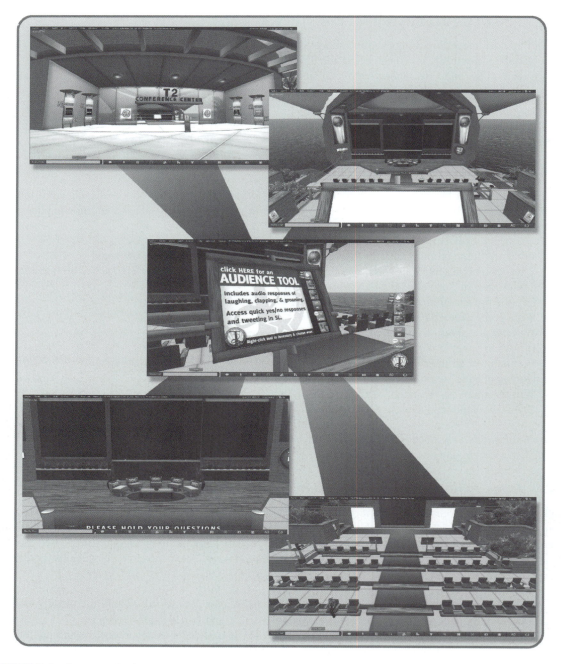

FIGURE 9.4 Screen grabs from a conference center in Second Life, T2 PTSD Education region. Entrance to conference center (top left), alternate camera position accessed by key commands when seated (top right), audience response and social media tool HUD (middle), avatar's starting camera view of stage when seated (lower left), and an alternate shot accessed by key commands when seated (lower right). This facility was created by 2b3d Studios team.

4. Make the screen part of the gathering circle, on the floor, or someplace where all the participants can view it easily.
5. Consider the use of whiteboards/learning interfaces, such as SLOODLE (Simulation Linked Object Oriented Dynamic Learning Environment) [14] or media on a prim [15] which can be setup in the Build/Edit/Texture menu.
6. Audio should be active so all who wish to can hear the discussion, but remind the audience members to mute their own mikes during the presentation. Members of the discussion should also be encouraged to add the salient points of their talk into the chat log so the idea is supported visually as well.
7. The space should be designed with a consideration of the "Design for All" standards (http://www.designforall.org/). Physical, visual, and aural accessibility are important.
8. Take the default camera positions of your attendees into consideration when you design the space. Make sure the entranceways and overhead elements are high enough so their third-person avatar's camera does not whack into anything as they enter the space.

9.4.2 Fostering the Ideagora Spirit by Personalizing the Space for Your Group

One of the most creative and prolific build groups in Second Life is the MetaHarpers Cabal founded by Arrehn Oberlander. A visit to their hangout will show you the kind of environment that exemplifies the Ideagora in its most creative form. In Figure 9.5, you can see a wide shot of their hangout in Second Life. It's a space filled with random objects from past and present projects that inspire a relaxed fun-loving mood,

FIGURE 9.5 A view of the Metaharper's hangout in the Harpers Region of Second Life. This is a collaborative/meeting space for the whole group decorated with mementos from their various projects in Second Life.

and open the conversation to a creative spirit. Blank walls inspire blank minds. Your environment has a direct impact on your creative energies, and the inclusion of art, toys, and other kinds of objects that represent your group's accomplishments, ideas, and sense of identity will enhance the collective imagination of the group. This collection of stuff should be curated as well so it stays in constant rotation, and the environment is always changing.

Now, before you go on to make your Ideagora into a curio shop, remember that the surroundings should be interesting and comfortable but not distracting. This is a fine balance and may take a bit of fiddling to get it right, but the richness these kinds of objects bring to the group experience is worth the time it takes to arrange them in your meeting spaces.

In his classic book and film *Social Life of Small Urban Places*, William H. Whyte, who worked with the New York City Planning Commission, lists the basic essentials of a shared public space [16, 17]. He and his staff filmed behavior in public meeting spaces all around the United States in the early 1980s. They observed that popular public spaces have the following elements in common:

1. There are lots of steps and places for people to sit and watch other people.
2. The area is not too sunken, too raised, or too large so that line of sight is lost.
3. There are water features such as fountains that can be accessed and played in.
4. There is food available.
5. There are shops nearby and an open-market feeling.
6. There is a sort of cave-like or slightly protected feeling to the area due to overhead trees or hanging, awning-like elements.

If you look at the ancient agora in Athens, Greece, on Google Earth, you see the remnants of just such a place. Here is the essence of it: If you provide an area where people can meet, mingle, communicate, and feel safe and yet are not trapped, great ideas will be fostered, just as the idea of democracy was fostered in the agora of Athens.

9.5   DESIGNING FOR THE FUTURE AND MOBILITY

Virtual meetings are just beginning to gain popularity. What is now a 2D webcast event will no doubt become an almost universal 3D experience that you access from your office on a daily basis. It will be driven by the need to pull together globally situated talent-diverse individuals for time-delimited projects within a user-friendly environment that is cost effective and can be accessed from any device.

9.5.1   INTERNET TRENDS TOWARD MOBILE PLATFORMS AND HOW THEY AFFECT DESIGN

In her 2012 report on Internet trends [18], Mary Meeker, a partner at Kleiner, Perkins, Caufield & Byers, raised some interesting points for discussion regarding how business will use the Internet in the future. The use of tablets, smartphones, and other mobile devices is rising rapidly worldwide, while the use of desktop computers is dropping. This clearly points to a need for "lightweight" viewers that will allow access to virtual worlds on a mobile device, and there are several in the early development stages. Web viewers like Pixieviewer (http://pixieviewer.com/) and Radegast's 3D viewer (http://radegast.org/wiki/Radegast) are competing with the more established Unity-based web viewers such as Jibe. Lumiya (http://www.lumiyaviewer.com/) has created an Android-based tablet app for Second Life, and as tablet use increases, more virtual world applications for them will appear. This in turn will probably have an impact on your design considerations, perhaps by limiting the amount of 3D detail you can do or the amount of texture memory you will have available. When you are designing for multiple platforms, you should always look at the smallest, most limiting one first. Make that your benchmark design and embellish the other versions later, once your design runs well on the smallest platform.

9.5.2 New User Interfaces: Touch, Voice, and Gesture

Meeker's report also shows us that we are interfacing with the online world more frequently in "natural" body-based ways; the GUI (graphical user interface) has given way to the NUI (natural user interface) as we touch, talk, and gesture toward our devices. It is not a big stretch to imagine voice-to-object creation. Kyle Gomboy (G23D Studio) has approached that with his new application, called 2Cube. This is a system that utilizes the Kinect motion capture data in unison with a 3D modeler, allowing users to create 3D models with their hands and voice. Think of a 3D model building and editing itself as the designers talk about its structure in a virtual meeting. How would you design a presentation room for that? Perhaps it should be a vast open space surrounded by seating, like an arena theatre, amphitheater, or agora?

9.6 PROJECT: BUILDING AN IDEAGORA FOR YOUR TEAM

This project is about making a space that encourages ideas and communication for your team members. It would be best done with a group of three to five people, but you can also try it yourself and show it to some of your buddies in OpenSim or Second Life. One version of an Ideagora mesh model is provided with this chapter's content (Ideagora.dae) and can be found at http://www.anncudworthprojects.com/ under the Virtual World Design Book downloads section. It has been designed as a modular system of screens, walls, and other parts that you can break apart and assemble in any manner you choose.

9.6.1 Setting Up the Terrain and Loading in the Elements for the Ideagora

9.6.1.1 Setting Up the Terrain
You will need a flat, clear rectangular area 50 by 35 meters to accommodate the model provided with this chapter. In Figure 9.6, the custom Ideagora terrain height map and its resultant landform are shown. This was designed to showcase the Ideagora model; you could alternatively put the model in a skybox or on a plateau if desired.

9.6.1.2 Loading in the Ideagora
After you have prepared the terrain (or platform), upload the Ideagora. dae file using the affiliated Ideagora_Physics.dae file to set the LOD under the Physics tab in the Upload menu. Now would be a good time to review the information about uploading procedures in Chapter 2, Section 2.3, if you have not already done so. Once you get the Ideagora model into your inventory, complete with textures, then drag it from your inventory, and center it on your available space using the x and y coordinates. Lower it into position on the z axis, when you have it centered on your terrain or platform. In Figure 9.7, the Ideagora is located at 128,128 at the center of the simulator region.

FIGURE 9.6 Terrain height map and the custom sim region made for the Ideagora installation.

FIGURE 9.7   Screen shot showing the Ideagora installed at the center of the region.

Remember the qualities of the popular small urban spaces described by William H. Whyte and his group at the New York City Planning Commission, mentioned Section 9.4.2. Using this basic installation, try to emulate those features in your Ideagora.

9.6.1.3 Personalizing Your Ideagora

Personalize your Ideagora with objects and graphic elements made by your team; set up a leaderboard, a wall of images such as "awesome team member of the month" or some method of identifying each member of the group in a special way.

9.6.1.4 Landscaping around the Ideagora

By adding landscaping and additional gathering areas around the Ideagora, you create space that allows for private casual conversations and provides an escape from the intensity of the central meeting area. Put in greenery and landscape elements, such as shown in Figure 9.8.

9.6.2 Set Up Shared Media

9.6.2.1 The Screens

There are two large 16:9 screens in the Ideagora. They are provided for you to display media you chose for your meeting. When you get the model loaded in, you should change the texture on the surface of the screen to a texture that indicates to the visitors there is a media channel present. Sometimes, visitors need to be reminded to turn on their media channels.

FIGURE 9.8   Screen shot showing the basic landscaping in the immediate surroundings of the Ideagora.

9.6.2.2   Editing the Model for Presentation of Media

The Texture tab of the Build/Edit menu is where you can assign media to a face of anything you build. Let's take advantage of this to add a media link to the surface of the screens in the Ideagora. Start by selecting the Ideagora, and going into Edit/Select Face mode. Select the face of the screen you want to affect, just as you did to put the Media channel reminder texture on it. Then change the setting in the Texture tab from Materials to Media with the dropdown menu on the lower left side. Once you do that, it will give you three options: Choose, Remove, and Align. Simply copy/paste the URL of the home page from the online web site you wish to display on the surface of your Ideagora screen. Allow for Auto Zoom, Auto Play Media, and Auto Scale, as you try it out for the first time. Click OK, and you are done. See Figure 9.9 for more visual information about this process. You can also deepen your knowledge about this Shared Media at http://community. secondlife.com/t5/English-Knowledge-Base/Shared-Media/ta-p/700145.

9.6.3   Check the Usability of the Ideagora

Now, you should invite a few friends over for a meeting. Have them rez a few items in the middle of the Ideagora and see how high you need to set the screen so all can see it and that the objects being rezzed are not overlapping the view. Strongly discourage the rezzing of very large objects in the space; there are sandboxes for that kind of thing. In fact, having a sandbox adjacent to the Ideagora is a good idea if your group is primarily concerned with large-scale 3D design.

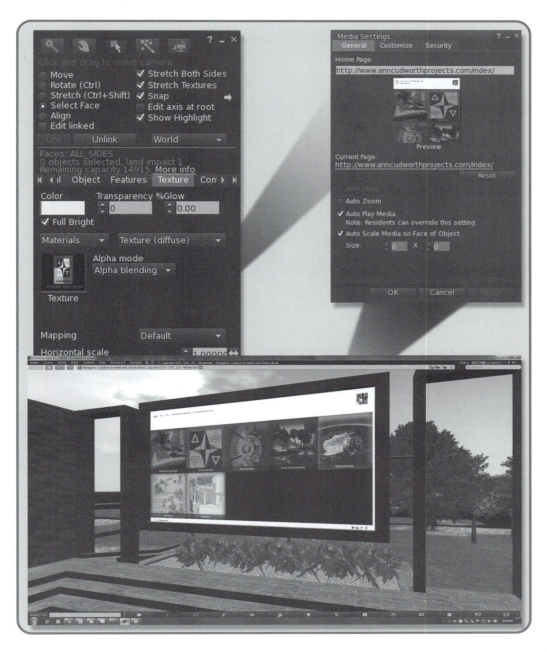

FIGURE 9.9   Screen shots showing an overview for installing media on the surface of the Ideagora. In the top left image, the Build/Texture tab menu in the Firestorm Viewer showing Media Channel Reminder texture and Materials setting. In the top right image, the secondary menu under the Texture tab, which is a dropdown menu from the Materials button, allows for Media to be assigned to any surface with a designated media texture. In the bottom image, the media screen displaying the designated web page on its surface.

FIGURE 9.10 View of Ideagora, showing the "Rubicon" water feature which can be used as a graphic marker of the Agree/Disagree vote in a meeting.

9.6.4 Emergent Usage of the Ideagora

The water features in this version of an Ideagora were initially added for decorative purposes, to give the environment one of the universal qualities desired in a public space, as discovered by William Whyte [16]. However, as this Ideagora was used on Alchemy Sims Grid, we discovered that they also served as visual markers for guiding the process of getting a consensus at a meeting. The small "river" and bridge in the middle of this Ideagora, could be declared the "River Rubicon" (in reference to Julius Caesar's historical decision to make war on Rome and Pompey), and that all who agreed with the concept being discussed should cross it, and gather on one side. Those who disagree would remain on the opposing side, perhaps needing further convincing. Emergent usage in your Ideagora design is one of the things you should be looking for and encouraging in your designs.

9.7 A BRIEF CONCLUSION

There is still a great need to be in the real "marketplace" every day, learning informally from elevator chats and impromptu meetings. There is also a great desire from the working public to have more control over their daily schedule. Creativity does not punch a time clock and having time to be in your familial/social network provides emotional support in your hectic life and nourishes your spirit. The common thread between these seemingly divergent needs is the desire to communicate ideas easily and clearly, no matter your location. What if your mission is to design meeting spaces that develop and support clear communication, no matter the time or place? Perhaps these environments have built-in multilingual translators or "speech-to-object" (say "cube" and one appears) 3D tools. Maybe the user can take advantage of "phase shifting" in the space and replay the media for people in another time zone. What if the new viewers could review and comment with voice chat in a previous meeting? Perhaps they can add verbal "Post-its" into the content for the next group to review? Let your imagination guide you as you design and build an Ideagora for your team.

REFERENCES

1. Cave Painting, Wikipedia article, http://en.wikipedia.org/wiki/Cave_painting. Accessed March 9, 2013.
2. Leckart, Steven, The Facebook-Free Baby, *Wall Street Journal*, May 12, 2012, http://online.wsj.com/article/SB10 0014240527023044511045773920411801389 10.html. Accessed March 6, 2013.
3. *Wikinomics: How Mass Collaboration Changes Everything*, Wikipedia article about the book written by Don Tapscott and Anthony D. Williams, Portfolio Books, 2006, http://en.wikipedia.org/wiki/Wikinomics. Accessed March 6, 2013.
4. Norman, Donald, *The Psychology of Everyday Things*, Basic Books, New York, 1988, p. 9, compared to by Soegaard, Mads, Affordances, 2010, http://www.interaction-design.org/encyclopedia/affordances.html. Accessed March 9, 2013.
5. Gibson, James J., *The Ecological Approach to Visual Perception*, Psychology Press, New York, 1986, compared to by Soegaard, Mads, Affordances, 2010, http://www.interaction-design.org/encyclopedia/affordances.html. Accessed March 9, 2013.
6. Murray, Janet H., *Inventing the Medium: Principles of Interaction Design as a Cultural Practice*, Kindle edition, MIT Press, Cambridge, MA, 2012, Chapter 2, location 697.
7. Lascaux—Interpretation of the Images, Wikipedia article, http://en.wikipedia.org/wiki/Lascaux#Interpretation_of_ images. Accessed March 9, 2013.
8. Harry, Drew, Designing Complementary Communication Systems, PhD thesis, pp. 44–86, submitted September 2012, http://web.media.mit.edu/~dharry/dissertation.pdf. Accessed March 5, 2013.
9. Hypatia, Wikipedia article, http://en.wikipedia.org/wiki/Hypatia. Accessed March 10, 2013.
10. McGonigal, Jane, *Reality Is Broken: Why Games Make Us Better and How They Can Change the World*, reprint, Penguin Books, New York, December 27, 2011, p. 268.
11. Robinson, Annabeth, Wikipedia profile, http://en.wikipedia.org/wiki/Annabeth_Robinson. Accessed March 10, 2013, and her website, http://www.annamorphic.co/uk/.
12. Scalable Virtual Worlds: Project, http://www.intel.com/content/www/us/en/research/intel-labs-scalable-virtual-worlds.html. Accessed March 11, 2013.
13. Aspect Ratio (Image), Wikipedia, http://en.wikipedia.org/wiki/Aspect_ratio_(image). Accessed March 11, 2013.
14. SLOODLE—Second Life and OpenSim Interface for Moodle the Learning Management System, http://www.sloodle.org/moodle/. Accessed March 11, 2013.
15. Streaming Media in OpenSim, http://opensimulator.org/wiki/Streaming_Media_in_OpenSim. Accessed March 11, 2013.
16. Whyte, William H., Social Life of Small Urban Spaces, http://vimeo.com/21556697. Accessed March 10, 2013
17. William H. Whyte, Wikipedia article, http://en.wikipedia.org/wiki/William_H._Whyte. Accessed March 10, 2013.
18. Meeker, Mary, KPBC Internet Trends @ Stanford—Bases, presented December 3, 2012, http://www.kpcb.com/insights/2012-internet-trends-update. Accessed February 28, 2013.

10 Virtual Goods and Design for Virtual Shopping Environments

Great things are not done by impulse, but a series of small things brought together.

—**Vincent Van Gogh**

10.1 WHY DO PEOPLE BUY VIRTUAL GOODS?

As game developers and virtual worlds designers work to build even more detailed immersive environments, and the resident population seeks to embellish their virtual surroundings, the need for virtual goods, clothing, furnishings, etc. keeps increasing. A virtual economy with its virtual marketplace has been part of virtual worlds and online games for many years now, and the phenomenon of how it works and why real people buy virtual goods has been the subject of many studies and reports. The three basic reasons why people buy virtual goods are (1) to establish and customize individual identity, (2) to communicate with others, and (3) to compete with others.

10.1.1 CUSTOMIZATION

Customization starts with your virtual identity. No player wants to keep the look of a default character from the game company; everyone wants to express their individuality. Virtual goods such as skins for your avatar, clothing, armor, and wearable accessories like hair and shoes are usually the first purchases a player will make and something players will continue to update. This will extend to other virtual attributes, such as pets, vehicles, and houses as the player seeks to gain status in the virtual community.

10.1.2 COMMUNICATION

Human beings, virtually represented or not, need to communicate. Virtual goods can be given as gifts to express love, friendship, and other sentiments. Virtual cards, flowers, jewelry, and toys are very popular. Body language in virtual worlds is just as important as it is in the real world. "Wearable" avatar animations, called Gestures, are created to express the nuances of communication across the spectrum of human emotion, and the market for them is enormous in Second Life as well as other virtual worlds, like Minecraft and IMVU.

10.1.3 COMPETITION

Invariably, people will want to gain status and wealth in a virtual world and will challenge and compete to get it. Virtual goods such as weapons, animations, magic spells, and the tools to make these are always popular. There are extensive online sites where players can buy various items to "level up" their character in the games.

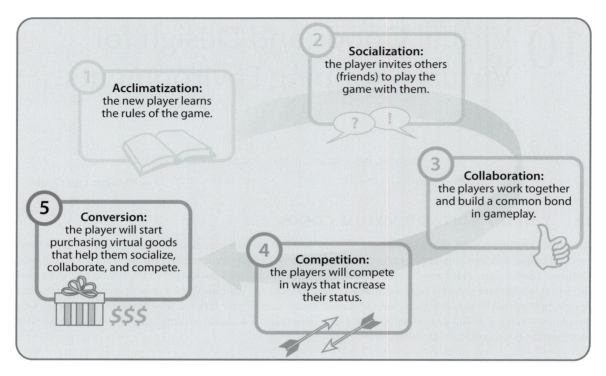

FIGURE 10.1   Chart showing the process of turning "players into payers" as defined by Dubit Limited, a UK-based game design and research company.

Understanding the main forces that drive consumption of virtual goods will allow you to intertwine your virtual content with game play and maximize the profit from your virtual goods market sales. Dubit Limited, a game design and research company in the United Kingdom, explains the five steps for turning "players into payers" [1]:

1. Acclimatization: The new player learns the rules of the game.
2. Socialization: The player invites others (friends) to play the game.
3. Collaboration: The players work together and build a common bond in game play.
4. Competition: The players will compete in ways that increase their status.
5. Conversion: The player will start purchasing virtual goods that help the player socialize, collaborate, and compete.

Once they have passed step 5, the cycle is complete. Now, the players have been turned into payers. This process is diagrammed in Figure 10.1.

10.2   CONSISTENT BRAND IDENTITY FROM YOUR LOGO TO THE ARCHITECTURE OF YOUR SHOP

Consider some of the greatest retail environments in the real world: the towering glass cylinder of the Apple Store in Shanghai, China; the wood-planked sweeping wall and "Staircase Theater" in Prada's New York flagship store; or the illuminated lotus blossom columns and golden statues of Harrods' Egyptian Room in London. Going to shop at these places is an event, an immersive experience that says as much about the brands they sell as it does about their sense of occasion. There are retail environments in virtual worlds that have the same impact. These are places such as Barnesworth Anubis' Prefab, the Furniture and Décor Shop in Demersal, the Curio Obscura shop built by Padora Wrigglesworth, and the Horizon Dream shop with designs by Marcus Inkpen (J. Matthew Root in real life) and Sharni Azalee. Images of these shops are shown in Figure 10.2.

As you set out to create the identity of your brand and its related design components, you should realize that you are embarking on one of the most challenging and exciting aspects of retail. This coordinated approach is fairly new in the history of advertising; only in the last 50 years or so have the marketing forces gathered information about a company to create simple, comprehensive image concepts that can stand the test of time. We can thank advertising legends like Saul Bass, Paul Rand, and the firm of Chermayeff & Geismar for the origin of this idea. As Wikipedia notes: "The visual brand identity manual for Mobil Oil (developed by Chermayeff & Geismar), [was] one of the first visual identities to integrate logotype, icon, alphabet, color palette, and station architecture" [2].

Let's launch our virtual store design with the idea of a sailing ship, *The Flying Cloud* (1851–1871). When you think of the famous *Flying Cloud*, what simple shapes come to mind? Now suppose you want to open a virtual shop that sells sailing ship models, full size ships and related nautical paraphernalia. How would you design the look of it? Should your shop have a sail-like design along the roof, like the Sydney Opera House in Australia? Or, should it look like the main deck of the *Flying Cloud* herself? Each style has a mood to convey to the visitor, and you should decide to what your customer base would best respond. Before you continue with detailed thinking about a potential *Flying Cloud* shop design, take a little time to consider these three elements in general terms: architectural style, signage/display, and color/lighting.

10.2.1 ARCHITECTURAL STYLE

Four thousand years of architectural ideas and innumerable descriptions of fantasy architecture may make the choice of architectural style hard for you. One of the best ways to get a handle on the "look" is to start a "look book." Find a binder or notebook somewhere and start collecting images that remind you of your content and themes. When you are defining how much your architecture should look like your product, consider these design extremes: In Flanders, New York, there is a shop that sells ducks and duck eggs called, simply enough, The Big Duck. It is easy to find this 20-foot high ferro-cement duck statue along the roadside, and once you realize it is also a shop, there can be no doubt about what kinds of products the shop sells. On the other end of the retail design spectrum is the featureless black or white box that is often seen in the modern stores. These "high-concept" retail environments provide support for the sale of all manner of goods since they imply no connection visually to one sort of content or another. Which one do you need? The oversized icon or the featureless box? There are more options than those two, of course. Choose your shop design elements carefully because strong visual architectural details will help your customers remember your shop, especially if the details are consistent with the look of your logo and products.

10.2.2 SIGNAGE/DISPLAY

You will quickly discover that signage and displays are 50% of your store design. This is your opportunity to make a direct connection between the 2D aspects of your store brand, the logo, the typeface, and the color palette and the 3D space where you are displaying your content.

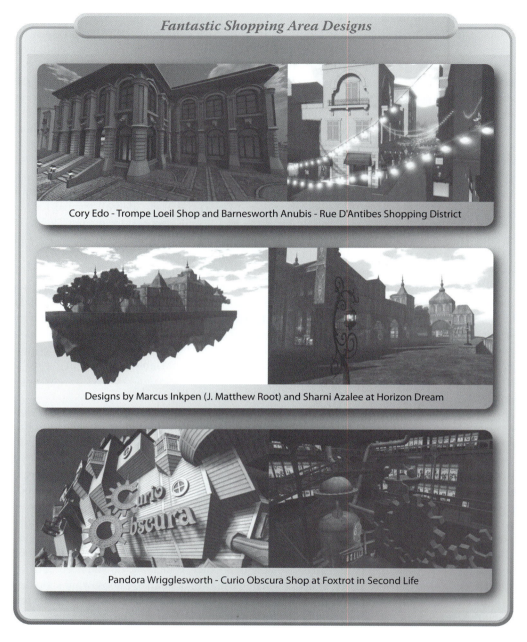

Fantastic Shopping Area Designs

Cory Edo - Trompe Loeil Shop and Barnesworth Anubis - Rue D'Antibes Shopping District

Designs by Marcus Inkpen (J. Matthew Root) and Sharni Azalee at Horizon Dream

Pandora Wrigglesworth - Curio Obscura Shop at Foxtrot in Second Life

FIGURE 10.2 (See color insert) Screen grabs from some of the fantastic shops in Second Life. Top image shows shops from the Hyde Park and Rue D'Antibes regions, middle image shows the floating shopping area in the Horizon Dream region, and bottom image shows a shop in the Foxtrot region.

One of the best places to display signage is on the floor of your virtual store because most avatar cameras default to a position that is high and pointing slightly down. Putting directional arrows into the pattern on your floor will help your customers navigate and not clutter the visual display field around your products.

Make the decision early on about the composition of your signage and set up a template in a program like GIMP (GNU Image Manipulation Program), Adobe Illustrator, or Photoshop. A square format is quite handy for this type of element since it allows for vertical and horizontal organization of the visual composition and maintains the consistency of an overall look. Try to include good, high-resolution images of your products on these signs and displays since images help persuade the customer to buy your goods.

10.2.3 COLOR/LIGHTING

Think of your favorite sports team uniforms or your national flag. There is no doubt you could pick the exact colors from that object from any color selector without hesitation. That is the kind of instant memorable impression your brand should make with its color palette. Once you have decided on the colors for your logo, tone them down into neutral tints to use inside your store. If you have the modeling skills, you should take advantage of mesh construction and utilize 3DS Max or Blender to build a model for your store with baked textures that add lighting effects on the walls and floors.

One excellent way to keep this all organized, especially if you work with several other content builders, is to create a "style sheet" for your logo usage and color palette. This is typically an 8.5 by 11 inch printout that shows the logo in color, black and white, and any other color type you want to allow. This document stipulates "official" usage of the logo and color palette, be it for in-store displays, websites, or signage. It will also call out the RGB (red, green, blue) values of the colors used, as well as hexadecimal values and PMS (Pantone® Matching System) numbers so that the logo is produced consistently across all forms of print and electronic media. You should have this available as a PDF document so that anyone who needs to use your logo for advertising or promotion can obtain the official guide from you instantly. Figure 10.3 displays a style sheet for the *Flying Cloud* nautical shop discussed in section 10.2. As you can see, everything is linked, and anchored visually to the oil painting image of the *"Flying Cloud."* There is a complete consistency between the logo, architectural style, and color palette of the shop architecture.

10.3 THE PHYSICAL ASPECTS OF AN EFFECTIVE INWORLD VIRTUAL STORE

You need to be cognizant of how people will interact with your virtual shopping spaces. There is no better way to learn this than to observe the traffic patterns and functionality of real-world places like shops, restaurants, and transportation hubs. What works in the physical world is a good blueprint for your virtual building after some adjustments for the larger avatar size, camera positions, and the ability to fly.

It is good practice to make use of a store map, especially if you have several floors of content. By providing a readily accessible, clearly visible map that is connected to a teleport system, you will create a pleasant and expedient shopping experience for your customer. It is good practice to make sure that you also provide a way for the customers to return to your teleport hub from each shopping area so they do not become lost trying to find the way back.

When your customers enter your shop for the first time, their avatars' camera has to load all of the textures within their line of sight and draw distance into their client viewer. You must consider what that rezzing time is for your customers and endeavor to make their initial experience a pleasant unfolding display of your most important products. One way to do that is to enfold your shopping space so that partitions and walls break up the views inside the store. This allows their viewer to load small sections at a time as the avatar walks

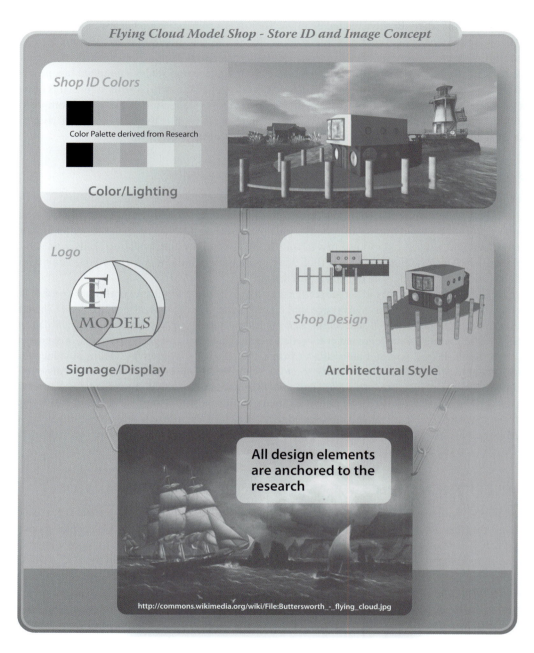

FIGURE 10.3 (See color insert) Chart showing the utilization of the aesthetic aspects from the *Flying Cloud* clipper ship painting for a shop design. This is visual research that "anchors" the architectural style, signage design, display design, color palette, and lighting in your virtual shop to a common theme or "look."

around to look at your shop. Remember that if you are fortunate to have a very busy shop, you must consider the performance of the server and how much lag your visitors are causing and experiencing.

It is highly recommended that you take a shopping tour of Second Life to see what the experiences are like at the major store areas, especially at times when the inworld population is high, and lots of people are shopping. Gaining a first-hand understanding of how virtual goods are displayed and sold will give you a good foundation for building shop areas that can handle crowds while providing displays with good visual clarity and ease of navigation.

The next sections break down some specific aspects of an effective store space. As a shop owner, designer, and content creator, you are undoubtedly aware that such things as: store size and scale, traffic patterns and types of display, shopping and social space, visual and aural ambiance, and the search listing and description settings are all important to your customers' experience and your sales.

10.3.1 STORE SIZE AND SCALE

As discussed in previous chapters, you know that the avatars' camera is often way above their head and behind them, looking down toward the back of their head and the floor. This affects the scale of your shop in several ways, especially where they enter and get their bearings. Initially, you should let them enter in a place that is high enough and wide enough so that they can take a good wide look around, but not cluttered with lots of content that bogs them down while their viewer loads it all. They should not have to enter through a doorway that bumps into their camera or have to reposition it to see what is around them. If you are in the business of selling small things like jewelry, accessories, or ship models, then you will need to display those not only in the actual scale of the object, but also with larger-scale detail images. Nothing is more aggravating to a customer than having to move a camera all over the place to see what your content looks like. For instance, in your *Flying Cloud* shop, you might put a lovely ship model in a central display at actual size and then install pictures of it on the walls, or on separate panels, to show close-ups of the details you have worked so hard to make.

10.3.2 TRAFFIC PATTERNS AND TYPES OF DISPLAY

Access your visuospatial sketchpad and recall the experience of entering a large department store. You probably remember how the pedestrian traffic is steered around several display cases, and everything is at eye level. This can be used to great effect when designing a shop in a virtual world too. Be mindful of guiding your customer through an advantageous traffic path that puts many attractive goods in their camera view. Think like a relaxed shopper, not an industrious content maker. What do you see when you walk into your shop and do not bother to move the camera? Anything located in a position that is higher than the default line of sight will not be noticed right away, so that area is where you will put your older (but still popular) content. Like any real-world shop, you want to put your special items right up front so they are noticed immediately. To keep them coming back, you need to constantly refresh any displays that are in the main entrance areas. Seasonal décor is typically displayed there, along with all the interactive buttons for your social media and the Second Life Marketplace links. However, you should avoid a cluttered entrance full of textures that are slow to rez.

Interactive devices scripted to display and sell your content have developed significantly over the last few years. Called vendors, or "rezzers," these are the vending machines of Second Life. Shop owners who sell complicated content such as prefab houses or vehicles, things that demand lots of space and server time to display, will find a vendor device useful. Judicious use of these in your store environment allows for a very dynamic display and will enhance your customer's ability to interact with your shopping environment.

Most of the time, the inworld shop owner will simply put the content for sale inside a simple box prim and sell a copy of that to the customer. To set up this simple built-in sales and display system for your content, follow these steps. First, apply a texture that has an image of the content, the price, and a simple description on the face of the box. Then, use the Viewer/Client Edit menu to set permissions for the customer to copy, modify, or transfer the content. Once the permissions are set up, put your content for sale in the box, and when you are done, set the price for the item with the Edit menu and put the packaged content out for sale in your shop. The customer should be able to right click on the package and buy a copy of your content for themselves in Second Life.

10.3.3 SHOPPING AND SOCIAL SPACE

There are several reasons to include a social area in your shop. Shopping is a social activity, and people who are doing it will sometimes want to sit down and chat while they decide on the next item they need or just hang out and see who else is shopping at that store. If you have a "sandbox" area, make it into an area where the customers can rez and try out their newly purchased products, others may want to watch and see how attractive it is. Do not overlook the value of providing a pleasant garden, café, or lounge for people to meet. With these kinds of social spaces, you will create a great deal of "stickiness" between your shop and your clientele and develop them into repeat customers.

10.3.4 VISUAL AND AURAL AMBIANCE

You should consider the visual and aural ambiance of your shop. Do the sky setting and time of day work to enhance the look of your content? You can set fixed sky and time-of-day settings under the Region/Estate/Environment menu if you own the island. Otherwise, a scripted greeting device (greeter) can suggest a WindLight setting for your customers when they arrive, although some may not bother to use them. To guarantee that your customers are enveloped in the right ambiance, you may have to enclose your shop inside a huge sphere or cube so that they only see the background sky color that you choose to show them. In terms of setting up the music for your shop, you should ask yourself: Does the music stream or media stream (if you are showing streaming video) work to connect my brand ideas to my customers? Some customers may not have their media channels on, so you should not consider it a reliable method of communicating information like sales announcements or store events. However, the correct choice in music can move people through your store space with ease and perhaps enchant them enough so that they stay longer and shop more. You can set these sound and media options with their respective tabs in the World/Parcel Details menu. For sound, simply add the URL of the streaming source you would like to hear in your shop. A comprehensive list is available (http://wiki.secondlife.com/wiki/Music_streams).

For media, you have several options; you could set up surfaces to display the web pages of your blog or the items you have listed on the Second Life Marketplace. You could display YouTube videos of your content being used inworld. It is your choice to utilize the media channel for audio, a web page, or a movie.

10.3.5 SEARCH LISTING AND DESCRIPTION

When you are setting up your land for your inworld shop, you should take advantage of keywords to make sure your shop comes up in the listings when a potential customer is using the search content function in a client viewer. Look at the World/Parcel Details menu, under the General tab. Here is your control panel for setting up your search keywords. In the Name section, make sure to name your parcel using your store name and what you sell. In the Description section, make sure that you include keywords that name the major products that you sell. Some shops simply list their biggest content items, while others add genre names or keywords like Steam Punk or Fantasy and activities like Role-play or Gaming so that their search comes up under larger categories. This strategy to be included in all large searches works sometimes, but often you may find your shop listed in the middle of a very long list. The best practice is to keep refining and updating these keywords so your store is shown in the top of a search list as often as possible.

10.4 SETTING UP YOUR SHOP IN THE ONLINE MARKETPLACE

As Linden Labs has developed the scope and functionality of its online marketplace, Second Life Marketplace (https://marketplace.secondlife.com/), more creators with content to sell have found that listing their goods online as well as showing them inworld has boosted their sales considerably.

James Warner Au, New World Notes creator and blogger, has been tracking the traffic on the Second Life Marketplace. As he said: "Here's some evidence of Second Life activity growth, at least where it matters most: According to Google AdPlanner, the SL Marketplace (Linden Lab's eBay style e-commerce site) now has 470K monthly unique users, over 50% in the demographically attractive 24–44 age range, with near gender parity" [3]. This kind of website traffic should convince you of the importance of an online shop as well as an inworld shop since many of your customers will use the online shop like a virtual catalogue to locate what they want to buy inworld. By taking advantage of a "Build It Once" approach, you can make this dual positioning of your content a relatively efficient process. You will also want to keep an eye on the marketplaces that are developing for the OpenSim grid and other grids in the Metaverse. With the "Build It Once" approach all your shops, online or inworld can share the same logo, tagline, branding elements, display images, descriptive keywords, and statements of store policies and mission.

10.4.1 LOGO, TAGLINE, AND BRANDING ELEMENTS ON THE SECOND LIFE MARKETPLACE

Your logo and branding elements will shine among the visual clutter of a shopping site, if you keep them simple. The square format, at 512 by 512 pixels, will look good both at your inworld shop and on the website masthead for your online shop, provided that it reduces well. The logo will be reduced for branding on each page, so it should be readable even at that scale, which is another argument for simplicity of its design. You should endeavor to coordinate the look of your online store with the style of your inworld store. That effort could also extend into the text you put in the descriptions and under your logo for a tagline. Another thing to strive for is multilingual versions of your online shop content. The European and Asian members of the Metaverse communities love to shop as much as the North Americans, so why not market to them in their own language? The Second Life Marketplace listings support the following languages: English, French, German, Japanese, and Portuguese.

10.4.2 DISPLAY IMAGES OF CONTENT FOR SALE ON THE SECOND LIFE MARKETPLACE

You will need to have at least one image of the content you are selling in your online shop. Sometimes, it is even better to have a view from various sides, especially if it is a piece of clothing. You should make a practice of creating signage for your inworld shop that contains multiple images so that you can utilize them in your online store as well.

10.4.3 DESCRIPTIVE TERMS AND KEYWORDS ON THE SECOND LIFE MARKETPLACE

Again, the keywords and terms are very important. They are the primary way of connecting with your first-time customers. Spend time to think of the descriptive terms your customers might use as they search for your content. This is time well spent and will return dividends in extra sales both online and inworld.

10.4.4 STATEMENTS OF STORE POLICIES AND MISSION ON THE SECOND LIFE MARKETPLACE

Also important is that you make a clear indication of your store policies and mission. If you want to offer a "no-questions-asked" return policy, make that clear on your shop site in the Second Life Marketplace as well as inworld. If your mission is to make the most realistic skins possible, then let the customers know that. Expressing your passion and commitment to your products will attract a loyal following, and you will have customers who believe in your brand.

10.5   USING SOCIAL MEDIA AND GAMES TO POPULARIZE YOUR CONTENT

Social media and the status of your content are intertwined these days. It is a remake of the old "word-of-mouth" advertising. Most people trust what their friends have to say about a product, and now, with the huge networks of "friends" they have on social media like Facebook and Google+, it is even more important to understand the cycles involved. The cycles of social media and content status are diagrammed in Figure 10.4.

Would you sell more goods if a game were involved? The answer to that is yes, but you must create content that works with the spirit of the game. Making your shop and brand attractive to popular game designers and event planners is just the first step. Do you think you could "gamify" your shop by creating an experience for the customers that makes each visit something new and exciting? One of the best aspects to having a virtual shop is that everything in it can become interactive. How can you enhance your customers' store experience without distracting them from their shopping mission?

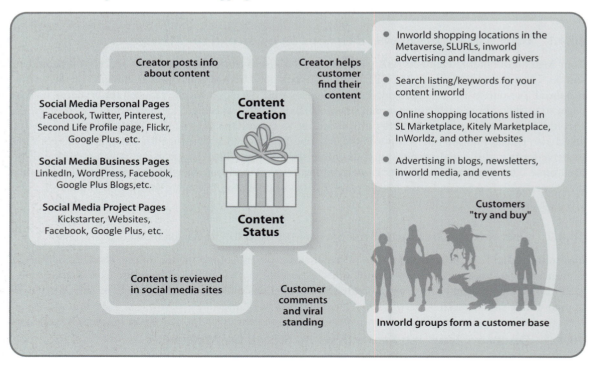

FIGURE 10.4   Diagram showing the relationships of content creation, content status, social media and advertising in a virtual economy.

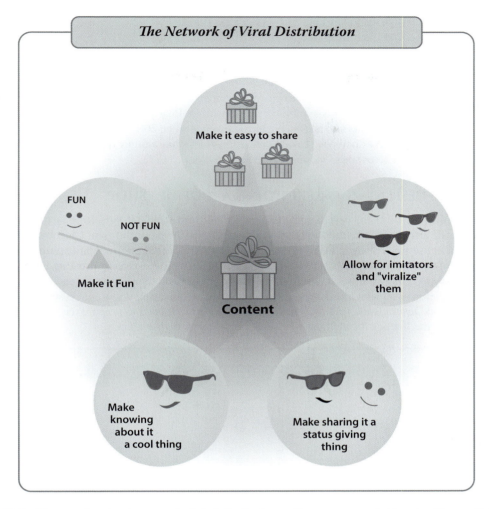

FIGURE 10.5   Diagram showing the network of viral distribution and how you can make it work with your digital goods and content in a virtual environment.

Here are some suggestions. Maybe you could create a series of "treasure chests" that they can try to unlock for a special limited edition product? Perhaps once they have become regular VIP customers, you can give them a special key that allows access to a private showroom. Maybe there are areas in your shop that shift in and out of our time dimensions, and to buy that special item, they have to be there just when it synchs up to our timeline. The sky is the limit with shopping interactivity.

In general, when you want the customers to take your content "viral," make sure it fits the qualifications in the list that follows. This interconnected system is diagramed in Figure 10.5.

1. Make it easy to share.
2. Make it fun.
3. Make knowing about it a cool thing.

4. Make sharing it a status-giving thing.

5. Allow for imitators and "viralize" them.

10.6 PERFORMANCE SPACES ADDED TO RETAIL

Fashion shows, cabarets, parties, and art openings are all opportunities for you to promote your content. One of the most successful examples of this symbiotic relationship is Phat Cat's Ballroom and Jazz Club at the Phat Land sim in Second Life. This sim has been a musical venue since 2007 and is surrounded by successful shops. One of the reasons these shops do so well is that Phat Cat's has a fancy dress/formal wear dress code in the club, and that necessitates some shopping for many visitors.

10.7 PROJECT: DESIGNING AND BUILDING A "POP-UP" SHOP

This chapter's project involves the design and creation of a "Pop-up shop" [4] for selling virtual goods. In the spirit of a "roadside attraction" like the Big Duck in Flanders, New York, or the giant Uniroyal tire in Detroit, Michigan, you will use super scale icons to make this store stand out on the virtual landscape. In Figure 10.6 is a screen grab of the completed shop, set up on the Alchemy Sims Grid. Creating this Pop-up shop will give you an opportunity to refine your basic building skills as you assemble the shop walls and create the content for it. However, before you download this chapter's content from http://www.anncudworthprojects.com/ in the Virtual World Design Book section and start to build, you will need to prepare the land for your shop, and make sure that the listings for the land will attract customers to your shop.

FIGURE 10.6   The completed Pop-up shop that you will create in this project, shown on Alchemy Sims Grid.

10.7.1 Laying the Groundwork

10.7.1.1 Preparing the Land for Your Shop

You are going to need at least a 20 m × 20 m square area to build this shop, allowing for some free space around it. If you don't own a parcel that large, you can practice this in a large sandbox area, or over it on a sky platform. Here are the steps for laying the groundwork on your land, also illustrated in Figure 10.7.

1. Turn on the Property Lines, under World/Show More/Property Lines, so you can make sure you are not going over into neighboring areas.
2. Use the terrain tool to flatten out the landscape on that parcel and to smooth the edges so there is a smooth transition to the next area.

10.7.1.2 Setting in the Foundation and About Land Permissions

Now that you can see the property lines clearly, let's set down a foundation prim, to make sure the shop will be situated nicely on the terrain, organize how the shop will be visible to the search engine and decide what kind of permissions will be available to the visitors. Figure 10.8 illustrates the visual progression of the following steps:

1. Create a 20 m wide × 20 m deep × 2 m high prim in the center (as closely as you can tell by eye) of your parcel. On a full region, the coordinates would be $x = 128$, $y = 128$.
2. When you have it centered, set the objects position to a set of whole number coordinates like $x = 195$, $y = 65$, and lower it in z so that it just pops up above the ground. Name this enlarged box prim "Foundation" and apply a tile or stone texture from your basic library to all sides of the box by dragging it into the Build/Edit window under the texture tab.
3. In the World/Parcel Details/About Land menu under the General tab/Name section, type in the name your shop, "Pop-up Shop for Lamps." Note, you can also access the About Land menu through the World/Location Profile/Places/Parcel menu. The Places menu combines all three sorts of land definitions: Parcel, Region, and Estate for your convenience.
4. In the World/Parcel Details/About Land menu under the General tab/Description section, type in as many keywords as you can think of that relate to lighting, lamps and home decorating. Note, this will serve to locate your shop in Second Life, but for OpenSim builds there is no metaversal search engine yet.
5. In the World/Parcel Details/About Land menu under the General tab/ section, set the group to whoever is building this shop with you. If you have not made a group for that yet, you can do so under the Comm/Groups/Conversations - Contacts menu on the top bar. Pick the Groups tab and use the Create button to set the group up so you can invite your co-builders to join you. Remember, once you set the land to the build group, they must wear their group tags to build on that parcel.
6. In the World/Parcel Details/About Land menu under the Options tab menu, make sure that Edit terrain is NOT set to Everyone, Fly is set to Everyone, Build is set to Group, and Object entry and Run Scripts are both set to everyone.
7. Further down in the same menu, You probably want to set the land to Safe (no damage can be done to an avatar's health) and turn on the No Pushing option so people cannot use push script containing devices like guns for griefing your customers. Show Place in Search should also be checked in its respective box. Check M for moderate content and choose "shopping" from the drop-down menu to indicate the category of your build.

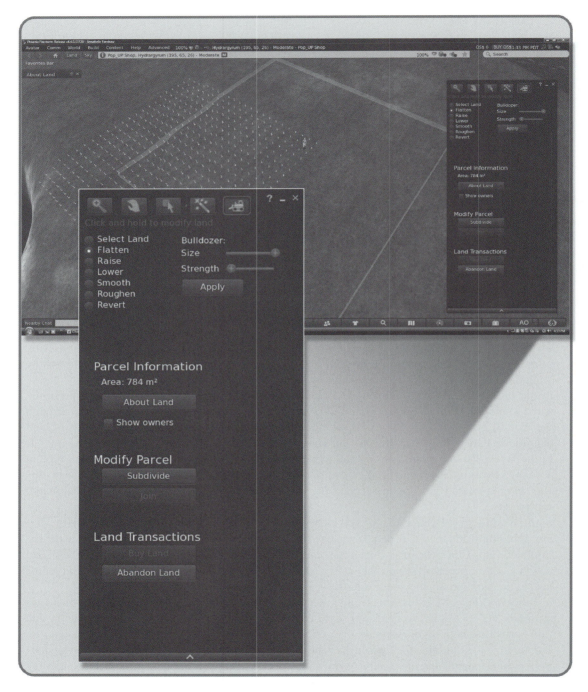

FIGURE 10.7   Screen grabs of virtual land and Land Tools menu showing the preparation of the terrain for installation of the Pop_up shop.

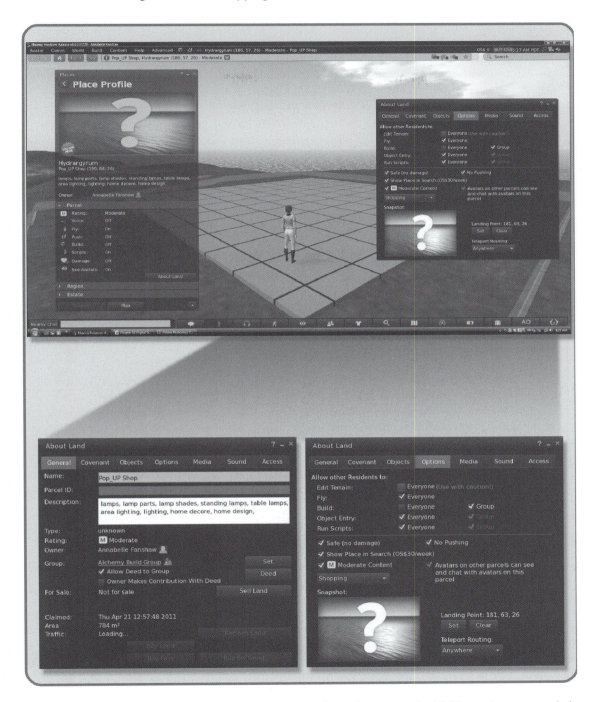

FIGURE 10.8 Screen grabs showing the About Land menus for setting up search visibility, and avatar permissions on the land.

8. At the bottom of the same menu, you have a space where you can drag in a snapshot of the completed shop, or perhaps your logo.
9. While you are still in the About Land/Options menu, walk to one end of the shop foundation, where the entrance will most likely be, and click the Landing Point/Set button to establish a Landing point. You can always adjust this and should check on it before you load landmarks into your greeter or give them out yourself. Leave the Teleport Routing set at Anywhere.

10.7.1.3 Setting Up Music for the Shop

Music can play a large part in setting the mood in your shop. This is added with streaming audio. The process is outlined in the steps below, and also illustrated in Figure 10.9.

1. Under the World/Parcel Details/About Land/Sound tab you can set up your streaming audio channel.
2. Choose a music URL from this list: http://wiki.secondlife.com/wiki/Music_streams, and copy/paste the URL from the page into the Music URL slot. It will be a series of numbers like this: http://108.61.73.119:8004/
3. Check the "Restrict the gesture and object sound to the parcel" box, the "Enable Voice" box, and the "Restrict Voice to this Parcel" box to prevent annoying sound bleed to your neighbors.

10.7.1.4 Setting Up Access and How to Ban Unwanted Avatars

Figure 10.10 shows you the steps to set up access and how to ban unwanted avatars. Please note, you can access all the land-based menus from World/Location Profile/Places, should you need to modify the parameters for a region, rather than a parcel.

1. In the World/Parcel Details/About Land/menu, under the Access tab, make sure that Allow Public Access is checked; you do not want to ban your customers.
2. The lower two boxes are where you can set up Access/No Access lists. Sometimes while you are building your store, you will just want the people in your build group on the land. In the Allowed Residents box, just add their names, deselect Allow Public Access. When you do that only your build group can teleport onto your land. Do not forget to open this again when your store is built.
3. Under the Banned Residents box is an Add button where you can list the names of the FlatterBots begging for money, avatars with a CopyBot program trying to steal your content, or griefers that may visit your shop and bother your customers.

10.7.2 Building the Shop Structures from Prefab Parts

Figure 10.11 gives a visual demonstration of the steps for building the shop wall structures from prefab parts.

Once you have downloaded the Chapter 10 content from the Ann Cudworth Projects website (http://www.anncudworthprojects.com) you should upload all the Pop_UP_Shop .dae files from into your inventory for use in the virtual environment, naming them the same way, once they have been uploaded. For instance, Pop_UP_Shop_Front_Wall.dae would become a linked object called Pop_UP_Shop_Front_Wall in your inventory. If you have not read the guidelines for uploads in Chapter 2, section 2.3, you should do that now. Follow the guidelines there for including physics shape files and textures in your uploads. Make sure you tuck all the parts away in a special folder when you have finished the upload, and make a copy of it just in case. As with other projects in this book, these shop elements come with alignment cubes, which you can see in the middle of the build in Figure 10.11. As noted in section 2.3, the upload may change the linking order of these elements. After you upload these models into your world and have them rezzed on the ground near each

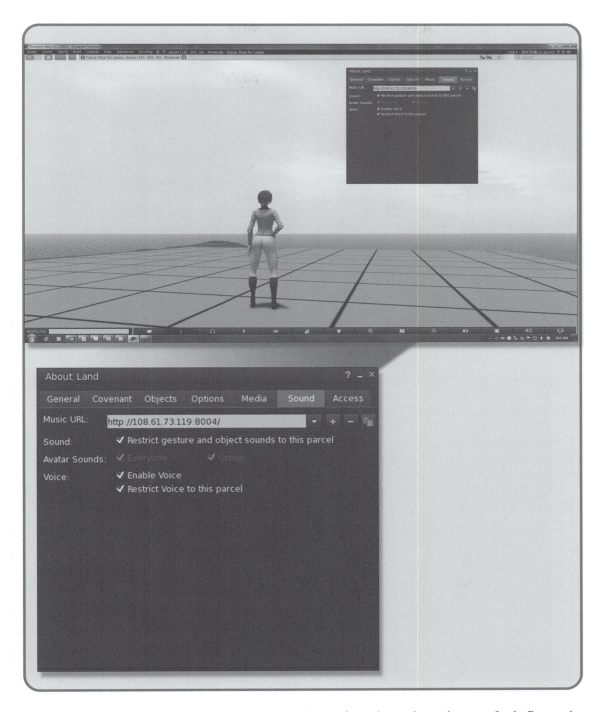

FIGURE 10.9 Screen grabs showing the About Land/Sound menu for setting up the music stream for the Pop-up shop.

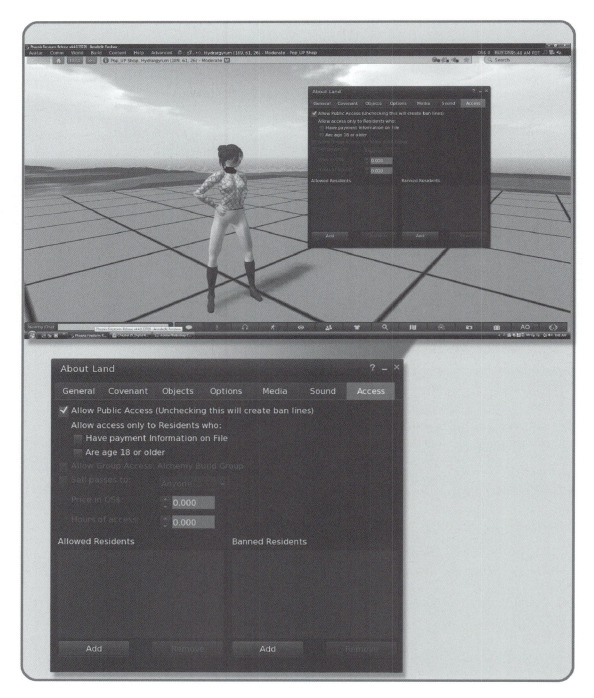

FIGURE 10.10 Screen grab showing the About Land menu and how it can be used to restrict access to the parcel while a Pop-up shop is being built.

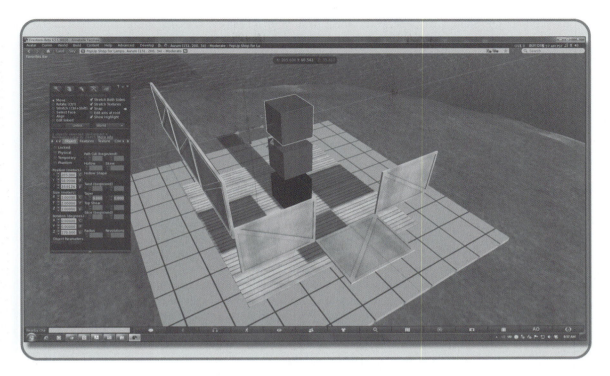

FIGURE 10.11   Screen grab showing the use of alignment cubes to assemble the floor, walls, and front door of the Pop-up shop.

other, check to make sure that the alignment cubes are the key prim on these elements. As you know, this is indicated with a yellow outline when you have the linked object (a wall section, for example) selected in the Build/Edit menu. If the .dae model files have not uploaded into your virtual environment with the alignment cube as the key prim, go into the Edit Linked mode (check the box on the Build/Edit menu), and unlink the alignment prim. Without moving it, deselect everything by clicking on the ground or sky. Now, re-select the model, and then the alignment cube, and link them back together. The cube should now be the key prim, and show a yellow highlight, while the rest of the model is highlighted in blue.

Do not unlink the parts of these walls until you have the whole shop assembled, want to remove the alignment cubes, and/or you want to make a hole for a window or doorway in the shop walls or ceilings. Since the shop elements are modular, you can always expand the shop infinitely, until you run out of land, of course.

10.7.2.1   Setting Up the Shop Floor and Walls

1. Drag the Pop_UP Shop_Floor object from your inventory and set the center in the same coordinates as the center of the foundation prim you have on your parcel. Reset the alignment cube to be the key prim for the Shop Floor, if necessary.
2. Drag Pop_UP Shop_Front_Wall object from your inventory onto the foundation in your parcel, reset the cube as the key prim if neccesary, and align it properly with the floor at the front of your shop, using the same coordinates as shown in Figure 10.11. The front wall has a ramp on it, the other walls are closed and flat.

3. Drag Pop_UP Shop_Left_Side_Wall object from your inventory, reset the alignment cube as the key prim if necessary, and set it up on the left side when you stand in the doorway facing into the shop. Align it to the center coordinates of the Pop_UP Shop_Floor.
4. Drag Pop_UP Shop_Right_Side_Wall object from your inventory and set it up opposing the left wall. Reset the alignment cube as the key prim if necessary, and make sure that the x and y coordinates match so that the walls are centered and parallel.
5. Drag Pop_UP Shop_Back_Wall object from your inventory, reset key prim if necessary, as you have with the other walls, and stand it up opposing the front wall. Make sure the x and y coordinates match with the front wall so they are centered and parallel.

10.7.2.2 Putting on the Roof and Giant Lamps

Please look at Figure 10.12 for a visual guide to the following steps:

1. Drag Pop_UP_Shop_Roof out of inventory and locate it above the top of the walls. Reset the alignment cube as the key prim if necessary on these objects.
2. Using the spinners in the Edit Object box, make sure that the roof has the same x and y coordinates as the floor prim and lower it into place on the walls.
3. Drag Pop_UP_Shop_Outlet_Plug out of inventory, and align it to the center of the roof.
4. Now, drag Pop_UP_Shop_Lamp_1 and put it in the back right corner of the roof, as you face the door, so that its plug matches in the socket, you will have to rotate it on the z axis 90 degrees.

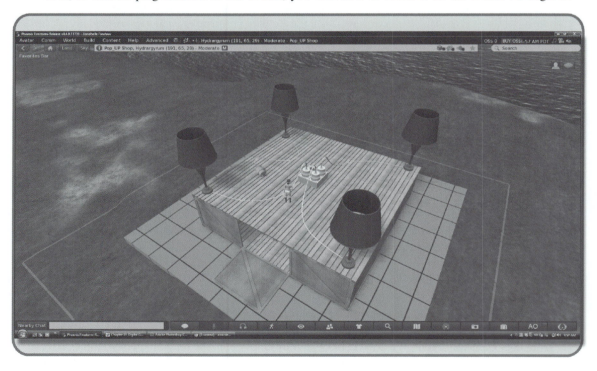

FIGURE 10.12 Screen grab of the almost completed Pop-up shop, showing the large lamps and their placement on the roof.

Continue clockwise around the roof surface, and continue with Lamp_2 on the front right corner (rotate this one 270 degrees in z), Lamp_3 is on the front left corner (rotated 90 degrees in z), and Lamp_4 (rotated 270 degrees in z) lands on the back left corner. Note that Lamp 4 has been left unplugged. You are doing great. The shop is really coming together.

5. Now that you have all of the shop assembled, go ahead and unlink and delete the alignment cubes from the shop components.
6. Select the whole shop, the big lamps on the roof, and then the foundation prim, and link them. This should make the foundation prim the key prim of the entire group. It will make the whole structure much easier to move about, should you need to relocate the shop.

10.7.3 Building Content, Setting Prices, Descriptions, and Listings

10.7.3.1 Making a Table Lamp Prototype
Figure 10.13 gives a visual demo of the steps for making a table lamp prototype.

The Table lamp prototypes are shown here as giant versions for clarity of illustration in the project. In fact, it is easier to make things this way, in a giant format, and then scale it down to the correct size once you have worked out all the details.

1. Create the first lamp base with a dimpled sphere prim and flatten the bottom side with a dimple that begins at 0.00 and ends at 0.80.
2. Use select/Shift key/drag Copy to drag the two additional prims up from the lamp base, in the same x,y location, just moving the new prims up on the z axis.
3. Change their forms into (1) a Path-cut Torus prim and (2) Ring prim to make the (1) neck and (2) shade of the lamp prototype.
4. Change colors, shininess, and transparency to make it look interesting.
5. Turn on the light feature of the lamp shade prim on the lamp and set it for a small radius, like 0.5 meters, so the lamp will light only its surrounding area when it's reduced to its smaller, realistic size.
6. Link the parts together by Shift selecting them, one at a time, picking the lamp shade last so it becomes the key prim (it will have a yellow halo, instead of a blue one if it is the key, when the object is in Edit mode).
7. Name the linked object Lamp Prototype and take it into your inventory to start your lamp stock.

10.7.3.2 Developing the Product Line
Figure 10.14 provides a visual of this section on developing the product line.

1. Drag a copy of the original prototype lamp out onto the ground from your inventory.
2. Name the lamp Pop_UP_Shop_Style_1_Lamp and set the description under the General Tab to "Your Shop Name_Cute Lamp" in various colors.
3. Set the permissions for Copy for the next owner and leave the rest of the Modify boxes blank.
4. Set the price at $1 Linden (if you are in Second Life) or whatever currency for which you think it will sell.
5. Shift/Drag copy 2 more of these lamps and edit the colors of the shade, neck, and base so you have a variety of colored lamps to display.
6. Name each lamp individually, perhaps by the predominant color at the end of it, such as Pop_UP_Shop_Style_1_Red. Make a copy of each one, stretch it to a smaller, more realistic size in the Build/Edit menu and take them back into your inventory in a folder you made called Lamps_Style_1_Final_size.
7. Save the original large prototypes in another folder, for more product development later.

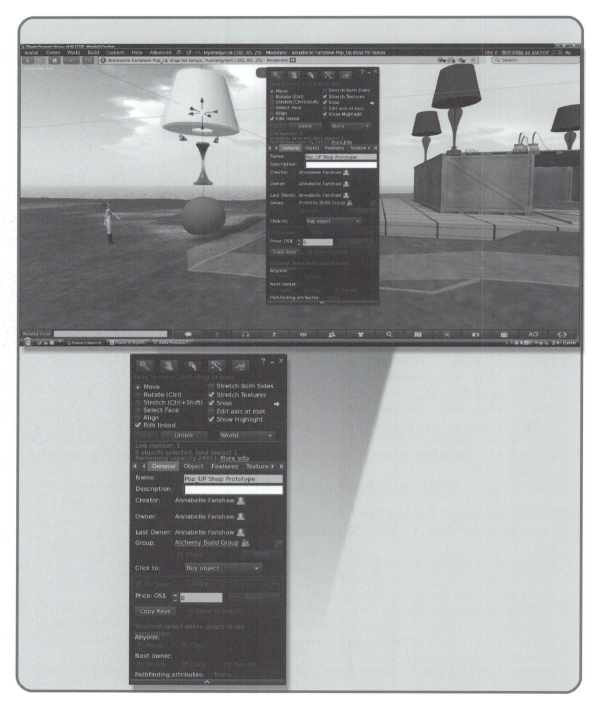

FIGURE 10.13 Screen grab showing the large scale creation of an initial lamp prototype using three basic prims.

FIGURE 10.14 Screen grab from OpenSim, shown initial creation of prototype lamps for the Pop-up shop.

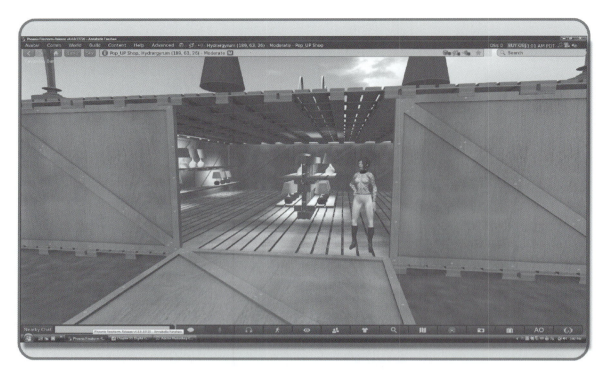

FIGURE 10.15   Screen grab from OpenSim showing the Pop-up lamp shop with stocked shelves displaying the virtual content.

10.7.4   Setting Up the Shop Display

10.7.4.1   Display Layout and Design for Selling

The visual explanation of this section on display layout and design for selling is provided in Figure 10.15.

1. Upload and drag out Pop_UP_Shop_Shelf.dae mesh model from your inventory.
2. Reset the alignment prim as key, if necessary, and put the shelves inside the middle of the shop.
3. Display your lamps on them—not too many; leave some blank space.

10.7.5   Adding the Signage, a Simple Shop Greeter, and a Note Card Giver

Now, we are going to put in signage for your shop and add a simple shop greeter and a note card giver.

10.7.5.1   Branding Your Shop Signage with the Logo

Upload the Pop_UP_Shop_Sign, and then drag it from your inventory onto the ground in front of the shop door. Orient the sign to the front left wall of the shop exterior as shown in Figure 10.16.

10.7.5.2   Making a Note Card for Your Shop

1. Using the inventory "create note card" function, make a new one for use in your shop greeter.
2. Name it "Welcome to the Pop UP Shop."

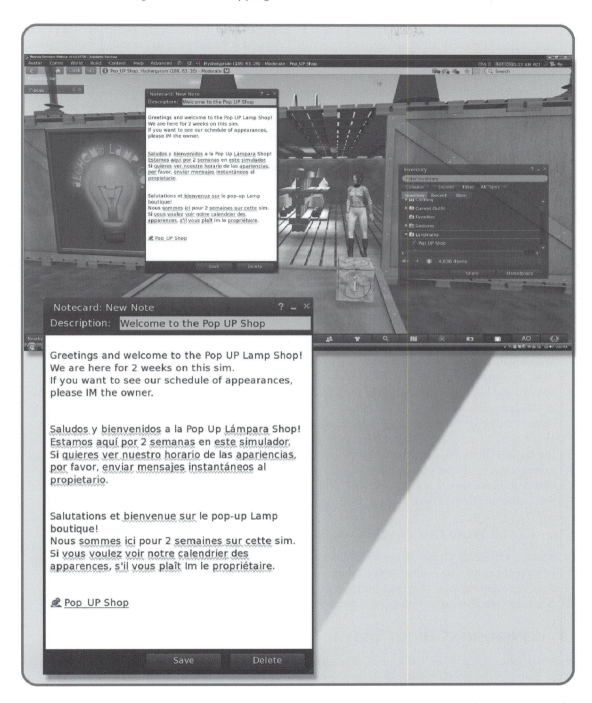

FIGURE 10.16 Screen grab from OpenSim showing the Pop-up shop welcome message in 3 languages with a landmark link, that will be placed inside the contents of the info cube.

3. Write a welcome message on it and use Google Translate to make a Spanish and French version of the text (unless you speak all these languages yourself). Add these translations to the text of the notecard, the Metaverse is international, and it's nice to give welcome in as many languages as you can.

4. Using the World/Parcel Details/About Land menu, go to the Options tab, stand on the spot where you want your customers to land, and reset the Landing Point.

5. Use the World/Landmark This Place menu, to create a landmark in your inventory for use with your greeting notecard. Drag this shop landmark from your inventory into the text box of the notecard you just made while its open on your screen. It will appear as a link that your customers can use to return to your shop.

6. Once you have added all of the information you would like to share on the note card, save it into your inventory and close the editor.

10.7.5.3   Set Up an Automatic Greeter and Note Card Giver for Your Shop

Figure 10.16 provides a visual explanation about setting up an automatic greeter in your shop sign and a note card giver in an "info" cube outside the door for your shop.

1. Go to http://www.3greeneggs.com/autoscript/ and make two scripts: (1) a script that gives a note card to an avatar when they touch the prim that contains it, and (2) an avatar sensing script that says something in local chat when the avatar approaches the prim that contains it. The second script should sense when the avatar is 5 meters away, and it should only give the message once so it doesn't become annoying.

2. Put the second script into the contents section of your store sign prim. Make sure the distance between the store sign and the store entrance is 5 meters or less, so the sign will greet the avatar on arrival with the message you want to say to them in local chat.

3. Now, set up the note card giver. Make a small texture that says "info" or just the universal circled "i" symbol and apply it to a cube. Drag the "Welcome to the Pop-up Shop" note card into the contents of this info cube and the note card giving script you just made. When your customers touch this info cube, it will give them the note card that includes the shop landmark.

4. Walk away to get out of the sensing range of the store sign greeter script. Select the sign, and in the Build/Edit menu, reset the script in its contents, and then walk back into range. The store sign greeter should say the welcome message to you when you are in range.

5. Check to make sure that your note card giver also is functioning by touching it. It should offer you the "Welcome to the Pop UP Shop" notecard.

10.7.6   Get the Word Out and Open for Business

1. Make a Customer Group in the Comm/Groups menu, and invite all your customers to join it for news updates on new content (more lamps!) and sale events.

2. Sponsor events at your shop and list them on websites and event guides.

3. Send out free content to your friends to advertise your new shop.

10.8   CONCLUSIONS ABOUT VIRTUAL COMMERCE AND SHOPPING SPACES

Congratulations. By now, at the end of this chapter, you will probably have a much deeper appreciation for how virtual goods are created, displayed, and marketed in a virtual world. There is a complex cross-promotional system developing between inworld and online retail sources. The Kitely Marketplace (http://www.kitely.com/market) is growing, and no doubt this and other markets will continue to evolve both in OpenSim and Second Life.

REFERENCES

1. Warneford, Matthew, Converting Players into Payers in Five Steps, Dubit Platform blog, October 24, 2010, http://www. dubitplatform.com/blog/2010/10/24/converting-players-into-payers-in-5-steps-html/. Accessed December 31, 2012.
2. Brand, Wikipedia article, http://en.wikipedia.org/wiki/Brand#Visual_brand_identity. Accessed December 30, 2012.
3. Au, Wagner James, Second Life Marketplace Grows to Nearly Half a Million Users, *New World Notes*, August 7, 2012, http://nwn.blogs.com/nwn/2012/08/second-life-.
4. Pop-up Retail, Wikipedia article, http://en.wikipedia.org/wiki/Pop-up_retail. Accessed January 10, 2013.

11 Sound Design for Virtual Spaces

The strange thing is that you take the emotional treatment that sound is giving, and you allow that to actually change how you see the image: You see a different image when it has been emotionally conditioned by the sound.

—Walter Murch [1]

11.1 DISCOVERING SOUND IN YOUR ENVIRONMENT

Let's prepare for this chapter by doing the following experiment: Get a piece of paper and a pencil and sit down in a comfortable spot; find someplace where you will not be bothered for a minute or two. In this experiment, you will close your eyes and focus on listening to the sounds of the environment around you. Start with the tiny sounds your clothes make as you shift to get comfortable and then open up the radius of aural awareness to take in the room sound. As you become aware of these sounds, note them as a list on the paper. Your list may look like this:

Close-by sounds I hear:
Creak of chair legs and back
Hum of computer fan
Clicking of hard drive disk
Hiss of oscillating fan in room

After 30 seconds of "close listening" and note-taking, close your eyes again and tune in to the largest possible range in your aural perception. Focus on listening to what is going on outside your immediate environment; try to listen to the world around you. Many of these sounds will be low frequency and capable of traveling over long distances. Now, your list might include these items:

Distant sounds I hear:
Hoot of the ferry horn as it departs the dock
Drone of an overhead passing jet
Whoosh of car tires on the street
General rumble of city traffic in the distance

You may be surprised that your list is long and full of complex sounds. When you focus on listening to your environment instead of just hearing it, you discover a whole symphonic tapestry of sound that your brain has tuned out so it may focus attention on input from your visual field. Even though you may not be actively listening, all that sound is reaching your brain quickly. In fact, your response to a new sound is 10 times faster than your response to a change in your visual field; you just do not pay attention to it unless your brain recognizes it as something unusual or as a threat [2].

This awareness, this capacity to listen and not just hear, is a fundamental tool for making captivating virtual environments. Each one of these environments should have a distinctive aural ambiance, just as your current physical world location does. If you create a sense of the layers and subtleties that the sound of your physical world has in all of your virtual projects, you will enhance the visitors' overall experience. With a virtual "soundscape" containing music, sound, and vocalization, your sonic environment will impart a sense of presence, direction, and emotion to all who visit.

11.1.1 GAME SOUND AND HOW IT IS ADAPTIVE AUDIO

Why is sound in a game so different from sound anywhere else, and how can this help you design better virtual environments? Fundamentally, there are three large categories of sound in a video game: (1) musical score and ambiance; (2) special sound effects (or FX); and (3) voice or dialogue. You can design all three of these, and the more you can compose and orchestrate these sounds, the more immersive and powerful the experience will be for the visitor or player. Many games accomplish this with an "adaptive" or interactive sound structure. The underlying musical score may fade away temporarily as new sounds become prominent, enhancing the fight action for the player. This audio is adapting and interacting with your player's advancement and actions in the space. The sound and music files are arranged in phased overlapping layers and triggered by the position and direction of the player's character in the game space.

Should your player retreat, a section of the theme can be replayed or looped to maintain the aural ambiance of the environment. Although a relatively new approach to audio, this technique has become popular in video game development because it gives the game programmer a flexible musical/sound structure that can easily be incorporated into the coding that drives the game play [3].

As you start to plan for the sound in your virtual environment, it is helpful to keep these approaches in mind. While the sound structures of your virtual environment may not be as complex as a high-level video game, having a clear plan of how the sound will transition, or "play," for a visitor is important for creating a harmonious immersive presentation. Look for rhythmic permutations, the "beat" of the space. Ask yourself if there is an underlying sense of tempo for building a soundscape. Does this tempo provide for sound transitions and changes of overlying themes in the virtual space? For example, perhaps there is a large machine in the nearby area, thumping and squeaking with wheels and gears in rotation. This kind of device would add a fundamental "heartbeat" to the underlying sounds in your environment and would actually serve as a location guide to the players as they navigate the space. Maybe there are scary monsters that approach and retreat from the vicinity as the player wanders through your environment. How you structure the sound events in a virtual environment is crucial to providing your visitor with a memorable experience. Figure 11.1 is a diagram of a maze-like virtual environment compared to a chart of the types and durations of sound events (triggered and ambient) as they are experienced by the visitor within the space. In this virtual space there are continuous looping sounds and infrequent sounds that may be triggered by the player's approach. There are also ambient sounds and musical themes the player will hear when exiting the space.

11.1.2 CONSIDERING MOVIE SCORES AND VIRTUAL SOUNDSCAPES

Sound is the only aspect of a virtual environment that can touch our bodies physically. When a sound is created, the vibrations pass physical energy through the air, move the tiny bones in our ears, and transmit the sound into our brains. Perhaps it is their physical aspect that gives sound effects and musical scores the capacity to evoke a whole spectrum of emotions in us. Most of you can probably hum the themes from *The Godfather* or *Star Wars* but also consider movies like *Wall-E* or *Apocalypse Now*. *Wall-E*, for the most part, has no spoken dialogue, and yet you know exactly what is going on thanks to Ben Burt's sound design [4].

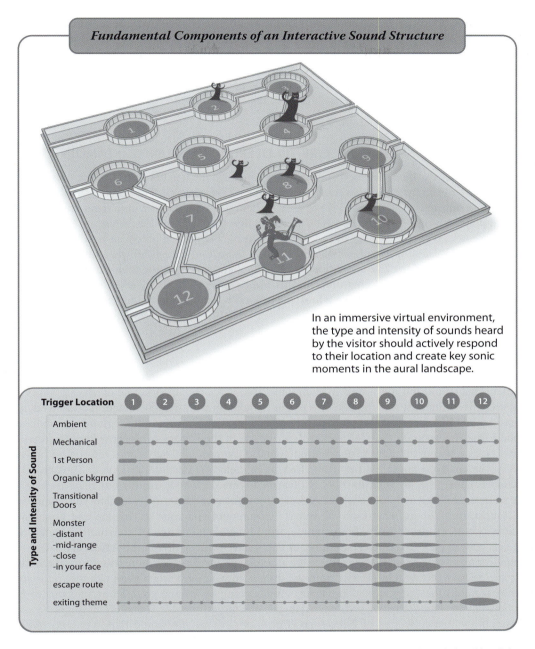

In an immersive virtual environment, the type and intensity of sounds heard by the visitor should actively respond to their location and create key sonic moments in the aural landscape.

FIGURE 11.1 Diagram showing a schematic of virtual spaces (top image) in a game, and the relationship of the sounds within the game to their trigger locations and duration (bottom chart image). By defining the occurrence of sounds based on players location in the virtual space, you create an interactive soundscape.

Apocalypse Now exhibits the genius of Walter Murch, who created a whole palette of helicopter sounds and used them for the "musique concrète" or "electronic music out of real sounds" for that film.

As you start your soundscape design, ask yourself these questions: What is the aural structure of the sound environment? Are there some "building blocks" of sound clips that can support your visual theme, just as the various helicopter sounds enhanced the surrealism and hyperrealism of *Apocalypse Now*? What sounds will support the "sense of space" as well as the emotion of the environment? What is the order of presentation for your sound clips to the visitor?

11.2 JUST A BIT OF SOUND THEORY TO DEEPEN YOUR UNDERSTANDING

The IEZA framework by Sander Huiberts and Richard van Tol at the Utrecht School of the Arts (2003–2008) is a useful structure to analyze and plan sound for virtual environments [5]. They divided all the game/virtual space audio into four major categories: (1) Diegetic, or sound coming from within the virtual environment, such as your player's footsteps; (2) Nondiegetic, or sound from a source outside the virtual environment, such as a musical score; (3) Setting, which includes things like surf sounds at an ocean beach; and (4) Activity, for sounds that are related to what is happening. Within these four categories, they defined four domains: Interface (I), Effect (E), Zone (Z), and Affect (A). While there is no specific recipe for creating the sound-scape structure of a given virtual environment, this framework can be a valuable tool to help you analyze your audio plans. For instance, let's take a look at the sounds from the Alchemy/Particles story sim region using this framework.

11.2.1 ALCHEMY SIMS STORYTELLING SOUNDSCAPE

When the Alchemy Sims build group created the Alchemy/Particles region in Second Life, they built an environment that would tell the visitor in sound and note cards the historic tale of an imaginary popula-tion that once lived there. It was the tale of a native population who was contacted, modernized, and then abandoned by an alien race that they called the Alchemists. The terrain of that region was subdivided and developed visually into areas that defined an "age" or era in the history of the now-vanished civilization. In Figure 11.2, you can see how a storytelling soundscape was laid out across the region of Alchemy. Essentially, the environs broke out into these four main areas: (1) Earthquake Dome, (2) Active Volcano, (3) Volcano Engine, and (4) Bathing Pool. Notice in Figure 11.2 how the various regions were defined by their sounds, shifting about on the IEZA scale from place to place. As you plan your soundscape on the IEZA grid, think about what kind of virtual environment you want to develop and how that would be balanced across the framework. For example, would the sound design of a virtual nightclub with live musical acts appear only in the Interface zone, or can it have some action in the Affect area? Does a "God game" environment with your avatar ruling over all creation and destruction represent itself mostly in the Affect zone? Would getting a large roar from the dragon in your cave when you poke him draw too much focus away from all the dripping and slithering sounds going on around you? Think in terms of how you want to balance the soundscape of your environment; one large Interface sound effect might be enough to counterweigh a whole collection of Zone-type effects, or perhaps you would like to balance Affect with Effect sounds. These choices are up to you.

11.3 BASIC QUALITIES OF SOUND IN A VIRTUAL WORLD

Sound, like light in a virtual environment, is digital information instantiated, modified, and controlled by the underlying game engine with its coded laws of physics and physical world qualities. In a virtual world, you

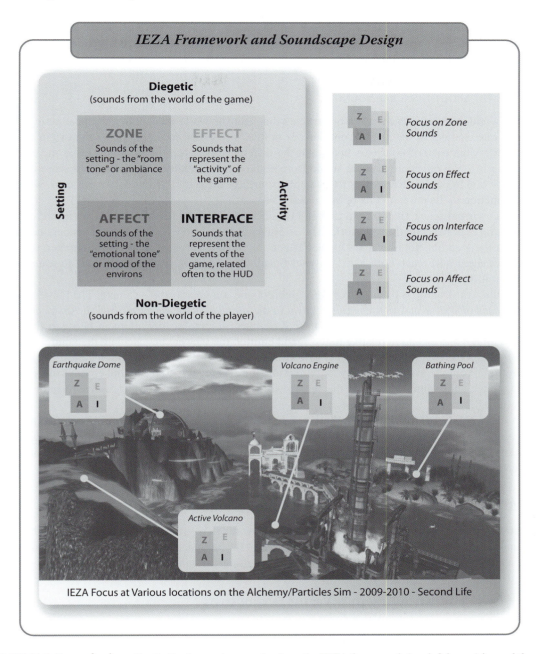

FIGURE 11.2 (See color insert) In the figure above notice how the IEZA framework (top left image) is used throughout the virtual environment (bottom image) to transition the visitor through various areas, while providing a sense of aural specificity (top right image).

can control the initiation of a sound, its duration and loudness, frequency of repetition or loops, with simple LSL scripts and sound clips in the contents of an object or prim. More advanced versions of these sound scripts control interactive qualities and create prolonged cascading sound effects for a seamless atmosphere.

11.3.1 A Bit about Binaural Sound

In the real world, most of us have two working ears that hear the world monaurally, each ear acting like one speaker or one channel to the audio cortex of our brains. You experience and locate the origin of sounds by comparing what each of your ears hears and the difference between the signals. This is the essence of binaural hearing. Not only can you hear sound from all directions simultaneously, but your sense of hearing also can function in complete darkness to locate the source of the sound—how unlike our eyes, which need light and function in the narrow cone of our visual field.

Audio in a virtual space, like Second Life and OpenSim is 3D sound, in other words, a virtual re-creation of our binaural experience in the real world. This is especially noticeable when you wear headphones and can clearly hear the location, volume, and Doppler effects. If you use speakers with your computer, the sounds from each of them will reach both ears, but your binaural recognition is diminished due to sound overlap and reverberation.

In a virtual world, audio is listened to by the "microphone" on your avatar's camera. The viewer identifies the coordinates of your avatar in the region relative to the sound emitter. By measuring the distance between your avatar and the sound emitter as well as the difference in angular measurement between the avatar's rotation (azimuth) and elevation relative to the sound emitter, the viewer can calculate the volume changes it needs to make in the two sound channels to give your ears the sense of distance and location for the sounds being emitted. From the avatar's velocity and direction of travel relative to the sound emitter, the viewer can calculate a pitch and volume change in the sound, which creates a Doppler effect, as your avatar flies by a sound emitter [6].

Much like a single lightbulb that is radiating light in a large dark room, the sound is emitted in a sphere from the center of the source and has a "falloff" range that dims it and cuts it off when you are too far away. That falloff effect is called attenuation in both audio and lighting. Attenuation is a variable that you can manipulate by changing the volume settings in a sound-playing script.

11.4 BUILDING BASICS FOR A SOUND ENVIRONMENT

Now that you have a deeper understanding of how sound works in a virtual world, you can start to build your own soundscapes. What kind of sound files do you need? If you look at the Second Life game engine, you see that it supports the kinds of sound and sound sources discussed in this section.

11.4.1 Types of Sound Supported in Virtual Environments

According to the game engine database at Devmaster.net (http://devmaster.net/devdb), these kinds of sounds and compression formats are supported by the Second Life virtual environment game engine:

3D sound. This kind of sound provides us with (1) the location of sound via two-channel binaural sound; (2) volume attenuation, or the fading of sound volume as the distance between the listener and the emitter increases; (3) Doppler effect, or the apparent change in pitch as a noise emitter passes the listener at high speed.

Streaming sound. This is sound brought in from a website URL through media on a prim.

FMOD. This advanced tool is free to use for noncommercial purposes (http://fmod.org/).

Ogg-Vorbis compressed format streamed. This is a common compression format.

QuickTime MOV video streamed. This is another common compression format.

Doppler effect. Doppler pitch shifting is the pitch-shifting effect heard by a listener as an emitter moves by quickly.

11.4.2   REQUIREMENTS FOR SOUND FILES WHEN IMPORTING THEM TO VIRTUAL ENVIRONMENTS

To import sounds into Second Life and OpenSim virtual environments, the absolute requirements for sound clips are as follows:

1. Sound clips saved as .wav format with the standard PCM (pulse-code modulation).
2. 16-bit/44.1-kHz/mono or stereo (converted to mono).
3. Length of less than 10 seconds. Your clip length can be 9.99 seconds but no longer; an 10.1-second audio file will fail to upload.

Note: Sound clips for Unity can be longer than 10 seconds in duration. For a "Build It Once" approach, try building your Unity sound from smaller units less than 10 seconds. Then, you can utilize audio that imports into virtual spaces like Second Life and OpenSim while maintaining a library for the longer audio themes in your Unity builds.

11.5   HOW TO CONTROL SOUND IN A VIRTUAL WORLD

Sound-making objects are created and controlled with the addition of LSL (Linden scripting language) scripts into the objects' content section via the object editor. The sound in Unity is controlled via C# or Unity Script (like Java script) or via Boo (a .net language like Python). Assuming you have the sound clip ready to go, you initiate and control the sound emission with various kinds of scripts that respond to things like avatar presence (a burglar alarm); avatar touch (a doorbell); the time of day (larks in the day, owls at night); wind direction (noise from a windmill); or location (parcel limited sound for the dance floor in your nightclub). The possibilities are practically limitless, just as our real-world sound-making devices are. A source of scripts and sample sounds accessed by their UUIDs (Universally Unique IDentifiers) to test these various types of sound activators for the Second Life viewers is available online (http://wiki.secondlife.com/wiki/Audio_Test). Within this old but still valuable wiki are many sources of information for the content creator. Here, you will find scripts for playing sound, looping sound, and synching various loops together for a bigger effect.

If you have a server available, sound clips can be played continuously and streamed on your region. This technique has been used successfully to create an overall ambiance for themed and gaming regions in Second Life. Care should be exercised with this approach, however, as having sound effects that appear to come from everywhere can seem disjointed and inappropriate to the visitor if there is no visual event or object to support the reason for the sound. This is best used for Zone and Effect sounds like wind, weather, and Non-Digetic sounds such as theme music.

Another factor to be aware of is lag and how it affects sound. One way to avoid awkward pauses in audio is to utilize a sound "preloader" function in your scripting. This will load the sounds when the object is rezzed in your environment so that they are ready to be activated on a touch event.

11.6   WHERE TO OBTAIN SOUND FOR YOUR 3D SPACES

You have built your beautiful house, car, or fountain now, and you need to give it an audio presence. Where do you obtain sound for your 3D spaces? Basically, you have two options: (1) download sound from sites on the Internet under varying license requirements, such as Freesound.org (http://www.freesound.org) and Soundsnap.com (http://www.soundsnap.com); or (2) make and record your own sound.

If you go with option 1, remember to check the licensing and permissions for use of the sounds you download and follow the guidelines.

If you go with option 2, your life is about to become more interesting. Recording your own sound, doing voice-overs, making sound effects, and even composing music for your virtual builds is creatively rewarding. Perhaps you have a secret talent as a Foley (sound effects) artist and can find ways to utilize the everyday objects in your household for making special effect sounds. Maybe your reading voice is pleasant to listen to, or your voice sounds great as the talking computer in your science fiction adventure build. You might even be a good musician and now have discovered that scoring music for the theme of your build in a virtual world has its own rewards. With readily available and affordable recording devices like the Zoom recorder (H series) (http://www.zoom.co.jp), you can record sound easily. There probably are many items you already own that will create the sounds you need for your soundscape. The key to making creative Foley sound is to listen to the sound the object makes without looking at it. Take a piece of plastic wrap, crumple it up, and roll it around in your hands beside your ear. It sounds like rainfall. Shake a piece of thin sheet metal, and you have the sound of thunder. All around you are objects that make interesting sounds if you shake, drop, squeeze, bend, or walk on them. It all starts in your imagination.

11.7   HOW TO EDIT THE SOUND FOR YOUR VIRTUAL ENVIRONMENT

Editing sound, like Foley work, is part art, part science. Sometimes you just need a simple file converter, and sometimes you need to bring out the heavy artillery. There are many good sound editors, and they range in price. A list of free downloads for Voxengo is available (http://www.dontcrack.com/freeware/audio-software. php/id/10753/downloads/Voxengo/). Audacity (http://audacity.sourceforge.net/) is a popular freeware program that runs on most platforms and has loads of features. FMod (http://fmod.org/) is free to use if you are editing the sounds for noncommercial purposes and provides very high end features and functionality. For people who like to work in the Adobe Creative Suite, Adobe Soundbooth (also known as Adobe Audition) has good interconnected functionality with Adobe Premiere and Adobe Photoshop, but this program is in the higher end of the price range. FMod under the pro license would fall into the superheavy artillery category in both cost and functionality. You may find yourself utilizing several sound editors depending on what your needs are for the project at hand.

In the edit phase, you should start to think about how your ultimate sound plan will come together. Most sound-editing programs give you the capacity to make stacked audio tracks. Just as you discovered in the very first part of this chapter, no environment (except an anechoic chamber) is without sound reflection and underlying ambiance, so you will be utilizing these audio tracks to create layers of sound for the visitor in your virtual world to discover. It is time to start thinking about the 10-second sound-layered plan for your environment.

11.7.1   Step by Step toward a Soundscape

Let us break down a soundscape step by step. Where do you start to build your sound design, what layer goes first, and how do you organize a soundscape? In general, you can rely on the following list of the five basic layers of sound to help you get started:

1. Baseline sounds in the world environment relative to your build's location (e.g., seaside or mountains).
2. Score or theme that sets underlying tone (e.g., horror, peace, loneliness, etc.).
3. General ambiance of your location, such as sounds of a marketplace, factory, or field.
4. Prop sounds, proximity activated as you pass through the environment, such as doors, a buzzing neon sign overhead, automated butler robots, and the like.
5. Sounds that are touch or voice/chat activated, perhaps part of a game you are playing inworld or part of the functioning of the space (e.g., magic doors, supersecret hideout entrances).

This list excludes voice chat and sound-generating devices an avatar may be wearing because those are transient events in your environment. While they are important elements, these sounds may not be part of every visitor's experience all the time, so they can be put aside for the moment while you build the environmental soundscape. Just bear in mind that if you need to allow for focus on specific sound emitters, the rest of your environmental sound should be made more subtle and localized to smaller areas. As you start to plan the soundscape for your next project, take the time to create a list of all the sounds you want to utilize.

There are just a few more things to consider when you set out to make your soundscape, and these are important factors about the volume of the sound you will bring into a virtual world. The volume of your sound is defined by a range of 0.1 to 1.0 with the sound scripts in Second Life and OpenSim. This is perfectly adequate if you are hearing the sound when your camera is in mouse-look and you are standing near the emitter. However, try to remember that most visitors will just trundle along with their camera floating above and behind their head. This will affect your soundscape design, and you will have to compensate for it by moving your sound emitters up to where most of the cameras are or tell the visitors to hear sound from their avatar location. This setting can be changed in the Avatar/Preferences/Sound & Media/Voice settings menu.

One method for getting the right amount of sound to the avatar's camera/audio listener is to have the emitter installed in a small prim or object. That way, to "see" it, they have to move the camera or avatar close, and by doing so, they bring the listener into the appropriate range for hearing the sound effects made by that object of interest. Another method is to set up a series of sound emitters, both high and low, at different volumes to reach the audio listener no matter where the visitor has the camera set. The best approach is to consider these methods, put a preliminary soundscape in place, and do a test walk through with your camera in many positions. From that walk, you can start to eliminate any extra sound emitters that have proved superfluous and add to the work the server has to do.

Another issue that pops up is a sound file that plays too faintly for the virtual world, even if you have it set to full volume in the scripting. If that is the issue, take a look at the clip in your sound editor and try "normalizing" the sound to bring the waveform up to 100%. You should also look at the bit rate of the sound encoding and use the lowest possible setting that gives you clear and undistorted playback in the virtual world. A setting of 64 kbps (kilobits per second) will work fine for speech and simple sounds and will create much less lag in the server than a file uploaded at 128 kbps [7]. Finally, make sure that, as you create, install, and test your soundscape, your headphones and the sound settings on your viewer are set to the default settings for your initial test walk so you can set a "baseline" for the audio experience. This will help you decide how you should ramp up the sound as the visitors explore the region and what visible devices you may need to add, such as signs and note cards to clue them in to changing their audio settings for the maximal experience in your build.

Although not much data are available, the client viewers seem to hit the top limit at 32 simultaneous sound emitters in any region. It is also wise to avoid putting too many looping sources close together; use only one or two within the range of hearing if possible.

11.8   PROJECT: MAKING AN AUDIO-BASED GAMING ENVIRONMENT

For this project, you will create a simple audio based navigation game inspired by the Norwegian folk tale "Three Billy Goats Gruff." The original story, as you may recall, is about the billy goats' trickery of a dull troll, who tried to eat one of them. In this game, the billy goats must navigate their way from their barn, through the market place, over the troll's bridges, past Troll Hall and the troll campsite, find a lost kid, and get to the safety of the orchard, all by using their sense of hearing to follow the audio cues. Because this is a sound-based game, it will be played in a relatively nonvisual environment, situated inside a black box honeycombed with internal black walls that limit views of the other player's avatars. The entryway corridor has signage and proximity activated sound clips that explain the game to the entering player. Once you get this project finished, invite some friends over to try it. You should be prepared for, and even encourage, emergent game play or the evolution of new game play within this sound-based game space.

11.8.1   PRELIMINARY GAME SPACE LAYOUT

Let's go through the steps for setup of the playing landscape. Figure 11.3 provides a visual display of these steps.

1. Download all the Chapter 11 content needed for this game from http://www.anncudworthprojects.com/, in the Virtual World Design Book Downloads section. This will include textures for the game board surface and maps, as well as the sounds needed for making the game. As you upload this content, make sure to name the sound and texture files with the same name. For instance, the sound file named Babbling_Stream.wav will become a sound in your inventory called Babbling_Stream.
2. Create a 100 meter wide (on the x axis) by 100 meter long (on the y axis) by 1 meter thick (on the z axis) box prim as your game platform. This can be a skybox platform or set up somewhere on a flat terrain. You will also need 100 meters more off the side to create the entrance to the game. So, count on using at least half a region (256 meters by 128 meters) to set this game up properly.
3. Apply the texture called 3BGG_game board image.png to the top face of the game board so you can lay out the sound emitters in their appropriate areas. As you can see, this is kind of a schematic map, that indicates the kinds of locations the players will visit aurally in this game space.
4. Create a 100 meter (x) by 100 meter (y) by 20 meter high (z) black box prim centered on your game board and set it to 99% hollow so you have high black walls surrounding the game space.
5. Create a path cut on that box, settings at Beginning (B)=0.025, and End (E) =1.00. This cut will open up an entrance to the game space for the players. You can see this in the bottom image, lower right corner of Figure 11.3.

11.8.2   THE SOUND EMITTER SETUP

Now, you will make the audio elements of the game. For this section, you will need the sound file called Test_123.wav that is in the contents provided with this chapter. Figure 11.4 has a visual description of this section. You will also need to wear a good set of headphones to do the rest of this project, so you can experience binaural sound.

1. Make three spheres, set them to phantom, and name them loop_sound, touch_sound, and proximity_sound, respectively, in the Object Name slot in the Edit menu. The loop and touch spheres should be 0.5 to 1 meter in diameter, and the proximity sphere should be 5 meters in diameter.

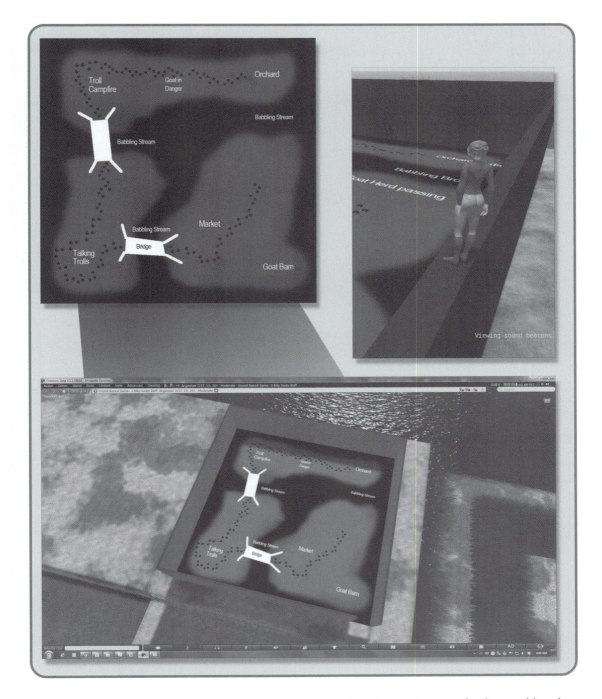

FIGURE 11.3 Screen grabs from OpenSim showing the initial setup of the game space for the sound-based game inspired by "Three Billy Goats Gruff."

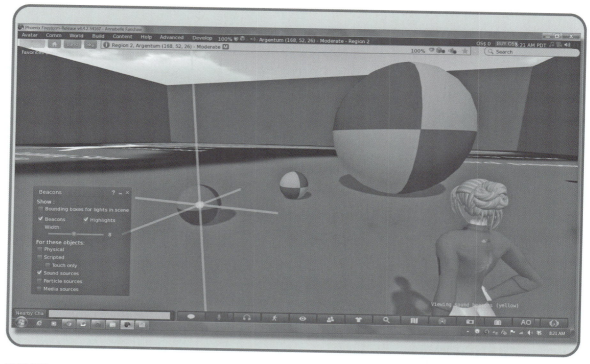

FIGURE 11.4 Screen grab for OpenSim, showing the process of making the basic sound emitters for looping sound, touch-activated sound, and proximity-activated sound. Foreground shows how sound beacons can identify the sound emitters.

2. *Note:* Turn on your sound beacons by checking the Sound sources and Beacons boxes in the World/Show More/Beacons menu. This will enable you to find the sound emitters when you make them transparent.

3. From the Script Me autoscript site (http://www.3greeneggs.com/autoscript/) make three kinds of scripts: (1) a looping sound that plays the sound repeatedly as soon as the object is rezzed from your inventory and the script starts; (2) one that plays sound when an avatar clicks on (touches) it; and (3) a script that plays a sound when an avatar gets into proximity. Set the sound in this last one to play repeatedly, if you wish, and trigger at the proximity distance of 5 meters. If you set it to only play once, repeat players will not hear these sounds a second time.

   a. In the loop_sound sphere, put in the looping script and Test_123.wav sound file from the chapter's content files. Check to make sure you can hear the looping sound from your mouse-look position.

   b. In the touch_sound sphere, put in the touch start sound script and the Test_123.wav from the chapter's content files. Make sure the sound plays once when you touch it.

   c. In the proximity_sound sphere, put in the proximity start sound script and Test_123.wav sound file. Take this sphere back into your inventory, rez it at least 10 meters away, and walk up to it. Make sure that the script plays the Test_123.wav file when your avatar walks near it.

Please note, you may have to give the server some time to load these sounds; they may not play immediately at first.

If the scripts are all working as expected, take a copy of the spheres, and put them in 3 folders in your inventory. Call the folders "Loop," "Touch," and "Proximity Sound Emitters" so you can find them easily.

11.8.3 MAKING THE SOUND EMITTERS SPECIFIC TO SOUND AND TRIGGER

1. Now, you should download and import the rest of the sounds provided with this chapter; make sure you have the following 14 "ready-to-go" sounds:
   a. Babbling_Stream.wav
   b. Boiling_Stew.wav
   c. Campfire_loop.wav
   d. Goat_help_me.wav
   e. Goat_saved_me.wav
   f. Goatherd_going_by.wav
   g. Herd_of_goats_loop.wav
   h. Marketplace_with_vendors_loop.wav
   i. Orchard_birds.wav
   j. Troll_eat_you.wav
   k. Troll_goat_stew.wav
   l. Troll_MMM_eat_stew.wav
   m. Troll_my_little_goat.wav
   n. Wind.wav

2. Drag out seven looping-type sound emitters from your Loop Sound Emitters folder and put in the sounds "Babbling Stream," "Boiling_stew," "Campfire," "Herd_of goats," "Marketplace with_ vendors," "Orchard_birds," and "Wind", respectively, removing the Test_123.wav file as you do. *Note:* The volume setting in these ScriptMe-generated scripts is found in the sound function line and set at 1 (the loudest) as a default. You may need to change that number when you have several spheres close together.

3. Now drag out two touch-activated sound emitters and put sounds d and e into their content inventories, one sound in each, removing the Test_123 as you do it. Touch it to make sure it works. Rename the emitter spheres "Goat_help_me_touch" and "Goat_saved_me_touch," make them phantom, and take them back into your inventory in a new folder called "TBG_sound_touch."

4. Drag out four proximity-activated sound emitters and put sounds j, k, l, and m in each. Put one sound into the contents of each emitter, removing the Test_123.wav file as you do. Walk away and then back to it to make sure it works and that the sound activates only once when you are 5 meters away from it. Rename the emitter spheres "Troll_eat_you_prox," "Troll_goat_stew_prox," "Troll_MMM_eat_stew_prox," and "Troll_my_little_goat_prox"; make them phantom; and take them back into your inventory in a new folder called "TBG_sound_prox." *Note:* This script will have to be reset or the object rezzed again for the emitter to produce the sound again for you to hear when you approach it, since it's scripted to play only once.

You will see an inworld view of this step in Figure 11.5; note that the sound emitters have a bright pattern on them for illustrative purposes only. You can make them any color you wish while you build; eventually you will make them fully transparent and invisible for game play.

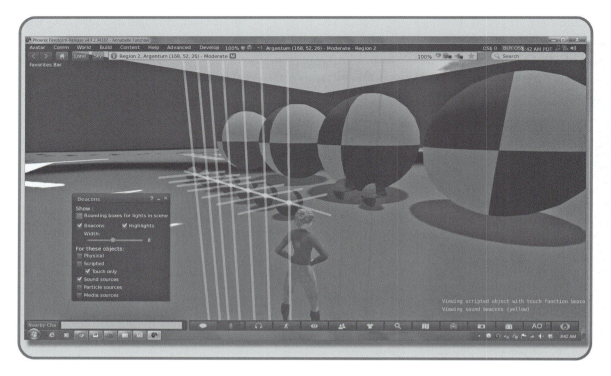

FIGURE 11.5 Screen grab showing the creation of the basic sound emitters for the game. The Beacons are turned on indicating the center of these touch-activated scripted sound prims, and while the sound script is running, the prim turns red.

11.8.4 LAYING OUT THE AUDIO LANDSCAPE OF THE GAME

Now that you have made all of your sound emitters, it is time to spread them out across the game environment to make the game soundscape for your players. Figure 11.6 provides an illustrated overview of this section.

Here are five basic factors to remember while you do this:

1. **Anchoring:** By using the game board graphic as a guide, locate your audio "anchors" first. Place the looping sounds of the marketplace, the goat barn, trolls, and orchard far enough apart and spaced over the landscape so that the players will have a sense of direction and can be relatively secure in their location on the game board. It is perfectly legal to put your emitters outside the box, above or below it, so that the sound is heard less by the players inside. Aim for being able to hear them all from a distance of 20 meters on a 50% volume setting in your headphones.
2. **Emergence:** Support the emergent nature of game play by putting sound in surprising locations and varying the height of the emitter off the plane of the game board so it sometimes coincides with the location of the default camera position.
3. **Layer:** You may also decide to layer/trigger a sound in a couple of ways. For instance, having a troll saying "MMMMM-goat stew" on a loop in the distance creates an atmospheric sound layer with an underlying threat factor. Placing a loud emitter with a proximity trigger running the same sound can make your players jump at the unexpected change of position and loudness of the troll's sound.

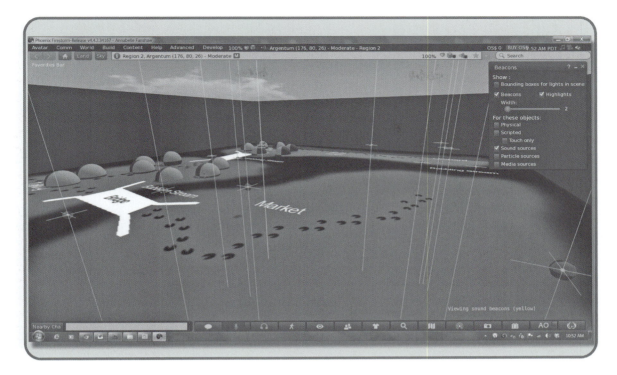

FIGURE 11.6 Screen grab showing process of laying out the sound emitters on the game board.

4. **Server load:** Be efficient and choose your locations carefully; try to make the space work with 20 or fewer sound emitters so there is time on the server for other kinds of sound in the sim.

5. **Testing:** Once you have placed your emitters, turn off your computer monitor, raise the volume on your headset, and try to find your way across the landscape. You should be able to navigate successfully from the goat barn to the orchid if your layout is good. The locations of the sounds should be clearly heard, and not piling up in one chaotic noise. If not, move the sound emitters around until you can.

11.8.5 MAKING THE SIGNAGE AND ENTRANCE

Figure 11.7 has an image of the setup for the signage and entrance. Even though this is a sound-based game, you will need some visuals for the players to help them orient to the arrangement of the space. It would be a good idea to show them a map of the game space and to make that map object a "proximity-activated" sound emitter that describes the space to someone who has limited vision. If you do this with a silly goat voice or a scary troll voice, your signage will set the mood of the game right away. Each sign that the players walk past should inform them about the game. To avoid confusion and too much overlap of sound, try to keep your signage to three or four signs. As you can see in Figure 11.7, the game audio landscape is described along the entrance hall with a series of talking signs; each one is activated by the proximity of the avatar. The avatar takes about 10 seconds to walk 30 meters, so by the time the avatar gets to the next sign, the first clip has ended, and the next one is ready to go. You can set these signs up for your version of the game by using these three images from the Chapter 11

FIGURE 11.7   Screen shot from OpenSim showing entrance to finished game. Aspects of universal design were utilized for the entrance to the "Three Billy Goats Gruff" audio-based game. Signs are visual as well as audible. They are self-illuminating for clear visibility even in the darkest WindLight settings.

content: BBG_intro_sign1.png, BBG_intro_sign2.png, and BBG_intro_sign3.png. The audio clips that go with them are: BBG_game_Audio_Hint1.wav, BBG_game_Audio_Hint2.wav and BBG_game_Audio_Hint3.wav.

11.8.6   How to Set Up for Play Testing Your Audio Game

Let's set up for play testing and add the final elements for use by a group of players.

1. Add eight black phantom partitions that are 100 meters long, 0.5 meters thick, and 20 meters high so the internal space is divided into 16 compartments. Do not link them to anything. In Figure 11.8, you will see how they are laid out. These are used to prevent people who are still looking at visuals on their monitor from seeing across the landscape and locating others who are nearby. This should also discourage them from using inworld voices to find one another if necessary.
2. Turn all the textures to black on their material settings so you cannot see the landscape map on the game board or the surrounding walls. Make all the sound emitters 100% transparent; check again that they are all phantom.
3. Put a black lid on the box and set the surrounding WindLight setting to Midnight or Phototools/Photo No Light if you want complete blackness. *Note*: If you use the No Light WindLight setting, you will need to make your entryway signage have a bright or self-illuminating setting so the players can find their way into the space.

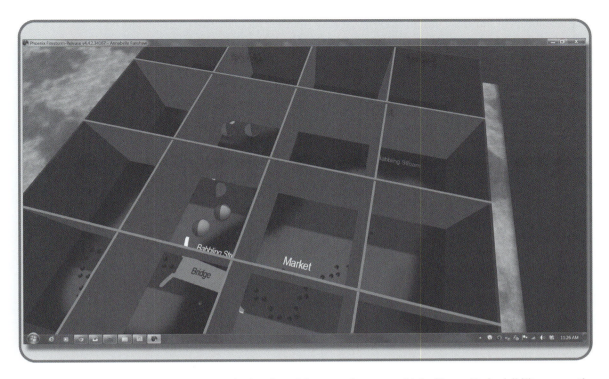

FIGURE 11.8 Screen grab showing how the interior of the game is set up with baffles to limit visibility across the game board.

11.8.7 PLAY TESTING AND SOME THINGS YOU CAN EXPECT

Finally you are ready for play testing; here are some things to remember:

1. Let the players go through the instructions and game play without any intervention.
2. Take notes and meet for a group chat afterward.
3. Tweak your audio landscape to make play harder or easier as the case may be. You might find that more visual barriers are needed or more sounds. Play testers tend to break your games, and that is what you should expect them to do. You may have to ask them to set their sound "roll off" to the minimum (under Avatar/Preferences/Sound & Media/General) so they can separate the sounds more easily, or perhaps you may need to turn down the volumes or set the sound emitters into more distant locations.
4. After five or six rounds of play testing, you should be ready to go public and open the game up for all.

As you observe how people play this game, make notes on human behavior and how it is affected by your design. Look for new ways to use audio in all of your builds. If you do see emergent game play, make notes on how it happens and what inspires it so you can utilize those qualities in your future designs.

11.9 FINAL THOUGHTS ABOUT SOUND DESIGN

Hopefully, you have been inspired to become a sound designer or at the very least a person interested in the potential power of sound as an immersive element in a virtual world.

12 Avatars and Nonplayer Characters

Henry Frankenstein: Look! It's moving. It's alive. It's alive... It's alive, it's moving, it's alive, it's alive,
   it's alive, it's alive, IT'S ALIVE!
Victor Moritz: Henry—in the name of God!
Henry Frankenstein: Oh, in the name of God! Now I know what it feels like to be God!

Frankenstein, Universal Pictures, 1931, screenplay by John L. Balderston

12.1 AVATARS AND OUR SENSE OF SELF

Your avatar, no matter what manifestation you choose—human figure, fire-breathing dragon, or anime doll—is the center of your experience in the virtual world. As a human being with a self-reflective mind capable of observing your own thoughts and desires, the creation of your avatar in a virtual world gives you the opportunity to experience social relationships in new ways, physical capacities that you may not have (flying), and another perspective on self-identity/cultural identity (possibly as another gender). As you can see from Figure 12.1, the avatar is at the center of all things. As you log into the virtual world, the basic avatar geometry takes on the body shape you have modified into your own virtual representation. Your virtual body is stretched or compressed, tinted or made invisible. Meshes and objects are added to create interesting things like wings and hooves. As you rez into existence, many layers are added. First, the shell of a shape is put on, then a gender with its associated clothing and attachments, and finally the social and virtual barriers that define your visibility to others and availability for social contact.

Avatars are the common denominators, the hub of your subjective experience, and the heuristic framework that allows you to observe relative scale and spatial qualities of the virtual environment. They are the representative self through which you can participate in communication (text chat, voice chat), and they are your cocreator (role-playing character) of the shared story in an MMORPG (massively multiplayer online role-playing game).

Be careful about choosing an avatar in cyberspace. The psychological/physical connection to our virtual selves runs deep in our minds. For many people, self-observation of their real body and thinking of their avatar light up the same areas of their brains during scans [1]. Studies about the phenomenon of "body transfer illusion" have demonstrated that a threat to your avatar's body, no matter how differently it looks from your actual body, will elicit the same physiological response as a threat to your real body [2].

At the Stanford Virtual Human Interaction Lab (http://vhil.stanford.edu/), there are several research programs that study the body transfer illusion as well as other avatar/human-related events. In one experiment, they found that people using avatars with superpowers to save a lost diabetic child in the virtual scenario would demonstrate a faster response to helping one of the lab assistants pick up a bunch of spilled pens after their virtual session was over [3]. The scientists at the lab have found that more ecological behavior (such as using fewer paper napkins) will be demonstrated by people after they participate as virtual lumberjacks in the toppling of a virtual tree. Testing results have also shown that composite avatars that blend your real-life face with a politician's face will make you more likely to vote for that politician.

237

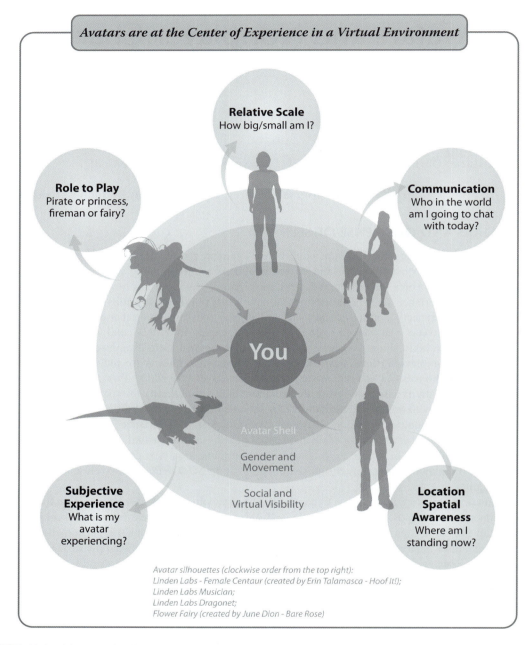

Avatars are at the Center of Experience in a Virtual Environment

Relative Scale
How big/small am I?

Role to Play
Pirate or princess, fireman or fairy?

Communication
Who in the world am I going to chat with today?

You

Avatar Shell

Gender and Movement

Social and Virtual Visibility

Subjective Experience
What is my avatar experiencing?

Location Spatial Awareness
Where am I standing now?

Avatar silhouettes (clockwise order from the top right):
Linden Labs - Female Centaur (created by Erin Talamasca - Hoof It!);
Linden Labs Musician;
Linden Labs Dragonet;
Flower Fairy (created by June Dion - Bare Rose)

FIGURE 12.1 Diagram showing the relationship of the avatar to the user in a virtual world. The avatar creates a layered framework that encompasses a range of experience including relative scale observation, communication, spatial awareness, subjective experience, and role playing.

12.2   THE IMPORTANCE OF AVATARS

Your own individuality is your most precious commodity. Even if you have an identical twin, you are still an individual personality with a unique collection of remembered experiences and interests. Your avatar provides you with the opportunity to reflect on this and add to your personal dimensions and self-identity. You may be putting on a character, playing a role, changing your gender or even your species, but at the core is your basic identity.

The following are some of the most important characteristics of an avatar:

1. *Images.* Avatars are your image, your reflection in a virtual world.
2. *Identification.* Avatars are how others will identify you, recognize you.
3. *Self-image.* Avatars reflect the self-image you have chosen.
4. *Icons.* Avatars can be icons or symbols of your beliefs.
5. *Aspirations.* Avatars can represent what you want to be.
6. *Body modification.* Avatars allow you to experiment with body modification.
7. *Nostalgia.* Avatars can be the mythological or cartoon characters of your childhood.
8. *Scale.* Avatars let you explore the scale variations of the body.
9. *Communication.* Avatars let you communicate and modify your voice.
10. *Storytelling.* Avatars let you tell stories and play roles in them.

12.3   DESIGNING THE LOOK OF YOUR CHARACTER

In essence, you need to get into your avatar's "character," which is part core personality, part projected values, and part reaction to outside forces. When you study theatrical acting, especially "method acting," you will encounter the GOTE method. Developed by Robert Cohen [4], this acronym helps remind actors about the qualities they should consider in developing their character. Briefly, here are those four qualities redefined for an avatar's character development.

1. **Goal:** What does your character want to do in this virtual world? For example, your character wants to be a great, wise teacher.
2. **Obstacle:** What obstacles will your avatar encounter? For example, the great wise teacher would encounter the obstacle of narrow minds and ignorance.
3. **Tactics:** How will your avatar attain goals? For example, the great wise teacher may start giving out books or scrolls filled with wisdom.
4. **Expectation:** What expectations of success does your avatar have? For example, the great wise teacher may realize that overcoming the obstacle of ignorance is a long, hard struggle, so the avatar will prepare accordingly.

By now, a picture of this great wise teacher may have formed in your head. Perhaps this avatar resembles Confucius (551–479 BCE) or Annie Sullivan, who taught Helen Keller (1866–1936), or perhaps this avatar resembles your high school physics teacher. Whatever visual image you have in your mind's eye can be developed in further detail by thinking like a costume designer. A costume designer will do research into the period of the character and will consider the socioeconomic status of the character as the costume is designed. These are valuable insights because they enrich the complexity, color palette, and overall shape of your avatar's outward appearance.

Last year, I asked Rafael Jaen, a noted costume designer and assistant professor of costume design at the University of Massachusetts, these two questions about costume design for avatars:

1. As a professional costume designer, what would you suggest to the first-time avatar builder?
2. How would you get to the "core" of the costume design and give the first-time designer a place to anchor their concepts?

His replies to me were as follows:

I take a two-step approach; the first step is to get into the character's spine; what are her/his motivations, underlying emotions, secrets and outward qualities. Will they need costume items that foreshadow these? I think of Blanche Dubois' entrance in Tennessee Williams' *A Street Car Named Desire*, the description of her dress looking like a "moth driven to the flame" symbolizes her undoing.

The second step is to look at the character's givens, including philosophy (or religion), socioeconomics, environment, weather, historical period, etc. These aspects translate directly to a character's silhouette. Expanding on the previous example, when we first look at Blanche we realize that she is of a different socioeconomic class and an earlier fashion silhouette; she is out of place.

The idea is to endow the character with emotions and qualities using visual design language (such as color, texture, and mass) to communicate the character's history and destiny at first glance.

As you design your avatar's costume, you may want to collect images from your research and make a "look book" of period clothing photographs and illustrations. Slowly, you may formulate a "backstory," a biography if you will, about the avatar. In this story, you may decide on the age, the gender, the social class, and a host of other details that support and compliment the meaning of your avatar.

If you desire to make an avatar that is a "new-and-improved" virtual representation of yourself, think a moment before you start shopping for clothes and shoes. Your avatar can represent your personal interests in a very visual way. For instance, if you are into English blues musicians, your avatar may look like one, or you may have an interest in mythology and horses and decide to combine the two subjects with an avatar that looks like a centaur. Likewise, you can wear or carry the tools of your trade. Attributes such as a hard hat, a tool belt, a briefcase, or a crossbow all indicate your interests and possibly your profession.

12.3.1 WHERE TO SHOP FOR YOUR AVATAR

In the online marketplaces, you will find the clothes, hair, skin, shoes, or other avatar components you need. Also, do not overlook the trade fairs, such as the Hair Fair, Fashion for Life in Second Life and other worlds. The Asset Store (http://unity3d.com/asset-store/) in Unity is filling with high-quality content as well. Another place to check is your own standard avatar inventory; there are often overlooked goodies in there.

12.3.2 MAKING YOUR OWN CLOTHING AND ACCESSORIES

Eventually, you may decide to create your own clothing and accessories for your avatar. There is a great collection of tutorials in the Second Life wiki (http://wiki.secondlife.com/wiki/Clothing_Tutorials). At this site, you will find the standard templates for clothing from Linden Labs and other sources. Making clothing for your avatar is a complex process, but extremely rewarding.

12.4   ANIMATING YOUR AVATAR

In a 3D world, the animations that move our avatars are actually a sequence of coordinates or "positions" for the skeleton inside the mesh surface of our virtual bodies. Like a puppeteer, the animation files (Biovision Hierarchy or BVH format in Second Life and OpenSim) move our bodies and give the avatar a sense of life. The most basic of these is called the "idle" animation. You see this when the avatars are standing, shifting their weight, crossing their arms, and so on. Watch closely, and you will see it cycle as the animation plays through a loop. If you decide to walk your avatar somewhere and press the Up Arrow key to send the avatar off, the idle loop stops, and the walk cycle begins. This is another loop, which repeats for as long as you are walking. Should you decide to fly, another animation kicks in as your avatar moves up in the air. Most people who have been in Second Life for a while will opt out of using the standard animations and wear an animation override (known as AO) on their avatar. These are attached prims, or head-up displays (HUDs) that contain a group of animations and possibly a screen menu for selecting them. For the record, animations should not be confused with gestures. Gestures can contain animation files, but they will also contain sounds and text messages. These are social tokens in virtual worlds and are often created to be given away and shared with a group.

12.4.1   HOW DO YOU OBTAIN ANIMATIONS?

The quick-and-easy way to obtain animations for your avatar is to buy them. The Second Life Marketplace has a large selection, and if you are in OpenSim, there are several websites that have free collections of basic animations. Maria Korolov keeps an OpenSim vendor directory list on her virtual worlds newsletter site, Hypergrid Business (http://www.hypergridbusiness.com/).

If you need a special animation, you can hand make your animations with the free software QAvimator (http://qavimator.org/). Mixamo also sells animations tailored specifically to the Second Life avatar, which you can create (http://www.mixamo.com/motions) and download as Biovision animation (BVH) files for use in Second Life or OpenSim. Due to the differences in skeletons and rigging, you cannot use the same skeleton and animations in Unity that you utilize in Second Life.

12.5   WHAT ARE NONPLAYER CHARACTERS?

Nothing makes a real country or virtual world more interesting than its peoples. In the virtual worlds of Second Life or OpenSim, real people come together as avatars to represent their cultures and aesthetic interests simultaneously across a virtual landscape. By doing this, they create a fascinating mosaic of virtual environments, pulsing with the sounds and sights of their collective creative imaginations. Despite high numbers of visitor concurrency, many popular user-built virtual environments experience the "crowded empty paradox" [5], the emptiness of vast structures echoing with few visitors and the false perception that no one is there. To be sure, some design changes could be added to the architecture and planning of these regions, social centers could be added, and entertainment venues provided as a possible antidote to the lack of a crowd. Another excellent way to enliven these empty spaces is with nonplayer characters (NPCs), who can serve as "ambassadors" to your virtual environment, providing the visitor with a point of contact, a guide to your region, and information about you and your creations.

NPCs provide us with the artificial life forms that add an extra dynamic to the environment; they give it a "heartbeat" if you will. The virtual environment designer's task is to make an environment that will support an NPC population and enhance the immersive game play experience for the player. A virtual world designer must recognize and capitalize on the human need to communicate and interact.

12.6 TYPES OF NPCS AND HOW THEY CAN BE USED IN VIRTUAL ENVIRONMENTS

To understand how NPCs support the visual depth and diversity of an environment, put on your walking shoes and take a 20-minute stroll through your real-world local marketplace, mall, or public park. While you are walking, take note of the people around you. Who is standing still, and why? Are they selling something, or maybe looking at a map? Is there a group of them chatting together, blocking traffic on the sidewalk? Do you see a couple sitting on a bench together, or maybe an old lady and her ancient poodle enjoying the afternoon sun? Inspiration and information about how to populate a street scene are right outside your door, and you should tap that resource for your virtual world scenes.

12.6.1 SETTING THE "STAGE": PROPER BEHAVIOR IN YOUR NPCS

Behavior, just like costumes or clothing, is period specific. When you start to think of the crowd design for your virtual space, ask yourself: What kinds of behaviors are appropriate for the time period I am representing, and how can I reflect that in my NPC animations?

Also, you will have to consider how many of these virtual background actors the server supporting your virtual environment will be able to control, especially if you have a busy sim full of running scripts and people-run avatars with lots of attachments.

Furthermore, you need to ask, how does adding NPCs to my sim enhance the visitors' experience of the environment? Do the NPCs in my region make them feel like the "leading actors" there?

12.6.2 CITY OF URUK: A SUMERIAN TOWN COMES TO LIFE

A significant example of NPC utilization in Second Life is the city of Uruk (http://www-staff.it.uts.edu.au/~anton/Research/Uruk_Project/). In this sim, the daily life in the ancient Sumerian city of Uruk, circa 3000 BC, is reenacted by numerous NPCs, playing out the roles of fishermen, potters, slaves, and royalty. Created in 2008 and ongoing both in Second Life and in OpenSim, this project was started with the collaborative efforts of Dr. Anton Bogdanovych, PhD, from the University of Western Sydney (UWS) and Alex Cohen, the senior digital information strategist at the U.S. Department of Energy. In Figure 12.2, you will see images taken from Uruk that show the resident avatars performing daily tasks such as pot making and fishing and an overall view of the city as it stands today in Second Life (http://maps.secondlife.com/secondlife/FAS/184/121/28).

12.6.3 ROLES THOSE NPCS CAN PLAY

How can we utilize NPCs on a sim? Let us count the ways. Here are some basic categories of NPCs, separated by their level of artificial intelligence (AI) and interaction:

1. *Non-AI:* mannequins, crowds for street scene, "regulars" at a bar or tavern, spectators, entourage, palace staff, village inhabitants, angry mob, flash mob, pacers for exercise programs, "hares" for people-based "hounds" to chase, weapons targets
2. *With partial AI:* receptionist, tour guide, companion, ensemble actor, maître d'
3. *With programmed/chatbot AI:* language tutor, teacher, presenter, therapist, near "background" actor, interactive actor/performer, bartender

FIGURE 12.2 Screen shots showing NPC characters in the virtual city of Uruk, Second Life, FAS region. This virtual environment was built to teach about life in a real world historical period (Mesopotamia circa 3000 B.C.). Images include: bird's eye view of the city (top left), an overview of city street (top right), some of the native population of NPCs (middle image), two fisherman (bottom left) and a potter working on his wheel (bottom right).

4. *Nonhuman types* that are not based on an avatar but still can interact with the visitor: talking trees, animals, environmental/spirit characters, fantasy characters such as fairies, signage that talks (good for "all-access design")
5. *Your custom NPCs* that fit your special creative vision for your sim

12.7 DESIGNING THE ENVIRONMENT FOR THE INCLUSION OF NPCS

The scale and numbers of people or avatars in a landscape provide its defining qualities. In most films, Fifth Avenue in New York City can be identified by its populous masses on the sidewalks, but when they want to make a shocking disaster movie, they show Fifth Avenue with those sidewalks empty, cabs parked everywhere, and no evidence of the resident population. As the designer of this virtual environment, you are also the director of these "background actors," your NPCs, and it is your job to make sure they help define the overall mood of the region to the visitor.

12.7.1 Key Components to Consider When You Design for NPCs

What kind of environment do you have? Is it a language-learning sim that looks like a French country village? Or, perhaps it is a mystic temple for consulting a virtual psychic. There are many sim concepts ready to be developed in virtual worlds [6], and they offer an opportunity to devise new ways to utilize NPCs in your environment. Here are some key components to consider:

Interactivity: What is the interactivity desired between the NPCs and the visitor? In your French country village/language-learning sim, do you want the visitors to practice French with every NPC they meet, or do you want to provide a scripted guide with a higher level of AI to take the visitors around? Learning a new language is accelerated by immersion, and having the NPCs only respond to French conversation would enhance that effect.

Progression: Consider that there could be concentric circles of increasing interactivity as the visitor moves into the most important part of the sim landscape. How would you design for that? For example, you may want to set it up so that as the visitor gets closer to the meeting room where the resident virtual psychic holds her séances the NPCs become more interactive and perhaps more difficult to pass. They can become "gatekeepers" and security on a sim, set up to provide access when given the correct password and to monitor the traffic and activities on the sim while you are not there.

Guided Flow: How can you relate traffic flow and the positions of your NPCs? A virtual landscape, as you know from the terrain designs discussed in Chapter 5, should "unfold" to the visitor as the visitor travels around it. Suppose you provided an NPC or two at special junctions throughout the sim that lead the visitors' exploration thorough your carefully designed terrain. These could be "native guides" or friendly locals or perhaps even reclusive "celebrities," who react to the visitor like they would to voracious paparazzi and run off in the opposite direction, subtly inviting the visitor to give chase.

Other Life—Biosystem: Recent developments in additional features have added Pathfinding to options available for nonavatar characters in Second Life. This could provide your environment with a freely moving animal or insect population that responds to an avatar presence. Basically, the Pathfinding system, when activated on a region and combined with the appropriate scripts in your animated character, will give the character the capacity to walk, crawl, or fly around the region, avoiding obstacles that have been identified by the Navigation Mesh, or NavMesh. There is much more information about it here on the Good Building Practices of the Second Life Wiki (http://wiki.secondlife.com/wiki/Good_Building_Practices/).

12.8 SETTING UP AND DESIGNING THE LOOK OF YOUR NPCS IN SECOND LIFE

Assuming you now have an insatiable desire to create your first NPC, let's talk about the initial steps you must take and how to design the look. In Second Life, you can make them by creating a new avatar account and signifying that it is a "scripted agent" or "bot" on the Scripted Agent Status tab in the avatar's account page. In Second Life, the bot support is quite robust, and you have the option of running that bot and controlling it with software in your computer such as Thoy's (http://slbot.thoys.nl) or running it as a server hosted bot via services like SmartBots (http://www.smartbots2life.com/) or Pikkubot (http://pikkubot.de). Since your bot is basically an avatar, albeit a machine-controlled one, you can alter its appearance just as you would your own avatar. When you create this bot in Second Life, you must log in on that account and set up its appearance. When that task is done, open another viewer window and log in as your usual avatar, make friends with your new bot, and send it some Linden dollars and inventory (not too much, just what is necessary). Now, you can utilize the stand-alone software options or the server-hosted options noted previously. Each of these options has websites and inworld facilities to help you set up your bot with their system; you only need to decide which service suits your bot usage the best. To help with that decision, look at the Second Life wiki (http://wiki.secondlife.com/wiki/Second_Life_bot_software_comparison).

While you think of the character of your bot, and by extension the appearance of your bot, you should ask yourself, what will make my design memorable? How can I support the message of the shop, region, or sim, and how can I add mannerisms to my bot's behavior that are appropriate to the period of its dress and character?

12.9 SETTING UP AND DESIGNING THE LOOK OF YOUR NPCS ON AN OPENSIM REGION

Setting up an NPC on an OpenSim region is actually simple. Basically, the NPC in OpenSim will be a clone of your avatar, wearing whatever your avatar is wearing when you make the clone. Again, you should push yourself to be creative with your clone's appearance and behavior to bring dynamic design into your environment. Scripts for setting up NPCs are available on OpenSim (http://opensimulator.org/wiki/OSSLNPC). Eva Comaroski has a great tutorial online at the Wizardry and Steamworks site (http://was.fm/opensim:npc) for creating a series of NPCs that follow a path, read a script to chat with you, and wander around.

12.10 NPCS AND THEIR FUTURE DEVELOPMENT

The classical age of NPCs has just begun. Every year, more developers and designers create smarter NPCs in their games and simulations. An artificial game character called UT^2 has been judged to be human by more than 50% of the actual humans playing against it, earning this NPC the coveted BotPrize for Human-like Bots [7].

NPC visual diversity is now possible by modifying avatars with genetic algorithms in their creation programs [8]. Imagine whole populations of NPCs walking around your environment, representing the genetic diversity you would find in any major city on Earth. Soon to come, no doubt, will be diversity of behaviors and animations running on those NPCs, which will not be read from a note card, but from a procedural program that actively changes in response to the environment [9].

NPCs can also save our lives. Disaster scenarios can be modeled using them as the endangered popula-tion, allowing city planners and first responders to identify and eliminate weaknesses in their evacuation plans [10].

You will probably find working with NPCs a challenge, but a rewarding one, so go ahead, Dr. Frankenstein, create some artificial life.

12.11   PROJECT: SETTING UP A BASIC AVATAR IN A VIRTUAL ENVIRONMENT

Virtual worlds with their own content making employees like Second Life have created avatar content for first-time players so that they may enter the world in a character of their choosing. This may not be the case with worlds you are creating on OpenSim, so it is important that you know about the basics of avatar setup and appearance. Once you become adept at this task, you may want to create alternate avatars for inventory storage purposes or have a couple of "lightweight" versions of your standard look for travelling around the Metaverse.

12.11.1   CREATING A NEW USER AND MAKING THE USER MANIFEST

Access the server for your OpenSim regions and make your new avatar or alternate (alt) avatar using the "create user" command in either the region command window or in the Robust Service window if you are running a grid of regions on OpenSim. The program will prompt you for the name, password, e-mail, and so on and then set up your new avatar with its own UUID (Universally Unique IDentifier) and account.

Log your new avatar into the world for the first time. In the Firestorm Viewer, what you will see is a cloud and probably a message that the clothes are downloading. In fact, there are no clothes, skin, or any parts for your avatar to download yet, so it will stay a cloud until you give it some (see Figure 12.3, picture 1).

You can solve this problem by opening the inventory window (the little suitcase icon on the bottom bar) and then selecting and right clicking on the Body Parts folder. When the drop-down menu opens, click on new eyes, hair, skin, and shape so that these are added to your inventory. Then, select them and right click to "wear" them (see Figure 12.3, picture 2). You will now have a skinned avatar with the basic hairstyle.

The next step, as shown in Figure 12.3, picture 3, is to create some clothing layers for your avatar. This is done the same way as the body parts. Go to the Clothing Folder in your inventory, select, right click, and create new underpants, undershirt, pants, and shirt for your first clothing layers and make sure to "wear" them. Continue by adding the available clothing layers to your avatar until you have them all.

12.11.2   LOOKING OVER THE CLOTHING OPTIONS AND LAYERS

You may have noticed that the avatar has 12 options when it comes to clothing layers. The basics are under-wear, pants, shirts, skirts, jackets, and the kind of layers you would have in the physical world. Let's focus on editing those first. Under Avatar/Appearance, you will see an edit menu showing what your avatar is wearing; in this case, it is called Avatar_basic_layers. Select the "wrench" (edit) icon in the top right corner so you can modify these items (see Figure 12.4, picture 1). Your avatar will go into a pose, so you can see how the adjustments will look.

The next menu that pops up has three tabs: Clothing, Attachments, and Body Parts. Since we are going to adjust clothing first, select the Clothing tab. As you can see, the list of what your avatar is currently wearing will be displayed (see Figure 12.4, picture 2). Go ahead and click the wrench (edit) icon next to the clothing item you would like to adjust to modify that layer.

When you get the layers for pants, shirts, jacket, and so on into edit mode, notice how you have two options in the top section, one for Fabric and one for Color/tint (Figure 12.4, picture 3). The Fabric option

FIGURE 12.3 Screen grabs from OpenSim. Initial steps for setting up a new avatar, skin, and undergarments.

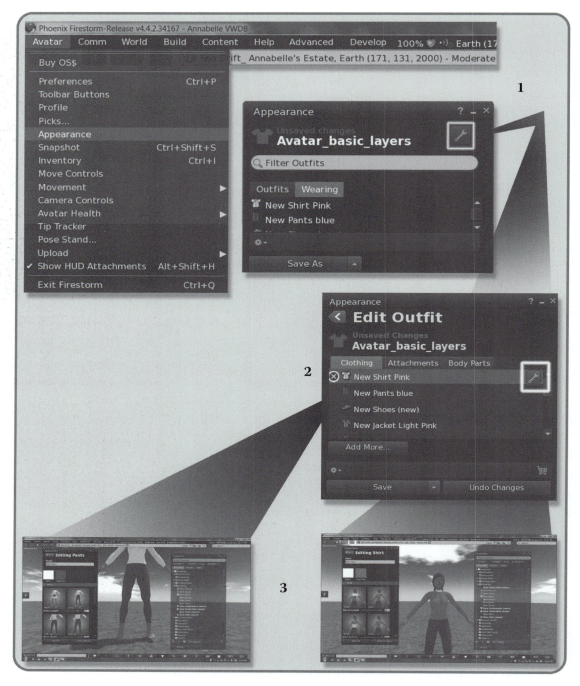

FIGURE 12.4 Screen grabs from OpenSim showing the menus for adjusting the clothing layers to make a basic set of clothes.

allows you to put a pattern on your avatar's clothing layers; this could also be an image of the seams and other surface detail that you would see on a garment. To create that kind of detail on your clothes, you will need to make your own fabric texture file that contains these details and is designed to align to the avatar's shape. Section 12.11.6 has some examples of these, but for now, let's focus on finding and coloring the various layers of clothes so you can see the default shapes and how they can be adjusted. You have already probably started to play with the sliders on the clothing layer edit page, so go ahead and get the pants, shirt, jacket, what have you into the color and fit you want.

When you are happy with the color and fit on each layer, click on the top Save arrow to go back to the main edit list.

12.11.3 Editing Eyes, Hair, and Skin

Now that you have set up your basic clothing layers, colored them, and fit them, let's go to work on the body parts. Jump back through the edit menu using the save arrow key on the top left until you are back at the main Appearance menu. This is the one shown in Figure 12.4, picture 2, it has three tabs, Clothing, Attachments, and Body Parts. Now, select the far right tab, called Body Parts. Under that listing, you modify the editable layers for your eyes, hair, shape, and skin. Select the eyes you are wearing and start adjusting your eye color and lightness. Note that the other qualities of your avatar's eyes, such as spacing, size, and position, are adjustable under the Shape layer. As you can see, the eye has a default iris texture already in its window (Figure 12.5, picture 1). You can make your own eye textures should you desire something different.

Jump back to the main menu and select the hair you are wearing to edit. Again, there is an option for adding your own hair texture, such as straight, fine or, abundantly curly (Figure 12.5, picture 2). Under the Hair menu are four categories: Color, Style, Eyebrows, and Facial (male avatars only). Please note that the standard avatar hair is not easy to adjust and usually produces somewhat unrealistic results. Most avatars opt for going to a no-hair setup (bald) and/or wearing a wig attachment. Good results can be achieved by combining prim-based hair attachments, the standard avatar hair, and a head tattoo for those close-to-skull details on the hairline. You should also adjust your eyebrows to match your hair.

Finally, select and edit your avatar's skin. As you can see from the avatar in the picture, all colors are available, so you can be blue if you desire. Also under this subcategory are the options for adding facial detail like lines, wrinkles, and freckles, as well as this kind of detail to the body. There is a makeup section for decorating the face and nails of your avatar as well.

12.11.4 Adjusting the Parameters of Your Avatar, Shape, Size, and Other Details

The Shape parameters are a large menu in the Appearance/Body Parts menu section which you can access by selecting the shape you are already wearing under the Body Parts tab in the main Edit Outfit menu. Select the shape you are wearing to edit it, and in the Shape menu, you will find the gender selector (top right corner), as well as tabs for Body, Head, Eyes, Ears, Nose, Mouth, Chin, Torso, and Legs (including foot size). Most avatars are well over the norm for height in human scale. As you can see from Figure 12.6, the range of avatar sizes is extensive.

For the purpose of demonstration, this avatar has been given large, pointy ears and some minimal makeup. Her height is 6.5 feet or 1.98 meters. That is tall for the average human female, but fairly common for the avatar female. Go ahead and tweak the shape settings until your avatar has a pleasing shape.

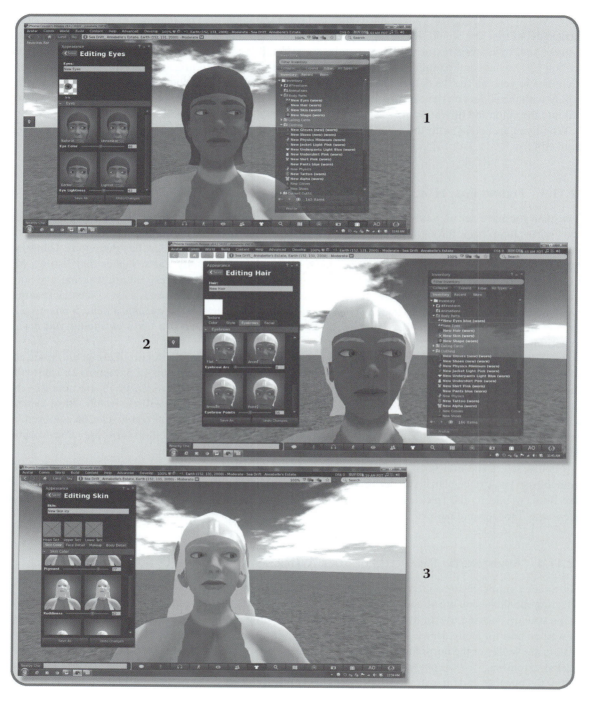

FIGURE 12.5 Screen grabs from OpenSim showing the menus for adjusting avatar hair and skin parameters.

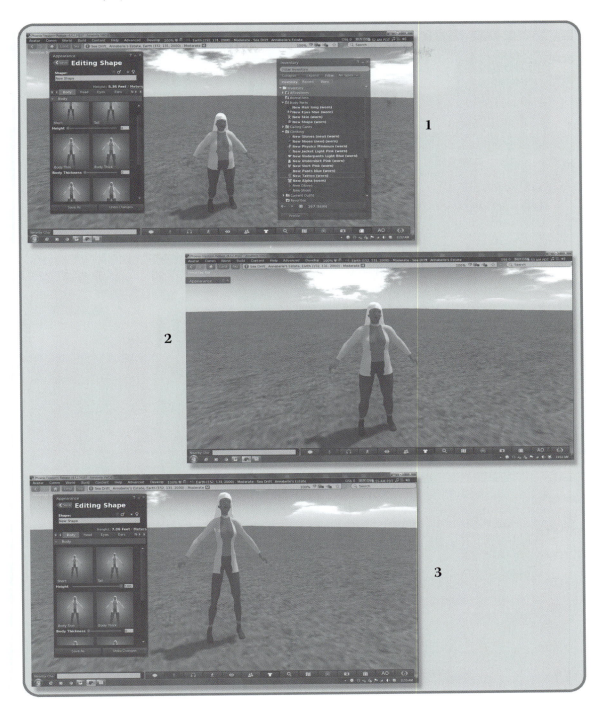

FIGURE 12.6 Screen grabs from OpenSim showing the menus for adjusting avatar height and shape.

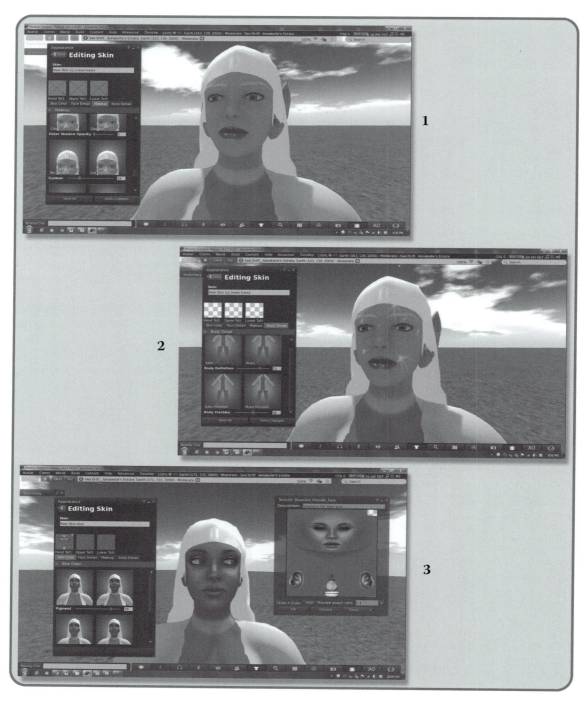

FIGURE 12.7 Screen grabs from OpenSim showing the menus for adding skin and tattoo layers.

12.11.5 Adjusting the Face, Adding a Tattoo or a Skin Texture

Further detail can be added to your avatar's face and body through the use of the makeup features in the Skin submenu, which appears when you edit the skin you are wearing in the main Edit Outfit menu. As you can see in Figure 12.7, picture 1, a little lip gloss and eyeliner have been added to the avatar's face. In Figure 12.7, picture 2, a texture file with an alpha layer has been added to make a white star tattoo appear on the avatar's face. Finally, in Figure 12.7, picture 3, a series of skin textures has been added to the avatar. Good skin textures are complex layered graphics files built up on templates. If you have an interest in making your own, probably the best place to start is at the Avatar Toolbox site (http://avatartoolbox.info/MakingAvatars.html). The blue skin shown here was developed from Eloh Elliot's skin resources (https://sites.google.com/site/another/resources).

12.11.6 Utilizing Texture Maps to Make Custom Avatar Clothes, Preparing Attachments

Now that you have been introduced to the basics of how the avatar clothing and body layers work, it is time to learn about how to add clothing details. In Figure 12.8, picture 1, the avatar is in the edit mode for her shirt. To the right is the texture map that creates the detail for the torso of her jacket and its sleeves. Again, like the skin, this is made from layered templates that are available from the Avatar Toolbox site or from Second Life's knowledge base. The textures for this jacket were created for Annabelle Fanshaw's avatars by Alaina Simcoe Toadpipe.

In picture 2 of Figure 12.8, the pants take on another texture to create a nice striped effect. Again, this texture was developed from the avatar clothing templates available at the Avatar Toolbox site. Finally, in picture 3, the avatar is preparing for the addition of a new hairstyle, one made from primitives or objects rather than just the basic avatar hair texture and shape changes. She has adjusted her hair layer to baldness so that it will not show around the prim-based hair she will add in the next step.

12.11.7 Adding Attachments for Hair

Early on in virtual worlds, it became obvious that for complex structures like hair an attachment would look better on the avatar. In Figure 12.9, picture 1, you will see that a multipart linked object that looks like a wig is being attached to the avatar's head. There are several places to attach hair; usually, it is connected to the skull or the nose, so it moves appropriately with the head movements. This particular hair came from OpenSim creations (http://opensim-creations.com/category/avatar/hair/) and was modified to make a more individual look. In the final image, picture 3, you can see the complete avatar, ready for action in her virtual world.

Finally, when you have found and edited all the clothing layers, added your attachments, and so on, click the Save As button and name it First Outfit. Now, all the layers and objects your avatar is wearing will be collected into a folder. If you decide to change it or make a green-skinned version, you will always have these settings saved for later usage.

12.11.8 Advanced Avatar Development

There is much, much more to avatars, of course. They are so important to us that we spend hours dressing and modifying them. Second Life has over 1 million items listed under the Apparel category. If you desire to get into more complex avatar design, there is much on the subject at Creator Resources shown in Second Life destinations (http://secondlife.com/destinations/howto/creator), and on sites like Avatar Toolbox. The avatar

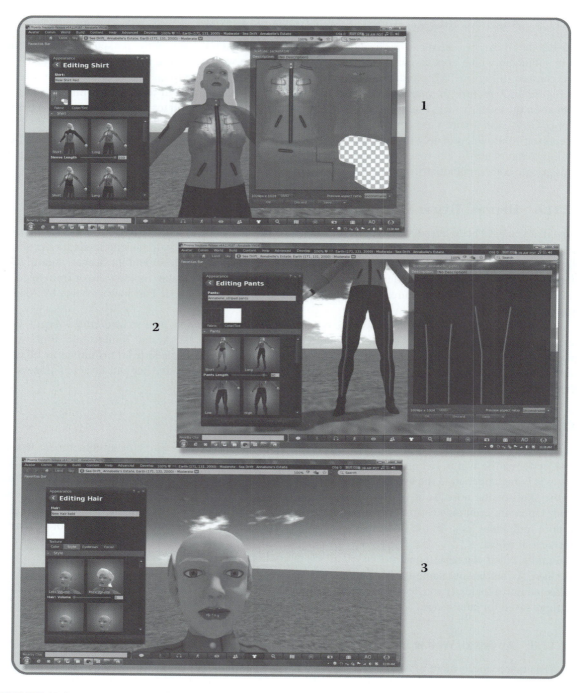

FIGURE 12.8 Screen grabs from OpenSim showing the menus for adding new clothing textures to the avatar, and preparing the head for the attachment of prim hair.

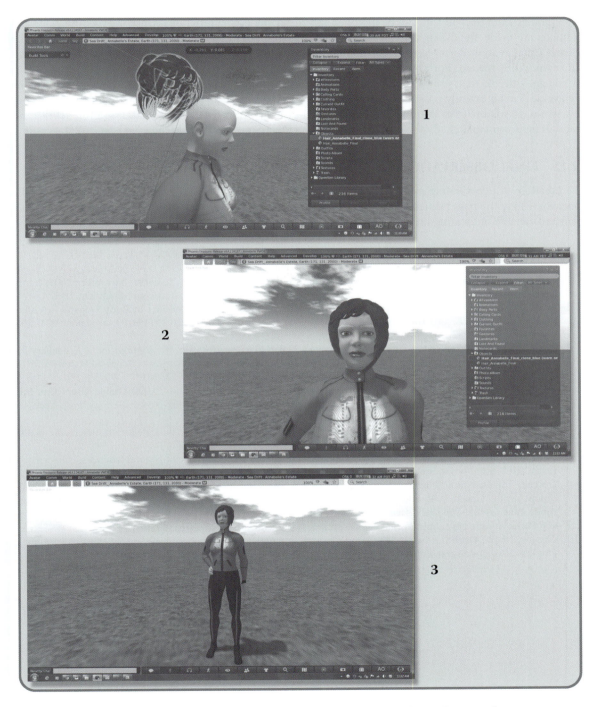

FIGURE 12.9 Screen grabs from OpenSim showing menus for adding a prim hair attachment to the avatar.

mesh models from Second Life can be modified in your 3D modeling programs. Once the modifications and additions are made, the avatar with new attachments can be reimported into Second Life or OpenSim. The Second Life Creation Portal has information and sources for your avatar's mesh models (http://wiki.secondlife.com/wiki/Creation_Portal).

You may desire that your avatar be represented as the same being on all the worlds you visit in the Metaverse. That is entirely possible. You can make note of your avatar shape settings and set them up in your new world. If you own the clothing and skin textures, you can transfer those as well. For a full set of tools that will help you build characters for Second Life and OpenSim, there is a Blender add-on called Avastar.

12.12   FINAL OBSERVATIONS

The creation of a captivating avatar that embodies your interests is an enlightening and enriching artistic endeavor. Enjoy the possibilities that avatar design unveils for you; it is self-expression in its most personal form and capable of creating inner growth through self-discovery.

REFERENCES

1. Callaway, Ewen, How Your Brain Sees Virtual You, by Ewen Callaway, *New Scientist*, November 2009, http://www.newscientist.com/article/dn18117-how-your-brain-sees-virtual-you.html. Accessed March 22, 2013.
2. Slater, M., B. Spanlang, M.V. Sanchez-Vives, and O. Blanke, First Person Experience of Body Transfer in Virtual Reality, *PLOS ONE*, 2010, http://www.plosone.org/article/info%3Adoi%2F10.1371%2Fjournal.pone.0010564. Accessed March 22, 2013.
3. Clark, Liat, Study: Embodying Superman-like Avatars Makes Gamers Altruistic, *Wired Magazine, UK*, January 31, 2013, http://www.wired.co.uk/news/archive/2013-01/31/superman-virtual-reality-atruistic. Accessed March 23, 2013.
4. GOTE, Wikipedia article, http://en.wikipedia.org/wiki/GOTE. Accessed March 23, 2013.
5. Au, Wagner James, The Crowded Empty Paradox: How a Virtual World with 75,000 Online Users Can Still Seem Abandoned, *New World Notes* blog, http://nwn.blogs.com/nwn/2010/01/the-crowded-empty.html. Accessed October 14, 2012.
6. Korolov, Maria, Hypergrid Business, Biz Plans, http://www.hypergridbusiness.com/category/resources/biz-plans/. Accessed October 20, 2012.
7. UT^2 Game Bot Judged More Human than Human, Computer Science, College of Natural Sciences, University of Texas, 2012, http://www.cs.utexas.edu/news-events/news/2012/ut2-game-bot-judged-more-human-human.
8. Trescak, Tomas, Anton Bogdanovych, Simeon Simoff, and Inmaculada Rodriquez, Generating Diverse Ethnic Groups with Genetic Algorithms, *VRST'12*, December 10–12, 2012, http://staff.scm.uws.edu.au/~anton/Publications/VRST_2012.pdf, accessed October 17, 2012.
9. Ken Perlin's home page, http://mrl.nyu.edu/~perlin/. Accessed October 23, 2012.
10. Korolov, Maria, OpenSim NPCs Simulate Disasters, http://www.hypergridbusiness.com/2012/06/opensim-npcs-simulate-disasters/. Accessed October 23, 2012.

13 Prototyping the Real World in a Virtual Environment

It will never cease to be a living blueprint of the future, where people actually live a life they can't find anywhere else in the world.

—Walt Disney speaking about EPCOT (Experimental Prototype Community of Tomorrow)

13.1 PROTOTYPING AND WORKFLOW: WHERE AND HOW DO VIRTUAL WORLDS FIT IN?

How do you get from inspiration to a real life prototype? Let's look at the flow of design ideation. As you can see in Figure 13.1, each step of a design process flows into the next, and concepts from some steps may possibly flow into noncontiguous steps as well. Design thinking is not usually a linear process; it is more like a "cloud" of ideas. In every step but the initial one, there is an opportunity for prototyping something as well as developing a new layer on the previous prototype.

As you can see in Figure 13.2, your initial design concept may be inspired by an interesting eight-sided goblet you found at a flea market. The octagon shape informs your design approach on every level. With the pleasing symmetry of this regular polygon, rooms feel circular but are easier to build and furnish. Interconnections between other rooms, buildings, and regions become simplified and organized due to the array of sides on this regular polygon.

Where do virtual worlds fit in this design cycle? Well, if you think about it, they fit in everywhere. All these design phases lend themselves to virtual world utilization. For instance, the development of an octagonal grid, created for a floor or for a city plaza, can easily be realized in any virtual world through the use of textures with an octagonal pattern on them or with octagonal geometry. In fact, the octagonal pattern can even be used on the land textures to visually embed the theme, and the terrain itself can be terraformed to octagonal patterns, perhaps resembling columnar basalt or stepped terrain. As far as building structures and furniture is concerned, you might find it interesting "that numerous Americans, from Thomas Jefferson to Orson Fowler, saw octagon architecture as a tool to cultivate new kinds of private 'selves'—stronger, healthier, more rational subjectivities capable of negotiating an emergent capitalist and democratic society" [1].

How would you convey this octagonal concept to your client, your peers, or your class? It helps to "reverse engineer" the workflow in your mind. Start from the date of the final presentation and who will be seeing the proposal. What are their needs, and how do they relate to the overall message? What methodologies will you adopt to answer their needs and develop the presentation of that message? Let's suppose your client wanted to launch a new resort and golf course called Octopus Bay in the Bahamas. Think backwards from the future goals to plan your project. In your mind's eye you look past the elegant octagonal paperweights that were printed as promotional items from the 3D model and think of how you spent lots of time discussing eight-sided ideas with your client and codesigners. Further back, you remember eight-sided buildings and furnishings that were designed and how they subtly supported the concept of eight-sided symmetry displayed

257

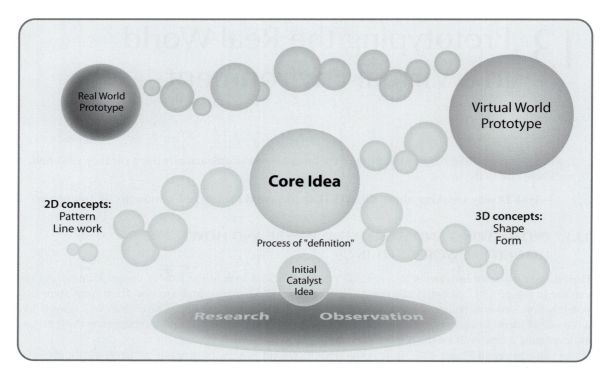

FIGURE 13.1   Schematic showing the cloud of design ideation, initiated from the ideas discovered with Research and Observation, catalyzed into and defined as a Core Idea that expands into 2D and 3D concepts and Prototypes for the real and virtual world.

by an octopus. All of these buildings were nested in a series of interconnected octagonal cul-de-sacs that spanned the octagonal network of your virtual designs. The clients were with you every step of the way, even from their offices in the Bahamas. In fact, they contributed some of the 3D design because they could get into the virtual world and rough out their ideas alongside you and your team.

The proposal was a success, and even now someone is looking at that goblet and thinking of another project (Figure 13.2). Remember, a virtual world environment, all of it, is a tool. It is an assembly floor for rapidly making models that embody ideas made visible to people everywhere. It is also a perpetual idea generator that can create its own internal source of content through the process of iteration and modification.

13.2   INTRODUCTION TO WORLDWIDE GROUP COLLABORATION AND WHY YOU SHOULD USE IT

On June 4, 2009, President Barack Obama spoke in Cairo and called for creating a new relationship between the United States and Islam [2]. Part of that initiative developed into a program called the Online Youth Network: Kansas to Cairo, which encouraged the development of existing online programs for international communications between young Americans and Muslims. One of the notable projects in this program involved David Denton, AIA, from the United States, and Amr Attia, owner of the PUD (Planning and Urban Development) architectural firm in Cairo. Denton and Attia had previously collaborated internationally on

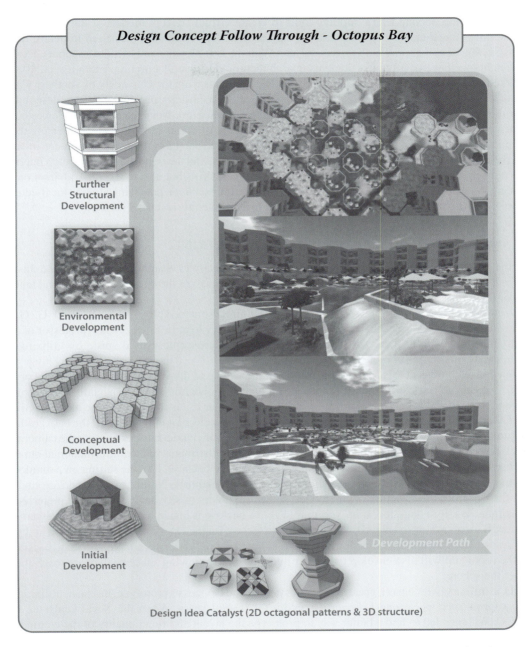

Design Concept Follow Through - Octopus Bay

Further Structural Development

Environmental Development

Conceptual Development

Initial Development

Development Path

Design Idea Catalyst (2D octagonal patterns & 3D structure)

FIGURE 13.2 Schematic showing a design concept flow through the design and construction of a virtual resort called Octopus Bay. The development path starts with an eight-sided goblet (bottom center) which in turn generates development of structures, landforms, and buildings (left side). It all comes together in the virtual world (three images on right side), and shown here are screen grabs from OpenSim including a top view, central lawn view, and long shot of the completed proposal build.

projects by utilizing Second Life's building tools to create virtual concept models of the architecture they were designing. Together, they created concept models that were eventually measured in detail, translated into construction drawings, and built on the real site. With the U.S. Department of State's support, Denton and Attia brought together two groups of students in architectural design collaboration. From Egypt, 40 students who worked with Attia at Ain Shams University and eight students from the University of Southern California School of Architecture who worked with Denton got together as avatars in Second Life to design a master plan for the area around the site of the new Grand Egyptian Museum. Near the end of the semester, five of the students from Cairo came to California and gave live demonstrations of their designs, meeting their U.S. counterparts in real life for the first time. This project returned far more than its investment in time and money; the cultural exchange between the two groups of students, and the opportunity to develop international design connections on both sides, contributed not only to their skills but also to their worldviews on culture and design. As a designer, you can encourage similar cultural exchange programs at your local educational institutions to enrich their students' experience and build a cross-cultural design network.

13.3   MATH, MOLECULES, AND MILITARY ENGINEERING

One of the great advantages of virtual environments is the capacity to design in unlimited scale. Just as you can make a full-scale replica of the Great Pyramids, you can also go in the opposite direction and make scale models of the tiniest things as shown in Figure 13.3.

Dr. Andrew S.I.D. Lang (professor of mathematics, Oral Roberts University); Dr. Peter G. G. Miller (School of Biological Sciences, University of Liverpool); and Dr. Joan L. Slonczewski (professor of biology, Kenyon College) have all taken that fantastic voyage into microscopic virtual space by utilizing virtual worlds to create prototypes of molecules.

Design considerations at this scale should focus on the clarity of the structure and consistency of colored labeling. It is easy to get lost in complex models of proteins or quantum shells, especially if the structure is too large to see as a whole on a standard camera draw distance, or if it is too small to see its connecting parts clearly. Other design elements to take into consideration with a molecular exhibit are (1) the background color and texture of the display, (2) the types of avatar access to the entire model besides craning the camera around it, and (3) the interactivity of the model and how many ways it distributes related information about itself.

The background behind a model is of paramount importance because, like the setting on a diamond ring, it supports the observation and understanding of the central element. Nothing in the background should distract the eye from the structure of the model, so neutral colors or sky backgrounds are preferred. If the model is in a visually congested area, you may want to enclose it inside a hollow phantom sphere that is large enough for an avatar to enter. If you put an alpha texture on the exterior face of the sphere and put your neutral color background on the inside face of the hollow sphere, you have a molecule that is visible from across the room and will also envelop the avatar into an isolated viewing space as they approach the model and enter the sphere.

The U.S. military, which has a great number of systems and devices to prototype, has been utilizing virtual world platforms such as Second Life and OpenSim for several years. When the Naval Undersea Warfare Center (NUWC) needed to find a better way to prototype the layout and functionality of the command-and-control center, they turned to virtual worlds for a solution [3]. What they discovered was that virtual world prototyping worked well with their security requirements, and that they saved significant amounts of time and money during their design meetings because the reviewers could visit the prototype from their desktop computers. Furthermore, they discovered that these prototypes could become functional training environments for people as avatars, and that real-time training scenarios could be run to test the efficacy of the prototype's overall design.

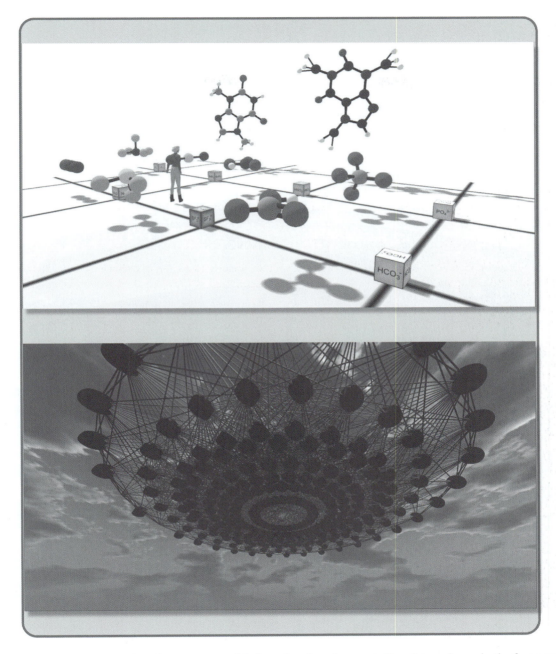

FIGURE 13.3 Science and math prototype models in a virtual environment. Top picture shows, in the foreground, molecule rezzers created by Dr. Andrew S.I.D. Lang (Hiro Sheridan in Second Life), and in the background are models of caffeine ($C_8H_{10}N_4O_2$) and theobromine ($C_7H_8N_4O_2$) created by Scott Rhoades. Bottom picture shows model of E8 mathematics created by J. Gregory Moxness. This model is an interpretation of two- and three-dimensional perspectives of the universe's subatomic particles.

FIGURE 13.4 Screen grabs showing a virtual prototype of a design for the command-and-control center at the Naval Undersea Warfare Center.

In Figure 13.4, the tech lead avatar shown in the top image is Douglas Maxwell (Maccus McCullough is his avatar name) as he sets up the testing area in Second Life. The bottom image shows two operators (as avatars) operating the BYG-1 Combat System. They were logged in to the Qwaq/Teleplace Clients (viewer) located in a different building from the combat system hardware, effectively desktop sharing the combat system software. This allowed the participants to remotely operate the combat system and perform target motion analysis tasks while their avatars were present in the virtual command-and-control center.

13.4 ENTERTAINMENT ENVIRONMENTS: PROTOTYPING THE PERFORMANCE SPACE

Creating entertainment spaces, in both the real and virtual worlds, involves projects that come with their own special set of design challenges. Although it is not typical for a Broadway show set designer also to create the architectural design of the theater, it can be a common experience in virtual world entertainment design. In fact, one of the most exciting things about creation of a theatrical production in a virtual world is that you can discard the concept of the theater building as a separate part of the entertainment design if you so choose. You have the opportunity to redefine space and the way it serves entertainment, so run with it.

For example, let's start with one of the most basic of entertainment spaces, the "black box" theater (Figure 13.5). In real life, these are empty spaces that have been painted black and provided with a modicum of theatrical lighting. This is an appropriate environment to explore your first virtual entertainment designs because it will be easy to build and modify. By utilizing the plan of an existing room or black box theater

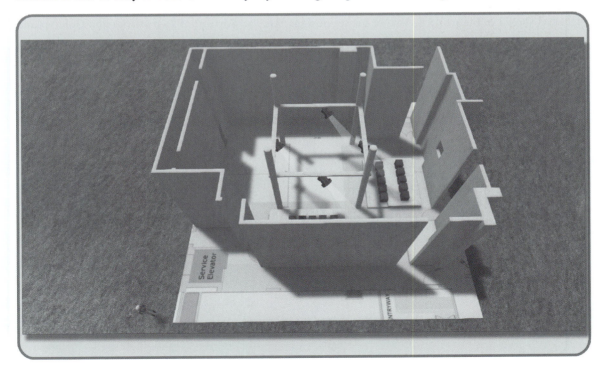

FIGURE 13.5 Screen grab from Second Life showing a virtual prototype of the Steinhardt Black Box Theatre, 82 Washington Square East, New York University, New York.

your group may have in real life, you can start with what is familiar and work toward the virtual possibilities. Here are the steps:

1. Obtain a scaled plan of your designated black box room as a clear JPG or PNG image file cropped to 1024 by 1024 pixels.
2. In the virtual world of your choice, import this image and apply it to the top face of a large work platform prim (primitive), making sure that the scale of the plan is accurate and an appropriate size for the use of an avatar. *Note:* if you want to prototype this for a real world build, then you should shrink your avatar to a maximum height of 6 ft.
3. Create the walls and other interior details, such as seat risers, columns, and doorways with new prims. As you build, make sure you label each component of the black box theater with clear descriptive names so you can easily find them.

Now, put on your design hat and think about how this space could be scripted and animated to serve the purposes of theatrical presentation. Walls can slide away for the entrance of set pieces and color, rotation, scale of the room can change; in fact, the whole theater can be "choreographed" to interact with the theatrical production, and you have not even designed one bit of "scenery."

If you invite the director and all the other creative staff into your virtual world to collaborate on this, a theatrical production can be prototyped right on your desktops.

Richard Finkelstein, a set designer in both real life and in Second Life, has taken this approach even further as shown in Figure 13.6. Two of his set designs, for *The Servant of Two Masters* by Goldoni and

FIGURE 13.6 Images of Richard Finkelstein's virtual set design prototype in Second Life of *Our Country's Good* (top left) and the real set version at James Madison University in 2011 (lower right).

Our Country's Good by Timberlake Wertenbaker, were visualized initially in Second Life and then built for the real stage productions at James Madison University in Virginia. As he said: "One remarkable difference in Second Life is that through the use of avatars, it is possible for the director to come INSIDE the visualization to interact in a more meaningful way with the proposed environment" [4]. Images of the set designs and their virtual prototypes can be seen on Richard Finkelstein's website (http://www.rfdesigns.org/VIRTUAL.HTM).

13.5   PROTOTYPING GAMES IN A VIRTUAL WORLD

Among the myriad prototyped items a virtual world is capable of creating, there is a place for games. Although some people would define the virtual world itself as a game, a virtual world is also an excellent place for designing a real-world game prototype. Such is the case of "Tribe," a game that Alchemy Sims developed to promote understanding of the stresses that indigenous peoples of the world have to contend with as they seek to preserve their tribal way of life (Figure 13.7). Ann Cudworth (known as Annabelle Fanshaw throughout the Metaverse) of Alchemy Sims collaborated on the game board design and game play structures with Deb Thomas of SillyMonkey games (http://www.sillymonkeyinternational.com/) on the OpenSim-based Alchemy Sims Grid (ASG). Essentially, the procedure was the same as if you were making the game prototype from real materials; they created a game document, decided on the rules, and worked out the game elements that would come into play. Where they had the advantage over real life was in the virtual play testing. Very easily, they could get people to log in to the ASG and play the game with their avatars. It was quite amazing to see people walking around on the large board, using the spinner, and picking up

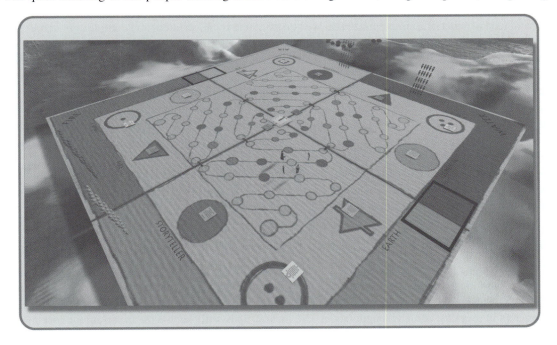

FIGURE 13.7   Screen grab from OpenSim on Alchemy Sims Grid of the prototype used for play testing "Tribe," a board game about the struggles of indigenous peoples.

the "chance" cards as they attempted to attain the game goal of preserving and increasing their tribal size. Emergent play developed as the game testers invented new aspects of the game goal.

13.6 PROJECT: PROTOTYPING A VIRTUAL SPACE AND MAKING A 3D PRINT FROM IT

In this project, we are going to make a maze. It has elements of architecture, entertainment, and gaming embodied in its structure and will provide an appropriate vehicle for learning about the process of prototyping a virtual space for the real world. For the purposes of this project, you will utilize a simple maze pattern to make a design that scales from an avatar-size playground to a handheld maze game.

Note: This project starts in SketchUp, a widely available free 3D program that will export models into OpenSim via the COLLADA (.dae) format and into the 3D printing devices via the SLT format. You could also make this maze model in Blender, if you wish. If you have a specific 3D printing service in mind, look at their preferred file format before you start modeling. While some will accept a COLLADA (.dae) file, others do not, so check the final specs and see what kind of export plug-in you may need. It is assumed you have basic knowledge of how to model in SketchUp, which is user friendly. The latest version of the program can be downloaded (http://www.sketchup.com/). If you do not want to make your maze in SketchUp, then feel free to download the premade Maze.dae file from the content included with this book into your virtual world and continue from Section 13.6.6.

Let's get started.

13.6.1 Making a Maze Pattern

First, you need a layout of a simple maze that will be printable by 3D printers and complex enough to generate a challenge for people who will walk through the avatar-size version. If you do not want to draw a maze of your own, there are many maze generators available online (http://www.mazegenerator.co.uk/ was used to make the pattern for this project), see Figure 13.8 for the initial maze design. Keep it simple; you can always increase the complexity of a maze later. *Hint:* Be aware that wall thickness is going to matter in the 3D print, so you want to design with that in mind. A quick check of the material options on the Shapeways website (http://www.shapeways.com/) indicates that the wall thickness should be between 0.7 and 5 millimeters depending on the material with which you choose to print. In this project, you will make the initial model with 1.5-millimeter thick walls.

Note: Ultimately, this model was printed in a ceramic material, which has less tolerance for thinness, so the walls were thickened to 4 millimeters for printing purposes. An image of this object in its ceramic 3D printed form is provided at the end of the chapter in Figure 13.19.

13.6.2 Setting Up and Building the Maze Base in SketchUp

1. In SketchUp, under the Window/Preferences/Template section, choose the Product Design and Woodworking Template–Millimeters because you want to make your initial model in the 3D printing size first and scale up from there (Figure 13.9). In the drawing space, make a plane that is 100 millimeters in overall width and length (about 3.92 inches). This will become the baseplate for your maze, allowing you to print a 3D game piece that you can hold in your hand. Extrude the plate 10 millimeters, so you have a box that is 10 millimeters high, 100 millimeters long, and 100 millimeters wide.
2. Import the maze as a texture into your SketchUp scene.

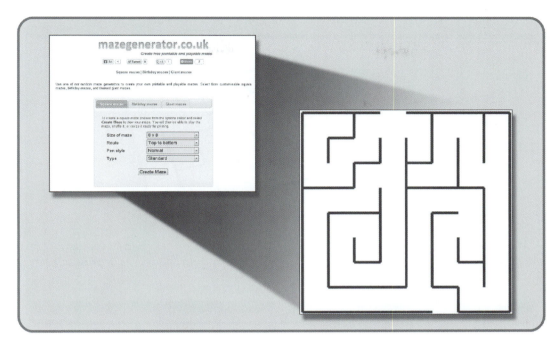

FIGURE 13.8 Screen grab showing the maze maker used to create the initial maze pattern.

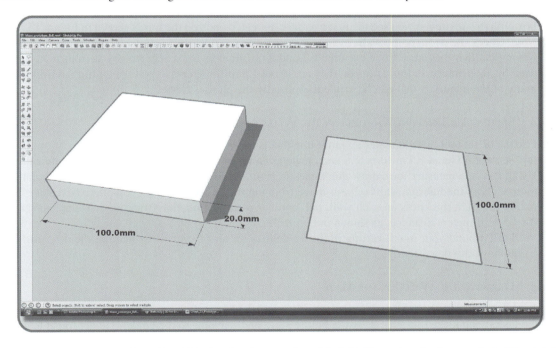

FIGURE 13.9 Screen grab from SketchUp showing the extrusion of the initial base plate for the maze in its 3D print size.

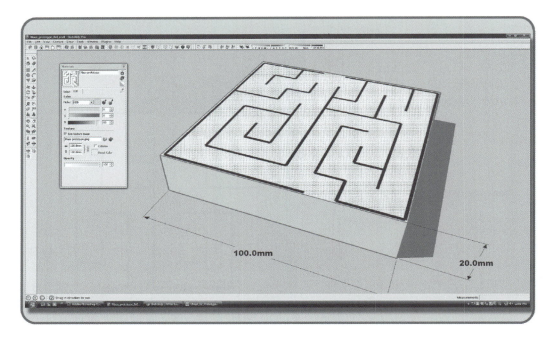

FIGURE 13.10   Screen grab from SketchUp showing the process of adding maze texture to the top of the model baseplate.

3. Pick a standard SketchUp material and add the maze pattern as a texture to it. Fill the top face of the box with this texture so you see the maze pattern, repeated once on the top as shown in Figure 13.10. *Note:* Check the width of the walls in your maze diagram as it has been stretched out across the box. Remember that they need to be between 0.7 and 5 millimeters to be accepted by various materials used by 3D printers. In this example, they are about 1.5 millimeters, so you are within the limits of many of the materials that can be printed, especially the plastics range.

13.6.3   SETTING UP DRAWING GUIDES FOR THE WALLS OF THE MAZE

1. Use the offset tool, which makes an inner line that is offset inward from the outer edges of your box top; set that offset at 1.5 millimeters and create an inner line on the top surface of the baseplate.
2. Using the tape measure tool, draw guidelines in from the middle of your outside edges and match them up with the internal walls of your maze from the image applied to the top of the baseplate. To obtain the right thickness on each wall, pull another parallel guideline from the first line and set it for 1.5 millimeters distance, as shown in Figure 13.11.
3. Work all around your maze, setting in the guidelines for all of your walls making them 1.5 millimeters in width consistently.

13.6.4   DRAWING THE WALLS OF THE MAZE

1. Now that you have the guides in place, draw all around the edges of your walls, following the pattern of the underlying maze image as shown in Figure 13.12 and snapping to the guides. Do not forget to add the doors again; the offset has closed them off. You can check to make sure you have all the walls filled in by coloring them with another material, replacing the texture you are using to guide your lines.

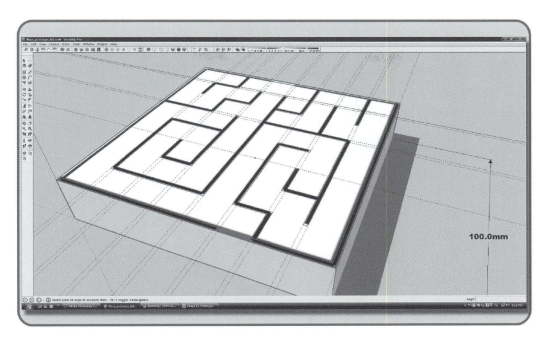

FIGURE 13.11 Screen grab from SketchUp, showing how to set the maze wall guidelines (dotted lines).

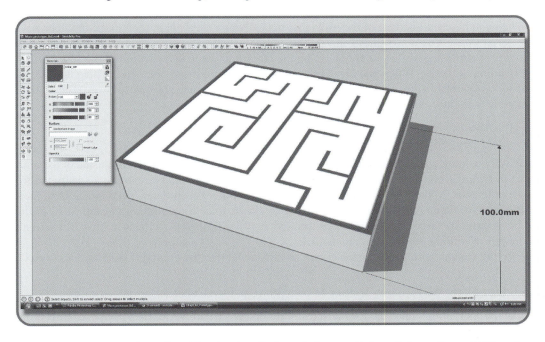

FIGURE 13.12 Screen grab from SketchUp showing final result from outlining all the walls, and filling them with another color material.

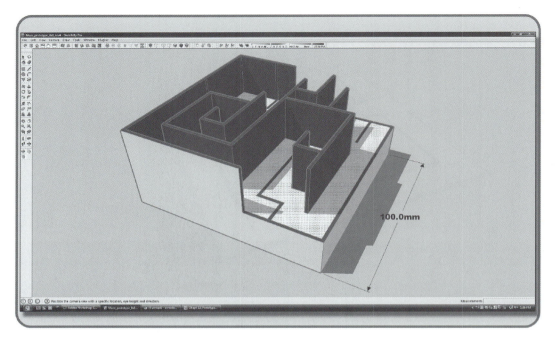

FIGURE 13.13   Screen grab from SketchUp showing the process of extruding the walls.

2. When you have outlined all of the walls and made them a solid color, then make the floor a white material. *Note:* You may want to change the outline color in Window/Styles/Edit to a red or green so it is easier to see while you are outlining the black-and-white maze pattern.
3. Extruding the walls. When you have finished all the walls, extrude them to the height of 25 millimeters as shown in Figure 13.13. Now, you should see the maze starting to form. The walls will extrude with the color you used to fill the top surface.

13.6.5 MAKING A HANGING TAB

You may want to hang up the printed object. If that is so, add a punched tab to the front side of the maze base as shown in Figure 13.14. Just draw in some cut lines on the face of the base, extrude a square tab from the front face of the box. Make a tab 10 millimeters thick and about 30 millimeters deep on the front face. Trim and add a hole for hanging the maze from a string or chain, something with a radius of 8–10 millimeters should be sufficiently large. In the prototype, printed at 100 millimeters to the side, this 10-millimeter tab should be just over three-eighths of an inch thick.

Note: In the virtual world, you can sink some of this model into the ground if the base looks too thick.

13.6.6 EXPORT THE MODEL AND IMPORT IT TO A VIRTUAL ENVIRONMENT

If you like the look of this maze and want to test it out in the virtual world, then save it as "my_prototype_maze.skp" and export it in the COLLADA (.dae) file format from SketchUp. This is under File/Export/3D model in the top menu. Take the default options when you export. You are going to export this model twice; make two files for uploading—the mesh model file called "my_prototype_maze.dae" and a physics file for it.

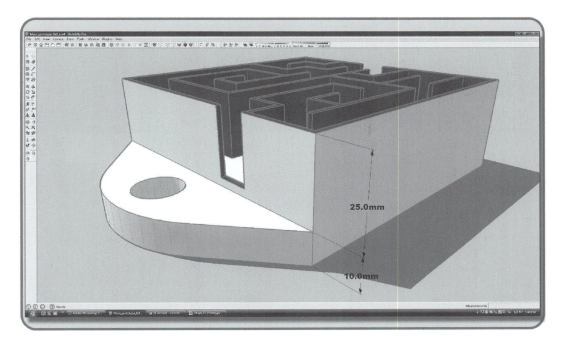

FIGURE 13.14   Screen grab from SketchUp showing the process of making the hanging tab.

Let's call that one "my_prototype_maze_physics.dae." *Note:* when you export the physics file, uncheck the Export Texture Maps box, in the Export Menu of SketchUp. Log in to your OpenSim-based virtual world with the Firestorm Viewer, and under Avatar/Upload/Mesh Model/ find your newly saved maze file and select it for upload. A large Upload menu box from Firestorm should appear. You will need to do a few settings on each page, so let's go over them. Note: in Chapter 2, section 2.3, the rules for uploading, known problems, and tips about how to reduce the costs of uploading are included. If you have not read these, please do so now.

Tab 1: Level of Detail Options. Make sure that the following items are selected on the Upload menu: Settings for Source are High=Load from File, Medium=Load from File, Low= Use LoD above, and Lowest = Generate. See Figure 13.15 for a screen shot of this menu.

Tab 2: Physics Options. Set Step 1: Level of Detail to "From File" and select the Maze physics file you made. Leave Steps 2 and 3 alone. See Figure 13.16 for a screen shot of this menu.

Tab 3: Upload Options. Now, you will scale this model up so it is big enough to walk around inside. Remember that right now it is only 100 millimeters. Scale it up by a factor of 200, and it will be 20 meters wide, plenty big for avatar use. If you put a special texture on it, then check the Include Textures option. See Figure 13.17 for a screen grab of this menu.

Other selections: Name the model at the top of the Upload Model menu, and select "Building Component" from the "This model represents..." list. You can display the textures on the model selected for upload, if you check the box in the lower right corner below the Preview box. When you are ready, click the "Calculate weights & fee," and then Upload when it gives you that option. In Second Life, the Upload Fee in Linden dollars, the Land Impact, and other statistics will be displayed below the Upload button. In OpenSim, these will all read 0, or TBD.

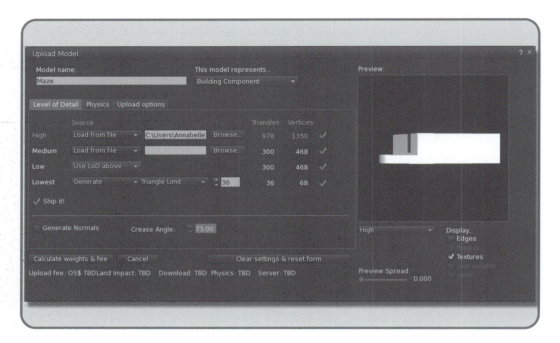

FIGURE 13.15   Screen grab from OpenSim showing the Upload Model menu, the Tab for Level of Detail.

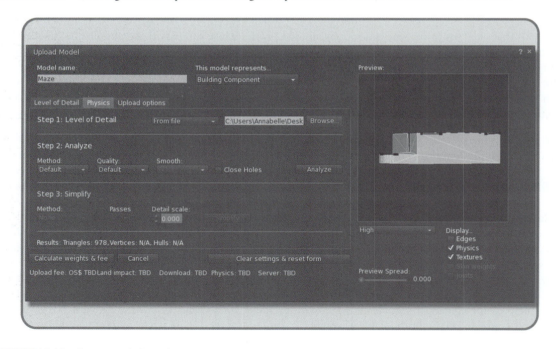

FIGURE 13.16   Screen grab from OpenSim showing the Upload Model menu, the Tab for Physics.

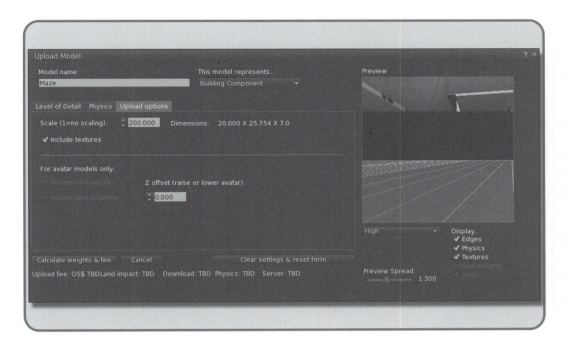

FIGURE 13.17 Screen grab from OpenSim showing the Upload Model menu, the Tab for Upload Options.

13.6.7 LOOKING AT THE MODEL INWORLD

When the model appears in your inventory, drag it down onto the ground near you as shown in Figure 13.18. Take a walk around the maze and see how it feels. You are doing great. Now, let's look at the results of the other side of the prototyping process: the creation of a real solid model.

13.6.8 SENDING THE MODEL TO BE 3D PRINTED

To send the model to be 3D printed, you will need a printable file, which can be exported from SketchUp using the STL file plug-in or from another 3D modeler like Blender to other file formats the 3D printers will recognize.

Shapeways (http://www.shapeways.com/) has a good system and online printing service, and you can even share the model with your build group via the Shapeways website. There are also many other 3D printing services, such as Sculpteo, 3ders, and i.materialize. Find the one that works best for you. Once the model has been accepted for printing, you will decide on the appropriate material to make the first one. One of the less-expensive materials is probably a wise first choice, although it may not have as much fidelity or allow for superthin walls. When you get your hands on the real model of the prototype, take a picture of it and share it.

As you can see in Figure 13.19, the ceramic version of the maze turned out well; all you need now is a tiny avatar to put inside it. Note that the walls were thickened to accommodate the ceramic material used to make the prototype.

Here are some additional things you may want to try: Make a machinima of a walk-through, stage a scene, or have a party. Play with the scale, try several models: one in real-world dimensions based on a 6-foot person, one in virtual world scale for tall avatars, and one for tabletop display in the virtual space.

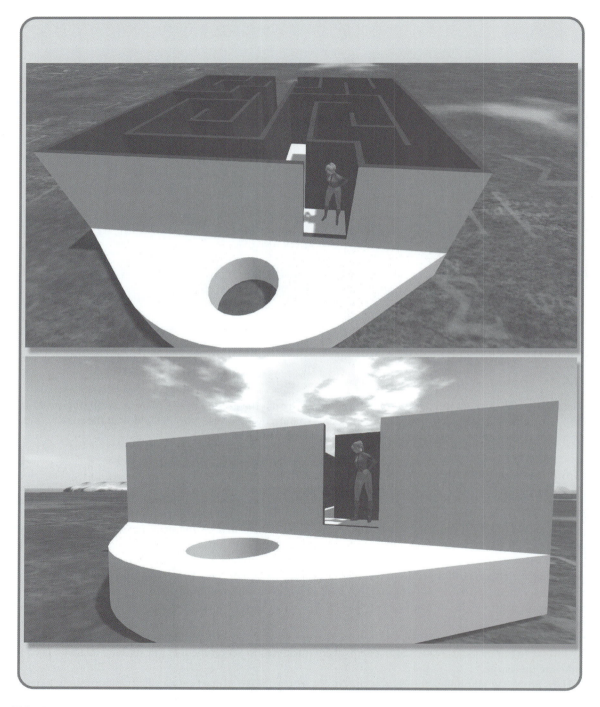

FIGURE 13.18 Screen grabs from OpenSim showing the maze mesh model on the ground.

FIGURE 13.19 Photo of maze model, created as a physical world prototype printed out of a ceramic material by Shapeways.

Brainstorm about your next project. Will it be an architectural project, a theatrical project, an art project, or perhaps some qualities from all of these? Your imagination is the only limit.

REFERENCES

1. Cheng, Irene, Forms of Function: Self-Culture, Geometry, and Octagon Architecture in Antebellum America, PhD dissertation, Columbia University, School of Architecture, awarded Carter Manny Award from Graham Foundation 2010, http://www.grahamfoundation.org/grantees/3768-forms-of-function-self-culture-geometry-and-octagon-architecture-in-antebellum-america. Accessed October 27, 2012.
2. Sokol, David, Kansas to Cairo, *Architectural Record*, June 2010, http://archrecord.construction.com/archrecord2/work/2010/June/Kansas_to_Cairo.asp. Accessed October 29, 2012.
3. Maxwell, Douglas, Steven Aguiar, Philip Monte, and Diana Nolan, Two Navy Virtual World Collaboration Applications: Rapid Prototyping and Concept of Operations Experimentation, NAVSEA Division Newport, Rhode Island, Combat Systems Department, *Journal of Virtual Worlds Research,* July 2011, http://journals.tdl.org/jvwr/article/view/2113/5551. Accessed October 31, 2012.
4. Stage Designs of Richard Finkelstein/Designing for Virtual Worlds home page, http://www.rfdesigns.org/VIRTUAL.HTM. Accessed October 30, 2012.

14 Scripting Basics for the Designer

There should be no such thing as boring mathematics.

—**Edsger Dijkstra**

14.1 INTRODUCTION TO SCRIPTING IN LSL

Just as movie actors need scripts to exchange dialogue with other actors and guide their actions on set, a virtual environment needs scripts written in a programming language to bring animation and interactivity to its vehicles, buildings, furniture, vegetation, and animals. Inside the contents of a chaise lounge, entry door, or a vehicle are scripts that communicate with the avatar, the server, and the client viewer. These scripts are programs written in languages such as Linden Scripting Language (LSL) for Second Life or OSSL, which is an API (Application Programming Interface) extention of LSL made for worlds based on OpenSim. In Unity, languages such as UnityScript, C#, or Boo are used, and you can code in C# for OpenSim as well.

Although scripts are an essential component to most virtual environments, they often present a seemingly inaccessible workspace for designers with little or no background in computer programming. In this chapter, the basic elements of a script are discussed, and samples of a few starting scripts are analyzed to help you, the designer, embark on your own path of discovery about scripting. If you are designing a more advanced virtual environment that involves complex interactive elements, you should consider hiring a scripter (or coder) to write the scripts you need. Guidelines about collaborating with scripters are provided in Section 14.6. Also included in this chapter are various sources online for pre-written scripts which you can adapt for your designs in Second Life and OpenSim.

14.2 DESIGN THINKING AND SCRIPTS

The idea of referencing and running a script program on the server from a 3D object in a virtual world may seem unusual to your designer's frame of mind, but in fact scripts are used by lots of virtual world content, and can easily become part of your design thinking.

14.2.1 Setting Design Goals for a Scripted Environment

Good design of script-filled environments starts with a clear set of goals. Let's suppose you wanted to build an Art Park in a virtual world. Start thinking about how scripting is incorporated into your design by asking the following questions:

1. What are the primary needs for scripting in this environment?
2. What are the secondary needs for scripting in this environment?

You might define the primary needs as: (1) avatar interaction with seating and viewing, (2) avatar interaction with signage and media on the sim, and (3) avatar movement to all parts of the environment.

Scripted objects used for these primary needs are the benches and seats in the viewing areas, various interactive signs and boxes to give the visitor informative note cards from the exhibits, and transportation devices (often teleporters, sometimes tour vehicles) that help the avatar move about, especially in a large virtual environment.

Now, what about secondary needs? To define them, consider these questions:

1. What if some of your artworks were interacting with real-time data gathered online?
2. What if your artworks "interacted" with the visitor, creating sound, movement, or other changes in response to their presence?

These secondary needs can directly affect the visitors' experience with the artworks in your Art Park and greatly enhance their understanding of your message. So, how do you decide what gets scripted in your Art Park? The essential questions to ask are the following:

1. What experience can be created for the visitor by using scripts?
2. How can scripted objects enhance that experience?
3. How can this environment be made more accessible to all through scripting?

Remember to consider "Design for All" access in your planning, with signs that can talk as well as be read, paths that guide with sound as well as directional pointers, and tour vehicles that give narration in sound and notes.

14.2.2   BUILDING A REACTIVE ENVIRONMENT

In a virtual world, architecture can take on a life of its own. Jon Brouchoud (Keystone Bouchard in Second Life) creates spaces with "reflexive architecture" and interactive forms. These structures react to an avatar's presence by changing properties, such as their scale, form, opacity, and color. If you are thinking about designing a building that has the capacity to move, change, and evolve its shape, you cannot help but develop an awareness of how the scripts inside the building elements will be working and how they relate to the linked structure of the building itself. In Figure 14.1, a "twist response" script developed by Keystone has been loaded into some brick columns, and, as you can see, the proximity of an avatar causes the columns to twist up.

As a designer, you also need to think of the interaction between an avatar and the virtual environment, not only the "reaction" of the objects to the avatar's presence, but the "interactivity" that a scripted design engenders. The plasticity of a virtual environment creates both design opportunities and complications for you in this regard. On the one hand, you could design a living room that rearranges its furniture to suit the owner's needs for space, but on the other hand, you may find an automatic furniture-arranging living room does not fully suit the very human need to be "hands on" when personalizing an owner's environment. Haptic technology is creating ways to let us touch and feel virtual objects but is still in its early development stages. For the time being, we still rely on screen-based graphic and textual interfaces to control and manipulate the objects and their properties in our designs. Make the following observations as you learn about scripting and plan for its inclusion in your virtual environment designs.

1. What interactive opportunities am I seeing in this virtual environment?
2. What are avatars doing with this designed environment that I did not expect?
3. Have I seen avatars playing games with available content not intended for gaming purposes or hacking/modifying it in some way?

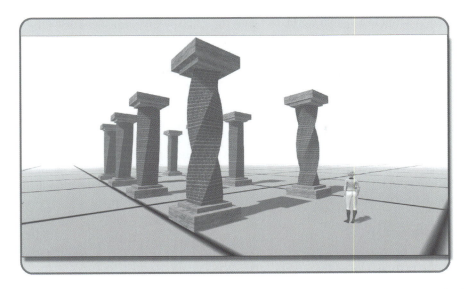

FIGURE 14.1 Screen grab from OpenSim showing architectural columns with "twist response" reflexive scripting, developed by Jon Brouchoud (Keystone Bouchard in Second Life). The LSL script makes them twist in response to avatar proximity.

These observations provide valuable insight into how interactivity can be developed and enhanced. Humans, and the avatars they inhabit, have a fundamental need to interact with their environment, and a good designer utilizes this to make his or her scripted designs part of a powerful and immersive environment.

14.3   AN OVERVIEW OF HOW LSL SCRIPTS WORK

Because writing commands out in binary or even machine language is cumbersome at best, we have developed programming languages like C, C++, C# (pronounced "C sharp"), Java, and so on to enable our communication with the computer. The scripting languages used in Second Life and OpenSim (LSL and OSSL) are related to, but different from, programming languages like C, C++, C#, or Java. LSL language and the scripts made from it are designed to help you communicate with the server about the things you would like your content to do, in a way that is easier to understand, manage, and modify.

There is a pivotal scene in the *Wizard of Oz*, the 1939 MGM film, when Dorothy discovers that the "great and powerful Oz" is just a middle-aged man pulling levers on a machine behind a curtain. Dorothy quickly comes to the realization that she could just as easily control these magical devices, and suddenly the whole status of Oz changes in her mind. People who write the scripts in virtual worlds may seem like wizards. Let us pull the curtain back, look at their tools, and try running the magic ourselves.

A script is really just a set of instructions that is running on the server and referenced by your content. You have probably seen a similar thing in real life. For example, look at this snippet of a script you might write for a movie scene.

Dorothy: Wow! That is some magic-making machinery you have there! [She moves forward.]

A script for objects in a virtual world shares several characteristics with that bit of screenwriting: (1) It identifies what (or who in this case) is directed to do something, and (2) it defines what that thing or person should say and do. A script in a virtual world, like a movie script, also has a specific structural format. It also utilizes color-coded text to identify its key components for easy reading.

Just as a movie script uses capitalization, indentation, and parentheses to let the reader quickly differentiate between who is speaking, what they are saying, and what they are doing, a virtual world script uses indentation and curly brackets {and} to identify its components and allow the scripter (coder) to keep track of what goes on in it.

14.4 ABOUT THE SCRIPT EDITOR

Fasten your seatbelts and turn on your brain. Log in with the Firestorm Viewer, and go to a sandbox or some land where you have build permission. Let's go ahead and create a few basic scripts inside of an object by using the new script button in the Build menu. When you double click on a script within the contents of an object, the Script Editor menu will let you examine the actual code of the script itself.

14.4.1 YOUR FIRST SCRIPT

We start this section by creating a cube. There are samples of basic scripts in the next sections for both Second Life (Table 14.2) and OpenSim (Table 14.3), so the world in which you start really doesn't matter. Figures 14.2 and 14.3 illustrate the process.

1. Activate the Build menu on the top bar of your viewer. Rez a cube and look down at the tabs in the Edit menu that appears. Find the last tab over, the Content tab as shown in Figure 14.2. Open the Content tab and click the New Script button.

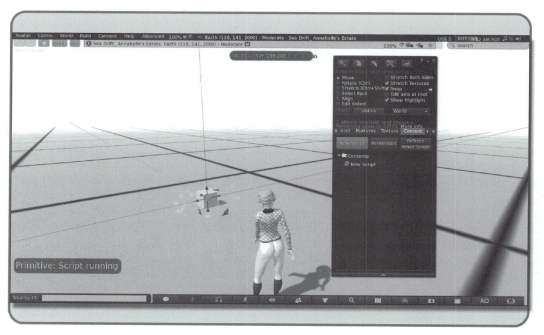

FIGURE 14.2   Screen shot from OpenSim, showing the process of adding a new script into a cube's content. Note how the object now says "Script running" to you in local chat as it runs the script.

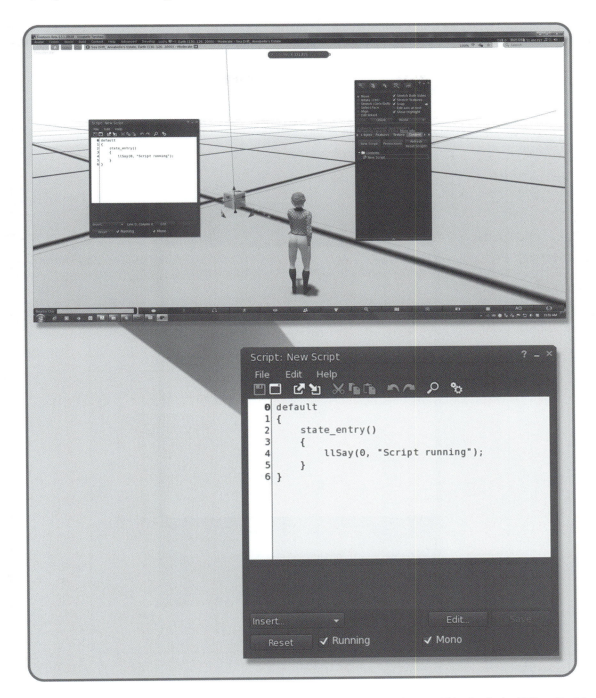

FIGURE 14.3   Screenshot of new script creation in OpenSim environment, shown within the Script Editor. Double click on the new script in the contents of an object to open the Script Editor.

2. When that is created, you should see "Script running" (OpenSim) or "Hello, Avatar!" (Second Life) appear in your local chat panel or on the lower left of the screen. Congratulations—you just created your first script, and it made the object talk to you.

14.4.2 THE SCRIPT TEXT EDITOR AND ITS PARTS

Before we dive into the actual script writing, let's look at the parts of this window called the Script Editor (Figure 14.4). Double click on the new script in the context window to open the Script Editor. Although it

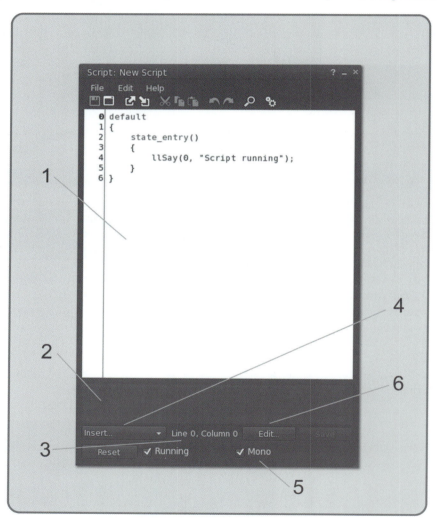

FIGURE 14.4 Screen shot of Script Editor menu showing (1) text entry window, (2) status box and error message window, (3) location indicator for cursor in text window showing line and column numbers, (4) drop down menu for inserting new functions, constants, and other script elements, (5) toggle for Mono, an open source scripting engine that can speed up the performance of a script and (6) opens up WordPad for editing and saving script as a document.

looks simple, this interface has significant functionality built into its parts. The Script Editor is a text editor and a compiler that translates (compiles) the textual symbols we use to write the script into a much more compact code for the server to run.

14.5 BREAKDOWN: FINDING THE PARTS OF A BASIC SCRIPT

If you look in the Script Editor window, and you have added a new script into an object on a virtual world running OpenSim, you will see what is shown in the two left-hand columns of Table 14.1. Initially, this writing probably looks like alien transdimensional driving instructions, but if you take it in bit by bit, so to speak, it will start to make sense. Remember the movie script sample and how that delineated between what was going on and who was saying it? That is happening here. In all the script examples shown in Tables 14.1 to 14.5 the actual script is written in the left-hand column and the "plain English" description of what the program is supposed to do is in the right-hand column for your comparison. Let's examine these two initial scripts from Second Life and OpenSim, line by line, starting with the one made inside a prim in the OpenSim environment.

14.5.1 A BASIC SCRIPT IN OPENSIM

In Table 14.1 is the starting script for an object in OpenSim, broken down by line and defined in plain English so you can see what those lines of code represent. When you read these scripts, pay close attention to the curly brackets { } because they enclose important parts of the script and tell the virtual simulation that interprets and runs the script where each section starts and ends.

Line 0 says `default`. What this means is that the object's script is in its default state when the script starts. States are the fundamental part of scripting; each object may be in only one state at a time but may transition through many in the course of running a script, if necessary. With the word *default*, the script is saying to the server, enter the first state and "start here." If you look at this script on your screen, you will see that the text is red. The Script Editor color codes various parts to help identify them. Default states are always indicated in red.

Line 1 shows the { symbol, which is a curly bracket, and if you follow along in the script editor and click your mouse cursor on it, it will indicate "Line 1, Column 1" just below the status box. This bracket encloses all the event handlers, functions and other scripting components that happen when the script enters its next state, where it will actually begin to do something. Events (and the event handlers that deal with them) come in many forms; they can be "listen" events that respond to something in the chat, "sensor" events that respond to avatar proximity, or "collision" events that respond to something colliding with the object containing that script, to name a few.

TABLE 14.1
A Basic Script in OpenSim

Line No.	Script Code	What It Means in English
0	`default`	"Start here."
1	`{`	This is where we start to have Events and Functions.
2	`state_entry()`	**Event:** transition to a new State and wait for instructions.
3	`{`	This is a new block of code.
4	`llSay(0, "Script running");`	**Function:** say in local chat channel 0, "Script running."
5	`}`	This is the end of a block of code.
6	`}`	All Events and Functions end here, and it is the end of the State.

Line 2 says state _ entry (). This is an event handler, the scripted receiver specific to an event that tells the server to execute the commands between the curly brackets { and } of the next text block. The state_entry () event handler activates when the script runs for the first time (an event) or when the script is saved or reset (an event). Please note, in general practice this script element is simply referred to as an "event," rather than an event handler. The event color code is blue in the Script Editor. A state is one of the basic parts of LSL scripting, and a script can only be in one state at any given time. In this tiny script, there are two states, *default*, and *state_entry*. States contain events by enclosing them with { and } in the structure of LSL.

Line 3 shows {, another curly bracket, but further right in the column. It has been shifted over to indicate to the scripter and to the computer that within this new state, there will be some more things to do. The curly bracket is saying that these new instructions will happen during this new state and only while the cube is in this new state.

Line 4 says llSay(0,"Script running"). This is a function named llSay(), followed by an indication of what chat channel the cube will announce the message "Script running" on. In this case, the channel is 0 and is indicated by the first number (or integer) in the line of code. The color code for functions is red in the Script Editor. A function is a member of a very large family of commands that do specific things in scripts. If you move your mouse down and click on the insert drop-down box below the status window, you will see a whole list of words starting with ll, and they are all functions available for use in scripts. Also, note that they have a name llSay(), for instance, and are followed by (). Note that this line ends with a semicolon, which is required for lines with functions in them.

Line 5 is the } or curly bracket to close the little code block that holds the llSay() function and its trailing number (or integer) for the chat channel and the string of text it has to say.

Line 6 is } and closes the state within which the cube performs its function of letting us know that the script is indeed running.

So, to recap what happened: The cube was made, and a new script was added. When that script was added, it opened in its default state. Then, the cube's script entered a new state, ran a function that made the cube say that the script inside the cube was running.

14.5.2 A Basic Script in Second Life

Now, for a slightly more complex starting script, let's take a close look at the starting script for a cube made in Second Life. Refer to the left two columns of Table 14.2.

As you follow along in your on-screen Script Editor looking at a starting script loaded into a cube made in Second Life, the first five lines should look very familiar. The basic start script for Second Life does the same things as the start script in OpenSim. However, instead of saying "Script running," it says "Hello, Avatar!" in the llSay() Function.

After the blank line on line 6, we see something new.

Let's analyze the rest of this script. If the mouse cursor is hovered on the lines while the Script Editor is open, the Firestorm viewer will give you hints regarding the functionality of each script element and its usage.

Line 7 tells you that this is an event; touch _ start (integer total_number) will activate the following function each time the cube is clicked by your mouse, or "touched" (an event).

Line 8 has the curly bracket {, indicating that we will have the start of another block of code in the script.

Line 9 has our old friend the function llSay() followed by the channel number, which is 0 in this case, and the statement "Touched." as well as the final semicolon that ends the line.

TABLE 14.2

A Basic Script in Second Life

Line No.	Script	What It Means in English
0	`default`	"Start here."
1	`{`	Start of the script.
2	`state_entry()`	**Event:** transition to a new State and wait for instructions.
3	`{`	This is a new block of code.
4	`llSay(0, "Hello, Avatar!");`	**Function:** say in local chat "Hello, Avatar!"
5	`}`	End of the block of code.
6		Blank Line.
7	`touch_start(integer total_number)`	**Event:** do something when you are touched, activate the Function.
8	`{`	Next block of code starts.
9	`llSay(0, "Touched.");`	**Function:** say in local chat "Touched."
10	`}`	End of previous block of code.
11	`}`	All Events and Functions end here, and it is the end of the script. Return to default State.

Line 10 closes that script block with the curly bracket }.

Line 11 closes the entire script and sends the script back to the default or standby, where it will wait for another avatar's touch to activate the `touch _ start` event and its `llSay()` function again.

14.5.3   CREATING A SCRIPT USING AUTOSCRIPT

Now, let's try making a script of your own with a little help from an online script generator. This process and the script it generates can be used in either OpenSim or Second Life.

Here are the steps:

Step 1. Repeat the same procedure as previously and generate a new cube prim or object with a new script in it. Click on the New Script in the contents and open the Script Editor again. It should have the same new script in it that the previous one did.

Step 2. Open your web browser and go to http://www.3greeneggs.com/autoscript/. Autoscript is the brilliant creation of Hilary Mason, a data scientist in her first life; she goes by the name of Ann Enigma in Second Life. As she describes in the introduction, the site "tries to map the way you think into the way the LSL interpreter thinks." Using this website will show you new ways to learn about scripting and how to think like a scripter. Autoscript gives you two sections of options. The top one covers some basic tasks that you would want the script to do, and the bottom one concerns itself with the activation and timing of that action.

For our first use of this, let's keep it simple.

Step 3. In the Script Editor window, select all of the old script in the text window and delete it out; you will be pasting in the new autoscript script and need a clean slate.

Step 4. Go back over to the autoscript window. Pick the radio button that says "change the object's color" in the top list and select "red" on the color drop-down text box that appears. Then, pick "when an avatar touches your object" in the bottom list. Click on the Make My Script button to generate the script. Select all of the new script that appears and copy/paste it into the empty script window. The new script should look like the code on the left side of Table 14.3.

TABLE 14.3

An Autogenerated Script

Line No.	Script	What It Means in English
0	`//This script was auto-generated by AnnEnigma's script autogenerator`	Notes about how the script was made. Will not be read because of // at the beginning.
1	`//available at http://www.3greeneggs.com/autoscript/`	Notes about where you can access the Autoscript generator online.
2		Blank Line.
3		Blank Line.
4		Blank Line.
5	`default`	"Start here."
6	`{`	New block of code, start of new State.
7		Blank Line.
8	`touch_start(integer total_number) {`	**Event:** do something when touched, and start of next block of code.
9		Blank Line.
10	`//change color!`	Notes about what will happen.
11	`llSetColor(<1.0,0,0>,ALL_SIDES);`	**Function:** change the color to an RGB percentage, on all sides (a **CONSTANT**).
12		Blank Line.
13	`}`	End of block of code.
14		Blank Line.
15	`}`	Script over, go back to default.

This one is 15 lines long because it uses extra spaces to keep the script clear and easy to read. Let's go through the lines again and look at the new things that have appeared.

Lines 0 to 1 are where Ann Enigma has made some comments about the script and where it came from. When a scripter puts a double backslash in front of any line in these scripts, the lines will turn into orange color-coded "comments," which will not be read by the compiler as part of the active script. This gives the scripter a place to add instructions and comment on the various aspects of more complex scripts.

Lines 2–4 are Blank Lines to keep the script clean and neat.

Line 5 contains our old friend default, the built-in command that sets up the initial state of the script. The cube is now waiting for an event to react to in the next state.

Line 6 contains the curly in bracket indicating the script block and new state will be starting.

Line 7 is blank for ease of reading the script.

Line 8 starts the now familiar touch _ start event, color coded as usual in blue. The line ends with another curly brace, shown like this {, and here is where the next script block will be starting.

Line 9 is left blank for clarity.

Line 10 has another comment. It says //change color! Here, the scripter is indicating that the next line contains a function that will change the color of the cube.

Line 11 has a new function to tell the object to do. This function, like the `llSay()` function, also needs some information, put inside its parentheses, called parameters. The typical syntax for the function and all that it expects to have on its line is this:

```
llSetColor(vector color, integer face);
```

What this means is that you must define the color in terms of red, green, and blue percentages, and you have to specify which faces on the object should change color. *Note:* you can find out the number of a particular face by selecting with the Build/Edit menu/Select Face and looking at the notation just above the tabs line on the menu interface.

As we discussed in Chapter 7, color is indicated by percentages (0% or 0 to 100% or 1) in a virtual world. Within this function, to obtain the color primary bright red, we ask for R = 1.0, G = 0, and Blue = 0, which is indicated between < and > or the pointy brackets, and would look like this `<1.0,0,0>` or this `<1.0,0.0,0.0>`. Leave the extra spaces out between the numbers; the commas will do the separation for the compiler.

To make sure all the sides of the cube change, we are going to use a constant, which is indicated in CAPS at the end of the function. `ALL _ SIDES` indicates that all the sides are chosen. It is important to use `ALL _ SIDES` in this little script because various primitives (or objects) will have varying numbers of sides. This will cover all possibilities from the one-sided sphere to the seven-sided hollow cube that numbers its faces from 0–6.

Line 12 is blank for clarity purposes.
Line 13 closes the script block that has the `llSetColor ()` function in it with the curly bracket or }.
Line 14 is blank for clarity purposes.
Line 15 closes the first script block and sends our cube back to the default state.

14.5.4 REVIEW OF BASIC SCRIPT ELEMENTS

Now, to recap what we have seen so far. We have looked at three very basic scripts in LSL. All of these scripts had a default state and other states enclosed by { and }. These states contained events such as `touch _ start`. We also had some LSL functions, such as `llSay()` and `llSetColor()`, and these functions asked for integers as well as constants. All of these terms and more are defined in much greater detail in the Second Life LSL Wiki (http://wiki.secondlife.com/wiki/LSL_Portal).

14.5.5 SOME NEW SCRIPT ELEMENTS: CONSTANTS AND VARIABLES

Let's introduce a few more new terms that are common to many LSL scripts and how they might have an impact on your design decisions.

Two of the most common elements in scripts are called Constant and Variable. Constants are values that never change, and are expressed in ALL CAPS. For example, ALL_SIDES contained in the function llSetColor(<1.0,0,0>,ALL_SIDES), is a constant.

Variables give you places to store data in the script for use as the server runs it. There are seven kinds of data that can be contained in a variable: string, integer, float, list, vector, rotation, and key. A string is a line of text enclosed in quotes, like "Hello Avatar," and an integer is a number, only a whole one, not fractions or decimals. A float is a number that has decimal places, like 1.0 or 2.5. Lists are special kinds of data enclosed in square brackets, [and], for example ["this is a list," 125, 2.34, <1.0,0.0,0.0>,<0.5,0.0,0.1,1.0>] and are often seen in scripts for texture animations and particle effects. A vector is 3 floats inside of pointy brackets < and >, such as the number for the color green, <0.0,1.0,0.0>. Rotations are 4 floats also in the pointy brackets and indicate the object's relative position to the axes of the virtual space and its angle of banking, for example <0.0,0.2,0.0,1.0>. A key is a unique number, or UUID (Universally Unique IDentifier) given to every texture, object, sound, avatar, and animation in the virtual environment. These numbers are generated randomly when the item is created or rezzed from the inventory and allow for the script to find the particular item in the simulation, connect with it, and run its code.

Let's sum up the concepts in LSL scripting. Oberon Onmura, one of Second Life's master scripters and art makers, described it this way to me: "I think of LSL as an 'event driven state machine' in which functions are nested within events which are nested within states. So a state is a defined environment, events reflect things that happen within that environment, and functions are the things that actually do stuff in response." Another way to think about it is to visualize the cause and effect you encounter in the real world. For instance, let's suppose you are taking an afternoon nap on the couch. Think of this as the "state" you are in. Your new puppy decides to jump up on your stomach, which is an "event." The nerves acting like "event handlers" in your abdomen feel the impact of canine weight and send signals to your brain which causes you to enter another "state," and you wake up. The brain sends signals acting like "functions" to your arms, so you can steady the bouncing puppy. More events can follow, and more states can be entered, and more functions can be triggered, all defining what happens in your real environment. LSL is designed to help create real world scenarios in a simulator environment, and that is why it has this specific structure. Now that you have the basic concepts, you are on your way to learning more about how to enhance the user's experience in your designs.

14.6   DO IT YOURSELF OR HIRE A SCRIPTER?

For some folks learning about LSL, scripting is like learning a foreign language. To really get the hang of it, you need to immerse yourself and do it every day for a few months. Learning LSL can be rewarding, but you will need to have the time for focused study or already be adept at another programming language like Java or C#. Making the decision to devote time for training in scripting will most likely be driven by the parameters of your project and your goals for self-development as a designer.

For instance, if you are designing and building an amphitheater with 50 seats and need a sit script for the audience in each chair, you might want to take the scripting task on by yourself. There are several tutorials online that demonstrate how to use this basic script and readily available free sit scripts in the LSL library that you could probably modify and use. Modifying existing scripts that are available to the community is a good way to learn about how to manipulate variables and use constants in an LSL script.

Another example of a good do-it-yourself project is particle script work. Just having one good working particle script can give you the foundation for creating everything from bonfires to snowstorms. The best place to acquire information and pre-written scripts is at the Particle Lab in Second Life, (http://maps.secondlife.com/secondlife/Teal/191/56/21).

Reach out to the community; there are several groups in Second Life, notably Builders Brewery, College of Scripting Music Science, and one named Scripts, where you can contact experienced scripters to share your efforts and ask for support. In OpenSim, many scripters exchange information on the OS Grid Forum (http://forums.osgrid.org/), and they keep a large script library there for all to use.

The best thing is to try it, see what works for you in the parameters of your skill level, and push a little bit harder each time to make more scripts for your inventory. It will give you not only more confidence as a virtual builder and designer but also more granular control over the behavior of your designs. The autoscript program

TABLE 14.4
Combining Two Functions in a Simple Script

Line No.	Script	What It Means in English
0	//This script was auto-generated by Ann Enigma's script autogenerator	Comment: where the script came from.
1	//available at http://www.3greeneggs.com/autoscript/	Comment: how you can get one.
2	//Note: You will need to copy both this script and a texture (named Texture_1) into your object	Comment: how to use this script.
3	default	"start here"
4	{	New block of code, start of new State.
5		Blank Line.
6	touch_start(integer total_number) {	**Event** = do something when touched and start of next block of code.
7		Blank Line.
8	//change color!	Comment: what the next Function does.
9	llSetColor(<1.0,0,0>,ALL_SIDES);	**Function** = change color to red, all sides.
10	//set the texture	Comment: what the next Function does.
11	llSetTexture("Texture_1",ALL_SIDES);	**Function** = change texture to the one inside the object's contents, all sides.
12	}	End of code block.
13		Blank Line.
14	}	End of script, return to default.

generates simple scripts that can be combined, and that also will broaden your LSL understanding. For example, the llSetTexture () function from one could be combined with the llSetColor () function in our previous example to create a more dynamic script for your cube. All you need to do is generate another script that changes the texture on the sides of the cube when touched. Copy and paste in the new lines of script from the second script into the first one, making sure that the new function is within the same brackets and state as the first one. To keep it simple in this example, both scripts begin with a touch _ start event handler. Table 14.4 analyzes the result of these two scripts combined. If you decide to test this inworld, note that the name of the texture has an underscore in it, "Texture _ 1," and is exactly how it needs to be named in the object's contents.

All that considered, nothing is better than working with a talented LSL scripter when you have a complex project. The creative synergy that can develop when the team is trying to do new things with scripting and building is well worth the fee that you may have to pay to obtain expert advice.

14.7   HOW TO TALK TO A SCRIPTER ABOUT LSL SCRIPTS YOU NEED

For most of this chapter, we have discussed the parts of some basic LSL scripts and how those parts work together. This knowledge will come in handy when you sit down with a scripter to design a complex script. Let's suppose you have a fancy apartment building in mind, and all the doors will be scripted to open at their owners' verbal command. Also, you would like the apartment owners to have the option of adding a guest's name to the door when the apartment is being lent. If you try to think about that like a scripter, what elements of an LSL script do you begin to see? Try to fill in the plain English/right side of the script analysis table (Table 14.5) first so you will have a list from which the scripter can work.

TABLE 14.5
Setting the Parameters for a New Door Script

Line No.	LSL Code	What You Want the Script to Do
?		The door has to rotate on its hinge.
?		The door has two States in its script besides the default; they are Open and Shut.
?		The door knows who the owner is; it has the owner's identity, called Key or UUID.
?		The door lets the owner update a list of people with access to the owner's place so they can enter.
?		The door needs to open on the owner's verbal command.
?		The door needs to shut by itself after some time or when the owner or guest touches it again.
?		The door makes a nice closing and opening sound.

This exercise should have shown you the following two things:

1. This kind of door script is probably beyond the abilities of a novice scripter.
2. There are many factors that can go into creating even the simplest things in a virtual world, especially if we want them to be interactive.

It is not typical to think of a virtual door as interactive, but in fact, doors most often are to some extent. A good scripter will make a nice, clean, readable door script with understandable comments on it. A great scripter will look for and suggest ways the door can be made more interactive and streamline the script to help the script run faster.

14.8   SCRIPTING AND VARIOUS PERFORMANCE PITFALLS

Every prim or object, every texture on them, every script in them, demands attention from the processor of the virtual machine that runs your sim. When this is overtaxed, we begin to experience "lag," which can manifest in various ways. Our chats and instant messages (IMs) start to show up out of order, making conversation difficult, or our avatars and their cameras jerk or just freeze in position.

The following is a list of some of the biggest lag producers in the scripting family as well as scripts that can interfere with the overall rendering of the virtual world on your screen:

1. Listener scripts that are utilizing the `llListen()` function to scan the region for chat to which they should respond. If there are a lot of these scripted objects, it will start to have an impact on the server's processing time, especially if these objects are all listening and chatting on the same channel.
2. Lots of changing textures or animation of textures on the surfaces of your build will demand significant processing time from your viewer.
3. Physics-based elements such as vehicles, moving animals, or even physical coconuts falling from a tree can add work for the physics engine and tax the region's processing response.
4. Object-embedded software scripts, such as URL givers that open a viewer or seek a database on an outside server, will add to the load.

When you need to use scripts like these in great quantities, you should keep an eye on the performance of the sim and check periodically to see if you are running efficiently. You can track the impact of your scripted objects with the performance tools provided in the viewer[1]. You will find the lag meter and the sim statistics window under the top bar menu, Advanced/Performance tools in Firestorm viewer. (Note, if your Advanced menu is not showing, it can be activated under the Avatar/Preferences/Advanced tab on the top bar menu.)

To keep an overview on the server, check the lag meter. The lag meter indicates client, network, and server lag, with "stoplight"-based graphic indicators for each lag type. Green is good, yellow indicates some drag on the system, and red is a serious problem with your connection or client.

After you have checked the lag meter, open the statistics window. As you read down the listings on the statistics window, note the frame rate given in frames per second (fps). A good range for frame rate is around 15–30 fps for a virtual world. This is much slower than what you would have in an action-based console game, but it is acceptable for the exploration of a virtual world space. Also look at these three things in the statistics window: Ping Sim, Packet Loss, and Time Dilation.

The Ping Sim value measures the time (in milliseconds) that it takes for a packet from the viewer to reach the server. A high number such as 150 milliseconds and above could indicate your network or Internet connection has a problem or is too slow, or you have just turned your draw distance up too high and are looking at thousands of objects within that view. Many things affect Ping Sim, and all should be taken into consideration.

If Packet Loss is greater than zero, there may be a problem with your network or ISP (Internet service provider) connection.

Time dilation is usually the best indicator for lag; the lower the number is, the better.

Remember, your viewer is doing lots of work, so much of what is considered "lag" may be caused by your graphics settings and the speed of your graphics card. Try always to have your graphics set for what is minimally acceptable unless you need to have ultragraphics performance for a snapshot or machinima.

14.9   DEBUGGING AND TESTING AND THE IMPORTANCE OF THOSE TASKS

Eventually, you and your scripter will create that special door or vehicle script that you hope will provide many useful options for the avatars that use the content you make. Now, how do you test it and add the qualities to make it bulletproof?

You should expect a thorough debugging of all new code from good scripters. They do this in various ways. They can run the code in test objects under various conditions, such as crowded sims or heavy lag, or they can utilize the Debug Functions that are available in the viewer to force the system into a demanding testing mode. Other ways they should test your new script is by running it under other operating systems, such as the Mac OS and Linux. Scripts that will compile and run in Windows may give error messages in the Mac OS or not run at all on a Linux-based machine.

Other reasons to test in various systems and conditions are the differences in various LSL editors and how they will report error messages differently to the script writers. In fact, there is an integer constant DEBUG _ CHANNEL that is reserved for script debugging and error messages. This is a special chat channel used for script debugging and error messages. The viewer will display chat on this channel in the script console to help the scripter find their errors.

The final test of good scripting will come when the object and its script are set up by the scripter to be tested under live conditions, called "play testing." These sessions are useful, especially if you and your scripter can have a wide variety of people test the item in question.

TABLE 14.6

List of Scripts Useful for Presentations in This Book and Location for Download

Related to this Chapter	Name/Type of Script	Where You Can Get It
4: 3D design	Information about scripts and usage	http://wiki.secondlife.com/wiki/Good_Building_Practices (not scripts but lots of info about building with them)
5: terrain	Teleportation and getting around	http://wiki.secondlife.com/wiki/CatTeleportation (various teleporters)
6: modeling	All sorts of texture manipulation scripts at the Texture Tutorial	http://maps.secondlife.com/secondlife/Livingtree/127/99/25 (the scripts are on the note cards given out in the Texture Tutorial pavilion)
7: color/particles	Control for particles and color changes	http://maps.secondlife.com/secondlife/Teal/195/59/25 (take the balloon to the Particle Lab: lots of scripts that control particles, sounds, textures, etc.) http://wiki.secondlife.com/wiki/Category:LSL_Color (shows most common color percentages) http://wiki.secondlife.com/wiki/CatColors (assorted color-changing scripts)
8: lighting	Controls prim to make it light up	http://wiki.secondlife.com/wiki/Category:LSL_Light (various types)
9: presentation	Camera controlling scripts	http://wiki.secondlife.com/wiki/CatCamera (various types)
10: interactivity	Signage and display	http://wiki.secondlife.com/wiki/CatTextures (various texture display scripts)
11: sound	Sound playing and looping	http://wiki.secondlife.com/wiki/CatMedia (various sound and media scripts)
12: avatar and nonplayer characters (NPCs)	Avatars, groups, and avatar presence	http://wiki.secondlife.com/wiki/CatAvatar (various ways to relate to avatars and groups) http://wiki.secondlife.com/wiki/CatTouchDetection (touch detection scripts) http://www.hypergridbusiness.com/opensim-content-providers/ and http://wiki.secondlife.com/wiki/CatAnimationOverride (posing and poseball scripts) http://atate.org/mscel/i-zone/npc/NPC-Scripts.lsl.txt (various NPC scripts) http://opensimulator.org/wiki/NPC (all about bots for OpenSim) http://was.fm/opensim:npc (step by step for making bots work in your OpenSim region)
13: prototyping	Scripts that relate to building	http://wiki.secondlife.com/wiki/CatHousing (scripts for doors, windows, etc.) http://wiki.secondlife.com/wiki/CatHolodecks (scripts for holodecks)
14: scripting	All kinds of scripts	http://wiki.secondlife.com/wiki/LSL_Library (the Script Library)
15: heads-up display (HUD)	HUD interaction	http://wiki.secondlife.com/wiki/CatHUD (just a few) http://secondview.wordpress.com/2007/12/05/scripting-snippets-7-creating-a-hud/ ("How-to" with scripts)
16: machinima	Whole blog article full of useful links	http://metaverse.mitsi.com/secondlife/posts/Camstudio/
Additional scripts	Chapter 7: spin script for moving prims around	http://wiki.secondlife.com/wiki/LlTargetOmega

14.10 MOVING ON TO MORE COMPLEX SCRIPTING

By now, you should be feeling more confident about LSL script structure and working with scripters. Like oil painting and creating sculpture, script writing for virtual worlds is a technically demanding art form and could provide a worthwhile challenge to you for many years to come. The magic and the wizard's tools await you.

14.10.1 OTHER SCRIPTS MENTIONED IN THIS BOOK

In previous chapters and those to come, LSL scripts are mentioned and can be utilized by you for your design purposes. Table 14.6 is a list of the scripts useful for projects in this book and provides links where you can get them online.

14.10.2 MAJOR SCRIPT LISTS FOR OPENSIM AND SECOND LIFE

Major script lists for OpenSim can be accessed at the following:

The OSgrid Forum now has a comprehensive list of major scripts at http://forums.osgrid.org/.
The Hypergrid Business OpenSim Vendor Content directory is available at http://www.hypergridbusiness.com/.

There are several sources for script lists for Second Life:

The LSL portal has a categorized library at http://wiki.secondlife.com/wiki/Category:LSL_Portal
The Second Life Script Library is accessed at http://wiki.secondlife.com/wiki/LSL_Library
A massive online collection of scripts is found at http://www.free-lsl-scripts.com/, collected and curated by Fred Beckhusen (Ferd Frederix in Second Life and OpenSim).
Another major contributor to Second Life and OpenSim is Eva Comaroski. You will find her invaluable collection of information and scripts at http://was.fm/start.

14.11 CONCLUSION AND ROAD MAP FOR LEARNING MORE

You have just dipped your toes into the vast and deep ocean of scripting for virtual environments. Hopefully, this has enticed you enough to consider furthering your studies in scripting. Where do you start to build a foundation in scripting?

Assuming that you have no programming experience, it may behoove you to start learning about scripting with LSL, then to deepen your understanding and gain more powerful control over virtual environments by adding C and C# to your course of study. Eventually, you will probably want to add JavaScript to your studies since Unity uses that as well as C#. There are many other great programming languages, of course—Python, PHP, and Java, to name a few. If you find a good project (maybe making a small game) that needs some scripting, that is probably a good place to start your education. Whatever course your interests take you in scripting, have fun with it!

REFERENCE

1. Using the Statistics Bar, Second Life Knowledge Base, http://community.secondlife.com/t5/English-Knowledge-Base/How-to-improve-Viewer-performance/ta-p/1316923#Section_.3. Accessed May 12, 2013.

Visuospatial Sketchpad

Measuring relative scale and deciding on distance

Comparing color and size of all objects

Compare related objects in memory

- shape
- size
- color
- texture

Compare

- shape
- size
- color
- texture

As we observe our surroundings, our eye sends visual and spatial information to our memory

Visuospatial Sketchpad

Memory

Visuospatial Sketchpad (inner eye): Stores and processes information in a visual or spatial form.

FIGURE 4.1 Schematic chart of the Visuospatial Sketchpad as it processes your observations on shape, size, color, texture and relative location of a 3D form into your memory. These observations are stored in the Visuospatial Sketchpad (inner eye) as a recoverable database of forms for your use in designing.

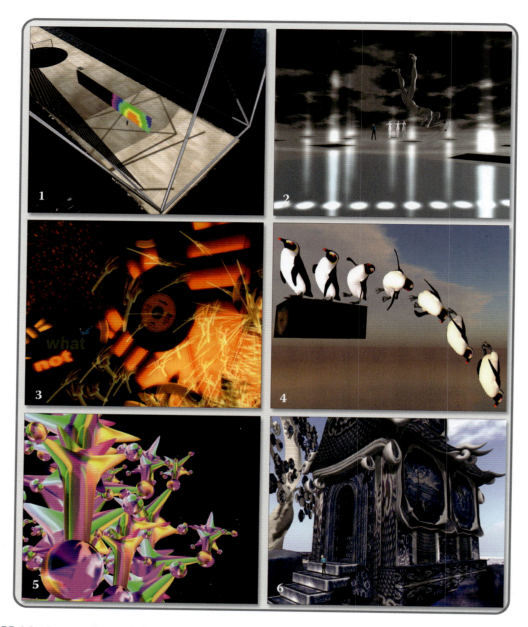

FIGURE 4.2 Images of artwork that embody the six primary principles of 3D design. From the top, these principles are (1) "Line," from a build by Werner Kurosawa (a Belgian architect and artist in real life) for the Linden Endowment for the Arts (LEA) Media Arts Center SE; (2) "Space," from *listen ...* , a sound-based exhibit by Alpha Auer (Elif Ayiter, an artist in real life) for the HUMlab exhibit "Tropophonia"; (3) "Shape," from *Le Cactus*, by Maya Paris (an artist working in the United Kingdom); (4) "Form" from *The Arrival of the Fish*, by Rose Borchovski (a Dutch artist in real life); (5) "Color" from *plante**, by Betty Tureaud (a Danish artist in real life); and (6) "Texture," from an educational project at the Possibilities Unlimited Museum, by Quinlan Quimby (artist and content creator for virtual worlds).

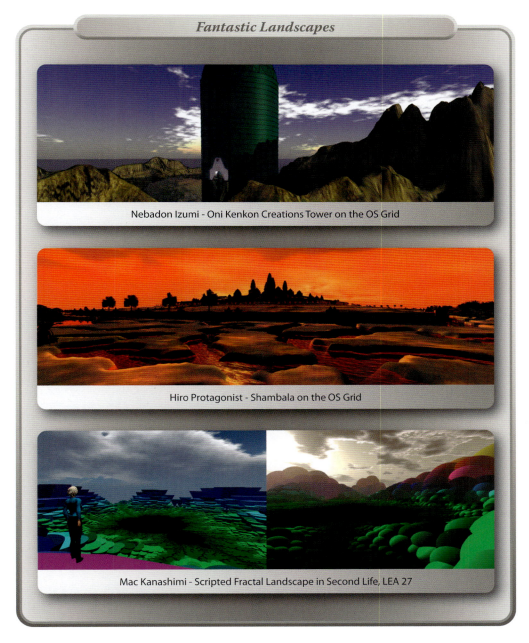

Fantastic Landscapes

Nebadon Izumi - Oni Kenkon Creations Tower on the OS Grid

Hiro Protagonist - Shambala on the OS Grid

Mac Kanashimi - Scripted Fractal Landscape in Second Life, LEA 27

FIGURE 5.2 Screen shots of amazing landscapes created for OpenSim and Second Life. Notice how they can vary in composition, with the usage of outlying mountain meshes (top image), composite terraforming that combines many regions into a whole large structure (middle image) and the creation of a landscape made from scripted objects (bottom image).

Terrain and Landscape Shots of Wheely Island

Wheely Island looking Southwest

Wheely Island looking East

Looking West at Sunset

FIGURE 5.16 Screen grabs in OpenSim from Alchemy Sims Grid, showing the finished Wheely Island terrain at sunset.

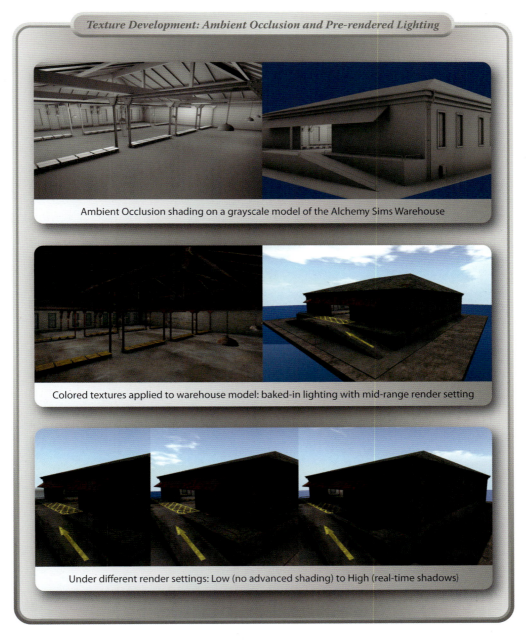

Texture Development: Ambient Occlusion and Pre-rendered Lighting

Ambient Occlusion shading on a grayscale model of the Alchemy Sims Warehouse

Colored textures applied to warehouse model: baked-in lighting with mid-range render setting

Under different render settings: Low (no advanced shading) to High (real-time shadows)

FIGURE 6.18 Screen grabs from OpenSim, Alchemy Sims Grid. The top panel shows the Alchemy Sims Warehouse model with just the ambient occlusion lighting on while it was being built in Blender. In the middle panel, the effect of ambient occlusion and the colored texture maps is displayed. In the bottom panel are three views of the warehouse showing various render settings available inworld and how they can enrich the image.

FIGURE 6.22 Screen grabs from Second Life and OpenSim, showing several examples of how external data can be introduced and utilized to create artworks in the virtual environment.

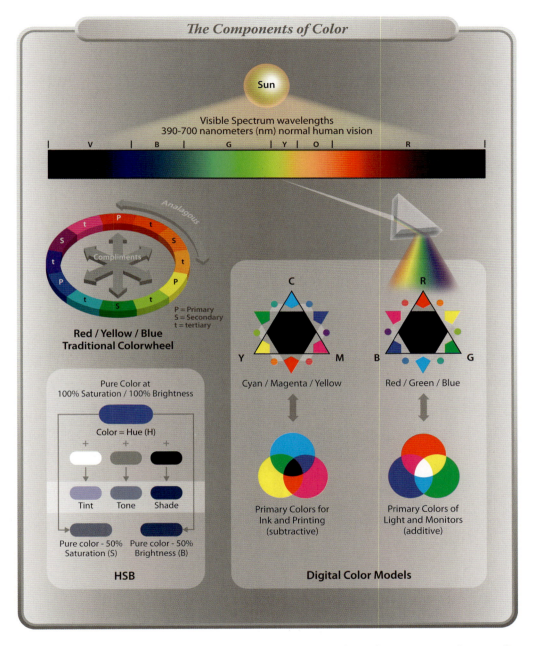

FIGURE 7.1 This chart shows the components of color. From the visible light color spectrum on the top, color models are pulled out to display the RYB (red, yellow, blue) wheel, CMYK (cyan, magenta, yellow, key-black) model and the RGB (red, green, blue) model. Subtractive color mixing is shown under the CMYK model and additive color mixing is shown under the RGB model. Also included is the HSB (hue, saturation, and brightness) structure, bottom left.

FIGURE 7.2 Screen grabs from OpenSim showing the texture tab in the Build menu (top right) and Color Picker sub-menu (top left) that provides color tools for the designer. In the lower left is a sampling of the saturation/luminance range on a series of prims.

FIGURE 7.3 Chart of color palettes by decade (1950–2010) based on color samplings from pop cultural images from these times.

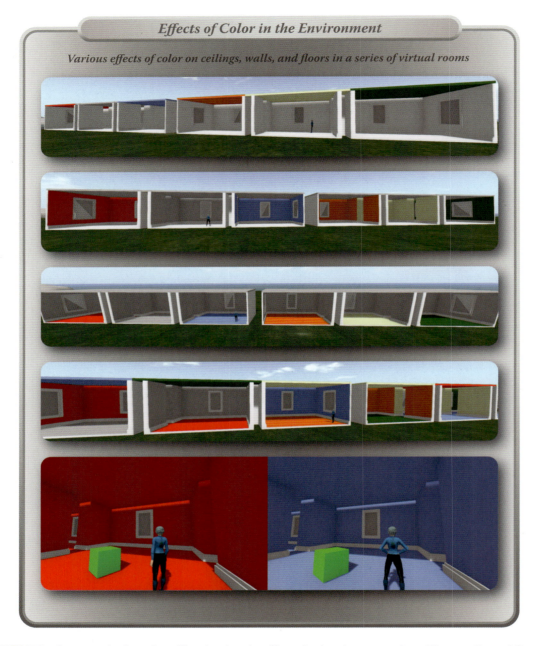

FIGURE 7.4 Screen grabs from OpenSim showing the effect of color changes on the ceilings, walls, and floors of interconnected rooms (top four images). In the bottom two images, the effect of a warm color on the perception of the virtual space is contrasted with that of a cool color.

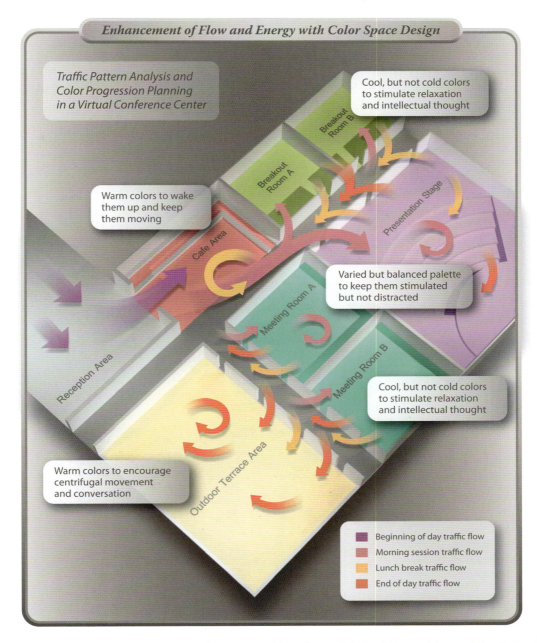

FIGURE 7.5 Chart showing a conference environment, and how the spatial circulation and interactivity during the event could be analyzed and influenced with a color space design.

Color Temperature of Light - Effects on Scene

12 pm

9 am

3 pm

10,000K
Midday Clear Sky

5,500K   5,500K

6 am

Color Temperature
measured in
degrees Kelvin (K)

6 pm

2000-3000K
Sunrise

Color Temperature changes in
the arc of a day and affects
the appearance of other
colors in the scene

2000-3000K
Sunset

Candle light
1500K

Candle light
1500K

Recreation of "Barry Lyndon" scene - shooting in "candle light." Shot on location at Academie Royale des Sciences, Languedoc Coeur, Second Life

Recreation of "Eyes Wide Shut" scene showing large range of color temperature. Shot on location in Bay City - Moloch, Second Life

FIGURE 8.1 Chart showing how the color temperature of virtual light effects the look of a virtual environment. These frame grabs from Second Life show how the color temperature of virtual light changes throughout the day cycle. These observations can be compared to the physical world color temperature scale in the middle. In the lower section, two scenes from Stanley Kubrick's films "Barry Lyndon" and "Eyes Wide Shut" have been re-created to display how color temperature in a virtual scene can be manipulated for machinima just as it was for these films.

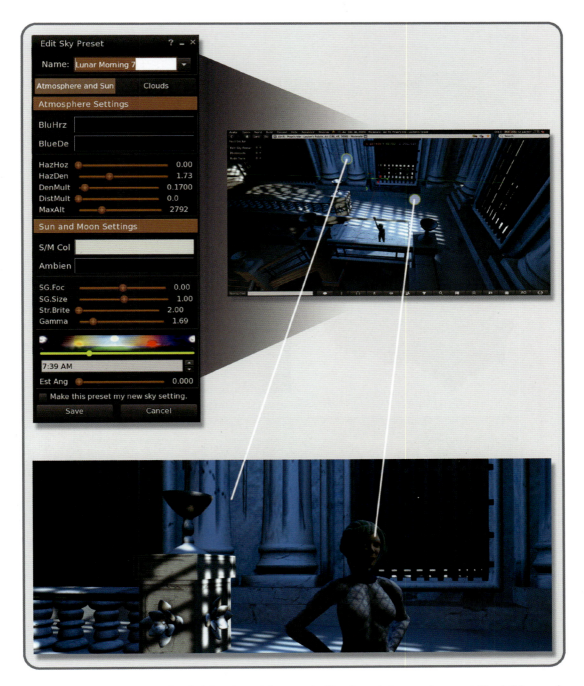

FIGURE 8.6 Screen shots showing lighting for a night scene inside a large indoor environment. Top left image shows the WindLight setting for Lunar Morning 7. Top right image shows positioning the background (fill) light on the left side and the front (key) light on the right side. In the bottom image, the lines point toward the targets of these lights.

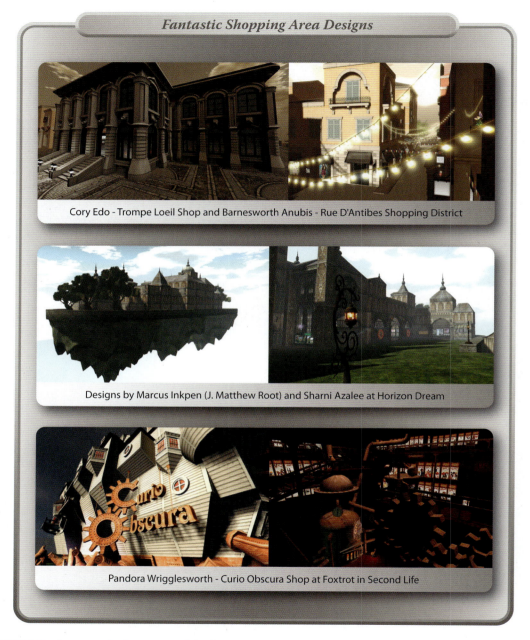

Fantastic Shopping Area Designs

Cory Edo - Trompe Loeil Shop and Barnesworth Anubis - Rue D'Antibes Shopping District

Designs by Marcus Inkpen (J. Matthew Root) and Sharni Azalee at Horizon Dream

Pandora Wrigglesworth - Curio Obscura Shop at Foxtrot in Second Life

FIGURE 10.2 Screen grabs from some of the fantastic shops in Second Life. Top image shows shops from the Hyde Park and Rue D'Antibes regions, middle image shows the floating shopping area in the Horizon Dream region, and bottom image shows a shop in the Foxtrot region.

FIGURE 10.3 Chart showing the utilization of the aesthetic aspects from the Flying Cloud clipper ship painting for a shop design. This is visual research that "anchors" the architectural style, signage design, display design, color palette, and lighting in your virtual shop to a common theme or "look."

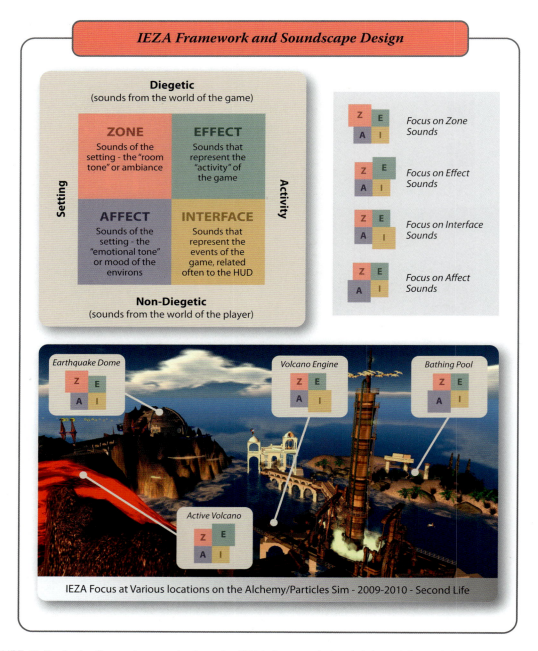

FIGURE 11.2 In the figure above notice how the IEZA framework (top left image) is used throughout the virtual environment (bottom image) to transition the visitor through various areas, while providing a sense of aural specificity (top right image).

15 HUDs in Virtual Environments

Never trust a computer you can't throw out a window.

—**Steve Wozniak**

15.1 WHAT ARE HUDS?

Not surprisingly, HUDs or heads-up displays are made from the same stuff that makes up the rest of your virtual world: prims and meshes, textures, and scripts. They are custom concoctions of shapes, colors, textures, and scripting that are created by content makers to help you access the functionality of their virtual products or to provide game-playing devices like tools, weapons, or counters. Instead of wearing a HUD on your avatar or walking your avatar into a HUD, you attach it to your screen. The HUD will occupy part of your computer's screen space in the position you choose until you decide to detach it. Let's explore how a HUD attaches itself to your screen by using a simple cube.

15.1.1 Attaching a Cube Prim to Your Screen to Test HUD Alignment

Follow these steps, illustrated in Figure 15.1, to see how a cube will align as a HUD to your screen:

1. Rez a cube on the ground and name it Test_HUD.
2. As you know, every cube has six faces. Change face 4 to a red color; keep the overall texture at the default "plywood" setting for now. With the Firestorm Viewer, you can find out what the face number is by selecting a face and checking the Build/Texture menu. The face highlighted is shown there just below the Link and Unlink buttons (see the highlighted box in Figure 15.1).
3. Once you have colored face 4, take the cube into your inventory. To attach a HUD is easy; simply find the Test_HUD object in your inventory, right click to open the Actions menu, and select Attach to HUD/Center. A red square should appear at the center of your screen; you are looking at face 4 of the cube, attached in the center position. This is shown in the lower image #3 of Figure 15.1.
4. To detach your Test_HUD cube from your screen, simply right click on it and pick detach from the pie menu.
5. Try attaching the cube in the other HUD locations and see how it looks in each one. In some cases, the Test_HUD may be mostly off the screen. This should indicate to you that the size of a HUD is just as important as the spot it is located on the screen.
6. Detach the Test_HUD one more time and save it in a new folder you have named HUD_builder for future use.

As you can see from your experimentation, there are eight possible starting positions for the attachment of a HUD. Let's consider the relative importance and "rank," if you will, of each position on the screen. Obviously, the center and center 2 on the drop down menu are the most dominant positions. Since they occupy the middle of your field of view, they would be used for HUDs that are of primary importance for a short amount of time, such as reading a text, looking at a map, or perhaps choosing the settings on an avatar

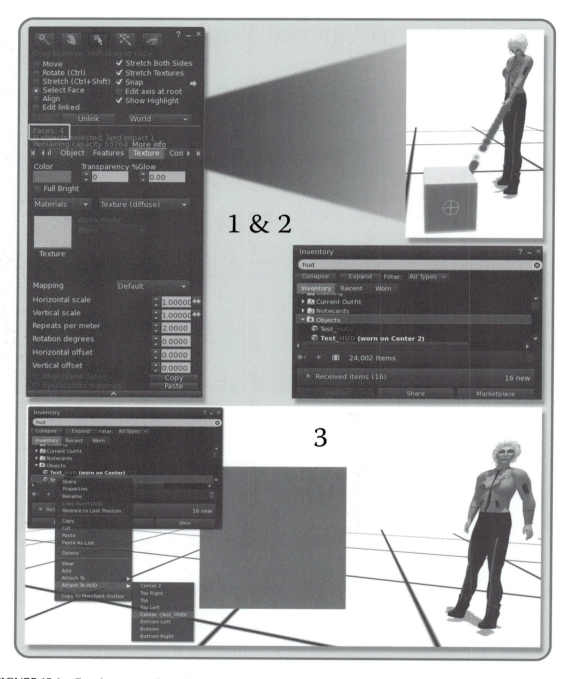

FIGURE 15.1 Creating a test cube and attaching it to a center HUD position. In parts 1 & 2 the cube is rezzed, and the #4 face is colored to identify it. This is the default face for attachment to the screen surface. In part 3, the cube, now a HUD, is attached to the center of the screen using the drop down menus.

attachment, such as the color of your new hair. Since HUDs cannot be "clicked through," a center-based HUD will block much of the mouse's target area and hinder building and interactivity with environmental objects. It is expected that this HUD will be detached soon after use so the user can see where he or she is going or can continue what he or she was building. The next most important positions are the bottom right and bottom left, and these are most often used for tools, weapons, and other things that game and combat systems utilize. The player should not have to move the line of sight too far from center to find his or her trigger or spell caster, or the consequences may be too horrible to imagine. Further down in the priority-of-use list are the drop down menu's remaining positions: top, bottom, top left, and top right. These positions are often used for HUDs that contain ongoing tools and systems used by the avatar, such as radar, chat language translators, animation overrides, and such. Positioning and content of the surrounding viewer in a virtual world game is subjective, and that can have an impact on the design you develop for your HUD. There are several studies about the importance of positioning in the HUD [1], and much consideration should be given regarding the possibilities for interaction when a HUD is positioned. Of course, the player/avatar in a virtual world can always edit the position, and often does, when seeking to make a custom screen interface.

In Second Life and OpenSim, the Firestorm Viewer acts like a gaming HUD by displaying the health meter on the top bar and many basic orientation and informational tools on the lower bar, at the very bottom edge of the screen. The buttons for these toolbars can be customized with drag and drop on your screen until you have a setup customized to your activities. Eventually, as you purchase content and activate the HUDs that come with it, you will find that there are too many HUDs on your screen. To remove one, simply right click it and select Detach in the pie menu; it will be whisked back into your inventory. If you think you have lost a HUD, it has most likely just attached outside the visible screen menu. Just select one of the other HUDs or attach a simple cube prim to the center HUD position, right click on that cube, and put it into edit mode. By using the middle mouse button, you can zoom out and find HUDs that have been attached outside the field of view and return them to your inventory. Simply reverse zoom to put the frame back into the correct screen size when you are done; the edges of the screen frame will be shown in your viewer as a white box to guide you back.

Sometimes, HUDs are heavily scripted and as such should be used with caution. When you are going to a large gathering, special event, or a place that has lag problems, it is prudent to remove as many of your HUDs as you can or, if possible, put them to "sleep" so they will not add lag to the sim with their running scripts. Furthermore, an avatar that is loaded with HUDs is difficult to teleport across sim lines. It is advised that you minimize or remove all of your HUDs if you are going to teleport around frequently.

15.2 TYPES OF HUDS

How many types of HUDs are there? Thousands—let's explore some of the most commonly found HUD types. *Note:* If you would like to do a design survey, significant numbers of various HUDs are available on the Second Life marketplace (https://marketplace.secondlife.com/).

Later in this chapter, you find a project showing you how to build one of your own: a URL giver HUD that can be customized for your favorite websites. Let's explore the various types of HUDs, arranged by usage or function, in the following sections.

15.2.1 ANIMATION OVERRIDES

Animation overrides can be an individual HUD or a customizable menu built into the bottom bar of the viewer interface. The Firestorm AO (animation overrider) interface (Figure 15.2) is one such HUD. The purpose of an animation override is to provide a place for storing and deploying all the avatar animations that go with the character you are wearing. These animations "override" the basic out-of-the-box animations

FIGURE 15.2   Screen grab from Second Life showing the range of animations that have been loaded into the Firestorm animation override (AO) HUD. This HUD can be accessed from the lower right bar in the Firestorm viewer.

that come as the default settings on a standard avatar. For instance, if your avatar works as a runway model, you would load all the animations for walking, strutting, turning, and bowing that you would need to put on a fashion display into the animation override HUD menu of the AO interface. In this menu, you can store sets of animations, so switching from the runway model to the pirate to the mermaid animation sets is quick and easy. In Figure 15.2, the avatar is demonstrating various stand poses that are loaded into the AO HUD.

If you are not using the Firestorm built-in AO, it is still possible to customize and augment the collection and sequence of animations with the use of note cards or button-based menus, there are many other kinds of AO HUDs available in the Metaverse.

15.2.2   Attachment Controls to Customize Hair, Clothes, Shoes, Animal Attachments

Often, the content creators like to give their customers the option of changing hair color and length, clothes, shoe color, or even pelt and eye color of their animal characters. Given the almost-infinite capacity for change in digital content, the choices may seem limitless. Unless you are doing a fashion show or having a really bad digital hair day, this kind of HUD would probably only be used temporarily and then detached back to the inventory.

15.2.3   Combat Systems, Spell Casting, and Spying

Let the battle begin. The HUDs for combat systems, spell casting, and spying are often sophisticated combinations of animation overrides, object rezzers, particle generators, and sensors. They can provide your avatar

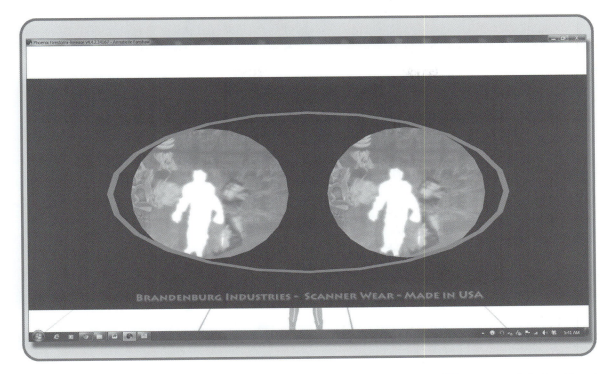

FIGURE 15.3 Singh's scanner wear HUD from "Inland: Search for the Sy." This HUD was part of the hunt-based game in Second Life and gave clues to the wearer about the game's back story.

with the capacity to push other avatars, deform them, create dazzling flashes of particles, and listen in on chat conversations half a sim away. Often complex, these HUDs can take up lots of screen real estate, and they may cause lag as well. These are not the kinds of HUDs you want to wear while teleporting.

15.2.4 GAMES

The game HUDs can provide the player/avatar with game components, give them special powers, and let them access other game-related qualities or objects. Sometimes, you will have to wear one just to stay alive. For "Inland: Search for the Sy," a game environment that Alchemy Sims built in 2010, there was a special HUD to help guide the players. In Figure 15.3, you can see how they used a full-screen HUD. These "scanner glasses" showed a series of slide images depicting what the missing owner (Dr. Singh) had seen just before he vanished in the game backstory and provided various clues about the game to anyone who recovered them.

15.2.5 INVITATIONS, ANNOUNCEMENTS, AND TOUR GUIDES

The art and performance communities in virtual worlds utilize HUDs in several interesting ways. Often, for their shows, artists will send out invitations and announcements that take the form of HUDs. Once attached to the invitees screen, these HUDs will deliver a nice display about the event. Landmark-giving scripts can be added to these HUDs to give the invitee direct access to the exhibit or the opening party as shown in

FIGURE 15.4 Screen grab showing an invitation HUD for "Inland: Search for the Sy," which gave out landmarks to invited guests so they could attend the event.

Figure 15.4. It is also common to find these kinds of HUDs at the exhibits themselves, and like a tourist that puts on the audio guide in a real-life museum, your avatar can attach these HUDs to access a built-in tour guide. Often included are internal teleport keys that will provide for easy use when visiting the multilevel exhibit.

15.2.6 Magazines and Books

Many publishers and writers utilize the magic of digital books in a virtual world, and weekly newspapers, magazines, art books, gallery guides, and exhibition catalogues are often delivered as HUDs. Often beautifully designed and displayed, they are an art form in and of themselves. There is an example of this in Figure 15.5, showing the catalogue book from the Beach Ride Art Park exhibition in Second Life 2010.

15.2.7 Multitool HUDs

There are dozens of versions of the multitool HUD all-purpose attachment for your avatar. In these highly useful devices, you will find menus that let you select protective devices like shields, offensive devices that dispel interlopers on your territory, as well as building rezzer tools and radar devices. An example of a fully matured and well-designed multipurpose utility HUD would be the Mystitool, developed by Mystical Cookie. This tool is widely available in Second Life and used by many of its residents. Its HUD is inconspicuous and yet when activated will provide the avatar with such things as privacy functions, security functions,

FIGURE 15.5   Screen grab from Second Life showing the exhibition catalogue from Beach Ride Art Park, shown as a HUD in the center position.

builder tools, teleport tools, and so on. The Firestorm Viewer has taken over some of these functions, but the Mystitool is still popular.

15.2.8   Photo Shoot, Camera, and Machinima Controls

Camera focus, movement, and lighting controls are crucial to virtual world photographers and machinima makers. A well-designed HUD for that purpose aggregates all the menus that control cameras and lighting in the viewer into one HUD for the photo shoot. This saves time for the photographer and gives much more control over the quality and content of the work. The Firestorm Viewer offers a Phototools menu in lieu of this HUD.

15.2.9   Radar, Location, and Teleport HUDs

As your avatar travels and teleports around the virtual worlds, you will collect landmarks from various locations that you may want to revisit. The capacity to store and retrieve them is often put into a HUD. This could be combined with a visible radar or virtual map access to give you a complete picture of who is around you on a sim.

15.2.10   Vehicles

HUDs play a significant part of vehicular design in virtual worlds. Just as in a real airplane or watercraft, you will have several dials to watch as you fly or sail across the oceans of a virtual world. This adds to the realism of the experience and gives your avatar a chance to interact with several highly scripted mechanisms in a visual way.

Even though this list could go on, you probably get the point. HUDs and their functionality are only limited by their creators' imaginations.

15.3   DESIGN CONSIDERATIONS

There is nothing in virtual worlds with the potential to be more useful than a well-designed HUD, and there is also nothing that can be more annoying when it is poorly designed. Given the popularity of HUDs, most avatars would probably feel naked and vulnerable if they did not have them on, and yet, they can block your view. At their worst, they make you feel disconnected by constantly reminding you of that monitor screen between you and the virtual environment. Since the early 2000s, video games have made some interesting developments in HUD design. Two major factors—the desire for increased immersion and the desire for more customization—are driving this evolution of the screen design. Since virtual worlds have the screen interface in common with video games, some of this video game HUD design development has a useful application in our virtual world HUDs. The next section asks some questions that help you design a better HUD.

15.3.1   DESIGN QUESTIONS REGARDING IMMERSION

What kind of immersion do I seek for my visitor/player/user, and how does my HUD design contribute to that? For instance, consider the minimized use of a HUD in games like Peter Jackson's King Kong by Ubisoft (Xbox 360) [2]. For much of this game, the HUD is not visible or is much reduced, purposely contributing to the "cinematic" feel by putting you in the movie within the game.

In Call of Duty 2 by Infinity Ward and Konami (Xbox 360), the health bar that is so ubiquitous in video games has been replaced by a simple effect in the viewing frame [1]. As your player's health declines to dangerously low levels, the screen frame pulses red around the periphery, an elegant yet obvious symbol of impending death for your player if you do not seek aid. These are but two examples of the recent thinking in how HUDs can be designed and used. Increasingly, the video gaming world is giving its players options in how their HUDs look and what elements they can contain. World of Warcraft by Blizzard Entertainment has been a leader in HUD customization [3]. As the player accumulates prizes, finishes quests, and acquires powers, the player also collects elements that can be arranged graphically into a custom HUD. This is an interesting idea to contemplate when it comes to designing HUDs for virtual worlds. Suppose your avatars could collect various parts of a HUD as they travel around the Metaverse? It is possible the avatar could accumulate the virtual equivalent of a passport, complete with different stamps that give them different powers, from each world visited? Perhaps the avatar would have to display them to return to that place or could trade them for other virtual goods.

15.3.2   DESIGN QUESTIONS REGARDING FLOW

How can my HUD be designed so that it contributes to Flow, and increases the likelihood of Flow, each time the player returns to the game? Let's suppose you could see the mind mechanism of a game player or an avatar inhabiting the virtual world. If they are performing a complex task with a matching level of competency, you will probably find that they have entered a state called *Flow* [4].

Perhaps you have experienced this sensation yourself. To be totally immersed in the world, focused on the task at hand, not cognizant of the time passing or even of your surroundings is to be in the state of Flow. Here, we find an optimal mental environment for performance, learning, and creative expression. In Figure 15.6,

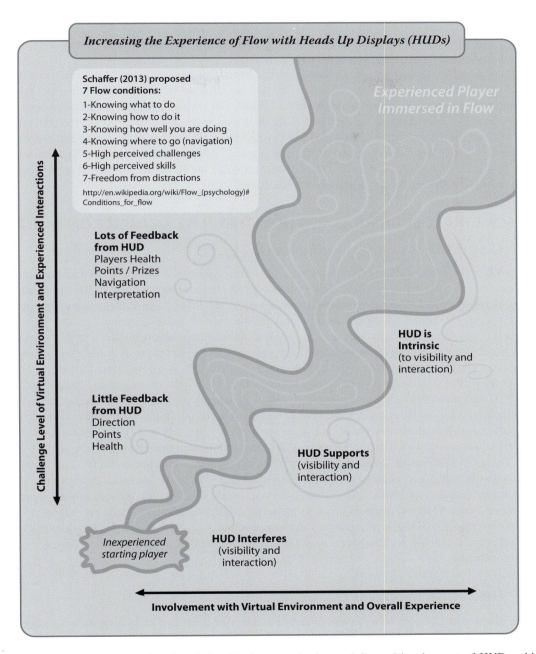

Increasing the Experience of Flow with Heads Up Displays (HUDs)

Schaffer (2013) proposed
7 Flow conditions:
1-Knowing what to do
2-Knowing how to do it
3-Knowing how well you are doing
4-Knowing where to go (navigation)
5-High perceived challenges
6-High perceived skills
7-Freedom from distractions
http://en.wikipedia.org/wiki/Flow_(psychology)#
Conditions_for_flow

*Experienced Player
Immersed in Flow*

**Lots of Feedback
from HUD**
Players Health
Points / Prizes
Navigation
Interpretation

**HUD is
Intrinsic**
(to visibility and
interaction)

**Little Feedback
from HUD**
Direction
Points
Health

HUD Supports
(visibility and
interaction)

*Inexperienced
starting player*

HUD Interferes
(visibility and
interaction)

Challenge Level of Virtual Environment and Experienced Interactions

Involvement with Virtual Environment and Overall Experience

FIGURE 15.6 Diagram comparing the relationship between the interactivity and involvement of HUDs with the quality of Flow experienced by the player.

you can see the relationship between the feedback levels of the HUD (left side) and the game support levels of the HUD (right side) and how that can increase the overall Flow experience when the appropriate Flow conditions (as defined by Schaffer; top left box) are met.

These are a couple of tough design questions perhaps, but not unapproachable. Players can and will adjust to just about any interface if they are determined to play the game or enter the world. Some virtual worlds have a notoriously steep learning curve for first-time visitors, and yet many people who have not been trained in 3D computer graphics skills do succeed and make their way in the world. Your job as the HUD designer is (1) to enhance the desire to take on that challenge by providing HUDs that are beautiful and simple to use, (2) create a HUD that can be customized to "fit" the players' needs (including the capacity to turn it off or severely minimize it), and (3) visually and functionally integrate the HUD into the visual environment so it does not interfere with the players' sensation of immersion.

15.4   SOME HUD DESIGN IDEAS AND HOW THEY HAVE AN IMPACT ON IMMERSION

15.4.1   Using HUDs for the "Cockpit Experience"

There are legions of virtual pilots in Second Life, and as OpenSim-based worlds develop and enhance their physics engines, they will also increase their vehicle content. In fact, the need for HUDs in all vehicles is always growing. As you design them, you will find several interesting design challenges inherent in vehicle HUDs. For example, before you spend months making the most beautifully detailed private jet complete with digital readouts on the cockpit dashboard, think about what happens when the avatar/player actually flies the plane. If the focus cannot be switched back and forth from your controls to the view out the windshield or if the HUD lags the vehicle so badly it does not perform well, you have missed the mark. There are several levels of HUD interactivity to be considered with a vehicle. First, is it easy to fly, and do you actually need a HUD to do that? Can you use the keyboard and mouse to move and accelerate/decelerate the vehicle? What other kinds of other functions for this vehicle would use a HUD? Things such as selection of color and details, driver position, attachable parts, and so on are probably best left to a HUD that the user/owner of the content can attach temporarily for the process of customization and then detach for the actual use of the vehicle. Things like altimeters, air speed indicators, and compass headings are useful for a pilot and should be designed as minimally as possible (in form and in scripting) to keep the lag factor down. Often, the pilot is flying in the "mouse-look" mode and cannot click on a specific HUD button without leaving mouse-look; this creates a serious hazard when engaged in an aerial dogfight with the Red Baron. Figure 15.7 is an example of a vehicle HUD shown in place as the avatar actually sits in the cockpit. This elegantly simple display helps the avatar fly a virtual version of the Boeing/Vertol CH-47 Chinook twin engine, heavy-lift helicopter with ease.

15.4.2   Using HUDs for Camera Control

Typically, the avatars' camera takes a position above and behind them and looks forward with a fairly wide angle as they walk or fly along in the virtual world. This is great when you are just out for a stroll, but what happens when you change into a tiny butterfly avatar and the camera needs to be much lower, or you decide to engage in virtual combat and the camera needs to be right beside your head? If you are an avatar designer or weapons specialist, undoubtedly you have included the camera adjustment with your content. Again, the same rules apply: keep it simple, keep it as low lag as possible.

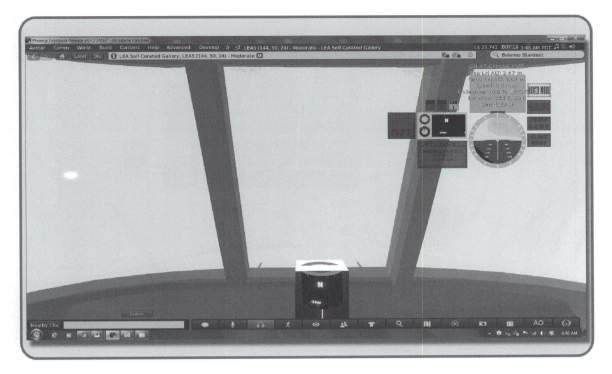

FIGURE 15.7 Screen shot from Second Life, showing the view out of the windshield and the HUD for a virtual Army CH-47 Chinook helicopter. The helicopter and interface were designed and built by Belenos Stardust, CEO Stardust Enterprises Incorporated.

15.4.3 Setting the Mood with a HUD

"Carry the concept through the design" are words to live by. A little window dressing can help the content maker set up the mental space in a user's mind for immersion and the creation of Flow. For instance, suppose you have designed a region that is a replica of the senate in ancient Rome. In fact, you have even set it up so that togas are required to be worn by the visitors to further enhance the immersion. Think how much a teleport HUD that looks like an old map or inlaid mosaic would add to this experience. Carry your design forward onto the screen and completely embrace the aesthetic of your particular design so that the user is never reminded of the other world by your graphics.

One of Second Life's premiere builders, Flea Bussy, creates beautiful HUDs for the creatures she designs. In Figure 15.8, you will see the Halloween Rat and the HUD (enlarged for image clarity) that goes with it. All the pictograms are clear identifiers of what the rat will do, making this avatar accessible to anyone, no matter what language the person reads and speaks.

15.4.4 Using HUDs to Play a Game

The potential of HUDs gives virtual world content designers the opportunity to be diabolical. Imagine a game where you have to build a tool, attaching it piece by piece to your HUD to stay alive, or you are creating

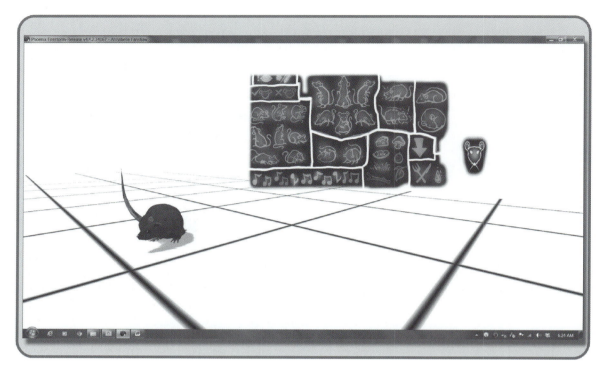

FIGURE 15.8 Screen shot from Second Life showing a Halloween Rat avatar designed by Flea Bussy and its related HUD. This HUD is an exceptionally fine design with great access for all users no matter their native language.

an onscreen playing board while you are solving the challenges of a 3D prize hunt game. The possibilities are endless, and given the ever-thinning barrier between 3D worlds and the 2D space of the World Wide Web, there can and should be more interplay possible between the 3D spaces and 2D websites with a HUD that can access them both. Linden Labs, the company that runs Second Life, created self-attaching HUDs for its Linden Realms project, adding the benefit of a seamless entry into game play environments and automatic setup of game tools for Linden Realms. In Figure 15.9, you will see how they attached a scoring HUD to your avatar as you enter the game through a special portal.

15.5   SOME THINGS TO REMEMBER WHEN YOU USE HUDS

The following recaps the most important points regarding HUD design:

1. Bear in mind the most useful screen position of your HUD and design for that. However, be aware that the user will change the position to fit personal needs or system, so your format should be adaptable and fit comfortably into any screen position.
2. Do not forget about lag and scripting considerations in your HUD. Always give the option of an "off" or "sleep" button if you can.
3. Plan on how you can rotate, scale, or otherwise transform the HUD on the screen so that it can be minimized to save screen space when the user needs to get it out of the way.

FIGURE 15.9 Linden Realms Portal and automatically attaching game HUD, created by Linden Labs, Second Life. As you enter through the portal (shown in the top picture), the crystal scoring HUD was attached to the top of your screen for use during game play (shown in the bottom image).

15.6   TOOLS TO MAKE HUDS

Let's get set up to make our first HUD. The buttons and framework for this will be created with the native prims in your virtual world through the Firestorm Viewer, so there is no need for any fancy 3D modeling packages yet. The textures for these buttons will be made in Photoshop or your preferred paint program, so go ahead and launch that.

15.7   PROJECT: CREATING A "FAVORITE LINKS" HUD

Start your HUD building with a simple one that allows you to access your favorite websites while you are logged in to your virtual world. You never know when you might want to post a snapshot or a cool quote, so this HUD can come in handy if you love social media or need to read your e-mail. It is assumed for the purposes of this exercise that you have a modicum of skills with graphics manipulation as well as 3D modeling and scripting. If you do not know how to manipulate images or edit them, it is recommended that you check out some Photoshop tutorials (http://www.photoshopessentials.com/) or some for GIMP (GNU Image Manipulation Program) (http://www.gimp.org/tutorials/). If you do not know how to create and edit prims or how to edit and load simple scripts, please go through Chapters 6 and 14 before you do this project.

15.7.1   CREATE AND UPLOAD YOUR BUTTON TEXTURES

For the purposes of this project, you should make three icons or select three logos from the three favorite places you like to visit on the web. Make each one of them into a 128 × 128 pixel PNG file. There is no need for anything larger because the buttons on this HUD will be petite.

Upload your textures as shown in Figure 15.10 through the Avatar/Upload/Image menu and find a quiet place or sandbox to build your HUD. From your inventory, retrieve the Test_HUD cube you made in Section 15.1.1 from your HUD_builder folder. If you do not have this, please go back to Section 15.1.1 and follow the steps to make one. As you probably recall, face 4 is the side that will attach to your screen when you "wear" this HUD. This is going to become the screen-facing side of your HUD button and where you will put the button textures you just made.

Next, change the color of the box to "blank" and select a color for the cube that complements the color of your icon texture, and apply that to all sides but face 4. Then select face 4 and apply your icon texture to it, as shown in Figure 15.10.

15.7.2   MAKING THE STACK OF BUTTONS AND BACK PLATE

Copy the cube two times in a stacked arrangement as shown in Figure 15.11, change their base color to complement your other two graphics and apply your button textures to them. Add one more prim to create a "back plate," or large semi-transparent frame for these three stacked buttons. Now, select the 3 buttons and then the back plate, and Link them in the Build/Edit menu. The key prim, or last one on the link chain should be the back plate, and it will indicate that by its yellow highlight when selected in the Edit mode.

15.7.3   INSERTING THE SCRIPTS INTO YOUR BUTTONS

Download the LSL script called "URL Giver for HUD" as shown in Table 15.1, to your computer's desktop. This chapter's content is available at http://www.anncudworthprojects.com/, under the Virtual World Design Book Downloads section. Click on the script to open it in WordPad or some other text editor, and copy/paste

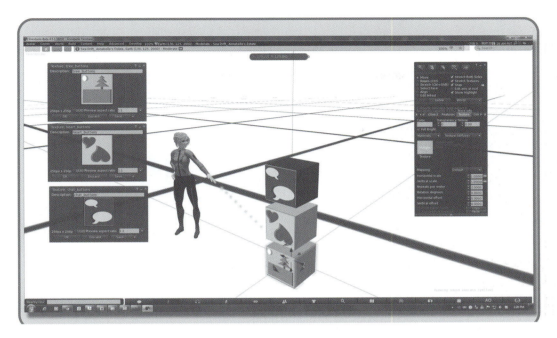

FIGURE 15.10 Screen grab from OpenSim showing the uploading and application of a button texture to the face of a prim.

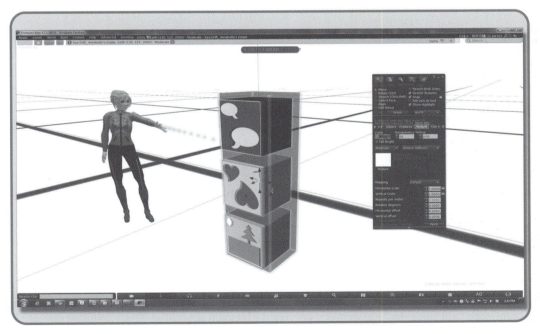

FIGURE 15.11 Screen grab from OpenSim showing process of making the structure of the HUD.

TABLE 15.1

URL Giver script – LSL Script for Favorite Website HUD

```
0   // In Line 6 add in the name of your desired webpage and the URL for it
    between the quotes. The script will make a menu appear on your screen
    asking if you want to go to that webpage. This script is modified from the
    public domain example script shown here:
1   http://lslwiki.net/lslwiki/wakka.php?wakka=llLoadURL&show_comments=0

2   default
3   {
4     touch_start(integer total_number)
5     {
6        llLoadURL(llDetectedKey(0), "Name of Webpage", "http://the URL of your
    desired webpage");
7     }
8   }
9
```

the contents into a new script you have made inworld. Name it "URL Giver for HUD" and save it into your inventory for installation in each of your HUD button prims.

Use the Edit Linked setting to select each button prim individually, and load a copy of the script into its contents using the Content tab on the Build/Edit menu as shown in Figure 15.12. Make sure to change the information in line 6 of each script to the name of the website site (such as "my home page") and the URL (such as http://www.myhomepage.com). Test each button to make sure it generates a blue "go to" card on your viewer and then takes you to the website you wanted as shown in Figure 15.13. If not, go back and check the scripts. (Did you miss a comma or semicolon?)

15.7.4   SETTING THE SCALE AND POSITION OF YOUR NEW HUD

First make a copy of your finished, scripted HUD and take that into your inventory as a backup. Now, scale the whole object down, as a linked object, until the size is approximately $x = 0.06$, $y = 0.09$, $z = 0.25$ as shown in Figure 15.14.

Name it "My favorite sites HUD_FINAL" or something like that and take it into your inventory. Now, select it in your inventory and attach it to the bottom right position of your screen using the menu that appears when you right click on it, just as you did in Section 15.1.1. It should appear in the corner, just as Figure 15.15 shows.

If it is not quite right, select the object and go into edit mode, scroll back so you can zoom out on the object, then scale the HUD down to the size you would like it to be or move it into a better position.

15.7.5   FINAL TWEAKS AND CONGRATULATIONS

Once the HUD is in position, double-check to see if each button will respond to your mouse and bring in a drop-down menu card from the Firestorm Viewer that will let you access the URLs you have chosen. If they all do, you are good to go. Sign in and tweet or post something about your new HUD. Now that you have scratched the surface on the topic of making HUDs, the virtual world is your oyster. Go ahead and create

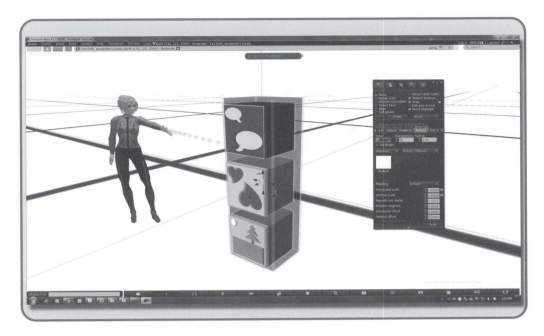

FIGURE 15.12 Screen grab from OpenSim showing the process of inserting the scripts in the HUD buttons.

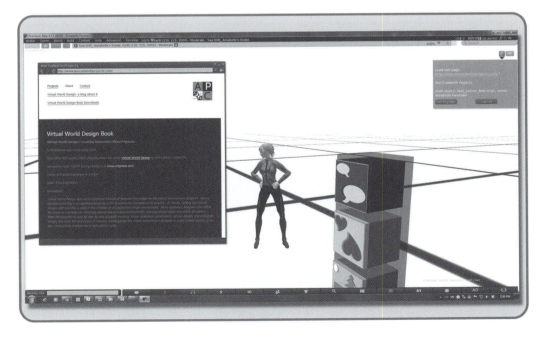

FIGURE 15.13 Screen grab from OpenSim showing the process of testing the HUD's scripting to make sure it accesses the URLs desired.

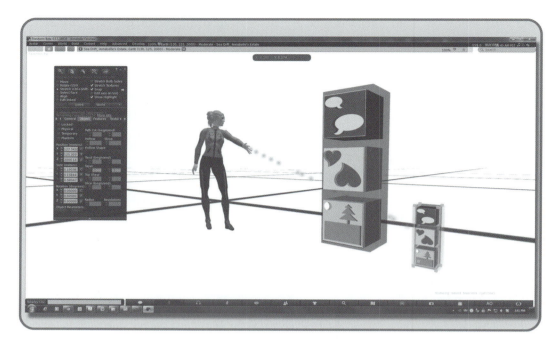

FIGURE 15.14   Screen grab from OpenSim showing the creation of the final HUD for screen display.

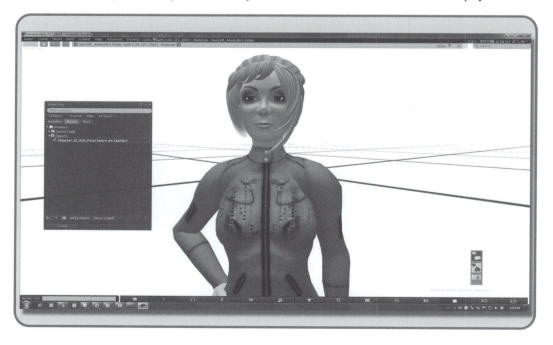

FIGURE 15.15   Screen grab showing the HUD in its final position attached to screen.

HUDs for all of your virtual environments. The objects you make will inform, entertain, and most of all support the message you have designed for your client.

15.8 CONCLUSIONS ABOUT HUDS

HUDs are incredibly useful when they are designed well and used appropriately. They are more than window dressing on the screen if they function to support Flow during the user's experience. Designing a good HUD requires careful planning and execution and perhaps even a specialist on your team. Utilize your imagination to combine the 2D and 3D experiences and create a holistic experience for your visitor. Unity utilizes a similar system. In Unity, the HUD is referred to more often as a GUI (graphical user interface). The same art you create in Photoshop or GIMP for your HUD buttons and labels can be used in Unity along with its native GUI creator (called UnityGUI) to make your game HUD. For more information on this, refer to the online Unity Reference Manual under Game Interface Elements [5].

REFERENCES

1. Fagerhold, Magnus Lorentzon Erik, Beyond the HUD User Interfaces for Player Immersion in FPS Games, Interaction design master's program, IT-Universitetet, Chalmers Tekniska Högskola, http://www.slideshare.net/DICEStudio/beyond-the-hud-user-interfaces-for-increased-player-immersion-in-fps-games. Accessed October 4, 2012.
2. Wilson, Greg, Off with Their HUDs! Rethinking the Heads-Up Display in Console Game Design, *Gamasutra*, February 3, 2006. http://www.gamasutra.com/view/feature/130948/off_with_their_huds_rethinking_.php?page=1. Accessed October 3, 2012.
3. Noom, Nathan, A Look through 14 Beautiful Video Game HUD Designs, *Inspiration*, February 25, 2010. http://feedgrids.com/originals/post/a_look_through_14_beautiful_video_game_hud_designs. Accessed October 3, 2012.
4. Flow (psychology), Wikipedia article, http://en.wikipedia.org/wiki/Flow_(psychology). Accessed October 4, 2012.
5. Unity3d.com, Unity 3D Scripting Guide for GUI, http://docs.unity3d.com/Documentation/Components/GUIScriptingGuide.html. Accessed October 7, 2012.

16 Machinima in Virtual Worlds

One of the most wonderful things in nature is a glance of the eye; it transcends speech; it is the bodily symbol of identity.

—Ralph Waldo Emerson

16.1 WHAT IS A MACHINIMA?

Machinima (a portmanteau of *machine* and *cinema*) is a video art form derived from screen animation captures in gaming and virtual world environments. 3D game environments and avatars are created or modified to create settings and actors for these short "movies." The Association of Machinima Arts and Sciences defines it as "animated filmmaking within a real-time virtual 3-D environment" [1].

Machinima has a long, rich history that evolved from the videos of the 1980s demoscene computer art and the 1990s games like Stunt Island, Doom, and Quake. "Quake movies" started to appear when scripts were added to the movies recorded off the screens of this first-person shooter game. Machinima's popularity continues to grow, and most virtual worlds and games offer a modicum of tools to the user that allow for the recording of screen action. Machinima has appeared in national television shows like *South Park*, "Make Love, Not Warcraft," in 2006; and *CSI: NY*, "Down the Rabbit Hole," episode 405, 2007, to name a couple of examples.

Second Life and the Linden Endowment for the Arts continually sponsor several machinima festivals. They have an entire region dedicated to making machinima called the MOSP (Machinima Open Studio Project), full of prebuilt locations, soundstages, and sets for public use. The MOSP can be visited at http://maps.secondlife.com/secondlife/LEA7/129/128/21 and followed at http://machinimasl.blogspot.com/. It is the brainchild of Chic Aeon, one of Second Life's noted machinimatographers.

16.1.1 THE USES OF MACHINIMA

From its early uses as a documentation device for "speed runs" through the levels in a first-person shooter game, machinima has expanded its usefulness into a broad-range media format.

Figure 16.1 (upper half) shows some screen grabs from a machinima Ann Cudworth (Annabelle Fanshaw in Second Life) created for a campus tour of the Virtual Center for the Science of Cyberspace.

Machinima has demonstrated its place in the teaching of medical, military, and safety procedures; in architectural and environmental fly through; as well as 3D concept presentations.

In the lower half of Figure 16.1, you will see some images from "Possibilities," a machinima about the display of data in a virtual environment. The machinima was recorded and edited by Ariella Furman (Ariella Languish in Second Life) at a data-display-driven Art/Sculpture Park built by Annabelle Fanshaw and Arkowitz Jonson (Ben Lindquist in real life) in 2010.

Machinima has provided a rich source of content and information for scholars and teachers of culture and media. These are two examples among the many available in this kind of machinima. Frame grabs from three machinima created by Lori Landay are shown in the top half of Figure 16.2. Lori Landay (L1Aura Loire in

FIGURE 16.1 Screen grabs from OpenSim and Second Life, showing two examples of machinima used for business purposes. In the top 3 pictures, the "SENDS" proposal machinima by Ann Cudworth (Annabelle Fanshaw in Second Life) and in the lower three pictures, "Possibilities," a machinima concieved, designed, and directed by Ann Cudworth, recorded and edited by Ariella Furman (Ariella Languish in Second Life).

FIGURE 16.2 Still images from machinima by Professor Lori Landay (L1Aura Loire in Second Life) and Professor Sarah Higley (Hypatia Pickens in Second Life). The top three images are from L1Aura Loire's works: "Mirror People" (top left), "Toggle" (top right), and "Transformations" (second row, left). In the lower section are three images from Hypatia Pickens: "Love Prayer" (top right and lower right) and "Cloud" (left).

Second Life) is professor of cultural studies at Berklee College of Music in Boston, Massachusetts, where she teaches visual culture and interactive media studies. She is an interdisciplinary scholar and new media artist who explores the making of visual meaning in twentieth- and twenty-first-century culture in her internationally recognized books, articles, and creative digital media. Included are three images from her works: "Mirror People" (top left), "Toggle" (top right), and "Transformations" (second row, left). All of these machinima are concerned with the virtual/physical world dichotomy and the reflection of ourselves in the virtual avatar. Below that in the lower half of Figure 16.2 is the work of Professor Sarah Higley (Hypatia Pickens in Second Life). Dr. Higley is an award-winning machinimatographer who is a professor of medieval studies, film, and cultural studies at the University of Rochester, New York. Her interests center around northern medieval languages, Old English, Middle English, Middle Welsh, and film courses (including machinima). She is utilizing virtual worlds to explore the creation of new media forms. In the lower section are three images from her work: "Love Prayer" (top right and lower right) and "Cloud" (left).

Machinima has arrived as an art form in its own right. The interface for making movies in Second Life has been part of the Second Life viewer for years, but now with accelerated graphics cards and large-capacity storage devices, the tools for sophisticated movie making are available. Virtual world viewers like Firestorm have upgraded the capacity to provide even faster frame rates for smoother video capture, as well as depth of field (DOF) and variable shadow settings.

In the realm of art-based machinima, a couple of notable standouts are Bryn Oh and tutsy NAvArAthnA. Bryn Oh designs and builds intricate virtual environments based on a loose diary of her experiences, which incorporate many aspects of technology and fantasy. She then creates machinima from the stories within that environment. Machinimatographer tutsy NAvArAthnA works in the surreal. His machinima "The Last Syllable of Recorded Time" won first place in the 2011 University of Western Australia's hugely popular machinima competition. In Figure 16.3, you will see screenshots from their work.

There is also some exciting machinima being done by the fashion photographers in virtual worlds. In Figure 16.4 are some images from Tikaf Viper, a noted fashion photographer and machinimatographer in Second Life.

16.2 DEFINING YOUR NARRATIVE AND PRESENTATION STYLE

The Latin word *camera* translates as "chamber" or "room." Therefore, you may take the term *first-person camera* to mean the metaphorical "room" or "point of view" from which you observe a world, real or virtual. If you were outside your body, looking at yourself and everyone else around, you would be using a "third-person camera" or point of view. These perspectives transition constantly from very personal up-close inspections to wide vistas full of many visual elements as you focus your virtual camera on the environment around you. Your interpretations become apparent to other observers when you record these observations and put them up on a screen as a machinima. Naturally, these visual observations are often accompanied by words of narrative, as evidenced by the numerous blogs that describe the experience of virtual worlds or "tell the story." Figure 16.5 shows a diagram of some of the interconnecting elements of your experience in a virtual world and the modes of storytelling. Essentially, there are two ways to present a story: You can talk about it (diegesis) or you can show it (mimesis). Both of these are going on simultaneously in most of the media produced today. In the center is your subjective experience. You see the visual elements in a virtual world as you observe the architecture, landscape and cultural design, characters of other avatars around you, and so on. You hear the narrative backstory when the avatars are role-playing, presenting a story, or even chatting in instant messaging (IM) or local chat. All of this contributes to your temporal and spatial experiences in a virtual world, as well as the various diegetic and nondiegetic elements that enter your awareness.

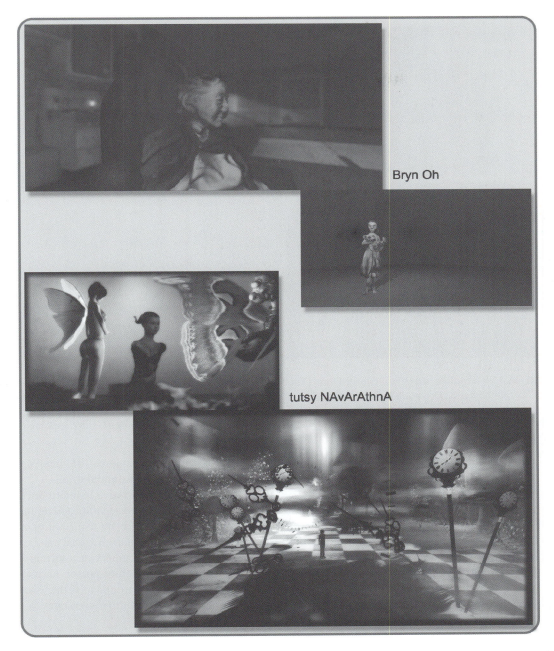

FIGURE 16.3 Still images from art-based machinima made in Second Life. In the top half are frames from "Virginia Alone" (top left) and "Gretchen and Teddy" (bottom right) by Bryn Oh. In the bottom half are frames from "The Garden of Delights" (top left) and "The Last Syllable of Recorded Time" (bottom right) by tutsy NAvArAthnA. Also shown in "The Garden of Delights" is the sculptural work by Claudia222 Jewell called Spirit, displayed at Art Screamer in Second Life.

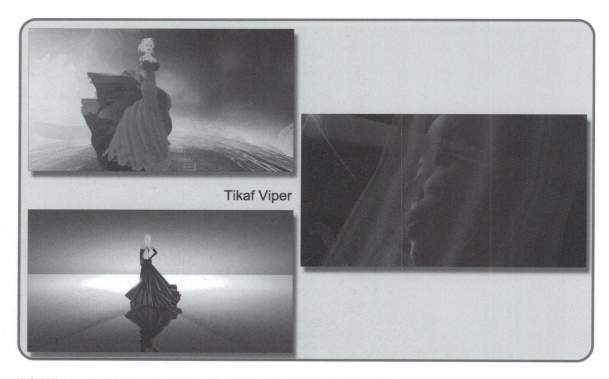

FIGURE 16.4 Machinima stills from Olivier Florio (Tikaf Viper in Second Life). On the right, "Carnival," shot on location in 2011 at the Rodeo Drive sim in Second Life. The Carnival show was produced by Agtaope Carter-Lane, who runs BeStyle District Agency. Left, two pictures from the 2011: A Year of Fashion, shot on location in 2012 at the Land's End sim (courtesy of the avatar Sudane Erato) and other locations in Second Life. The model is Federica Galtier, wearing designs from Jador and Vega Celli.

Furthermore, your attention can be further divided by the effects of camera position, real-life interruptions, your avatar's position in space, the Internet connection you have, and other circumstantial things.

Narrative is clearly evident in literature, film making, or theatre, but when narrative is intertwined with virtual environments that contain immersive 3D design, it becomes much harder to separate and define. In a socially based virtual world, several kinds of narrative happen simultaneously. You are using your personal camera, your point of view, to record and store your visual choices as a personal narrative that can be experienced collectively, in the 2D environment of a blog page and in the 3D environment of a virtual world. This personal narrative you are collecting may contain someone else's first- or third-person narrative, so the collective mix can be deep with meaning. A fine example of this type of environment is the War Poets Exhibition in Second Life created by the University of Oxford, United Kingdom (http://www.oucs.ox.ac.uk/ww1lit/secondlife).

It can be visited in the region called Frideswide in Second Life (http://maps.secondlife.com/secondlife/Frideswide/128/128/21/). Within this virtual wartime environment, you walk the trenches of the World War I Western front, seeing and feeling the dismal conditions while listening to sound clips of poetry and journal entries written by the soldiers who experienced it. There are also places for viewing video clips from current-day historians, who explain what happened there. Figure 16.6 is a screenshot of the "gas attack" section, which combines moving particle-based text from the historic descriptions and poetry of the time

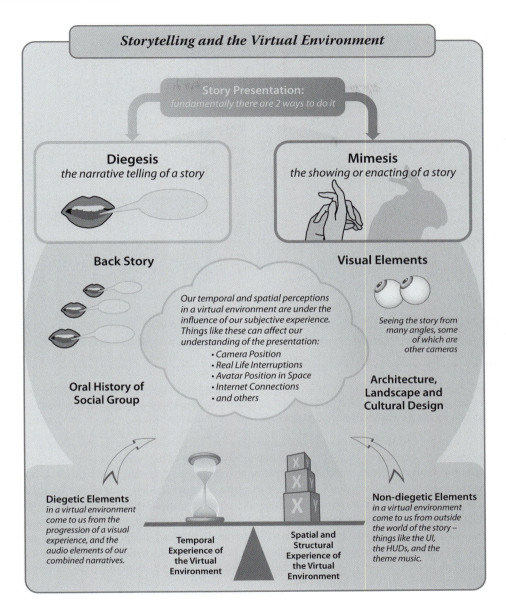

FIGURE 16.5 Chart showing the methodology of storytelling and how that involves the virtual environment. The story is presented initially with Diegesis, and/or Mimesis. The virtual world story environment contains verbal things such as backstory and oral history, and visual things like architecture, landscape and cultural design. Also entering into that enviroment are diegetic elements of combined narrative, and audio, as well as nondiegetic elements like the UI and HUDs. Underlying the whole are the temporal, spatial, and structural elements the avatar experiences. Furthermore, the perception of the story can be influenced by a number of factors such as camera position, real life interruptions, avatar position, internet connection, etc.

FIGURE 16.6   Screen grab from Second Life showing the First World War Poetry Digital Archive, Frideswide region. A complex recreation of the trenches used in WW1 exhibits poetry written by the soldiers of that war. This area relates the experience of a mustard gas attack in sound, landscape, and visual text particles.

with audio recordings of the same material. You experience both diegesis (the narrative telling of a story) and mimesis (the showing or enacting of a story) simultaneously in this virtual environment.

Spatial structure and temporal structure can become subjective in virtual environments, and that will influence the progression of narrative. One primary example of this is called *phasing*. In World of Warcraft and other MMORPGs (massively multiplayer online role-playing games), the server holding the game content will selectively reveal (or phase) the content visible to a player depending on the quests the player has achieved [2]. When a group of players is colocated and communicating, differences in what each one will see in the environment can lead to confusion. The World of Warcraft server puts a "phased" icon near the player's name card, but the group involved in a conversation or quest together may forget these differences in the heat of battle.

If you decide to ponder this phenomenon, ask yourself these questions: How does the verbal/visual language of my virtual environment create its own linguistic relativity? For instance, does it support the Sapir-Whorf hypothesis that semantic structures will influence the observer's perception of the world? And if so, how does that shift my understanding of a world, influence my social connections within the virtual world, and impact my personal narrative? [3].

That is probably enough theory for now. You can revisit these concepts after you learn about how cameras, their positions, and framing relate to narrative. Knowing how to set up a camera shot to support your chosen style of narrative is critical to the success of your machinima.

16.3   VISUAL NARRATIVE AND THE CAMERA

How is the position and framing of a camera view involved with the visual narrative or story of an event? Think about a sporting event for a minute. The rookie is facing the veteran. Half the spectators are expecting the veteran to succeed, and the other half of the crowd is hoping the rookie will show up the overconfident veteran and beat him at his own game. This game is televised nationally, and somewhere in the TV production facility of the stadium, a director is deciding what camera shots to use while the story of this time-honored contest unfolds.

Now, sit down in the director's chair and ask yourself: How would I tell this story? If you read back through the description, you will see that four shots have already been described: (1) the face of the rookie, (2) the face of the veteran, (3) the fans of the rookie's team, and (4) the fans of the veteran's team. Since the story is just beginning, you can keep the framing wide and also let the observer see the full body shots of the rookie and veteran, as well as groups of fans in the crowd shots.

As the competition escalates, it is a good time for a closer shot. Television directors of sporting events, of debates, and other kinds of contests will move the camera in closer and closer to the faces of the participants as the competition becomes more intense. "Tight" shots, or shots framed very close to the face, will build tension in the observer's mind and transmit the drama of the event. And so it goes—the director's job is to choose the framing, camera angle (or position), and movement of each shot and present them in an order that allows for the narrative story of an event to unfold to the observer. With media such as episodic television and feature films, the shots are usually made out of order for the convenience of the production crew, location availability, and other factors. After all the shots are accumulated, they are assembled by the editor into a progression that tells the story. This technique has been used for decades to create narrative stories, and it is still a widely used methodology.

But, what of virtual environments? Now, we can invite the observer into the Bates Motel or the Temple of Doom to create his or her own subjective experience and narrative in that space. We can populate the environment with cameras driven by artificial intelligence (AI), or "camera creatures," that respond to our gestures by lighting and framing the scene and characters within it [4].

Just as the novel and cinema created new ways of telling stories, perhaps games and the virtual environments that hold them will create a place for narrative to evolve into something else [5]. Janet Murray calls this new form of storytelling "cyberdrama." She observed the existence of a "game-story" and defined the new genres as "the hero-driven video game, the atmospheric first person shooter game, the genre-focused role-playing game, and the character-focused simulation" [6].

In your preparation for making a machinima, you need a good understanding of the visual language of the camera and the structures that narrative can take so that you can break the rules and still have a coherent final product. In the structure of a play, you begin with "stasis" or a balanced equilibrium in the environment [7]. To drive the narrative and give us a story to follow, the element of "intrusion" is introduced: war, plague, religious leader, and so on. What transpires after that leads to the dramatic nature of the narrative, allows for the intertwining of character plot lines, and eventually allows for some sort of climax and conclusion or "ending." These are the general guidelines of a linear plot utilized by plays, films, and some video games, but they do not completely apply to 3D environments. When you create a narrative-based 3D environment, there is the "narrative of exploration" experienced by the visitor, there is the "narrative storyline" that guided you to create the environment, and there is the "event narrative," which is continually created by the events and actions of the avatars within your environment. You may choose to make a machinima that follows any one of these narratives or possibly all three. What kind of machinima you choose to make about a narrative-based 3D environment is up to you. As Napoleon Bonaparte said, "Imagination rules the world."

16.3.1   Types of Camera Distance and Their Narrative Qualities

We all know familiar shots; we see them again and again, all day long, in the more than 5000 images we see each day [8]. In fact, we have seen them so often, that many of these camera shots have an iconic feeling to them. Where would the sweeping historical drama be without the wide, establishing shot showing the armies gathering? How can we know about the heroine's deeply held secrets without a close-up of her face or eyes? In Figure 16.7, take note of the narrative apparent in these camera shots that relate to the distance of the camera from the subject of interest. Notice how each shot has a different emotional tone and impact just by how far away the camera is. Here is a numbered list, with the name of the type of shot in bold, and one sort of narrative thread that could be attached to it:

1. **Extreme wide:** "Here is where our story starts/ends."
2. **Wide:** "Wow, look at all the people around."
3. **Medium:** "Who is that interesting person?"
4. **Tight, half body:** "I am really interested in them."
5. **Head shot:** "She is looking at me!"
6. **Close up:** "I think she likes me!"
7. **Extreme close-up:** "I think she loves me."

16.3.2   Types of Camera Angles and Their Narrative Qualities

The angle of the camera, especially as it relates to the eye line or the direction the eyes of the character are looking, has a great effect on the psychology of the observer. A neutral eye line is parallel to the floor when the character is looking straight ahead. Sometimes, the character's gaze is "cheated," and the character looks a little more toward the camera than toward the person with whom they are conversing during the scene. Figure 16.8 shows the various major camera angles as they relate to eye line. The following is a numbered list with the name of the camera angle (or view) as well as a narrative thread:

1. **Eye line:** "I am your equal."
2. **Low, under chin:** "I am your subordinate."
3. **High, above eye line:** "I am your superior."
4. **Worm's eye:** "You are really important/I am really unimportant or I am invisible."
5. **Bird's eye:** "I know all; you are my prey."
6. **Dutch tilt:** "I am confused; I am tilting my head to understand." This shot is also known as Dutch angle, oblique angle, German angle, canted angle, or Batman angle.

16.3.3   Types of Camera Moves and Their Narrative Qualities

The movement of a camera and the dynamic force that movement adds to the meaning of the image are frequently used in all forms of motion photography. For example, take a look at the 1939 version of *Mice and Men* produced by the Hal Roach Studios and starring Lon Chaney Jr. as Lenny and Burgess Meredith as George. There is a camera pullback in the barn as George realizes he has to kill Lenny. He puts the gun in his belt, turns away from his friend, and walks out the door to do it. The camera acts like someone who just heard a terrible secret and backs off in horror, widening the scene, as George walks toward the door [9].

In Figures 16.9 and 16.10, the major categories of camera movements are displayed along with icons that show the camera position and movement required to make the shot. Two numbered lists are provided next with the name of the type of shot and movement along with the narrative thread.

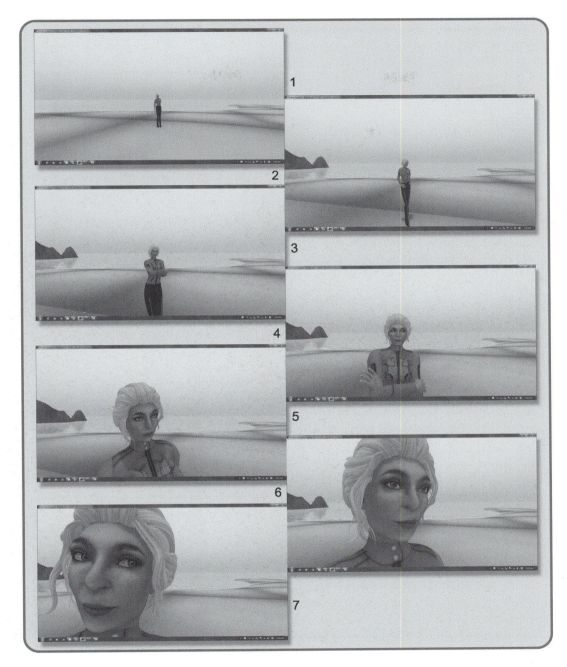

FIGURE 16.7 Camera narrative in shots related to distance of camera from subject. There are seven basic kinds of shots: (1) Extreme wide: "Here is where our story starts/ends." (2) Wide: "Wow, look at all the people around." (3) Medium: "Who is that interesting person?" (4) Tight, half body: "I am really interested in them." (5) Head shot: "She is looking at me!" (6) Close up: "I think she likes me!" and (7) Extreme close-up: "I think she loves me."

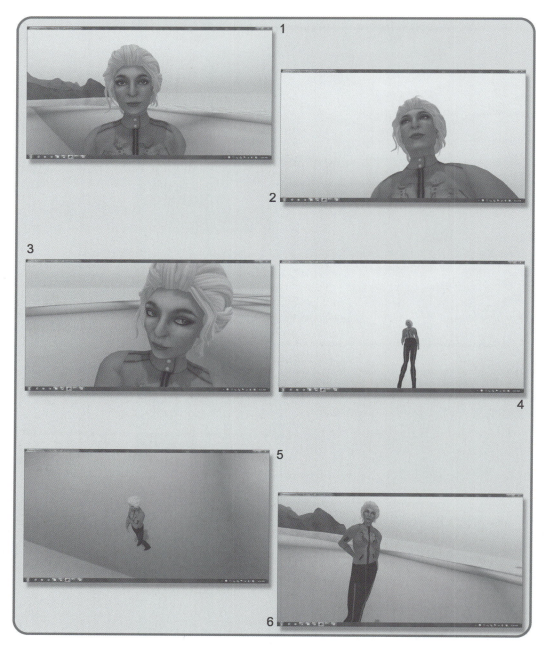

FIGURE 16.8 Camera narrative related to camera angle. There are 6 basic kinds of shots: (1) Eye line: "I am your equal." (2) Low, under chin: "I am your subordinate." (3) High, above eye line: "I am your superior." (4) Worm's eye: "You are really important/I am really unimportant or I am invisible." (5) Bird's eye: "I know all; you are my prey." (6) Dutch tilt: "I am confused; I am tilting my head to understand." This shot is also known as Dutch angle, oblique angle, German angle, canted angle, or Batman angle.

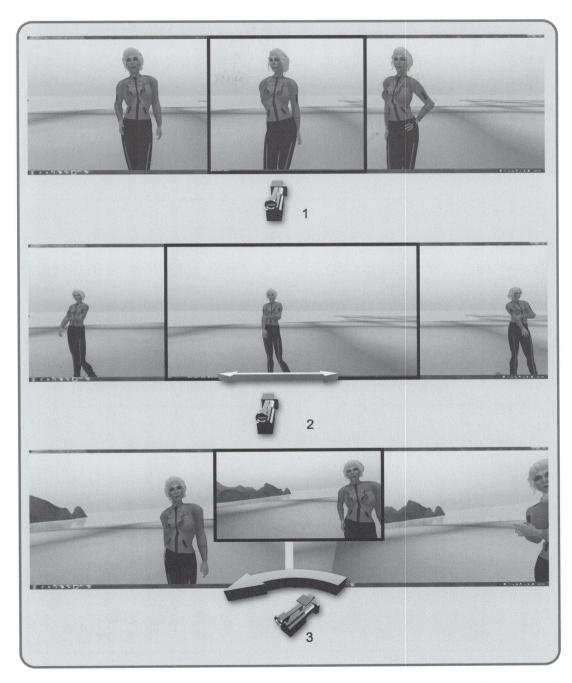

FIGURE 16.9 Camera moves as related to narrative quality. The three shown in this figure are: (1) Static shot: "The world is all out there; I see it all." (2) Dolly track left/right, straight line (crab): "I am moving through the space timeline." (3) Pan left/right, swish pan: "What—over there?"

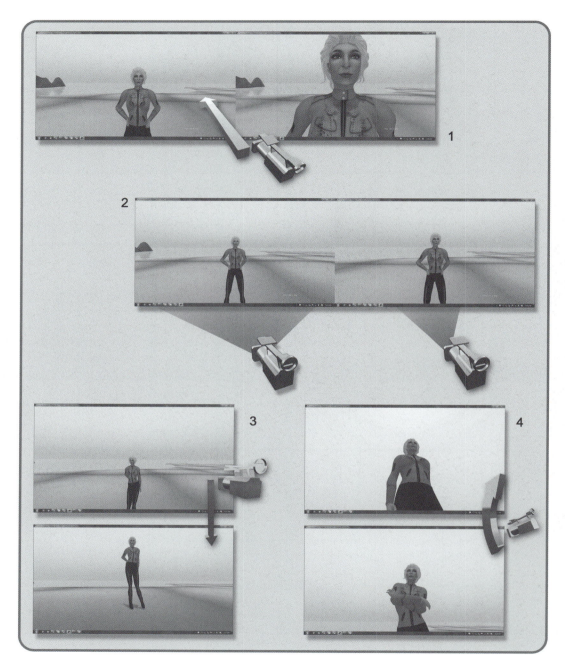

FIGURE 16.10 Camera narrative related to camera moves. The 4 moves shown in this figure are: (1) Push in, pull out: "You want a piece of me?" (2) Zoom in, zoom out: "I really want to know what you are thinking." (3) Ped up and ped down (moving the pedestal of the camera): "I think I will look at/hide from someone." (4) Tilt up and tilt down: "Hear what I am saying and look at what I am showing you."

In Figure 16.9, there are the following shots:

1. **Static shot:** "The world is all out there; I see it all."
2. **Dolly track left/right, straight line (move like a crab):** "I am moving through the space timeline."
3. **Pan left/right, swish pan:** "What—over there?"

Figure 16.10 has the following shots:

1. **Push in, pull out:** "You want a piece of me?"
2. **Zoom in, zoom out:** "I really want to know what you are thinking."
3. **Ped up and ped down (moving the camera pedestal):** "I think I will look at/hide from someone."
4. **Tilt up and tilt down:** "Hear what I am saying and look at what I am showing you."

16.3.4 SCRIPTS AND STORYBOARDS: WHY THEY ARE CRUCIAL TO YOUR SUCCESS

The backbone of your project, and its "spirit guide," is the script (or backstory or written play). The manual for the assembly of your camera images into a machinima is the storyboard. Both of these are essential for any machinima project. They will help you plan your project, and that planning saves time and money.

Let's suppose you have decided to make a machinima based on the timeless plot of a rags-to-riches story. Cinderella, Aladdin, and other favorite childhood stories follow this plotline. Essentially, there are three acts in these stories. Act 1 is about the hero's (or heroine's) life, which may or may not be an unhappy one. Act 2 is about how the hero is introduced to the possibility of a wealthy life but is prevented or distracted from achieving that life by events and actions of other characters in the story. In Act 3, the hero attains the monetary or spiritual wealth in accordance with the changes made in their natures by the events that have transpired. This plot is your guide, along with the events, characters, and their social interaction inside the story. It is your job as the machinimatographer to show the audience what these are, to create a visual story from the sequence of actions and interactions in the story.

You can do this by breaking down each act into "scenes." If you list them and the location where they take place, a pattern will emerge. For instance, for *Cinderella*, you may have a list of scenes and locations that look like this:

Act 1
    Scene 1: Cinderella's childhood, father dies, leaves her with evil stepmother.
        Location is grove of woods by Father's grave.
    Scene 2: Cinderella's current position as maid to two stepsisters and stepmother.
        Location is the kitchen of stepmother's house.
    Scene 3: Royal ball invitations come to the house, and all but Cinderella prepare.
        Location is the drawing room of the stepmother's house.
    Scene 4: Fairy godmother helps Cinderella attend the royal ball.
        Locations are Cinderella's room and exterior of stepmothers' house.
  Act 2
    Scene 1: Cinderella arrives at the ball and attracts the attention of the prince.
        Location is the ballroom of the royal palace
    Scene 2: The prince and Cinderella fall in love; it gets late, and she leaves him abruptly.
        Location is the garden terrace of the royal palace.
    Scene 3: The prince, left with a glass slipper, vows to find the mysterious Cinderella.
        Location is the steps of the royal palace

Act 3
   Scene 1: The evil stepsisters try to put the prince off his search.
      Location is the drawing room of the stepmother's house.
   Scene 2: The prince keeps searching and eventually finds Cinderella.
      Location is the well outside the stepmother's house.
   Scene 3: The prince and Cinderella get married and live happily ever after.
      Location is the ballroom of the royal palace.

When you take a script or story and break it down like this, it becomes easier to see how a chain of connected images will tell your story in a coherent manner. Now, imagine telling the story from the prince's point of view. When does his narrative start? What events and locations does his character encounter besides those he has in common with Cinderella? Each character should bring a backstory to your machinima. You could enhance this with what the character says, what the character's body looks like, and what the character is wearing.

Figure 16.11 is a sample page from a storyboard to demonstrate how it can be laid out on a page. Note how things like camera movement, angle, and dialogue are included beside the image. If a storyboard is organized in this way, it creates a document that will guide your entire machinima crew.

16.4   TOOLS NEEDED FOR MACHINIMA

Assuming you already have a location and the avatars to play the parts in your story, there are three basic tasks you need to do when you make a machinima: (1) record the sound and images from the computer; (2) incorporate additional sound/music; and (3) edit the visual content following the narrative guidelines and storyboard. Each of these tasks requires that you have a computer capable of handling heavy image processing, a good Internet connection, and a good amount of storage (either on your computer disks or in the cloud). A good place to check for all related equipment and software is in a Second Life wiki (http://wiki.secondlife.com/wiki/Machinima). There, you will find people to help, places to shoot, and software and equipment lists for each platform.

16.4.1   THE BASIC SETUP FOR RECORDING

Assuming that you have a good computer that on most days rezzes each scene quickly and have a high frame rate (15 frames per second [fps] or higher) in a full sim like a Second Life Info Hub, you are probably in good shape for making some machinima. Do everything you can do to improve your performance, like turning off all other programs, lowering your draw distance, and so on. There is a checklist available (http://wiki.secondlife.com/wiki/Making_movies#Improve_your_performance). To make your video and sound capture, Fraps (http://www.fraps.com/) is one of the most popular recording programs used by Windows users, and Snapz Pro X (http://www.ambrosiasw.com/utilities/snapzprox/) is popular with the Mac-based crowd.

16.4.2   BASIC EDITING

Making a storyboard pays off in the editing process. Once you have chosen the editing software for your system (there is a good list of options at http://wiki.secondlife.com/wiki/Machinima#Software), you can proceed to load the best versions of the scenes you recorded into the program and start your "rough cut." A complete well-organized storyboard to guide you during the shooting schedule will ensure that you have all the recorded scenes you need for the creation of your machinima. You may decide to go back and do a couple of reshoots

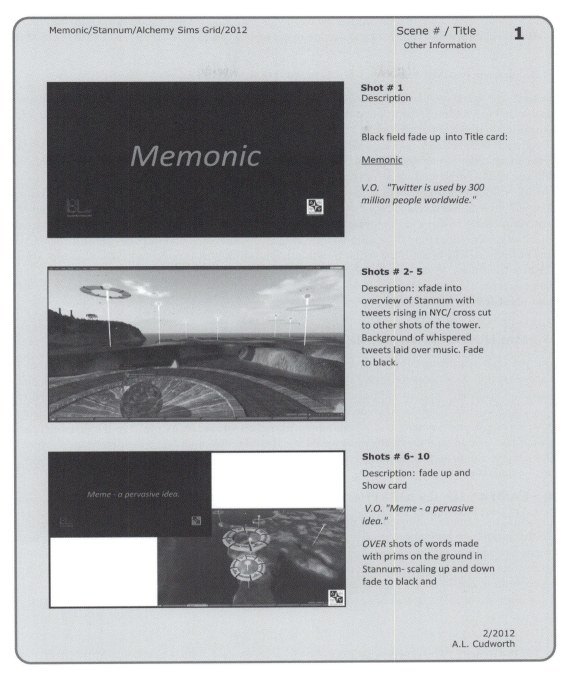

FIGURE 16.11 A storyboard used for creation of machinima about "Memonic," a real-time Twitter display in a virtual landscape created by Ann Cudworth (Annabelle Fanshaw in Second Life) and Ben Lindquist (Arkowitz Jonson in Second Life).

because you had some creative ideas during the editing process, and having a solid storyboard will allow for that flexibility. You will be editing from a standpoint of "let's be creative" not "now we have to organize this."

16.4.3 Sound and Musical Score Sources for Your Machinima

Sometimes, the sound is where you start on a machinima. Such is the case in music videos. If you are making a music video machinima, bear in mind that you will still need a storyboard because it provides the crucial organization of all the nontextual ideas.

If you need sound effects, making your workspace into a Foley studio to create and record unusual sounds for your machinima is not too difficult. Sound-recording equipment has become more cost effective and should you need to grab wild sound or record sound effects for your machinima, look toward the Zoom line of recorders (http://www.samsontech.com/zoom/) as an affordable line of equipment. If you prefer to buy your sound effects, SoundSnap (http://www.soundsnap.com/) has a good collection available. The Music Bakery (http://musicbakery.com/) provides a solid source of royalty-free music for backgrounds and scores if you need them. Stereobot (http://www.stereobot.com/), an offshoot of SoundSnap, has music available with a variety of licenses. The Machinima Artist Guild (http://slmachinimaarts.ning.com/) often has lists available of Creative Commons, free-to-use music.

There is a great deal of information about sound and sound effects in Chapter 11, so please refer to that chapter for additional information.

16.5 MACHINIMA POLICY AND YOUR WORK

Before you start making machinima in any virtual world, take the time to read any policies they may have in place regarding your rights for making images of their inworld content. In Second Life, there are specific policies for snapshots and machinima (http://wiki.secondlife.com/wiki/Linden_Lab_Official:Snapshot_and_machinima_policy). Make sure you read them carefully and secure the permissions you need from the landowners whose environments and avatars whose likenesses you are including in your machinima images. You would be wise to treat this just as you would a real-world film shoot. Take the time to create your own versions of general, talent, and location releases so you have written permission on file for each project.

16.6 CAMERA TOOLS AND PHOTOTOOLS IN FIRESTORM

Before 2011, the camera commands, WindLight environments, shadows, and other settings were scattered across the interface of most client browsers. William Weaver (Paperwork Resident in Second Life), a real-life photographer and filmmaker, created his own collection of tools, called Phototools; now, they have been integrated into the Firestorm Viewer. You will find them under World/Photo and Video/Phototools. As you go through these next sections, the various tabs in this menu are introduced and discussed. This is a great tool for machinima makers; it accesses all the things you need without cluttering the screen with open menu windows.

16.6.1 Phototools Breakdown by Tab

16.6.1.1 WindLight Tab
Figure 16.12 shows the opening page, "WL" (WindLight) tab, of the Phototools menu and how it can be used to drastically affect the color and composition of the surrounding sky and water as well as the main light on a

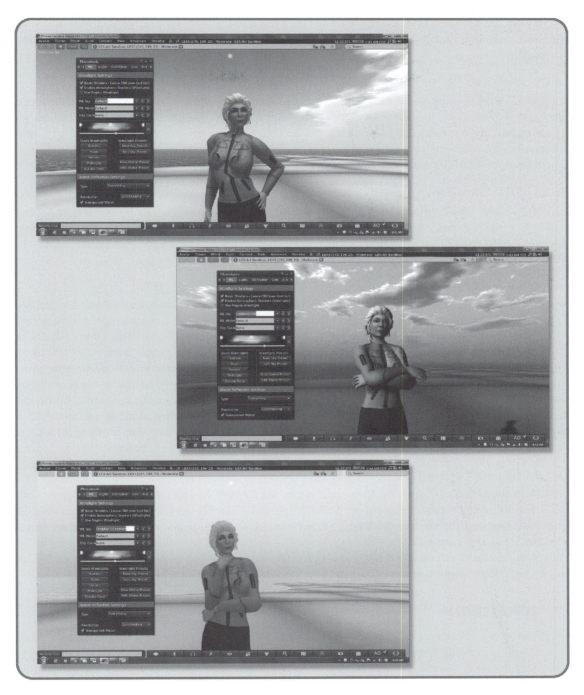

FIGURE 16.12 Screen grabs from Second Life showing three examples of the WindLight settings, all adjusted from the Phototools menu on the Firestorm viewer.

scene. Try out some of the sliders and settings and take a few snapshots. (*Note:* Snapshots open under Avatar/Snapshots.) More information about the WindLight system and how it affects the lighting of your scene is in Chapter 8.

16.6.1.2 Light Tab

In Figure 16.13, the contents under the Light tab are displayed. In the top left corner is an enlargement of the Light menu in Phototools. As you can see, the scene has three sources of light: moonlight, a standard point light on the left, and a projector light on the right. The Phototools tab enables you to affect the lighting and shadows as well as the Ambient Occlusion settings and Specular Highlight settings in the view. In the lower right corner is the Build/Features tab, showing how the point light in the scene is set up.

16.6.1.3 DOF/Glow Tab

Figure 16.14 shows the Phototools DOF and Glow settings available under that tab. By utilizing these depth and glow settings, images you make in a virtual world can take on more realistic lens effects. The range of focus and movement of the focal plane for the scene are controlled with a variety of sliders, as shown in the images.

16.6.1.4 General Render and Aids Tabs

In Figure 16.15, two related menu tabs are displayed: General Render settings and Aids. By changing the Draw Distance under the General Render settings, you can "dial in" the actual elements of the scene to the rendering levels you want. Note that in the top picture the avatar is looking at some empty islands, and in the lower picture, the islands are full. This represents a Draw Distance change from 32 to 600 meters. By making judicious adjustments on this menu, the frame rate can be increased in a complex scene without degrading the quality of the image. One of the key rendering settings is Draw Distance; make sure you only have what you need so the graphics card is creating images from only the necessary objects. In the lower image, the Aids menu is shown, which offers you some interesting tools. Most of these Interface Aids are for your information about the scene. Obviously, the highest frame-per-second reading is your goal here, and having the Quick Stats to refer to while you adjust the General Render settings is handy.

16.6.1.5 Camera Control Tab

Figure 16.16 shows the last tab in the Phototools menu, the Camera control tab. This menu page is a compressed version of the menu that opens at World/Photo and Video/Camera Tools, which saves you from opening two menus while you are shooting a machinima. All the controls for a regular camera are here, as well as the 3D mouse settings.

You will find more detailed information about these tools, from the guy who created it, on William Weaver's blog (http://paperworkshows.blogspot.com/p/home-page.html).

16.7 CONCLUSION

The competent use of cameras in a virtual world is one of the basic skills a designer should have for presentations as well as creating layers of video for a design. The best way to become cognizant of the quality of machinima possible is to subscribe to as many channels in Vimeo and YouTube as you can. Great machinima is being made on a daily basis, and you can learn a lot from watching others. You should also volunteer to be on a machinima project so you can see how other groups organize their shoots and how that affects the final project. Finally, remember: it is your world and your story, so tell it well.

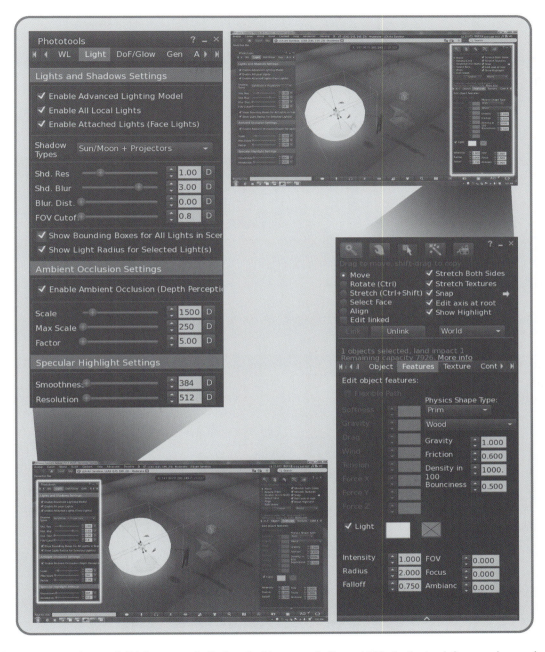

FIGURE 16.13 Phototools/Light menu tab displayed with a scene in Second Life. In the top left corner is an enlargement of the Light menu in Phototools, from the lower left image. In the top right image you can see a scene that has three sources of light: moonlight overall, a standard point light on the left, and a projector light on the right. In the lower right corner is the Build/Features tab, showing how the point light in the scene is set up. *Note:* The Advanced Lighting in the Avatar Preferences/Graphics menu must be turned on to activate projector lights.

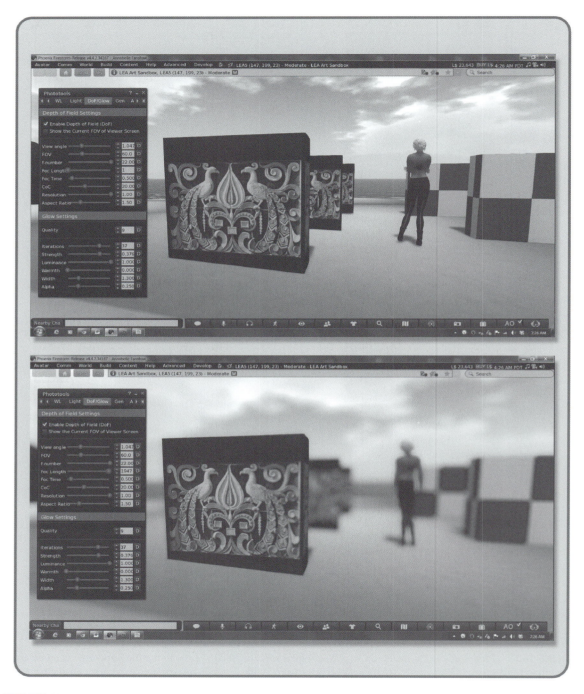

FIGURE 16.14 Phototools/DOF (depth-of-field) menu showing the change and range of focus (top image compared to lower image) available in the screen image.

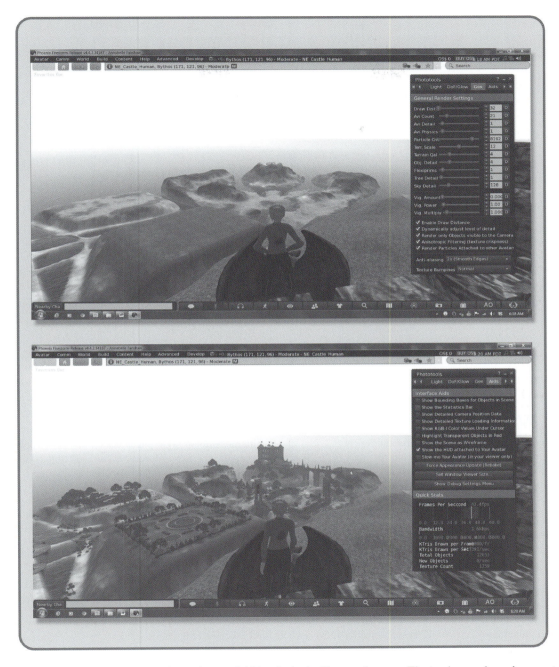

FIGURE 16.15 The General Render settings and Aids tabs in the Phototools menu. The top image shows how content can be culled out of a shot when necessary by lowering the Draw Distance. The bottom images shows the Quick Stats part of the Phototools menu, that allows you to check on performance and maintain the optimal settings for machinima image capture.

FIGURE 16.16 The 3D Mouse Settings in the Phototools menu and the Viewer Camera Menu Settings. Use of a 3D mouse will allow for dynamic moving shots not easy to accomplish with a standard mouse.

REFERENCES

1. Academy of Machinima Arts and Sciences—List of Machinima Festivals, Wikipedia article, http://en.wikipedia.org/wiki/Academy_of_Machinima_Arts_%26_Sciences. Accessed via https://developer.valvesoftware.com/wiki/Source_Filmmaker on March 30, 2013.
2. Phasing, World of Warcraft wiki, http://www.wowwiki.com/Phasing. Accessed March 26, 2013.
3. Benjamin Lee Whorf, Wikipedia article, http://en.wikipedia.org/wiki/Benjamin_Lee_Whorf. Accessed March 26, 2013.
4. Tomlinson, Bill, Bruce Blumberg, and Delphine Nain, Expressive Autonomous Cinematography for Interactive Virtual Environments, Synthetic Characters Group, MIT Media Lab, http://www.ics.uci.edu/~wmt/pubs/autonomous-Agents00.pdf. Accessed March 18, 2013.
5. Cieply, Michael, Saving the Story (the Film Version), *New York Times*, November 17, 2008, http://www.nytimes.com/2008/11/18/movies/18story.html. Accessed March 28, 2013.
6. Cyberdrama, Wikipedia article, http://en.wikipedia.org/wiki/Cyberdrama. Accessed February 26, 2013.
7. Ball, David, and Michael Langham, *Backwards and Forwards; A Technical Manual for Reading Plays*, Southern Illinois University Press, Carbondale, IL, July 7, 1983.
8. Story, Louise, Anywhere the Eye Can See, It's Likely to See an Ad, *New York Times*, January 15, 2007, http://www.nytimes.com/2007/01/15/business/media/15everywhere.html. Accessed March 29, 2013.
9. *Of Mice and Men*, produced by Hal Roach Studios, 1939; viewed on YouTube, scene appears at 1:38:25, http://youtu.be/axEQK_MGFu8. Accessed March 29, 2013.

17 The Future, Design, and Virtual Worlds

The distinction between the past, present and future is only a stubbornly persistent illusion.

—Albert Einstein

17.1 SOME PREDICTIONS FOR THE FUTURE AND THEIR IMPACT ON YOUR DESIGN OUTLOOK

In 1996, Bob Cringely wrote: "People care about people. We watch version after version of the same seven stories on television simply for that reason. More than 80 percent of our brains are devoted to processing visual information, because that's how we most directly perceive the world around us. In time, all this will be mirrored in new computing technologies" [1]. Bob Cringely was right; this progression toward visually based computing technologies is occurring universally. Just think about how much more graphic our screen interfaces have become, replacing text with images of wrenches and gears meaning "this is the edit button, and that's the settings button."

We are due for some major changes in our relationship with computing technology. Here are three factors that will contribute to this new experience: (1) the end of Moore's law, (2) increased adoption of haptic technology, and (3) increased levels of customization available to consumers for all the products they buy.

17.1.1 THE END OF MOORE'S LAW

Yes, all things must end someday. "Moore's law" [2], a speculation by Gordon E. Moore in 1965, that the computer chip performance would double every 2 years has been falling short of that mark for a few years now. This is not necessarily a disaster; rather, it is an opportunity for the computer industry to rethink and redefine the computer from the chips up. Already, we have seen the development of computers shift focus to include cloud computing so they can expand their capacity, the development of more effective software, and the increased intercommunication of the devices we use daily.

17.1.2 INCREASED ADOPTION OF HAPTIC TECHNOLOGY

A laptop with a tactile touchpad may be sitting on your desk, and your mobile phone may be giving you haptic feedback on every incoming e-mail. Haptic technology [3] is being subsumed into our interfaces everywhere.

17.1.3 INCREASED CUSTOMIZATION OF PRODUCTS

From websites offering customizable T-shirts, posters, and coffee mugs to online 3D printing of your own designs, customization [4] is driving our consumer market from "designer content" toward "user-designed content." Think about what that means for virtual worlds for a minute. The options for designing and modeling your own custom worlds, containing touch interactive elements, and downloading real versions of your digital creations increase every year. Virtual versions of the fitting room, the test drive, or a night on the beach are waiting for further development, and with that progress will come new employment opportunities for virtual designers.

17.2 EMERGING TECHNOLOGIES AND NEW DESIGN METHODOLOGIES

In the automotive world, designs for new cars are made by utilizing design technologies that span 40,000 years. Starting with a rough drawing (a method that started with prehistoric cave art), the car designer moves the design to a computer model, and from that a full-size car is made from clay utilizing human- and machine-created sculpture [5]. Designers in all practices have an enormous selection of tools and techniques available to them. Let's look at a few of the newer ones.

17.2.1 LASER SCANNING AND 3D MODEL MAKING

Why do you need to model something that already exists when it can be scanned? You should not have to undergo the tedious process of re-creating something digitally if you are willing to try some of the consumer-based technologies available like Autodesk's 123D Catch, Reconstruct Me, and KScan3D. For a higher level of scanning over much larger areas, a LIDAR (light detection and ranging) system is used. These scans are made to map archeological sites, subterranean caverns, and landscapes. With the digital information in these scans, virtual objects can be created to fit seamlessly onto real landscapes in the composite image, such as the castle in the background of your favorite fantasy television show [6,7].

17.2.2 DIGITAL PRINTING AND FABRICATION

The 3D printing "revolution" is just starting. With the popularity of this technology and the relative affordability of the printers, like Buccaneer, Printrbot Simple, and Makibox A6 LT, a designer with knowledge of 3D modeling and 3D print preparation can have a product prototype-making machine right in his or her own studio. Or, the designer can start a business selling original 3D models in the 3D printing marketplaces.

17.2.3 AUGMENTED REALITY AND IMMERSIVE ENVIRONMENTS

If you are a designer of large things like houses and landscapes, augmented reality (AR) and immersive head-mounted displays are probably of interest to you. These technologies are also undergoing substantial development. The Junaio application can be downloaded to your phone for viewing virtual objects in your real surroundings, and the Metaio company provides a platform for developing all sorts of AR applications. The Oculus Rift has some potential for providing the designer with a way to display his or her 3D designs, such as an architectural walk-through of a CG house that has been loaded onto the Unity platform.

It is not much of a stretch to think of Google Glass providing us with an architectural overlay filling in the details on your new house site or revealing the underlying archeological layers of the Eternal City of Rome, while you stroll its streets on vacation.

17.3 HOW THE NEW TECHNOLOGIES ARE INTERTWINING

In the process of writing this book, several technologies intertwined. The initial concepts and project plans were developed on the 3D modeling system of SketchUp, meetings about the design and content were held weekly in a virtual world created by OpenSim and Second Life code, and most of the figures that illustrate it were created by taking screen shots of virtual content with the FRAPs and Screen Hunter Pro software. This book would not have been possible a decade earlier. Every year, designers have more options for combining their methodologies for design and presentation of design with new tools and software.

In the process of utilizing these technologies, it will be smart to remember the concepts of "Build It Once." A wise designer would constantly look for new technologies that support a streamlined design process, augment the communication within the team, and support a client's needs. Like the car designers, you will be accessing the knowledge and techniques from the last 40,000 years and choosing the critical path method that works best for you and your company.

17.4 WHEN DO WE GET THE HOLODECK?

As you may recall from the virtual worlds timeline in Chapter 1, the television show *Star Trek, the Next Generation* introduced the concept of the "holodeck" to audiences worldwide in 1987. Now, more than 25 years later, converging streams of technology make this more reality than fantasy. Gartner's hype cycle for emerging technologies looks at technologies that have a great deal of promise for the future, lots of hype, or both. In 2012, the folks at Gartner's decided to focus their hype cycle chart on the concept of "tipping points," or technologies that are poised to make a significant impact in our lives and how we use technology.

"We are at an interesting moment, a time when many of the scenarios we've been talking about for a long time are almost becoming reality," said Hung LeHong, research vice president at Gartner.

> The smarter smartphone is a case in point. It's now possible to look at a smartphone and unlock it via facial recognition, and then talk to it to ask it to find the nearest bank ATM. However, at the same time, we see that the technology is not quite there yet. We might have to remove our glasses for the facial recognition to work, our smartphones don't always understand us when we speak, and the location-sensing technology sometimes has trouble finding us. [8]

In the 2012 report, Gartner's identified several technologies that they felt were at the tipping point. Among them were "Internet of things," big data, 3D scanners, and HTML5-Web GL. These are all interesting technologies to be sure, but how can you prepare for what is coming? Are we getting closer to having a holodeck? In the near future, will you be designing for one? Let's look at the convergent timeline in Figure 17.1. As you can see, a very broad base of interrelated technologies are pushing into the future and establishing the foundation of a working holodeck. We still have some hurdles to clear, our computers need to understand our vocal commands better, and we need develop advanced 3D projection systems in order to realize the complete illusion of the holodeck. It is difficult to actually pin down a date when the holodeck might appear, but we humans tend to actualize a future that we have taken time to think about and plan for [9]. Perhaps if we could create a worldwide linked database, the process of actualizing our dreams would become more robust and predictable.

One thing is for certain: The holodeck will need designers. Even with procedural creation of environments and landscaping, a designer will still be needed to decide how the whole environment goes together. What an exciting project that will be.

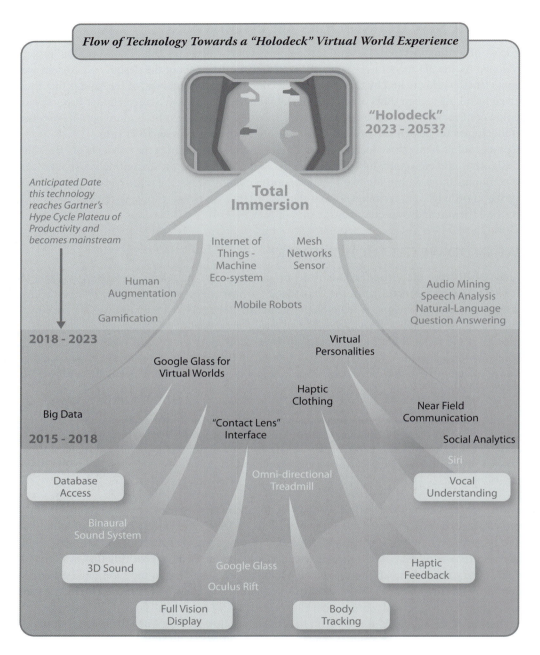

FIGURE 17.1 Diagram showing possible flow of technology over time that will lead towards the development of a "holodeck" virtual world experience.

REFERENCES

1. Cringely, Robert X., http://www.cringely.com/2013/04/03/accidental-empires-chapter-17-do-the-wave/. Accessed August 12, 2013.
2. Moore's Law, Wikipedia article, http://en.wikipedia.org/wiki/Moore's_law. Accessed August 12, 2013.
3. Haptic Technology, Wikipedia article, http://en.wikipedia.org/wiki/Haptic_technology#Fourth_generation_haptics. Accessed August 12, 2013.
4. Eliason, Erik, Three Reasons Why Mass Customization Is the Future of Consumer Products, Huffington Post, March 21, 2012, http://www.huffingtonpost.com/erik-eliason/mass-customization_b_1313875.html. Accessed August 12, 2013.
5. McCosh, Dan, Driving; Most Cars Are Born as Models of Clay, *New York Times*, March 7, 2003, http://www.nytimes.com/2003/03/07/travel/driving-most-cars-are-born-as-models-of-clay.html. Accessed August 12, 2013.
6. *Lightcraft Technology, Post Production Workflows*, tech manual for postproduction using lidar, http://www.lightcrafttech.com/support/doc/post-production-workflows/tracking-refinement-with-pftrack/. Accessed August 12, 2013.
7. Laser Scanning Buildings, website home page, http://www.laser-scanning-buildings.co.uk/. Accessed August 12, 2013.
8. Gartner's 2012 Hype Cycle for Emerging Technologies Identifies "Tipping Point" Technologies that Will Unlock Long-Awaited Technology Scenarios, press release, 2012, http://www.gartner.com/newsroom/id/2124315. Accessed June 12, 2013.
9. Spreng, R. Nathan, and Brian Levine, Doing What We Imagine: Completion Rates and Frequency Attributes of Imagined Future Events One Year After Prospection, *Memory*, 21, 458–466, 2013, http://www.academia.edu/1975294/Doing_what_we_imagine_Completion_rates_and_frequency_attributes_of_imagined_future_events_one_year_after_prospection. Accessed August 12, 2013.

Glossary

Additive Color: a color mixing system for light, in which red, green and blue light will combine to create white light.

Affordance: a term popularized by Donald Norman in 1988, which referred to the actual and perceived qualities of an object or its design that implied to the observer how it could be used. For instance, the affordance of a doorknob and its inherent usage is implied by its shape and position on a door.

Ambient Light: in 3D computer graphics, ambient lighting is represented by a widespread distribution of soft light of one color over the objects of an entire scene. This effect is created with rendering settings on the textures of 3D objects, as well as by the addition of diffuse sources of light into the scene.

Ambient Occlusion: a realtime lighting effect applied when the Advanced Lighting is selected in the Firestorm viewer (Avatar/Preferences/Graphics/). This creates the effect of soft shadows and shades of gray in areas that are occluded or blocked from the source of global illumination. This effect also found in 3D modelers like 3DS Max and Blender, and used for creating additional lighting detail in a scene.

Anechoic chamber: an echoless soundproof room used for audio testing.

API (Application Program Interface): is a system or group of programming directions, instructions or standards that allows the user of one program to access specific parts of the program or data from others, or to ask one piece of software to perform services for another program.

Atmospheric perspective: the creation of a sense of perspective within a landscape by increasing color fade and blurriness of background elements as they retreat in distance from the viewpoint.

Avatar: a 3D figure, sometimes human, and sometimes another species that represents a person, or an artificial intelligence program inside a virtual world. An avatar communicates and interacts with the other people or their avatars.

"Baking" Lighting: creating special textures for objects in a 3D scene that have the highlights and shadows rendered (baked) onto their surfaces, in addition to the colors and patterns inherent to the texture itself. This approach to creating content adds the effect of lighting to a scene without the need for any real time shadow rendering by the graphics card.

Binaural: hearing sound from two microphones, two channels, or two ears. This is how people with normal hearing perceive the world. Comparison by the brain of the two signals tells us where the sound is located and if it is moving.

COLLADA (.dae) file: a Digital Asset Exchange file format (.dae) used to exchange 3D content between 3D modeling programs and to upload those mesh models into virtual worlds and gaming engines.

Composition: arrangement of items in a 3D design to create a balanced image from all visible sides. This includes lighting, sound, and the elements of Line, Space, Shape, Form, Color, and Texture.

Design for all: see Universal Design

Diegesis: to tell a story with the use of a spoken narrative, as opposed to Mimesis, which is telling a story by visually acting it out.

Doppler Effect: this effect, also known as Doppler pitch shifting is the pitch shifting effect heard by a listener as a sound emitter moves by quickly. The relative velocities of the emitter and listener are compared and the resultant calculation used to change the pitch of the emitter's sound.

First person camera: a point of view provided by a game or avatar's camera that does not allow the person playing to see themselves, but only the view as they would see it from their eye position, similar to "mouse look" in Second Life. Usually found in "first person shooter" games and may allow the players to see their hands and weapons for aiming purposes.

Frustum: the pyramidal shaped volume that a projector creates from the start of its beam until it hits a plane or intersecting surface.

Gouraud shading: developed by Henri Gouraud, this kind of smooth shading uses the vertex normals (normal average of all surrounding planes) and the interpolation of many vertex intensities across the surface of a 3D polygonal model to produce the effect of a smooth surface. This kind of shading produces a smooth light-to-dark transition in the shadows of the geometrical surface.

Griefing: actions or activities by avatars with the intent of making the experience of a virtual place unpleasant or threatening. Often involving push scripts, overloading the location with prims, or broadcasting a loud noise via the voice chat channel.

Grid: a collection of regions laid out in a rectilinear grid system, interconnected via a simulator grid service for transport of avatars, messages and content across the virtual landscape. Represented in a map form for the players to orient themselves to the environment, a grid can include thousands of regions. These regions can be grouped to form "Continents" or a "Main Land."

Harmony of Dominant Tint: a method of unifying elements in a design or artistic composition by coloring all of them with the same tint, which visually harmonizes the composition.

HMD: (Head Mounted Display): devices such as the Oculus Rift that project a stereoscopic image on a display screen, or the Virtual Retinal Display that projects a virtual world image directly into the eyes. These devices bring the visitor into a state of deeper immersion in a virtual world.

HUD (Heads Up Display): a graphic element within the player's visual field that allows the player to access menus, activate programs or scripts, or gives information for the purposes of enhancing the virtual environmental experience.

Ideagora: a hybrid term that combines the words "idea" and "agora" (ancient Greek public space), and is used to represent places on the Internet where people can meet in a virtual space to exchange ideas, and build things together. Don Tapscott and Anthony D. Williams first used this word in "Wikinomics: How Mass Collaboration Changes Everything," (ISBN 1591841380), December 2006.

IAR (Inventory ARchive): a file saving process which collects all the content assets of an avatar's inventory into one single file, allowing that data to be moved and loaded into another OpenSim installation or transferred to another avatar's inventory.

IEZA framework: a concept framework, created by Sander Huibers and Richard van Tol at the Utrecht School of the Arts, for the purpose of organizing and defining the audio used in virtual environments.

Immersion: the shift in a player's perception as their attention focuses on the virtual world and its activities. This effect, enhanced with the use of headsets and/or viewers such as the Oculus Rift, utilizes sound effects, music, and visual images to envelop the player in the experience of the game.

Inworld: pertaining to the virtual location of an object, sound, animation or avatar entity that is experienced and/or manipulated through the client viewer while the user is logged into a virtual world.

Instantiation: the process of creating an object within a virtual space by accessing a prebuilt element, or bringing in pre-built content. All content is an "instance" that represents the underlying data. This process is also known as "rezzing," or to "rez" an object. An object is rezzed by dragging it from the avatar's inventory list to the virtual ground, or building platform.

JIRA: bug tracking software for projects and programs created by Atlassian. The name is a truncated version of Gojira, the Japanese name for Godzilla.

LSL (Linden Scripting Language): a language based on the Java and C programming languages and used throughout Second Life and OpenSim virtual worlds to direct an object in that world to do a series of tasks. LSL scripts are located in the contents of objects in the virtual world environment. An avatar can wear these scripted objects, examples are scripted hair, scripted clothing, and scripted interface tools. These scripts are interpreted and executed by the server running the virtual world environment, and seen by the user through the client viewer when they are logged into a virtual world.

Material: in the 3ds Max modeling system and in virtual worlds, a composite of the shader code and the texture maps. It is used on the surface of a 3D object to create its unique look. In some cases, "material" is used interchangeably with "shader." See also shaders and textures.

Mesh: a common term for the geometric forms made in modeling programs such as 3dsMax and imported into a virtual environment.

Mimesis: to tell a story by acting it out, as opposed to Diegesis, which is to tell a story with vocal narrative.

MMORPG: an abbreviation for Massive Multiuser Online Role Playing Game, which in its simplest form is a virtual environment that allows for a number of people to log in remotely and take the roles of various characters in order to play the game.

NPC (Non-player character): a character in the virtual world who is not controlled by a person during the game and may be interacting with the players by utilizing artificial intelligence code.

OAR (Opensimulator ARchive): like the IAR, a file saving process that allows for the collection of all the elements on a sim; the terrain, objects contained on it, the scripts, textures, and all parcel and region data into one file for distribution and reconstitution of the build on another system.

OpenSim: also called Open Simulator, an open source computer based platform that creates a virtual world or virtual environment. It is the 3D web, where instead of web pages, there are 3D regions linked together through servers on the internet.

OSSL (OpenSim Scripting Language): an extension of the LSL or Linden Scripting Language used in Second Life, also provides for extra functions that an Open Simulator based virtual world understands.

PCM (Pulse-code modulation): the uncompressed audio format usually found with a .wav audio file, commonly used in virtual worlds.

Per Pixel Lighting: a technique used by the computer to render out lighting effects based on the illumination calculation for each pixel in the scene. While this requires more graphics processing, it can be used to create much more visual detail in the scene.

Per Vertex Lighting: a technique used by the computer to render out lighting effects by calculating the illumination at the vertices of a 3D object in the scene, and interpolating the lighting across the surface of its faces.

Phasing: a selective display of environmental qualities, objects, and non-player characters utilized in various MMORPGs (Massive Multiplayer Online Role Play Games) to enhance the game, and keep the environment changing for the players.

Point Light: a light source that emanates from one central point, such as a hanging light bulb would in a dark room.

Poseball: a 3D object in a virtual world, often a sphere, that contains an LSL script and animations or poses. This enables the avatar to take up positions, or poses on such things as furniture, and vehicles.

Prim (or primitive): a simple 3D shape created in a virtual world. Also called "objects" (when rezzed in Second Life), these are used by the residents to build houses, roads, and other content that creates the world. The basic collection includes cube, cylinder, sphere, torus, prism, ring and tube.

Quaternion rotation: one of the two methods of rotational representations used in LSL scripts to define how an object will rotate in space. Consists of x,y,z variables to represent the axes of rotation and the s variable to represent the angle of rotation. The other method used is Euler rotation, which employs yaw, pitch and roll as vectors.

Real Time: the creation of a series of rendered images rapidly enough to produce the illusionary effect of objects and avatars moving at the same pace as one would observe in the real world.

Region: the virtual land, mountains, islands, or possibly open water, in a virtual world. This land can come in various sizes, but would typically be 256 meters by 256 meters in size if you were in Second Life or Open Sim. Regions created in a mega region format are subdivided into parcels set with individual permissions for visitor access, media playing, build rights and other qualities desired by the region owner.

Rez: term used in Second Life, OpenSim to describe the process of creating an object in the world, either by using the viewer's Build Edit/Create menu to "rez an object" or by dragging content from the avatar's inventory onto the virtual ground so that it can be seen and manipulated by the avatar. From the programmers term "resolve," and first used in the movie "*Tron*" Walt Disney Productions 1982.

Script: a set of instructions written in such program languages as LSL (Linden Scripting Language for Second Life), UnityScript (for the Unity game engine), C#, (pronounced "C sharp"), and others too numerous to mention. These scripts will activate and control the behavior of building elements, objects, avatars and non-player characters.

SL (Second Life): a persistant virtual environment or world created by Linden Labs in 2003, and it is accessed via the internet with free client viewer interfaces such as Firestorm, Second Life viewer, or Imprudence. Most of the content and design of the world is created by the residents, some of whom make a business of building and selling digital goods. OpenSim is a direct spinoff of this world, and the foundation of a new generation of 3D virtual worlds.

Shader: a set of computer instructions utilized to create shading, lighting, and special effect such as cartoon looks on the objects in a scene. By using various algorithms to affect the overall look of the rendered scene, they can create an almost infinite range of effects. See also material and textures.

Shadow Map: a virtual shadow created in a 3D environment. A shadow map is made from the comparison of a the light's position (x,y,z coordinates in a scene) to the lit objects position in a scene. This comparison by the rendering engine creates a depth map (depth buffer) of the object from the light's point of view and saves it in the graphics memory. In this grayscale depth map, as the objects surfaces recede from the location of the light, the black level increases, defining a "light space" for each light source. When a point in the scene is rendered from the camera view for your display screen, two spatial qualities are compared, 1) where that point is in the scene (world coordinate or x,y,z), and 2) where it is in light space (the depth map information). By comparing these two sets of information through various matrices, the rendering engine decides what is shaded and lit and creates a shadow map.

Simulation: also called sim, this is the virtual environment produced by the server when it is running a virtual world program such as OpenSim or Second Life. The word "sim" is often used interchangeably with "region," to signify one simulation area.

Sim-on-a-stick (SoaS): a portable version of an OpenSim virtual region distributed under Creative Commons, that can be run off a USB stick since it contains a portable server program as well as the Wifi admin panel for avatar logins. This program was developed by Dr. Christa Lopes (Diva Canto in SL) and is distributed from a site administered by Ener Hax at http://simonastick.com/.

Specular highlight: the highlight or "hotspot" on the surface of a shiny object that gives a clear indication as to the color and position of the lights in a 3D scene.

Spotlight: a spotlight is created in Second Life and Open Sim by selecting the light function in the Build/Edit/Features tab menu and applying to a prim. This kind of light source will have Field of View qualities, as well as focusing capacity. It may also be called a projector light when it is displaying a texture image with its light field. The effects of these lights can only be seen when the Advanced Lighting module is activated in the Avatar/Preferences/Graphics menu.

Texture: a 2D graphic image such as a photograph, or illustration that is applied to the surface of a 3D model to create its unique qualities. For instance, a photo of bricks might be applied to a large box, to create the illusion of a brick wall object.

Third person camera: the visual perspective on a scene in a virtual world that has the cameras point of view behind and slightly above the avatar or character the camera is following. This point of view, which can be partially controlled in some games and completely controlled in virtual worlds, allows for the player to view surrounding areas, see the approach of other players, and to see their own avatar as they direct it on a course through the environment.

Transform: the process of calculating the graphical information received from a moving point of view in a 3D scene and creating a 2D image from it. This process is happening when your avatar is walking through a 3D environment, and you are viewing it on a computer screen.

Universal Design: a "universal" approach to making the design of an environment, virtual or real, accessible to all people. This includes creating easy access to the space, redundancy of information in both audio and visual formats, directions and information in more than one language and color palettes that can be seen clearly by all. This is also known as "Design for All."

UUID: also called a "Universally Unique Identifier," an alphanumeric code that identifies each asset, instance of the object, avatar and land parcel.

Vertex: on a 3D model, the point where the lines or edges of a surface start. Many 3D modeling programs allow for the manipulation of these points in order to "sculpt" the form of the 3D model.

Virtual Reality: a computer generated 3D enviroment created for the purpose of enabling people to visit a simulacrum of our real world or a completely imaginary world. This kind of reality is enhanced for the player with large screens, stereoscopic displays, sounds played through a headset, and haptic feedback to create a compelling immersive experience.

Visuospatial Sketchpad: a component of human memory that initially starts with collection of short-term memories, and caches them into the working memory for recall later. This is a valuable tool for designers since it provides them with a vast store of visual, spatial, color and movement information that can be recalled at will.

Wireframe: a viewer mode that removes the surface rendering, and shows only the lines and vertices of the 3D model. In the Firestorm viewer, the wireframe mode can be accessed in the Developers menu, which along with the Advanced menu, is activated on the top bar of the Firestorm interface after the basic installation is done. The key commands are (Ctrl+Alt+D) and then (Ctrl+Alt+Q) to turn on these hidden menus.

Useful Links by Topic

DESIGN FOR ALL

Able Gamers: http://www.ablegamers.com/
Design for All Foundation: http://designforall.org/

IMPORTANT BLOGS AND WEBSITES FOR VIRTUAL WORLDS

Hypergrid Business: http://www.hypergridbusiness.com/
New World Notes: http://www.nwn.blogs.com/

IMPORTANT WEBSITES FOR FREE OR LOW COST APPS

Audacity-Sound editor: http://audacity.sourceforge.net/
Backhoe Terrain editor (Mac): https://www.macupdate.com/app/mac/28291/backhoe
Bailiwick Terrain editor (PC):   http://www.spinmass.com/software/Bailiwick.aspx
Blender—3D creator: http://www.blender.org/
Color schemes: http://colorschemedesigner.com/
Fraps—Video capture: http://www.fraps.com/
Gimp—2D editor: http://www.gimp.org/
Maze Generator: http://www.mazegenerator.co.uk/
Scripting (automatic):   http://www.3greeneggs.com/autoscript/
Unity (game engine):   http://unity3d.com/unity

IMPORTANT WEBSITES FOR TUTORIALS AND TECHNIQUES

Avatar Toolbox: http://avatartoolbox.info/MakingAvatars.html
OpenSim Artist Home: http://opensimulator.org/wiki/Artist_Home
Prototyping scenic design in Second Life/Richard Finkelstein: http://www.rfdesigns.org/VIRTUAL.HTM
Robin Wood Ent.:   http://www.robinwood.com/
Second Life Tips and Tricks: http://community.secondlife.com/t5/Tips-and-Tricks/bg-p/blog_tips_and_
                                     tricks
Second Life Wiki: http://wiki.secondlife.com/wiki/Good_Building_Practices

IMPORTANT LOCATIONS IN THE VIRTUAL WORLDS FOR TUTORIALS AND EXAMPLES TO VIEW

All listed below are in Second Life:
The Particle Laboratory * Learning Center, Teal (190, 48, 301)—General
The Vehicle Laboratory * Learning Center, Slate (204, 27, 267)—General

Ivory Tower Library of Primitives, Natoma (210, 163, 28)—General
Texture Tutorial, Livingtree (128, 100, 25)—General
TRANSIENT PARCEL TESTS—TERRAFORM FOR A LIMITED TIME ONLY!, Here (130, 125, 23)
　　—General
Uruk- FAS, FAS (203, 83, 27)—General

RESOURCES FOR CLIENT VIEWERS AND SOUND EQUIPMENT

List of viewers for Virtual Worlds:　　　http://wiki.secondlife.com/wiki/Third_Party_Viewer_Directory
System Requirements for Virtual Worlds:　http://secondlife.com/support/system-requirements/
Zoom Sound Recorder:　　　　　　　　　http://www.zoom.co.jp/products/h4n

RESOURCES FOR OPENSIM HOSTING

Dreamland Metaverse:　http://www.dreamlandmetaverse.com/
Sim Host:　　　　　　　http://www.simhost.com/
Sim-on-a-stick:　　　　　http://simonastick.com/

RESOURCES FOR OPENSIM CONTENT

Free Scripts and Tutorials:　http://www.free-lsl-scripts.com/
OpenSimulator:　　　　　　　http://opensimulator.org/wiki/Main_Page
Wizardry and Steamworks:　　http://was.fm/start

RESOURCES FOR SECOND LIFE CONTENT

Second Life Wiki (A little out of date, but lots of good info): http://wiki.secondlife.com/wiki/Main_Page

RESOURCES FOR DEVELOPMENT

Devmaster game engine database site, DevDB:　http://devmaster.net/devdb
ArchVirtual:　　　　　　　　　　　　　　　　http://archvirtual.com/
Autoscript—Script me!:　　　　　　　　　　　http://www.3greeneggs.com/autoscript/

Index

A

Able Gamers, 351
access, 12, 206
accessories, 240, *see also* Attachments
acclimatization, 192
actors, use of virtual worlds, 9
additive color, 345
Adigard des Gautries, Erik, 39
advertising, 216, *see also* Viral distribution
affordance, 172–173, 345
Agile development, 30
Alchemy Sims Grid (ASG), 6, 8, 222
alignment cubes
    heads up display, 295–297
    modular virtual classroom project, 66
ambient light, 345
ambient occlusion
    defined, 345
    lighting, 164
    textures, 120
anchoring, 232
anechoic chamber, 345
angles, 324
animals, 298
animation, *see also* Movement
    avatars, 241
    overrides, HUD, 297–298
    textures, 119
announcements, 299–300, *see also* Viral
    distribution
Application Program Interface (API), 345
applications, terrain and landscapes, 91
apps listing, free or low cost, 351
architects, use of virtual worlds, 9
architectural style, brand identity, 193
ArchVirtual website link, 352
art and data visualization systems,
    124–126
artists, use of virtual worlds, 9
ASG, *see* Alchemy Sims Grid (ASG)
atmospheric perspective, 345
attachments, 253, 298, *see also specific
    part*
audio-based gaming environment project
    audio landscape, 232–233
    entrance, 233–234
    game space layout, 228
    overview, 228
    signage, 233–234
    sound emitter setup, 228, 230–231
    testing, 234–235
    trigger, 231
audio landscape, 232–233
aural ambiance, 198, *see also* Sounds and
    sound design
automatic shop greeter, 216
autoscripts, 285–287
Autoscript-Script me! website link, 352
avatars, *see also* Non-playing characters
    (NPC)
    accessories, 240
    advanced development, 253, 256
    animation, 241
    attachments, 253
    backstory, 240
    banning, 206
    clothing, 240, 246, 249, 253
    creating a new user, 246
    defined, 345
    designing look of, 239–240
    details, 249
    eyes, 249
    face, 253
    hair, 249, 253
    height, 249
    importance of, 239
    layers, 246, 249
    parameters adjustment, 249
    project, 246–256
    sense of self, 237
    shape, 249
    shopping for, 240
    size, 249
    skin, 249, 253
    summary, 256
    tattoos, 253
    texture maps, 253
    user manifestation, 246
Avatar Toolbox, 351

B

Backhoe Terrain Editor (MAC), 351
back plate, 308
backstory, avatars, 240
Bailiwick Terrain editor (PC), 351
baked lighting
    defined, 345
overview, 159, 161
textures, 112–113, 120
balance, 46–47
banning, 206
Barragan, Luis, 73
behavior, 242
benchmark examination, 81, 83
best practices, 16
binaural sound, 224, 345
biosystem, 244–245
Blender, 351
blogs, 9, 351
Bonnard, Pierre, 155
books, 300
boxes, 104
Bradbury, Ray, 99
branding and brand identity
    architectural style, 193
    color, 195
    display, 193, 195
    elements, 199
    lighting, 195
    overview, 192–193
    signage, 193, 195
Build Editor menu, 113–119
building methodology, 100, 102–103
building with primitives
    art and data visualization systems,
        124–126
    boxes, 104
    cylinders, 104
    defined, 347
    details, 123
    focal points, 123–124
    landmarks, 123–124
    meshes, 108–109
    overview, 103
    prisms, 104
    project, 120–124
    rings, 108
    sculpt maps, 109–112
    spheres, 106
    summary, 126
    textures, 112–113
    3D timeline/résumé project, 120–124
    timeline base, 122–123
    torus, 106
    tubes, 106
buttons, 308